Issues and Applications of Case-Based Reasoning in Design

Issues and Applications of Case-Based Reasoning in Design

Edited by

MARY LOU MAHER
University of Sydney, Australia

PEARL PU
Swiss Federal Institute of Technology, Switzerland

Ψ Psychology Press
Taylor & Francis Group

NEW YORK AND LONDON

First published 1997 by Lawrence Erlbaum Associates, Inc

Published 2014 by Psychology Press
711 Third Avenue, New York, NY, 10017

and by Psychology Press
27 Church Road, Hove, East Sussex, BN3 2FA

Psychology Press is an imprint of the Taylor & Francis Group, an informa business

Cover design by Kathryn Houghtaling

Library of Congress Cataloging-in-Publication Data

Issues and applications of case-based reasoning in design / edited by Mary
    Lou Maher, Pearl Pu.
      p. cm.
    Includes bibliographical references and index.
    ISBN 0-8058-2312-3 (c). — ISBN 0-8058-2313-1 (p)
    ISBN 978-0-805-82313-4 (pbk)
    1. Computer-aided design. 2. Case-based reasoning. I. Maher,
    Mary Lou. II. Pu, Pearl.
    TA174.I78 1997
    620'.0042'0285—dc21   96-49426
                                                    CIP

Publisher's Note
The publisher has gone to great lengths to ensure the quality of this reprint but points out that some imperfections in the original may be apparent.

contents

list of contributors

ALEXANDER, PERRY
Knowledge-Based Software Engineering
Laboratory
Department of Electrical and Computer
Engineering and Computer Science
University of Cincinnati
Cincinnati OH 45221-0030 USA
email: perry.alexander@uc.edu

AYGEN, ZEYNO
Engineering Design Research Center
Carnegie Mellon University
Pittsburgh PA 15213 USA
email: zeyno+@andrew.cmu.edu

BHATTA, SAMBASIVA R.
NYNEX Science & Technology
500 Westchester Ave.
White Plains NY 10604 USA
email: bhatta@nynexst.com

COYNE, ROBERT
Engineering Design Research Center
Carnegie Mellon University
Pittsburgh PA 15213 USA
email: coyne@edrc.cmu.edu

DAVE, BHARAT
Architecture and CAAD
Swiss Federal Institute of Technology (ETH)
Zürich 8093 Switzerland
email: dave@arch.ethz.ch

DOMESHEK, ERIC A.
Institute for the Learning Sciences
Northwestern University
Suite 300, 1890 Maple Ave.
Evanston IL 60201 USA
email: domeshek@ils.nwu.edu

FALTINGS, BOI
Laboratoire d'Intelligence Artificielle
Departement d'Informatique
Swiss Federal Institute of Technology (EPFL)
1015 Lausanne Switzerland
email: faltings@lia.di.epfl.ch

FLEMMING, ULRICH
Department of Architecture and Engineering
Design Research Center
Carnegie Mellon University
Pittsburgh PA 15213 USA
email: ujf@edrc.cmu.edu

GOEL, ASHOK K.
College of Computing
Georgia Institute of Technology
Atlanta GA 30332-0280 USA
email: goel@cc.gatech.edu

HINRICHS, THOMAS R.
Institute for the Learning Sciences
Northwestern University
1890 Maple Ave
Evanston IL 60201 USA
email: hinrichs@ils.nwu.edu

KOLODNER, JANET L.
College of Computing
Georgia Institute of Technology
Atlanta GA 30332-0280 USA
email: jlk@cc.gatech.edu

MAHER, MARY LOU
Key Centre of Design Computing
University of Sydney
NSW 2006 Australia
email: mary@arch.su.edu.au

NARASIMHAN, S.
Robotics Institute
Carnegie Mellon University
Pittsburgh PA 15213 USA

NAVIN-CHANDRA, D.
Robotics Institute
Carnegie Mellon University
Pittsburgh PA 15213 USA
email: d.navin-chandra@isl1.ri.cmu.edu

PU, PEARL
Laboratoire d'Intelligence Artificielle
Swiss Federal Institute of Technology (EPFL)

1015 Lausanne Switzerland
email: Pearl.Pu@imt.dmt.epfl.ch

PURVIS, LISA
Department of Computer Science
University of Connecticut
U-155 Storrs CT 06269 USA
email: purvis@cse.uconn.edu

SCHMITT, GERHARD
Architecture and CAAD
Swiss Federal Institute of Technology (ETH)
Zürich 8093 Switzerland
email: schmitt@arch.ethz.ch

SHIH, SHEN-GUAN
Department of Architectural Design
National Taiwan Institute of Technology
Taipei Taiwan China
email: shih@taipei.dt.ntit.edu.tw

STROULIA, ELENI
Research Center for Applied Knowledge
Processing (FAW)
Helmholtzstr. 16
89081 Ulm Germany
email: stroulia@faw.uni-ulm.de

SYCARA, KATIA P.
Robotics Institute
Carnegie Mellon University
Pittsburgh PA 15213 USA
email: katia_sycara@isl1.ri.cmu.edu

TSATSOULIS, COSTAS
Center for Excellence in Computer-Aided
Systems Engineering
Department of Electrical Engineering and
Computer Science
University of Kansas
Lawrence KS 66045 USA
email: tsatsoul@eecs.ukans.edu

SNYDER, JAMES
Engineering Design Research Center
Carnegie Mellon University
Pittsburgh PA 15213 USA
email: james_snyder@edrc.cmu.edu

VOSS, ANGI
GMD—GermanNational Research Center for
Information Technology
D-53754 Sankt Augustin Germany
e-mail: angi.voss@gmd.de

preface

This book brings together a wide ranging collection of major contributions to the area of case-based reasoning in design. The idea of case-based reasoning has captured the interests of many design researchers because designing is so reliant on situated experience. It seems that a good designer is one that not only has a formal education in his or her profession or speciality but also has sufficient experience in the generation and development of design solutions. Case-based reasoning systems exploit the representation of situated experience.

In this book we tried to create, for those interested in developing case-based reasoning systems for design, a significant case library. The case library, as is typical of case-based design systems in a domain where there is no formal knowledge, is descriptive rather than formal. However, as an informal description of experiences in building case-based design systems, this book provides a broad range of experiences.

The contributors to this book were initially selected from the participants in the Workshop on Case-Based Reasoning in Design at the International Conference on Artificial Intelligence in Design '94. The chapters represent a more complete description of their case-based design systems than can be found in the workshop notes.

The development of a book of this kind starts with an initial idea and is only possible with the commitment and hard work of the authors. We would like to thank the authors for keeping to our schedule and producing a significant contribution to the field of case-based reasoning in design. Although the authors contribute the content, the presentation as a coherent book is only possible with the effort of the editors and more importantly, the preparation of the document itself. A special thanks to Fay Sudweeks for the immeasurable effort she gave to producing the camera ready copy.

Mary Lou Maher
Pearl Pu

chapter one

INTRODUCTION TO THE ISSUES AND APPLICATIONS OF CASE-BASED REASONING IN DESIGN

MARY LOU MAHER
University of Sydney

PEARL PU
Swiss Federal Institute of Technology

This book is a collection of chapters written by researchers that have been developing case-based reasoning (CBR) applications to design problems. This chapter provides an introduction to the book by giving an overview of the applications covered by the book and identifying a range of issues addressed by the authors of the following chapters.

1. Introduction

Design is believed to be one of the most interesting and challenging problem-solving activities ever facing artificial intelligence researchers. Knowledge-based systems using rule-based and model-based reasoning techniques have been applied to build design automation and/or design decision support systems. Although such systems have been met with some success, difficulties have been encountered in terms of formalizing generalized design experiences as rules, logic, and domain models. Recently, researchers have been exploring the idea of using CBR techniques to complement or replace other approaches to design support.

Motivated by a cognitive observation that humans often rely on past experience to solve new problems, Schank (1982, 1986), Kolodner, Simpson, and Sycara (1985), and Riesbeck and Schank (1989) pioneered the CBR approach. CBR systems (Bareiss, 1991; Hammond, 1989; Kolodner 1988; Kolodner, 1993;

1

Riesbeck and Schank, 1989) solve new problems by using knowledge gained from solving similar problems in the past. In general, a case-based reasoner

> *finds* (retrieves) those cases in a case base that solved problems similar to the current problem;
> *adapts* the retrieved case(s) or solutions to fit the current problem;
> *evaluates* the adapted case; and if evaluation is not satisfactory, repairs the adapted case, the adaptation algorithm, or a combination of both.

CBR can be considered as an alternative to paradigms such as rule-based and model-based reasoning. Rule-based expert systems capture knowledge in the form of if–then rules, which are usually identified by a domain expert (Davis Buchanan, and Shortliffe, 1977). Model-based reasoning aims at formulating knowledge in the form of principles to cover the various aspects of a problem domain (Davis, 1982). These principles, which are more general than if–then rules, comprise a model that an expert system may use to solve problems. Model-based reasoning (MBR) is sometimes called "reasoning from first principles". Instead of generalizing knowledge into rules or models, CBR is an experience-based method. As Schank (1982: 22) put it, "an expert is someone who gets reminded of just the right prior experience to help him in processing his current experiences." Thus specific cases, corresponding to prior problem-solving experiences, comprise the main knowledge source in a CBR system.

This book includes a collection of chapters that describe specific projects in which CBR is the focus for the representation and reasoning in a particular design domain. The chapters provide a broad spectrum of applications and issues in applying and extending the concept of CBR to design. Each chapter provides its own introduction to CBR concepts and principles. In this introductory chapter, we provide an overview of the range of applications and issues addressed in the subsequent chapters.

2. Applications of CBR to Design

The idea of using CBR techniques to assist or automate the design process is almost as old as the CBR field itself. Hinrichs' JULIA (1988) and Navinchandra's CYCLOPS (1988) appeared in the proceedings of the First Case-Based Reasoning Workshop (Kolodner, 1988). Following that, two more case-based design (CBD) systems, Kritik (Goel, 1989, 1991) and Archie (Goel, Kolodner, Pearce, Billington, and Zimring, 1991) were introduced. More recent developments of CBR in design are described in a special issue of AI EDAM edited by Pu (1994) and in a book that describes the general concerns of CBR in design (Maher, Balachandran, and Zhang, 1995). Even though the various implementations of CBD systems address different design activities, a common feature is that they all show that the design domain enlarges the scope of CBR issues and applications.

The applications of CBR to design have ranged from largely informal domains, such as meal planning, to analytical domains, such as the design of mechanical devices. The range of applications included in this book are shown in Table 1.1.

Table 1.1. Design domains represented in this book.

Design Domain	Name of System	Chapter	Authors
Architectural design	Archie	Chapter 2	Domeshek, Kolodner
	CADRE	Chapter 3	Faltings
	CADRE	Chapter 11	Schmitt, Dave, Shih
	SEED	Chapter 4	Flemming, Aygen, Coyne, Snyder
	FABEL	Chapter 12	Voss
Assembly sequence planning	Composer	Chapter 10	Pu, Purvis
Car configuration design	Composer	Chapter 10	Pu, Purvis
Communications systems	ASPII	Chapter 11	Tsatsoulis, Alexander
Fire engine design	PANDA	Chapter 11	Tsatsoulis, Alexander
Meal planning	JULIA	Chapter 6	Hinrichs
Mechanical devices	FAMING	Chapter 3	Faltings
	CADET	Chapter 8	Narasimhan, Sycara, Navin-Chandra
Physical devices	Kritik	Chapter 5	Goel, Bhatta, Stroulia
Software specifications design	BENTON	Chapter 11	Tsatsoulis, Alexander
Structural design	CASECAD CADSYN	Chapter 7	Maher

The design of physical devices requires an understanding of the causal behavior of the devices as well as previous experience with the design of such devices. The representation of causal behavior is directly addressed in the development of Kritik through the use of Structure Behavior Function models, in CASECAD and CADSYN through the use of Function Behavior Structure models, in CADET through the use of Interactive State Diagrams as a graph-based representation of behavior, and the use of constraints in FAMING. The integration of causal knowledge with CBR needs to be resolved in a CBD system that includes adaptation. The systems described in this book provide a set of alternative methods for resolving the integration issues.

Design usually involves the development and understanding of complex systems. The complex representations needed to adequately capture a design case has introduced challenges to CBR systems. Many of the chapters in this book address the issues in the use of CBR for the design of complex systems: ASPII through the domain of communication systems, PANDA and the configuration of fire engines, BENTON in the design of software specifications, FABEL in the design and layout of mechanical services in buildings, SEED in the domain of architectural layout of buildings, and CASECAD and CADSYN in the structural design of buildings. Generally speaking, these applications require the representation and reuse of parts of cases, typically organized as a hierarchy of subcases. In addition to the representation of complex design cases, these systems also address the need for domain knowledge that is represented separately to the design cases—either as rules, models, or constraints.

The development of CBR for design domains in which there is little formal or theoretical knowledge is addressed in the development of CADRE and Archie as CBR approaches to architectural design and the development of JULIA for meal planning. The CADRE project focuses on areas of architectural design that could be formalized, such as the geometric constraints on floor plans; where the Archie project looks at how issues of importance during conceptual design can be articulated and presented to designers as multimedia. JULIA develops a formal representation of a previously informal task. The lack of formal knowledge in design affects both the ability to define a formal and consistent representation of design cases and the role of adaptation as a human-centered activity or an automated process.

As can be seen in the subsequent chapters, the applications of CBR to design have identified and driven research in new directions. Many of the issues raised in the development of these systems has lead to a broad range of issues, as described in the next section.

3. Issues in Developing CBD Systems

The application of CBR to design raises a common set of issues, regardless of the domain of application. The issues can be broadly classified as representation and control issues. Representation issues include what is in a design case, how is a design case represented, how is a design case indexed, and how is design case memory organized. Control issues concern the general process model of a CBD system. That is, when and how is a design case retrieved, how is a design case adapted, is a case going to be presented to the user for inspection before a solution is offered, and how is an adapted design case evaluated. These issues have been addressed through the development and implementation of CBD systems, where each system resolves the issues within the context of their project focus. In addition to the general issues, the authors of the chapters in this book have raised a number of other issues such as the appropriateness of CBR for design in chapter 11 (Schmitt et al.) and the development of large project-based CBD systems in chapter 12 (Voss).

In the following sections, we address some of these issues and refer you to the individual chapters for detailed discussions. The goal is to provide a general overview of the chapters as well comparisons among them.

3.1. REPRESENTATION OF DESIGN CASES

Before discussing the representation of design cases, it is useful to look at how cases are considered in CBR. One view is that a case is a story or a lesson to be learned (Kolodner, 1994). Other views express cases as information about the context as well as solutions of a problem (Maher et al., 1995), or a case records the process by which a problem is solved (Flemming, 1994). The purpose of a case is to facilitate solving a similar problem in a similar but different context in the future.

A design case presents a complex problem. A common issue raised in the applications described in this book is that a design cannot be told in a single case (or story). Design involves reasoning about the rationale, the structure, the behavior, the constraints among structural elements, the decision of tradeoffs of an artifact. Most design cases you see in this book are complex and involve a representation of subcases.

The size of a design case is an important consideration both for representation and organization of cases. Design cases can be divided into smaller chunks, as in Archie for conceptual design and Composer for configuration design. A similar approach is to break cases into a hierarchy of subcases, as is done in CASECAD and CADSYN for structural design, JULIA for meal planning, Kritik for the design of physical devices, and PANDA for fire engine design. One approach is to represent a case as different views of the same design as done in the FABEL project.

Resolving the issue of "what is in a design case?" is done in many different ways in the systems described in this book. Design cases can be lessons whose purpose is to help designers interpret a previous design experience in a similar context as done in Archie. Design cases can be represented as constraint satisfaction problems and their solutions so that when a new design problem is encountered, the solutions can be retrieved and applied with minimum changes as done in Composer. Design cases can contain:

- models of the function, behavior, and structure so that the retrieval and adaptation of a case can focus on one or more aspects of a design as in Kritik, FAMING, CASECAD, and CADET;
- plan actions, components of physical systems, and specification elements as in PANDA;
- images, gestalts, tuples of values as in FABEL;
- multimedia such as text, CAD drawings, object-oriented models as in CADRE, CASECAD, and Archie; and
- a solution generated by a design module, an associated problem specification, and the technology or method used to create the solution as in SEED.

The variety of ways in which designs can be represented introduces issues for retrieval and adaptation, or simply provides a richer presentation of design information to the user.

Contrary to initial observation that case acquisition should be straightforward, most design stories told by designers or found in design documents are not easily formed into cases that can be indexed and classified for reuse. A systematic approach is needed to identify a uniform representation and parse design stories into these formats. Chapters 2, 4, 7, 11, and 12 discuss issues related to case acquisition. One approach is to use design models to guide case acquisition. Another approach is to use the design documentation directly and build the case memory around the existing documentation. Alternatively, the SEED project proposes that the design case memory be automatically developed through the use of the design environment.

In summary, regardless of the techniques used to describe a design case, the most important question when defining a case representation is what information in the design facilitates its reuse. Then the issue of how the CBR tool uses the design case representation as part of the design process (for retrieval only or for retrieval and adaptation) helps determine the implemented representation of a design case.

3.2. INDEXING AND RETRIEVING DESIGN CASES

The indexing and retrieval of design cases can be done informally, where the user browses and selects a relevant design case, or formally, where the system accepts a new problem definition as input and presents a set of relevant design cases as output. The use of informal approaches to design case retrieval is done in Archie, CADRE, and CASECAD. This approach addresses the need for flexibility in developing an understanding of the new design problem through browsing and retrieving design cases. The effectiveness of the informal approach depends on the number of designs in case memory and the richness of the indexing scheme.

The more formal approach makes assumptions about how a new problem is described and uses the specification for pattern matching. The most popular formal method of indexing and retrieving is to use a set of feature-value pairs to describe a design case. The new problem is then described as a set of feature-value pairs and this set is matched with design cases in memory. A close match is one that has many features in common with the specifications. Although there is variety in the algorithms used for comparing, this approach is used in CASECAD, CADSYN, Composer, JULIA, FABEL, SEED, ASPII, PANDA, and BENTON.

Other approaches to finding a relevant case are to index and retrieve based on function as in Kritik, to retrieve based on matching images or gestalts as in FABEL, to retrieve based on a hierarchy of problem specifications as in SEED, and to retrieve using graph-based representations of behavior as in CADET. A common issue discussed when developing indexing and retrieval schemes for design cases is the need for flexibility and allowing the new design specifications to change or be refined. Kritik and FABEL present approaches for qualitatively measuring the distance between new designs and cases, and CASECAD and CADET present methods to modify the new design specification based on the cases retrieved. In addition to flexibility is the need for efficient retrieval when case memory becomes very large. In Composer, a method called structural matching is used so that certain features of a case become labeled and matching only occurs with respect to this set of labels, reducing a significant amount of time for retrieval.

Another retrieval-related issue is the level of abstraction and the need to decompose a problem in order to find a relevant design case/subcase. In JULIA and CADSYN, the problem specification is decomposed if a case cannot be found to solve the entire problem. In Composer, case retrieval attempts to decompose the problem in such a way that all parts of a problem correspond to some existing cases.

3.3 DESIGN CASE ADAPTATION

Case adaptation has been regarded as such a difficult task that it has been said that one should avoid case adaptation at all cost. Whereas it might be possible and it may make sense to avoid adaptation in other domains, to avoid adapting design cases could be interpreted as copying another's design. One approach to the difficult issue of design case adaptation is to leave it to the human designer as in Archie. Here we discuss the issues and approaches taken in the applications described in this book.

In many of the applications, design case adaptation has drawn from the observation that a design can be described as features that are interrelated by constraints. The development of the constraints and their relevance to a new design becomes part of the formalization of the reasoning in CBD. For instance, in one design, the color of a car being red has to do with it being a sports car. When the case is adapted to a different type of car, this constraint is no longer important. On the other hand, being a four-door sedan, the size of the trunk has to be enlarged. The management of constraints in terms of which constraints are active and which are not, and the modification of values assigned to constrained variables are more generally called constraint satisfaction problem solving.

For example, JULIA and CADSYN formulate case adaptation as constraint satisfaction problems (although in JULIA it is called constraint posting). JULIA handles dynamic constraint variables as well. That is, adaptation of a case can cause some variables to participate or withdraw in a CSP, such as adding a side dish variable for an Italian course.

Composer adapts cases by retrieving a set of existing cases, each one being a solved CSP. When all of them are stitched together, there are numerous violations of constraints. A simple backtracking algorithm will be computationally too exhaustive to repair all conflicts. Composer uses a minimum-conflict repair heuristic on top of the backtracking method in order to reduce the complexity. For similar concerns, but in a domain of continuously valued variables, CADRE preprocesses the adaptation problem by sorting out which variables are independent and which ones are dependent. Only the dependent variables have to be verified for consistency if their corresponding independent variables have been modified. This process is called dimensionality reduction.

PANDA, ASPII, and BENTON use a rule-based approach to case adaptation when a single case can be modified, or resort to component replacement and constraint checking when subcases are retrieved. FABEL offers a variety of adaptation methods that depend on the aspect or view of the case being adapted and use techniques such as generate and test and constraint satisfaction. SEED views case adaptation as the addition, removal, or modification of design units.

Another approach used in case adaptation is to combine MBR and CBR. The cases provide the starting point of the solution to a given problem. Models provide knowledge to fix the areas where cases do not quite satisfy the current problem specification. In Kritik, case adaptation is considered as a diagnosis and repair problem, and case evaluation is a simulation process.

3.4. OTHER ISSUES

Last, but not least, two chapters discuss issues that are very important to CBD projects. In addition to technical discussions, Chapter 12 in describing FABEL provides insights on managerial concerns and chapter 11, in describing CADRE, discusses ethical considerations of design case adaptation. FABEL is a large project involving multiple industrial and research partners, each with their own perspectives and modules for which they are responsible. The development of CADRE raises interesting questions, such as does CBR prohibit designers' creativity? Or, if a design is a result of numerous case combinations, is it considered plagiarism? We leave you to read their chapters to see how they have resolved such issues.

4. Summary

In summary, the development of CBR for design applications raises a number of issues that can be addressed within the paradigm of CBR but may also introduce a number of issues that are not readily addressed by this paradigm. The chapters in this book provide a broad range of applications and issues that have been studied in a research environment. The results of the studies are presented in a way that allows the reader to apply the methods and techniques developed by the authors to another CBD system.

References

Bareiss, R. (ed.): 1991, *Proceedings of the Case-Based Reasoning Workshop*, Kaufmann, San Mateo, CA.

Davis, R., Buchanan, B., and Shortliffe, E.: 1977, Production rules as a representation for a knowledge-based consultation program, *Artificial Intelligence*, 8(1): 15–45.

Davis, R.: 1982, Expert systems: Where are we? And where do we go from here?, *Report AIM-665*, Massachusetts Institute of Technology, Cambridge, MA.

Flemming, U.: 1994, Case-based design in the SEED system, *in* G. Carrara and Y. E. Kalay (eds), *Knowledge-Based Computer-Aided Architectural Design*, Elsevier, New York, pp. 69–91.

Goel, A.: 1989, *Integration of Case-Based Reasoning and Model-Based Reasoning for Adaptive Design Problem Solving*, Doctoral Dissertation, The Ohio State University.

Goel, A.: 1991, A model-based approach to case adaptation, *Proceedings of the Thirteenth Annual Conference of the Cognitive Science Society*, Lawrence Erlbaum Associates, Hillsdale, NJ.

Goel, A., Kolodner, J. L., Pearce, M., Billington, R., and Zimring, C. A.: 1991, Case-based tool for conceptual design problem solving, *Proceedings of the Third DARPA Workshop for Case-Based Reasoning*, Kaufmann, San Mateo, CA, pp. 284–290.

Hammond, K. J. (ed.): 1989, *Proceedings of the Second Case-Based Reasoning Workshop*, Kaufmann, San Mateo, CA.

Hinrichs, T. R.: 1988, Towards an architecture for open world problem solving, *in* J. Kolodner (ed.), *Proceedings of Case-Based Reasoning Workshop (DARPA)*, Morgan Kaufmann, San Mateo, CA, pp. 182–189.

Kolodner, J. L. (ed.): 1988, *Proceedings of the First Case-Based Reasoning Workshop*, Kaufmann, San Mateo, CA.

Kolodner, J. L.: 1993, *Case-Based Reasoning*, Kaufmann, San Mateo, CA.

Kolodner, J. L., Simpson, R., and Sycara, K.: 1985, A process model of case-based reasoning in problem solving, *Proceedings of the International Joint Conference of Artificial Intelligence*, Kaufmann, San Mateo, CA, pp. 284–290.

Maher, M. L., Balachandran, B., and Zhang, D. M.: 1995, *Case-Based Reasoning in Design*, Lawrence Erlbaum Associates, Hillsdale, NJ.

Navin-chandra, D.: 1988, Case-based reasoning in cyclops, a design problem solver, *in* J. Kolodner (ed.), *Proceedings of Case-Based Reasoning Workshop*, Kaufmann, San Mateo, CA, pp. 286–301.

Pu, P. (guest ed.): 1994, Special Issue: Case-based design systems, *Artificial Intelligence in Engineering, Design and Manufacturing*, 7(2).

Riesbeck, C., and Schank, R. C.: 1989, *Inside Case-Based Reasoning*, Lawrence Erlbaum Associates, Hillsdale, NJ.

Schank, R. C.: 1982, *Dynamic Memory: A Theory of Learning in Computers and People*, Cambridge University Press, Cambridge, UK.

Schank, R. C.: 1986, *Explanation Patterns: Understanding Mechanically and Creatively*, Lawrence Erlbaum Associates, Hillsdale, NJ.

chapter two

THE DESIGNERS' MUSE:

Experience to aid conceptual design of complex artifacts

ERIC A. DOMESHEK
Northwestern University

JANET L. KOLODNER
Georgia Institute of Technology

This chapter presents the background and motivation for the development of a class of computerized design aiding systems we call case-based design aids (CBDAs). CBDAs focus on the needs of designers engaged in conceptual design, the earliest design stage in which the designer analyzes the problem specification, discovers the design issues that need to be addressed, and works out a solution framework. CBDAs make a library of design cases available to designers as they are doing conceptual design, allowing easy access to useful cases. In effect, a CBDA makes access to the experiences of others easier and extends the set of available cases. The ways access is provided to these design cases is intended to fit with the process of conceptual design. Thus, CBDAs are organized to support browsing directed at four different ends: initial problem orientation and issue discovery; issue understanding and elaboration; directed issue and tradeoff exploration; and proposal critiquing and evaluation.

1. Conceptual Design

Over beer one night while visiting a high school friend who had grown up to become a NASA engineer, one of the authors fell into conversation about this friend's work on the design of a new telescopic camera for a space probe. It happened that the engineer was just beginning to think about how he would design the lens cover for his camera. As he sketched the important issues and outlined his initial design ideas, what unfolded was a glimpse of conceptual design. His problem gives a good idea of what typically goes on during that early stage of problem exploration, idea generation, and trade-off analysis.

What were the important issues for his design problem? The camera needed a lens cover because it would contain delicate optics that must be shielded from dirt and contamination during early stages of the mission. During launch, the cap would have to remain secure despite extreme vibration. In flight, the cap and its mechanism would have to survive temperature extremes and gradients. Ultimately, despite the beating taken along the way, the mechanism would have to remove the cap from the camera as the probe approached its target. The mechanism would only have to work once, but it absolutely had to work, or NASA would have a billion-dollar piece of scrap floating beyond the reach of repairs.

There are two things to note about these deliberations. First, during this stage of design, he was discovering what was important about the problem. The process that leads to these discoveries, which we call *problem exploration*, is a process of playing scenarios through in the head to discover what is important about them. By knowing how things worked on other space probes, this designer was able to focus on a set of important issues. Second, the issues he was concerned with were considered at a fairly high and nonspecific level. At this point in the design process, coping with dirt and vibration, accounting for temperature, and ensuring reliability were not hard-quantified requirements.

What were some of his initial design ideas? He was pretty sure that he would build the lens cap out of a transparent material; then, if the cap removal mechanism failed, the probe could still get some use out of the camera. Having anticipated a possible failure (the cap staying jammed shut), he planned for a fall-back option. He also expected that the cap would be spring-loaded so that the only operation required to remove the cap would be to unsecure it; once unsecured, the cap would simply pop open, and there would never be any need for a mechanism to close it up again. Having identified a constraint in the situation (one-time operation of the opening mechanism), he was able to exploit it to simplify his design.

Again, in order to understand conceptual design, we note the kind of ideas he was generating. He was proposing strategies for coping with potential problems and exploiting problem constraints. He was not interested in the details of the design and its parts. He did not know nor care about the transmissivity of any particular lens cap material, and was not ready to worry about the spring parameters. What this means is that for this work, it did not matter very much that he had the skill to calculate torques or the knowledge to choose parts from catalogs. His primary leverage during this conceptual design process was familiarity with mechanical configurations in general, and past space probes in particular.

This held true for what became the focal problem in his initial design: the tradeoff between securing the cap during launch and unsecuring it for use. Ensuring the former would tend to complicate the later. Designing secure latches with a simple unlatching mechanism is, again, a fairly generic problem. As the engineer and computer scientist pursued this narrow task, it became clear that the most important knowledge in these deliberations were what kinds of mechanical configurations can achieve certain ends, and what accumulated experience says about the pros and cons of each option.

Despite its relative simplicity, this real-life scenario has illustrated many important points about the conceptual design of complex artifacts. This was not radical brainstorming: The engineer was not worrying about how to gather images from a space probe, or even how to protect the optics of an imaging device—he was just worrying about how to secure and then remove a lens cap. In truth, this was quite typical of conceptual design: The issues he was worrying about, the level of detail at which he was doing his reasoning, the fact that he was both exploring issues and generating initial strategic responses, the way he evaluated strategies, and the way he focused on a salient tradeoff are all characteristic of design during the conceptual stage.

Conceptual design, although a small part of the entire design process, is crucial to the overall success of many projects. As artificial intelligence researchers, we have been studying the process of conceptual design, particularly for complex artifacts such as buildings and aircraft. Our aims are both to understand the process and to develop tools to help people do the job better. Prescriptive design methodologies often miss the mark on what people are really doing when they do design. We are trying to offer a general description of the conceptual design process: Conceptual design involves exploring for problematic issues, generating ideas about possible solutions, noting interactions that are likely to require tradeoffs, making initial strategic commitments, and, often, generating a few focal commitments that can drive much of the rest of the design.

We have paid particular attention to the important role played by experience during successful conceptual design. In particular, previous design cases, whether a designer's own, ones relayed by another designer, or ones found in a magazine or file cabinet, provide grist for a number of the decisions made during design. They raise issues that need be taken into account, suggest strategies for resolving design issues, provide illustrations of how to carry out design strategies, warn about possible interactions between multiple issues and their associated strategies, and help project the possible effects of designing something a certain way. The practices of real designers tend to support the applicability of CBR to design. This chapter reports on our ongoing efforts to turn this observation into the basis for a class of computer-based design aiding tools.

2. A BRIEF HISTORY OF CBDAS

The concept of a CBDA grew from the more general idea of a case-based decision aid. CBR (Kolodner, 1993) started with the observation that cases were often useful in solving problems. Several members of the CBR community noticed that both novices and experts seemed to seek out cases when confronted with problems. Although case adaptation, merging of ideas from several cases, and case-based critiquing seemed to come naturally, these human reasoners did not always have access to relevant cases when they could use them. At the same time, CBR researchers found that creative case adaptation, merging, and critiquing were hard for computers.

Out of these observations came the idea of building human-computer systems for CBR: The computer aid would serve as a well-stocked, well-organized, and reliable external memory for past experiences; the person would be in charge of reasoning based on the available cases (Kolodner, 1991). This idea has since been developed in several domains: autoclave loading (Hennessy and Hinkle, 1992), architectural design (Domeshek and Kolodner, 1992), aircraft subsystem design (Domeshek, Herndon, Bennett, and Kolodner, 1994), user-interface design (Barber et al., 1992), trust bank accounting (Ferguson, Bareiss, Birnbaum, and Osgood, 1992), and tax consulting (Slater and Riesbeck, 1991).

A major issue in designing these systems was the content of cases and the form in which to present cases to human reasoners. Whole complex cases are too big to present at one time to a person (Domeshek and Kolodner, 1991; Pearce et al., 1992).[1] On the other hand, every large case can be partitioned into a set of interesting and useful lesson-bearing narrative chunks. It is these chunks, sometimes called stories (Schank, 1991), that are at the heart of case-based aids.

Stories capture past experience, recording real-world situations and analyzing their outcomes. Stories provide useful information for reasoners who are faced with similar situations and who must make decisions about how to cope with them. Stories are most effectively told in a vivid first-person voice by those who lived through, or were affected by, the situation. In some systems, stories are video segments of interviews in which experienced workers tell their most interesting war stories (Ferguson et al., 1992; Slater and Riesbeck, 1991). In our design aids, stories are text and graphic presentations that report evaluations drawn from many sources. The following is an example of a story (see also Figure 2.1) in the **Archie-II** CBDA for the conceptual phase of building design (Domeshek and Kolodner, 1992):

---

[1] Consider the case of the house you live in—not huge as cases go, but too large to present to anyone at one time. On the other hand, you might have an interesting story to tell about the design of your kitchen, the placement of your living room window, or the design of the tile in your bathroom, and so on.

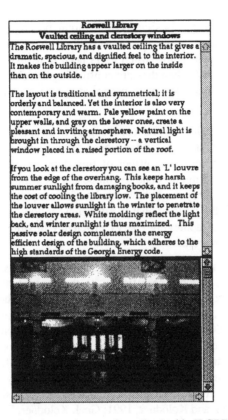

Figure 2.1. A sample story from the Archie-II CBDA.

The Roswell Library has a vaulted ceiling that gives a dramatic, spacious, and dignified feel to the interior. It makes the building appear larger on the inside than on the outside.

The layout is traditional and symmetrical; it is orderly and balanced. Yet, the interior is also very contemporary and warm. Pale yellow paint on the upper walls and gray on the lower ones create a pleasant and inviting atmosphere. Natural light is brought in through the clerestory—a vertical window placed in a raised portion of the roof.

If you look at the clerestory, you can see an L louver from the edge of the overhang. This keeps harsh summer sunlight from damaging books, and it keeps the cost of cooling the library low. The placement of the louver allows sunlight in the winter to penetrate the clerestory areas. White moldings reflect the light back, and winter sunlight is thus maximized. This passive solar design complements the energy efficient design of the building, which adheres to the high standards of the Georgia Energy code.

Most case-based decision aids are further characterized by an assumption that the user is engaged in an ongoing problem-solving task or goal-directed process (e.g., a designer using a design system might be engaged in design, or in evaluating the design of another designer). Stories have the greatest value when users are ready to hear them—when users need to assess a situation similar to one analyzed in a story, when they are confronting a decision for which the story offers advice, or when they have proposed a course of action that the story critiques.

A case-based decision aid and a user engage in an extended dialogue: The user composes a series of situation and response descriptions, which elicit a series of stories from the system. The effect of this iterative process is to refine an understanding of the situation and to compose a well-thought-out response. For example, the earlier story might have resulted from a query about lighting, and in that context raises the issue of energy efficiency; follow-up queries might dwell on different ways of achieving energy efficiency in situations where shielded clerestory would not work.

CBDAs are an application of the basic case-based decision aiding insight to the task of design, or more specifically, to the conceptual design of complex artifacts. This work is a natural outgrowth of combining the idea of case-based aids with a long-standing research program in CBD (Goel and Chandrasekaran, 1989; Hinrichs, 1992; Kolodner and Penberthy, 1990). Archie was the first, and is the longest running, CBDA project. The original Archie system (Pearce et al., 1992) let users partially describe a building and in return offered documentation on similar buildings. That first version taught us many lessons about how experience needed to be packaged if it was to be accessible and useful to a designer (Domeshek and Kolodner, 1991; Goel, Kolodner, Pearce, Billington, and Zimring, 1991; Pearce et al., 1992).

The primary lesson of the original Archie was that records of entire designs were too large and unwieldy to be very useful to working designers (Pearce et al., 1992). What we had to do instead was to carve what was known about existing artifacts into smaller presentations, each focused on making a particular point. These lesson-bearing chunks became the stories of the Archie-II system. For instance, the earlier story focuses on the way light is handled in the main hall of the Roswell library, describing the interaction of ceiling height, coloration, window placement, and sun shielding, but leaving out everything else about the design of the building.

A second consequence of experience with Archie was our reconceptualization of stories as rich multimedia presentations employing the formats and conventions natural to the designers we aimed to support. Figure 2.1 shows the earlier sample story as it appears in the current version of Archie-II, accompanied by a photograph illustrating how the clerestories bring in light. Figure 2.2 shows a floor plan of the building under discussion. Whenever possible, Archie-II presents evaluative stories paired with relevant design documentation to aid story interpretation. Experience with the original Archie also led us to focus on creating systems in which designers could quickly browse through a growing collection of small lessons, as well as among different artifacts and their natural forms of documentation. The facilities we have developed for browsing are discussed in the next section. Those facilities were shaped by consideration of how the different phases of the conceptual design process require different access pathways.

Since setting off in this new direction, there have been several rounds of implementation. An initial SuperCard mock-up of Archie-II was superseded by a first Lisp implementation. That stand-alone implementation was later replaced by a version built on top of our own CBDA shell, a tool built in Macintosh Common Lisp. The shell, called Design-MUSE, is now in its second major revision, and a new architectural database is being constructed to take full advantage of recently added features. We later the experiences we have had using Design-MUSE to construct and run CBDAs, primarily in educational settings.

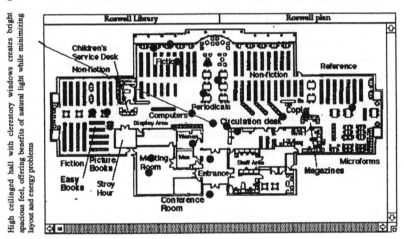

Figure 2.2. Design documentation for the story in Figure 2.1.

3. Browsing in a CBDA

This section aims to answer two primary questions: What kinds of information should be in a CBDA? How should the system's contents be made accessible? We know that people need access to cases during conceptual design and we know a system will be more helpful if it predigests those cases into lesson-bearing stories. What else might be needed to get the most value out of stories during conceptual design?

We note that the kind of support a designer needs is likely to shift during the course of conceptual design. Accordingly, we organize our discussion of CBDA contents and access by considering a likely browsing sequence reflecting different phases of conceptual design. We identify four phases:

1. Orientation and issue discovery.
2. Issue understanding and elaboration.
3. Issue and tradeoff exploration.
4. Proposal critiquing and evaluation.

3.1. ORIENTATION AND ISSUE DISCOVERY

When starting out on a new project, a common way to get oriented is to study similar completed projects. For instance, an architect designing a manufacturing research center told us how he had traveled the world to visit such buildings at other universities and corporations. The point of such an initial survey is to explore broadly what the artifact must accomplish, what might be difficult or problematic, and how a design might achieve the desired ends. CBDAs are set up to provide access to design documentation based on partial descriptions of major design goals, constraints, and environmental factors. In Archie-II, an architect designing a new public library might start by searching for libraries of an appropriate size range in suburban settings. The result would be documentation on those buildings in the system's library that come closest to fitting that description.

Figure 2.2 shows a sample of such building documentation displayed in Archie-II's Design Pane. One important feature of that display is the way the CBDA highlights lessons by using the standard architectural convention of annotating design graphics. In the left margin, a short note summarizes important design features ("high ceilinged hall" and "clerestory windows") and their effects ("bright spacious feel" and "minimizing layout and energy problems"). That annotation is tied to a dot on the floor plan indicating the part of the building being discussed. Many such dots are scattered over the floor plan, each indicating that there is something noteworthy about the design—each dot represents a story to be told. Clicking on a dot or on its corresponding annotation causes the related story to be displayed. The set of dots whose annotations actually appear in the left margin at any given moment depends on the set of stories selected as relevant at that time.

In the context of the current discussion, the important point is that the user can be led from an initial undirected survey of some existing artifact to a more detailed consideration of the lessons that can be learned from that artifact. The linkage from design documentation to stories is the first step in drawing the designer into a deeper understanding of the issues they face and of design options available to them.

3.2. ISSUE UNDERSTANDING AND ELABORATION

A story describing something that worked out well or led to trouble in a previous design can serve to raise an issue; but on its own, it cannot give a full understanding of the possibilities and interactions that might have arisen in other situations. A full grasp of any issue usually requires some general understanding of what is at stake and what strategies are available for coping, as well as how the problems and possible solutions are likely to manifest in a variety of contexts. Accordingly, CBDAs provide not only specific stories, but also general problem and response[2] statements that provide context for interpreting stories. Design documentation associated with stories allows the story to be interpreted in the broader context of the design case it is embedded in; problems and responses associated with stories generalize the points of stories and help readers to recognize those points.

For instance, Figure 2.3 shows the story from Figure 2.1, but this time, the screen shot includes a pair of flanking panes that display a related problem and response. The problem shown in Figure 2.3 points out the general desirability of having (some) natural light in a library and the difficulties with arranging for that light using normal windows. The response suggests a general way of arranging for light to be brought into reading areas in libraries. The story provides a concrete example of carrying out the response.

Stories, problems, and responses have symbiotic relationships. A problem statement associated with a story helps highlight the significance of the design features described in the story, whereas the story makes the general description in the problem statement more concrete. A story associated with a response provides a concrete illustration of how to carry out the general solution described in the response statement; the response statement points out the attributes of the story that the reader should focus on.

Because problems and responses may apply to several stories, they can serve as organizers of related stories, providing access to related similar situations. This helps a designer to explore the ins and outs of some design issue, for example, the range of ways in which a design problem manifests itself, the different ways its solutions can be carried out, the range of situations in which some response is applicable, and so on. Together, a set of stories can illustrate when a particular response strategy is appropriate and when it might fail, a variety of ways a general response might be implemented, or some of the pitfalls inherent in adopting a type of response. In addition to having several stories flesh out a response, CBDAs assume there are usually several responses available for

---

[2] A *response* here is taken to be a general but fragmentary solution strategy.

each identified problem; in design, it is rare that there is only one way to cope with an interesting problem.

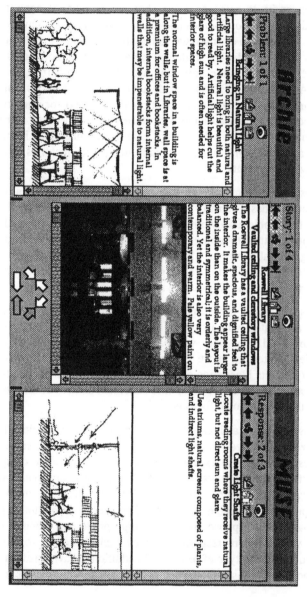

Figure 2.3. Problem/response/story grouping from Archie.

Just as we led the designers from their initial survey of similar artifacts to consideration of the significant stories of those artifacts, so we now want to lead the designers to a deeper understanding of the issues raised by those stories. Annotation dots on design documents indicate the availability of lesson-bearing stories. The triangle formed of six arrows symbolically linking the Problem, Response and Story panes indicate that the designer may traverse a network of linked presentations to explore issues in depth. When viewing a presentation in any of these three panes, the user may choose from pop-up menus associated with these arrows to select related presentations in either of the other two panes.

3.3. ISSUE AND TRADEOFF EXPLORATION

Problems, for the most part, represent interesting interactions among design issues that require some kind of trade-off for the best resolution. Through the kinds of browsing we have sketched so far, issues can be identified, interactions noted, and responses explored. But as designers get deeper into conceptual design, they will generate their own concerns with other issues and tradeoffs. At some point, a more focused mechanism for finding lessons becomes useful. For this phase, CBDAs provide search facilities based on user-specified interests, including design issues and partial-artifact specifications. Stories (and problems) are not only linked to design documents and to other lesson materials, but they are also indexed directly. The trick is to invent an indexing language in which it is possible to express many of the concerns that might arise during conceptual design.

For instance, having browsed through the set of stories clustered around the problem and responses in Figure 2.3, an architect would have some good ideas about ways of bringing natural light into a library and allowing for book stacks. In the course of starting to lay out study areas for visitors and work areas for employees, the architect could reasonably become concerned with how decisions about natural lighting might impact the users' sense of having private space to work in. Having arrived at this concern on her own, she needs a way to query the system about this issue.

Figure 2.4 shows the Find window from Archie-II with a query asking for problems arising from the interaction between getting natural light into work areas and the provision of adequate privacy for workers. The format of queries in this window (how they appear to the user) is one of the current areas of active work. The content of such queries, however, is sufficiently settled that Figure 2.4 can be used as a good basis for discussion.

The first thing to note is that a query can be composed of multiple interests that may be in competition and thus may require some tradeoff. In Figure 2.4, the first interest includes the old issue of getting natural light into the users' work areas; the second interest mentions the new concern about the users' sense of privacy. When the system scans its library for problems that share features with this query, it will prefer problems indexed by both issues.

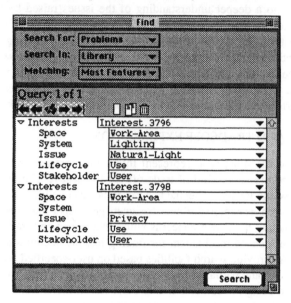

Figure 2.4. Find window from Archie with query for problems.

The second thing to note is that design issues are construed broadly, and explicitly so. Not only are there many possible choices for the Issue slot of the query form, but there are separate slots in which to specify the phases of the artifact's life cycle during which the issue might matter (Life cycle) and the particular class of people who might be concerned about the issue (Stakeholder). Thus, a user can pose queries about quite specific issues, such as an owner's concern about costs during maintenance, or the neighbors' concern about safety during construction.

The third thing to note is that in addition to talking about issues (further specified by life cycle and stakeholder), queries may focus attention on particular parts of the artifact. In Archie-II, we currently recognize two main principles for carving artifacts into parts: physical contiguity and functional relatedness. The Space slot provides a way for the designer to designate a physical part of a building. The System slot is where the designers can designate a functional subsystem. In Figure 2.4, both interests are focused on those spaces that are work areas; the first interest further specifies that the designer is concerned with the building's lighting system (whereas the second interest implicates no subsystem in particular).

Each of the five slots of an interest specification has a defined set of fillers from which the user can choose. Users are free to specify multiple fillers for each slot, or to leave slots blank. Once a query is composed, the user can request the CBDA to search. The result of a search is a new, selected set of presentations in some pane. The left part of Figure 2.5 shows the Problem pane following a search using the query in Figure 2.4; the first of four partially matching problems is on display. The right part of Figure 2.5 shows the index that was assigned to the problem displayed on the left. Note that this index is similar to, but richer than, the search query. The index includes many more descriptive terms and sometimes uses slightly different terms than the query. The system's nearest-neighbor partial matching algorithm can tolerate such differences, producing a graded sense of similarity between descriptions.

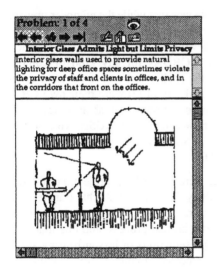

Figure 2.5. First result of Figure 2.4 problem search (with matching index).

3.4. PROPOSAL CRITIQUING AND EVALUATION

At some point in the conceptual design process, users will have developed their own sketchy proposals and at that point, the system ought to be able to offer more focused critiques. This is an area where the current version of Archie-II is weak. To better support critiquing and evaluation, the system would have to allow for more detailed descriptions of partial design solutions than it currently does. This is also an area of active development in the ongoing Archie project.

4. Experience with Design-MUSE and CBDAs

The first version of Archie-II, built in reaction to the original Archie, was demonstrated widely and aroused interest in the Advanced Design Division of Lockheed Aeronautical Systems Corporation (LASC). A small project was launched to build a CBDA supporting conceptual design of aircraft subsystems. The resulting MIDAS system focused on lessons about design tradeoffs in the initial design of aircraft hydraulic systems (Domeshek, Herndon, Bennet, and Kolodner et al., 1994). In about 6 months, with coaching from our group at Georgia Tech, a junior LASC engineer gathered and documented three dozen stories plus related problems and responses, developed an indexing system, and constructed a prototype CBDA.

What made the MIDAS project possible was that while the engineer prepared the specific information on aircraft and hydraulic system design, we were generalizing the capabilities originally developed for Archie-II into a generic CBDA shell supporting creation of new CBDAs for any kind of complex conceptual design. An important goal of the shell effort was to devise a simple interface affording domain experts the capability of growing their own CBDA libraries. MIDAS was first constructed on top of our initial shell prototype. As that prototype evolved into the shell we now call Design-MUSE, we continued to use MIDAS as a sample case library; MIDAS now runs in version 2 of Design-MUSE (as illustrated in Figure 2.6).

We learned several interesting things from the MIDAS project, not the least of which was how some of the ideas initially developed in Archie transferred to another design domain. What first attracted LASC's interest was the understanding that conceptual design was a critical process, and one that could benefit from easy access to multimedia presentations of lesson-bearing stories evaluating previous designs. LASC also liked the mixture of stories with more concrete design documentation and more general discussions of issues and tradeoffs, and they appreciated the variety of access paths provided by linking these various materials. When it came to the indexing framework, we found that the five dimensions used in Archie-II transferred directly to the aircraft domain, although the fillers did not. Table 2.1 shows the indexing vocabulary used in MIDAS (except that the system dimension, which for this prototype had only the single item *hydraulic*, has been omitted). The indexing vocabulary for Archie-II is too extensive to list in this chapter, and is also under active revision. The column listing MIDAS's components corresponds to Archie-II's spaces dimension, but obviously there is no overlap in the terms provided.

Likewise, the issues dimension shares little between the two systems other than the inclusion of similar classes of issues (e.g., parameters, pitfalls, requirements). The life cycle and stakeholder dimensions showed the greatest commonality between systems, although even here there are variations, and we consider many more stakeholders in the case of buildings.

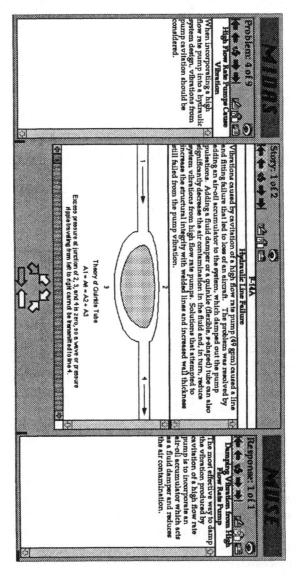

Figure 2.6. Problem/response/story grouping from MIDAS.

TABLE 2.1. Indexing vocabulary from MIDAS.

Components	Issues	Life Cycle
Accumulator	*Parameters*	Design
Actuator	Electric	Fabrication
Controller	Flow-rate	Assembly
Converter	Material	Test
Filter	Power	Transport
Fitting	Pressure	Use
Fluid	Volume	Maintenance
Heat-exchanger	Weight	Repair
Landing-Gear	*Pitfalls*	Disposal
Manifold	Contamination	
Motor	Cavitation	
Pressure-transducer	Temperature/Heating	*Stakeholder*
Pump	Vibration/Acoustics	Builder
Reservoir	Leakage	Customer
Sensor	*Requirements*	Designer
Valve	Effectiveness	Mechanic
Wiring	Efficiency	Pilot
	Installation	
	Range/Payload	
	Safety	
	Life Cycle	
	Affordability	
	Producibility	
	Deployability	
	Supportability	
	Reliability	
	Maintainability	
	Survivability	
	Flexibility	
	Vehicle-growth	
	Life-cycle-cost	
	Environmental-impact	

There were also three less-expected results. The first we probably should have expected—we were confronted with the importance of the social dimension when it comes to knowledge acquisition. We had imagined the bulk of our materials would come from interviewing a senior design engineer, but unfortunately, we found this expert to be quite reticent about sharing his war stories. Whether due to the security-conscious culture at LASC, a misconception of what we were asking for, a low valuation of his anecdotal experiences, or a high valuation of his special expertise, our expert told few stories.

The second interesting point, however, was that this same expert seemed delighted to share documents from his personal library and, partly as a result of his attitudes, we learned that there is much useful but normally inaccessible information in documents that could be organized by a CBDA. For instance, there are many studies evaluating trials of new technology in existing aircraft, and reports are often written documenting system failures. These are rich veins of experiential knowledge.

The third interesting discovery was that a CBDA library would not have to be tremendously large to be useful. Instead of the thousands of stories we had imagined, the Lockheed engineers seemed convinced that a system with as few as a hundred stories might be useful in a narrow domain, and with just several hundreds would be quite useful over much of the initial utility subsystem design. As a trial of our small prototype system we compared the results of a published design trade-off study examining alternate hydraulic system operating pressures with information gathered from searching in MIDAS; MIDAS provided quick access to the equivalent information and actually did a better job of raising issues and citing precedents.

As a final benefit, we also learned much about the usability of some of our interface concepts, as day-by-day feedback from our Lockheed collaborators helped shape many of the features of the evolving CBDA shell. Everything from screen layouts to label choices and icon designs was criticized. The range of linkages among presentations was simplified. More support was developed for entering, linking, and indexing materials.

4.1. ADDITIONAL EXPERIENCES BUILDING CBDAS

The MIDAS project ended in August of 1993. By then, however, we were well on our way into the first major revision of the CBDA shell. By January of 1994, Design-MUSE Version 1 was available, and we put it to use in a graduate course on CBR run by Kolodner (Domeshek and Kolodner, 1994). The goal was to gain more experience with supporting CBDA construction by people whose primary expertise is in domain content rather than indexing techniques. During a 10-week quarter, small groups within the class used Design-MUSE to produce five new CBDAs:

- **Next-Archie**: A revised-extended version of the Archie CBDA for building design, aimed especially at student architects. (Design education)
- **Composites**: An advisor to help with decisions about replacing metal parts of aircraft with parts made from composite materials. (Redesign)
- **DSP-Aid**: A guide to formulating design problems in the Decision Support Problem (DSP) methodology so they are suitable for analysis using DSP software tools. (Design process)

- **GT-SCARES**: An online trouble log to help in diagnosing and coping with satellite failures. (Diagnosis and debugging)
- **Dream-Car**: An advisor for consumers considering purchase of a new car. (Situation assessment)

As with MIDAS, we learned some interesting things from having domain-savvy AI novices build case libraries using our shell. First of all, these systems are not all CBDAs as we had originally conceived them. Although all aim to support decision making with respect to complex artifacts, they vary quite a bit in terms of what decisions they support. Some have little to do with design, per se.

Second, this exercise generated more divergence in the indexing frameworks. When we gave each student group their copy of Design-MUSE, we provided an initial index framework with five dimensions: part, system, issue, stakeholder, and life cycle. We also supplied a basic set of primitives for the fillers of the stakeholder and life cycle dimensions. None of the groups stuck with this initial framework. This was not terribly surprising in the case of systems such as GT-SCARES or Dream-Car, which were not primarily concerned with aiding designers. It is more interesting in the cases of systems like Composites and DSP-Aid. Next-Archie stayed much closer to the initial framework. The variety raises questions about how we can most effectively generalize our design-aiding work and build support into our shell so it gets easier for domain experts to build new CBDAs.

About the same time as this first class experiment, another project at Georgia Tech's Center for Human-Machine Systems Research began to test some of the core ideas of CBDAs, but without directly using Design-MUSE. Ockerman's recently completed work (1995) describes the CMS-Browser, a system she built to facilitate design reuse by NASA software contractors. She constructed a repository for analyses of several independently developed satellite command management systems. Those analyses were broken up into focused discussion of particular parts and issues and cross linked so as to facilitate comparison across projects. Evaluation tests at NASA suggested the system would be effective at helping designers recognize commonalties across software systems at a conceptual level.

4.2. BUILDING EDUCATIONAL APPLICATIONS OF CBDAS

Development of Design-MUSE continued, and related CBDA projects began to focus more on educational applications. During the winter quarter of 1995, Version 2 of Design-MUSE was exercised, again in Professor Kolodner's class. This time, three groups of students worked to produce three parts of a single case library on the topic of sustainable technology and development. One group focused on cases of industrial pollution, another on sustainable development and resource management, and the third on industrial accidents. The merger of these three pieces by Narayanan produced Susie (SUStainable technology Interactive Education). The faculty who run Georgia Tech's three quarter sequence on sustainable technology are currently considering whether to use Susie as a seed library for their students to learn from, and then extend.

The best example of work towards educational CBDA applications is CLIDE (Case Library for Industrial Design Education). Initially being assembled in the fall of 1995, CLIDE is intended to support two new courses on product design in the Industrial Design Program at Georgia Tech. The goal is that students in the first course (focusing on Design Case Studies) will extend CLIDE each quarter; then, beginning in 1996, students in the second course (dealing with Collaborative Product Design) will make use of the resulting case library. Both courses will be offered every quarter.

4.3. EXPERIENCE USING CBDAS IN EDUCATION

The first attempt at educational use of a CBDA (for end-user browsing as opposed to system construction) occurred in the Spring quarter of 1994 in the Georgia Tech College of Architecture. A version of Archie-II, stocked with information about libraries and courthouses, was made available to students in two studio sections that were involved in a library design competition. One of the two sections was composed of sophomore undergraduates, the other of second-year Masters students. We worked with the students only during the later half of the quarter, spending about 2 weeks with the undergraduates (just before they submitted their designs), and then 2 more weeks with the graduates (just after they had submitted theirs).

After group introductions to the system, each of our dozen students spent one or two hour-long sessions working through exercises we had designed. The first session's exercise involved critiquing an existing library on which we provided documentation; the second session, which was held only for the graduate students, involved critiquing their own designs. A couple of students also came back at other times simply to browse the system for their own interest.

Our pedagogical goals included familiarizing students with a range of past designs and reinforcing the habit of critically assessing design by consistently linking actual outcomes to relevant design intentions. We wanted to start evaluating our CBDAs both with respect to their use in teaching and with regard to their general usability, and the usefulness of their information content for conceptual design. The results were a bit mixed, but still encouraging. All the students liked the idea of the system, but the graduate students appreciated the actual content far more than the undergraduates. Interestingly, the undergraduate studio instructor judged that those students who used the system had gotten a lot out of their limited exposure, even though there was no way to directly trace any details of their designs to their use of the system. As for instilling a critical attitude in which designs are habitually related to intentions, there is no evidence as to whether or not any of the students absorbed that lesson.

Overall, the first studio experience was positive enough that Archie-II has been undergoing continued development in preparation for another, more substantial, classroom trial now tentatively scheduled for the Winter 1996 quarter. With the help of one of Georgia Tech's studio instructors, a new corpus of materials bearing on the design of tall buildings is being assembled. As with the other educational applications outlined earlier, our goal is to have students both contribute to the case library, and use it to support their own design work. We believe that both exercises should have significant pedagogical value.

5. Related Work

Using CBR in design (Hinrichs, 1992; Faltings, Shih, and Schmitt, 1992; Sycara, Navin-Chandra, Guttal, Koning, and Narasimhan, 1991; Hua, Smith), using cases to support design (Domeshek and Kolodner, 1994; Nakakoji, 1993; Oxman; and Oxman1993; Voss et al, 1993), or simply capturing design cases in process (Conklin and Begeman, 1989) have all become popular areas for research. There are now a variety of projects that have looked at ways to use cases to aid designers (including many in the domain of architecture). Surveying those projects reveals a set of issues where different researchers have taken different stances. Here we focus on the following issues:

1. What kind of design is supported?
2. What kind of users are assumed?
3. What kind of case materials are provided?
4. How are case materials made available to the designer?
5. What does the program let designers do with case materials?

5.1. WHAT KIND OF DESIGN IS SUPPORTED?

Most work on AI in design has focused on detailed design, often in simplified circumstances. This holds true for work on CBR in design and, to some extent, even for work on CBDA. For instance, Nakakoji's main domain was kitchen configuration using a limited pallet of possible kitchen components. Interestingly, the FABEL project, based on the ARMILLA model, aims to document the entire history of complex buildings at all levels of detail. In contrast, CBDAs are aimed squarely at conceptual design of complex artifacts. In this our work is most similar to Oxman and Oxman's information repository.

5.2. WHAT KIND OF USERS ARE ASSUMED?

We imagine two kinds of users in our work: professional designers and students. To satisfy both audiences, we must address the issue of how a case library might differ when targeted for students and when aimed at professionals. Our assumption has been that student designers are designers, although they are still learning, and therefore much of the help that is useful to professionals is useful to students. We also assume that professional designers, no matter how expert, learn from seeing critiques and analysis of other projects. Thus, we believe the form and content of case libraries for these two distinct user groups might not be very different. It is true that some lessons appropriate for a student would be too elementary for a professional (and likewise, some cases of interest to a particular practitioner would be too idiosyncratic for a student). Nonetheless, many of the design points illustrated by the successes and failures of existing buildings are of interest to both groups of users. Because users control what issues they focus on, a representative and well-documented case library can serve both user groups well. On the other hand, it might be appropriate to supplement a student system with basic information about standards and guidelines—resources that a professional might access more rarely. One thing we must remember is that a case library is but one resource available to designers as they design; it need not provide every shred of information a student or professional designer might need.

To pursue the notion of difference further, however, we can imagine more focused CBDAs diverging for students and professionals. A system for students might focus on a famous designer, an important design style, or on a group of precedent-setting buildings. Oxman and Oxman (1993) have pointed out that in architecture, some precedent-setting buildings recognized as breaking boundaries or setting standards are important for working designers to be familiar with. Because these buildings are well-studied and documented, CBDAs could be used to present them to students. At the other extreme, a CBDA might be built for a particular narrow group of professionals—perhaps the members of one design firm—reflecting the idiosyncratic experience of their particular design practice.

There are several more interesting ways in which a CBDA might be tuned for student use. First, student designers might not be familiar enough with the vocabulary of a domain to be able to use an indexing system based on the categories and shared concepts of experienced practitioners. A student-oriented system might focus on providing appropriate scaffolding (Collins, Brown, and Newman, 1989; Wood, Bruner, and Ross, 1975;) to introduce students to the vocabulary and concepts of the domain. Similarly, one can assume that students, initially unfamiliar with carrying out conceptual design, might need help in deciding what to investigate at any time and in recognizing the most important places to focus attention during their deliberations. The guidance provided here should be such that it helps students learn to do design. As far as we know, nobody is working directly on the problem of scaffolding for student designers.

5.3. WHAT KIND OF CASE MATERIALS ARE PROVIDED?

No matter the source and no matter the audience, we believe the most useful case libraries for conceptual design will emphasize certain kinds of case materials—in particular, lessons and documentation augmented by generalized problems and responses. We suggest avoiding masses of unanalyzed design data. Much detailed information on artifacts is irrelevant to conceptual design lessons and can be excluded from such a system. Likewise, online catalogs of parts for configuration are not needed to support conceptual design.

The bias toward conceptual design differentiates CBDAs from other design aids that use cases. Were CBDAs to be broadened to cover other phases of design (and this might be an interesting direction in which to move), materials needed for those other phases (e.g., extensive detailed design documentation, extensive descriptions of component parts) would need to be integrated into the presentation framework as well.

5.4. HOW ARE CASE MATERIALS MADE AVAILABLE?

CBDAs provide several means of navigating or browsing a case library, and we have discussed these extensively in Section 3, justifying the particular means we provide by appeal to the process of conceptual design. The kinds of access provided depends not only on the demands of conceptual design, but also on the availability of certain classes of presentations. Most other systems do not provide such a rich variety of materials, and thus cannot provide linkages, for instance, between documentation and evaluation, or between general and specific information. Except in systems where focused presentations address particular issues and interactions, the kind of interest-based indexing promoted by Design-MUSE is not a useful technique.

Irrespective of the exact content of indexes in a system, the system might take a stronger hand informing queries. A proposal due to Gomez de Silva Garza and Maher (1996) suggested a way in which the accessibility of indexed information might be improved through letting the system itself suggest components of search cues when a partially formed query indicates the user is interested in related areas.

Ultimately, we want to see CBDAs integrated with work environments, somewhat like that provided by Janus (Nakakoji, 1993), but with greater flexibility in response to the demands of conceptual design of complex artifacts. Such a system could watch a designer's work in progress and offer appropriate advice and information based on evolving design proposals. Nakakoji (1993) described case delivery in the restricted case of detailed kitchen design. Further work in this direction requires, at the very least, a more completely fleshed out online conceptual design environment. Initial steps in this direction are described in the final section.

5.5. WHAT CAN BE DONE WITH CASE MATERIALS?

The final issue is what a designer can do with retrieved case materials. Even in as complex a domain as architecture, most CBD systems try to make pieces of retrieved cases fit into a new design (Hua et al., 1992; Nakakoji, 1993). Because these systems are aimed toward more detailed design, they emphasize a direct kind of reuse that is usually inappropriate during conceptual design. Instead of expecting a designer to reuse a particular part of a building configuration (aided by parametric adaptation to fit new circumstances), we expect our designers to use cases to learn a lesson that can then be applied to the novel circumstances of the new situation. This might require radical reconfiguration when combined with all the other ideas and lessons picked up during browsing.

We do not yet know exactly what kind of aid we should provide to designers to help them with this merging process. The closest related work would probably , be systems that focus on design rationale capture or design space exploration (Conklin and Begeman, 1989). Although these systems do not emphasize access to lessons, they do suggest ways to help a designer organize the kinds of insights such lessons might impart.

6. Future Directions

This chapter has brought the story of CBDAs up to the present. We have built a series of trial CBDAs, we have developed a domain-independent CBDA shell, and we have conducted some preliminary trials of these systems, looking both at the construction of CBDAs and at their use in educational design settings. As the work has progressed, our vision has evolved. From our current vantage point, we can pick out several features that are central to the structure of CBDAs:

1. CBDAs are intended to support designers working on the conceptual design of a complex artifact.
2. The primary support a CBDA offers is easy access to prior experience.

3. Huge design cases are broken up into small lesson-bearing stories; stories are linked to general discussions of design issues and design strategies, emphasizing the trade-offs inherent in most complex design situations.

4. The issues highlighted in a CBDA encompass the entire life cycle of an artifact and represent concerns of all stakeholders.

5. All presentations can make appropriate use of whatever media forms are natural to working designers.

6. The presentations are organized so they are accessible in ways that fit the needs of the different phases of conceptual design.

The major task before us is to demonstrate the utility of CBDAs on a larger scale. The pending exercises—continued stocking and student use of CBDAs for architectural design, sustainable technology, and product design—are steps in this direction. Further progress in a corporate environment such as LASC appears to require major commitment of resources, not only to gather, prepare, and enter materials, but also to support reimplementation of the system to cope with real world requirements such as multiplatform portability, efficient centralized data storage, and standardized presentation formats. For many smaller companies, it might be sufficient to simply rebuild the system for Windows PCs.[3]

Our experiences so far have turned up several needed improvements; we are currently working on some of these. One deficiency we intend to address is the way that the indexing system is presented to the user. Currently, the query interface is almost totally transparent: The menu-driven fill-in-the-form interface (as shown in Figure 2.4) reflects exactly the structures that are used internally (by the system) for indexing; the hierarchical menus of filler choices reveal much of the conceptual space of index terms. The result is not as comprehensible or as usable as might be a system that buffered the user a bit more, presenting choices in a way more tailored to the mature practitioner's understanding of the domain. Another deficiency is in the expressiveness of the indexing system. Although we have worked hard on capturing the cross-domain dimensions of story indexes, our story indexes do not allow specification of the larger design a story is part of. Thus, one can ask the system for stories about lighting but not for stories about lighting in thick buildings.[4]

A related issue is the extent to which we have captured the appropriate generalizations for easing indexing across domains and for a variety of conceptual

---

[3]Work on indexing video clips in the VID project (Gordon and Domeshek, 1995), a tangentially related effort at Northwestern University's Institute for the Learning Sciences, might ultimately facilitate the move of CBDAs to the popular Windows platform by establishing basic data-handling infrastructure.
[4]A thick building is one that is so deep or wide that lighting from the outside cannot be used to light the center. Large, square buildings are thick.

design tasks. Our experience with the student-built CBDAs indicates we have not yet crisply characterized what should be in an index. We also know that we are not yet doing a good job of supporting the critiquing of partially-specified user design proposals.

One way in which we hope to improve design proposal critiquing is by building up the design environment of which a CBDA is supposed to be a part. CBDAs already include a notebook facility in which designers can clip and save interesting presentations they find while browsing, and to which they can add their own annotations. That notebook should grow into a more fully fleshed-out analog of a designer's notebook—a workspace that allows (and ultimately facilitates) sketching, calculating, and perhaps even drafting or modeling. An idea of what we intend can be gleaned from initial work directed at linking Archie-II to a sketch pad that recognizes some aspects of freehand drawings (Gross, Zimring, and Do, 1994). In this prototype, bubble diagrams of building floor plans sketched by a designer serve as queries to the CBDA library, which retrieves designs with similar structure (and then provides access to their evaluative stories). This is a direction we hope to expand significantly in the future.

Our emphasis on educational applications of CBDAs has increased the importance of providing appropriate scaffolding for student designers. We expect to pursue both of the directions suggested earlier: helping students learn the vocabulary of the new design domain (reflected, for instance, in the CBDA's indexing system), and helping students through the conceptual design process itself (in part by focusing them on relevant information that will help them make progress).

One final extension of CBDA capabilities is also being pursued: Efforts are under way at Georgia Tech to embed a CBDA information resource in a distributed collaboration environment. Design of complex artifacts is a process that necessarily requires teamwork over an extended period of time. The CaMile environment (Guzdial, Rappin, and Carlson, 1995) was designed to support structured group discussions that can make reference to documents prepared in any of a variety of normal microcomputer applications. A particularly useful class of documentation to reference during collaborative design discussion is the sort of case material available in a CBDA. Information on existing artifacts can be used to introduce alternatives, cited to justify design decisions, or referenced to buttress arguments during ongoing design debates. The Design-MUSE/CaMile environment allows cases to be referenced during collaboration; it also allows discussions about cases to be accessed while perusing the case library. Finally, the combination system provides the opportunity to provide definitions and illustrations of design vocabulary and context to novice users as part of an integrated system.

The future of case-based support for design seems bright. We have had much success with our experimental systems and generated interest from a variety of designers and design organizations. The ongoing construction and use exercises will expand both our case libraries and our experience with using CBDAs. Initial integration projects already under way will tie CBDAs to design tools and collaboration environments. Refinement of Design-MUSE continues, reflecting our accumulating experience of system use and our evolving understanding of what is common in conceptual design across domains. In short, we believe we can look forward to progress on a variety of fronts that will lead both to more usable systems and a better understanding of the place of CBR in design.

Acknowledgments

Thanks to Craig Zimring, our constant collaborator throughout the Archie project, and to Hari Narayanan, who has taken up the reins of the project this last year, helping to create Susie, and CLIDE. Thanks also to Ashok Goel, Michel Conan, Dale Durfee, Richard Billington, Anna Zacherl, Vijaya Narayanan, Marin Simina, Ellen Do, Osman Ataman, Husam Khalil, Ali Malkawi, Ameen Farooq, Marcia Herndon, and Andrew Bennett, who have all contributed to or influenced Archie and MIDAS. This work has been supported in part by the Defense Advanced Research Projects Agency, monitored by ONR under contract N00014-91-J-4092, by the Lockheed Aeronautical Systems Company, and by EduTech. All views expressed are those of the authors.

References

Barber, J., Bhatta, S., Goel, A., Jacobson, M., Pearce, M., Penberthy, L., Shankar, M., and Stroulia, E.: 1992, AskJef: integrating case-based reasoning and multimedia technologies for interface design support, *in* J. S. Gero, (ed.), *Artificial Intelligence in Design '92*, Kluwer Academic, Dordrecht, NL, pp. 457–476.

Collins, A., Brown, J. S., and Newman, S. E.: 1989, Cognitive apprenticeship: Teaching the craft of reading, writing, and mathematics, *in* L. B. Resnick (eds), *Knowing, Learning, and Instruction: Essays in Honor of Robert Glaser*, Lawrence Erlbaum Associates, Hillsdale, NJ, pp. 453–494.

Conklin, J., and Begeman, M.: 1989, gIBIS: A tool for ALL reasons, *Journal of the American Society for Information Science*, 40(3), 200–213.

Domeshek, E. A., Herndon, M. F., Bennett, A. W., and Kolodner, J. L.: 1994, A case-based design aid for conceptual design of aircraft subsystems, *Proceedings of the Tenth IEEE Conference on Artificial Intelligence for Applications*, IEEE Computer Society Press, Washington, DC.

Domeshek, E. A., and Kolodner, J. L.: 1991, Towards a case-based aid for conceptual design, *International.Journal of Expert Systems Research and Applications*, 4(2), 201–220.

Domeshek, E. A., and Kolodner, J. L.: 1992, A case-based design aid for architecture, *in* J. S. Gero (ed.), *Artificial Intelligence in Design '92*, Kluwer Academic, Dordrecht, NL, pp. 497–516.

Domeshek, E. A., and Kolodner, J. L.: 1993, Finding the points of large cases, *Artificial Intelligence for Engineering Design, Analysis and Manufacturing*, 7(2), 87–96.

Domeshek, E. A., and Kolodner, J. L.: 1994, End-user indexing of design lessons, *Working Notes from the AAAI-94 Workshop on Indexing and Reuse in Multimedia Systems*, pp. 119–125.

Domeshek, E. A., Kolodner, J. L., and Zimring, C. M.: 1994, The design of a tool kit for case-based design aids, *in* J. S. Gero and F. Sudweeks (eds), *Artificial Intelligence in Design '94*, Kluwer Academic, Dordrecht, NL, pp. 109–126.

Ferguson, W., Bareiss, R., Birnbaum, L., and Osgood, R.: 1992, Ask Systems: An approach to the realization of story-based teachers, *The Journal of the Learning Sciences*, 2(1), 95–134.

Goel, A. K., and Chandrasekaran, B.: 1989, Use of device models in adaptation of design cases, *in* K. J. Hammond (ed.), *Proceedings: Workshop on Case-Based Reasoning*, Kaufmann, San Mateo, CA, pp. 100–109.

Goel, A. K., Kolodner, J. L., Pearce, M., Billington, R, and Zimring, C.: 1991, Towards a case-based tool for aiding conceptual design problem solving, *in* R. Bareiss (ed.), *Proceedings: Case-Based Reasoning Workshop*, Kaufmann, San Mateo, CA, pp. 109–120.

Gomez de Silva Garza, A., and Maher, M. L.: 1996, Design by interactive exploration using memory-based techniques, *Knowledge-Based Systems*, 9(1), 151–161.

Gordon, A. S., and Domeshek, E. A.: 1995, Conceptual indexing for video retrieval, *in* M. Mayfield (ed.), *Working Notes: IJCAI '95 Workshop on Intelligent Multimedia Information Retrieval*, Montreal, Quebec, pp. 23–38.

Gross, M. D., Zimring, C., and Do, E.: 1994, Using diagrams to access a case base of architectural designs, *in* J. S. Gero and F. Sudweeks (eds), *Artificial Intelligence in Design '94*, Kluwer Academic, Dordrecht, NL, pp. 129–144.

Guzdial, M., Rappin, N., and Carlson, D.: 1995, Collaborative and multimedia interactive learning environment for engineering education, *ACM Symposium on Applied Computing 1995*, ACM Press, Nashville, TN, pp. 5–9.

Hennessy, D., and Hinkle, D.: 1992, Applying case-based reasoning to autoclave loading, *IEEE Expert*, 7(5), 21–26.

Hinrichs, T.: 1992, *Problem Solving in Open Worlds: A Case Study in Design*, Lawrence Erlbaum Associates, Hillsdale, NJ.

Hua, K., Smith, I., Faltings, B., Shih, S., and Schmitt, G.: 1992, Adaptation of spatial design cases, *in* J. S. Gero (ed.), *Artificial Intelligence in Design '92*, Kluwer Academic, Dordrecht, NL, pp. 559–575.

Kolodner, J. L.: 1991, Improving human decision making through case-based decision aiding, *AI Magazine*, 12(2), 52–68.

Kolodner, J. L.: 1993, *Case-Based Reasoning*, Kaufmann, San Mateo, CA.

Kolodner, J. L., and Penberthy, L.: 1990, A case-based approach to creativity in problem solving, *Proceedings of the Twelfth Annual Conference of the Cognitive Science Society*, Lawrence Erlbaum Associates, Hillsdale, NJ, pp. 978–985.

Nakakoji, K.: 1993, Case-deliverer: Making cases relevant to the task at hand, *in* S. Wess, K.-D. Atthoff, and M. M. Richer (eds), *Topics in Case-Based Reasoning*, Springer Verlag, Berlin, German, LNAI837, pp. 446–457.

Ockerman, J. J.: 1995, *Case-based Design Browser to Aid Human Developers Reuse Previous Design Concepts*. Unpublished Masters Thesis, Georgia Institute of Technology.

Oxman, R., and Oxman, R.: 1993, PRECEDENTS: Memory structure in design case libraries, *in* U. Flemming and S. Van Wyk (eds), *CAAD Futures '93*, Elsevier Science Publishers, Amsterdam, pp. 273–288.

Pearce, M., Goel, A. K., Kolodner, J. L., Zimring, C., Sentosa, L., and Billington, R.: 1992, Case-based design support: A case study in architectural design, *IEEE Expert*, 7(5), 14–20.

Schank, R. C.: 1991, *Tell Me a Story*, Charles Scribner, New York, NY.

Slater, B. M., and Riesbeck, C. K.: 1991, TaxOps: A case-based advisor, *International Journal of Expert Systems Research and Applications*, 4(2), 117–140.

Sycara, K., Navin-Chandra, D., Guttal, R., Koning, J., and Narasimhan, S.: 1991, CADET: A case-based synthesis tool for engineering design, *International Journal of Expert Systems Research and Applications*, 4(2), 157–188.

Voss, A. (ed.): 1993, Similarity concepts and retrieval methods, *FABEL Report #13*, Gesellschaftfur Mathematik und Datenverabeitung mbH.

Wood, D., Bruner, J. S., and Ross, G.: 1975, The role of tutoring in problem-solving, *Journal of Child Psychology and Psychiatry*, 17, 89–100.

chapter three

CASE REUSE BY MODEL-BASED INTERPRETATION

BOI FALTINGS
Swiss Federal Institute of Technology (EPFL)

For applying CBR to design, adaptation and combination are essential. They require adaptation knowledge defining the parts of a case that can be changed without compromising its function. We have investigated model-based interpretations for providing this knowledge. An interpretation is a functional model given by the user to explain the structure given by a case. It defines the intended functions and provides constraints on the structure that avoid violating them. Because the interpretation may be different from that used in the design of the case, creative reuse of cases is also possible. This chapter reports on the results of this investigation with two CBD programs: FAMING for mechanism part shapes and CADRE for buildings.

1. Introduction

Design is traditionally regarded as an activity where unstructured thought is of prime importance to allow innovation to arise. However, in the modern world, a designer has to consider an enormous amount of technical details that are hardly compatible with this requirement. Furthermore, design is now often carried out in a team where decisions must be shared with colleagues. Human intelligence is insufficient for this environment; designers require an artificial intelligence designed for problem-solving in highly structured and constrained domains.

Conventional CAD systems do not fulfill this goal: They are only drawing tools that provide no understanding and, consequently, no support for the design itself. Knowledge-based systems, such as the ICAD system (Wagner, 1990), are being used increasingly and successfully in large companies such as Boeing or

General Motors. Currently, operational systems are based on deductive rule systems that require a large knowledge-engineering effort to construct and maintain. Case-based and model-based reasoning promise a significantly lower development cost and could make the technology accessible to a much wider range of users:

- *Cases* model knowledge and experience of a specific designer; the base of cases can be built up at almost no expense by recording previous designs.
- *Models* encode general principles shared by a large community; they need to be developed only once and their development cost can be shared.

In this chapter, we show how we have applied these principles in two prototype design systems for mechanical and building design.

Most automated design systems use abductive reasoning where a structure is synthesized from components such that it fulfills a desired function. However, such abduction is computationally tractable only when components can be assigned functions in a way that is independent of their context of use, the no-function-in-structure principle (DeKleer and Brown, 1984). This condition is given in electronic circuits, in particular digital circuits, and design automation has become commonplace in this domain.

However, the no-function-in-structure principle does not hold in domains that require a geometric layout, such as mechanisms and buildings. Here, the space of good designs is very sparse, and any particular component is likely to be useful only in very particular contexts. Figure 3.1 illustrates this situation. Predicates P1 through P3 and Q1 through Q3 are used to distinguish good from bad designs. Note that each predicate has been invented with a particular example in mind: P1–Q1, P2–Q3 and P3–Q2 cover the three positive examples shown here. It is more practical to model this design knowledge as parameterized prototypes (Gero, 1990) of complete designs. In a prototype-based system, good designs are described as variations of prototypes, as indicated by the arrows in Figure 3.1. These approximate locally the complex shape of the space of good designs (indicated by the dashed line in Figure 3.1). There exist several commercial tools for such parametric design.

Defining libraries of prototypes is a tedious process that only large companies can afford. In general, knowledge is available in the form of cases of earlier designs, and models of how they work. The novelty of my approach is that I directly adapt cases of particular earlier solutions to new problems, using models to define the admissible modifications. I extend this idea, first proposed by Goel (1991), by grounding all models a systematic theory founded on constraint reasoning. This makes the models straightforward to formulate and combine and avoids the expensive knowledge engineering associated with the functional models used by Goel.

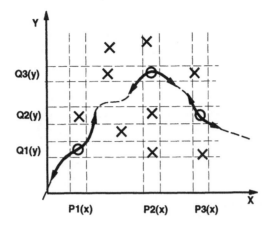

Figure 3.1. The set of good designs (circles) among the bad designs (crosses).

To illustrate the approach, we have implemented two prototype systems:

- FAMING for CBD of part shapes in mechanisms, and
- CADRE for CBD of buildings.

Both systems allow innovation by case modification, combination, and reinterpretation. They focus only on the aspects concerning reuse of a particular case and do not provide any support for selecting a suitable case. Because cases have to be selected according to their adaptability to the current problem, I consider that this case indexing problem can only be addressed after the questions of adaptation and combination have been solved. In many other domains where CBR has been applied (Kolodner, 1993), adaptation is straightforward and most research has focused on the case indexing problem. In the current state of the art, selection of a suitable case constitutes the 1% inspiration that is hard to reproduce in a computer program. FAMING and CADRE then take over the remaining 99% perspiration by automatically proposing novel designs that implement the designer's inspiration.

2. Case Interpretations

CBR is a technique where past solutions are reused or adapted to solve new problems. In CBD, specific design precedents are reused for new problems. Because designs can never be reused exactly, a key issue in CBD is how to adapt a case to a new problem. One can distinguish two types of adaptation:

- *Modification*, where small changes are made to a single case until it fits the requirements.
- *Combination*, where two or more cases are combined into a new design.

For adaptation, it is crucial to know what changes can be made to a design case without perturbing its function. This knowledge, which we call *adaptation knowledge*, must be provided in addition to the model of the structure stored in the design case.

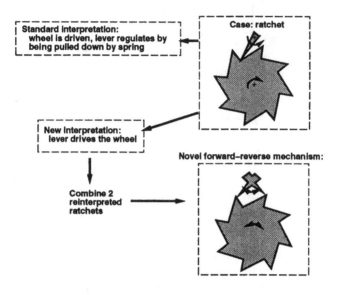

Figure 3.2. Artifacts are interpreted in terms of SBF models.

Our approach to provide adaptation knowledge for cases is to interpret them in terms of SBF models (Davis, 1984; Gero, Lee, and Tham, 1992; Goel, 1991; Sembugamoorthy and Chandrasekaran, 1986; Umeda, Takeda, Tomiyama, and Yoshikawa, 1990). An SBF model consists of three parts:

- *Structure*, usually a CAD model of the device itself and provided by the case.
- *Behavior*, a model of what the device does in a particular circumstance.
- *Function*, a model identifying what is important about the behavior.

Cross-references between aspects of the three parts define how each element of the structure is responsible for aspects of the behavior, and how aspects of the behavior are in turn responsible for the function of the device. This provides the knowledge of how modifications to the structure affect behavior and function. By associating an SBF model, called an *interpretation*, with a case, it becomes an intelligent object that is capable of adapting itself to fit new specifications and environments.

Following common design methodologies such as that of Pahl and Beitz (1988), I assume functions and thus SBF models to be qualitative. A qualitative model differs from a quantitative one in that it specifies properties that hold over ranges of parameter values. This makes it possible to express functions that hold over a range of situations, such as "block any counterclockwise motion." Another reason for using qualitative models is that they make it possible to determine all possible behaviors of a device, not only a particular snapshot valid for one particular scenario. This is required for expressing certain specifications, such as "parts A and B should never lose contact, no matter what orientation the device is held in." Finally, through the connections in a qualitative SBF model, constraints on qualitative function can be mapped to constraints on the structure.

In an intelligent object, structure is interpreted as implementing a function through a behavior. This interpretation is subjective to a particular use of the structure; reuse might imply a different interpretation. For example, a pen may be intended for writing, but can also be used as a pointing device. SBF models provide the language that allows the user to indicate what function the case should be reused for. Figure 3.2 shows an example where a ratchet device is reinterpreted using a different SBF model than intended by the original designer. Combination of two such devices results in an innovative design of a forward-reverse-mechanism, a device that transforms an oscillating input motion into a rotation that advances two steps forward and one step backward with each oscillation (this example is described in detail in Sun and Faltings, 1994). Such reinterpretation is the source of much innovation in design (Wills and Kolodner, 1994).

3. FAMING: A Case Study in Mechanism Design

FAMING (Faltings and Sun, 1994; Faltings and Sun, 1996; Sun, 1995; Sun and Faltings, 1994) is a system for supporting the creative design of elementary mechanisms, also called *kinematic pairs*. A kinematic pair consists of two parts with one degree of freedom: either translation in a fixed direction or rotation around a fixed axis. The part shapes restrict the relative motion of the two parts; this restriction implements the function of the pair. Examples of kinematic pairs are ratchets and clock escapements. Kinematic pairs are usually arranged in chains that transmit and transform motion between the terminal members. For example, in a mechanical clock the regular motion of pendulum is transformed through a kinematic chain into a motion of the hands.

FAMING is short for Functional Analysis of Mechanisms for Inventing New Geometries, but also means invent in Mandarin Chinese. Although the theories underlying FAMING are more general, the program itself has been restricted to devices consisting of two rotating parts; this covers, for example, all parts of a mechanical watch or clock.

3.1. STRUCTURE, BEHAVIOR AND FUNCTION IN FAMING

Figure 3.3 shows the structures that implement the three models for structure, behavior and function in FAMING, and how they are related through reasoning processes.

3.1.1. Structure: Metric Diagram

The metric diagram is a CAD model that defines a kinematic pair as two 2-dimensional objects consisting of vertices and edges between them. Each vertex defines two symbolic parameters; in the case of rotational freedom, an angle for its orientation and a scalar for its distance from the center of rotation of the corresponding object.

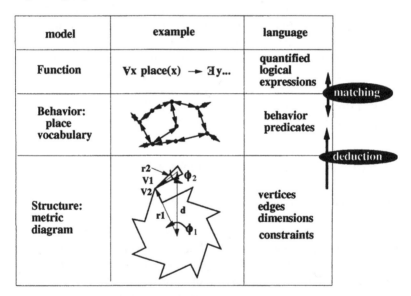

Figure 3.3. Representations of structure, behavior and function models for mechanisms.

Based on the metric diagram, a *shape feature* (which may involve both objects) is defined by a set of vertices and edges, and a set of constraints that must hold simultaneously for the shape feature to be present. For example, the shape feature which corresponds to the possibility of the top of the ratchet's lever being able to touch the wheel (v_1 touching v_2 in Figure 3.3) can be expressed as follows:

- must exist: vertices v_1, v_2
- constraints: $\{|d - r_1| < r_2\}$

3.1.2. Qualitative Behavior: Place Vocabularies

Textbooks on the subject explain kinematic behavior qualitatively by sequences of kinematic states. A kinematic state is defined by part motions and a contact relationship. For a kinematic pair, part motion is modelled qualitatively by a combination of signs that define the directions of each part's motion: $+, 0, -$, or $*$, which stands for any of the three values. The set of possible contact relations depends on the part shapes. We call each different contact relation a *place*.

Figure 3.4 shows the different types of contact relations that are possible for kinematic pairs with two rotating objects:

- *Edge-edge contact* or *point-point contact:* is maintained only when both objects do not move and thus is a zero-dimensional place.
- *Point-edge contact:* is maintained in a coordinated motion of both objects and thus is a one-dimensional place.
- *No contact:* both objects are free to move and thus this is a two-dimensional place.

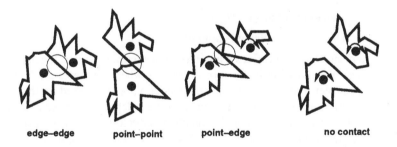

edge–edge   point–point   point–edge   no contact

Figure 3.4. Different types of contact relationships between two rotating objects.

When motion allows direct transition from the contact in one place to those in another, the places are adjacent. Places and their adjacencies form a graph called the *place vocabulary* because it defines the terminology for referring to states of the mechanism. The place vocabulary forms a mathematical structure called a *cell complex*. More details about the place vocabulary theory of qualitative kinematics can be found in Faltings (1990).

Depending on the place, only particular qualitative motions are possible, modelled by the predicate allowed-motion(x,d) where d is a vector of two signs. Motions can cause changes in contact relations. Arcs in the place vocabulary are formalized by the predicate transition(x,y,d), which is true whenever a motion in direction d can cause a transition from place x to y.

3.1.3. Function

There has been much recent work on formalisms for representing function in design. Most researchers consider function to be a causal relation between an environment (or context) and a particular behavior, and are concerned mainly with vocabularies for specifying these causal connections (Gero, 1990; Umeda et al., 1990).

In kinematics, there is only one form of causality, that of pushing on a part contact. In any particular state, the allowed-motion predicates allow predicting the behavior in an external environment and thus determine the function of the device. Often, functions are properties of sets of states, for example, that there exists a certain sequence of states. We therefore formulate functions in two levels:

- a *functional feature* defines a property of a particular state or set of states, and thus always takes at least one state as an argument. An example of a function feature is that a place blocks the externally imposed motions (M_{ext})

    blocking - place$(x, (M_{ext})$:

    $(\forall d \in M_{ext})\neg$**allowed - motion**$(x,d)$

- a *device function* defines a property of the entire behavior. It consists of a logical expression in functional features where all states are bound by quantifiers, and a specification of an environment assumed for this device function. I assume the environment to be independent of the mechanism state. An example of a device function is the following specification of a ratchet function. A ratchet is a device that blocks motion of a wheel in the clockwise direction, but freely allows it in the other direction.

    for $M(x) = \{-, *)\} \wedge F_{est} = \{(*, +)\}$:

    $(\forall y)\{\neg(\exists C)$**cycle**$(y, C) \wedge$

    $(\exists z)($**blocking - place**$(z, M(x)) \wedge$ **possible - path**$(y, z))\}$

This (partial) specification states that under the assumption that the first object turns clockwise, and the second object is pushed counterclockwise, no reachable place leads to a cycle and all states can eventually lead to a blocking state.

Because it is very cumbersome for designers to formalize functions, functional features as well as device functions are predefined in a library. The designer must intervene only when truly novel functions are considered.

3.2. CASE REUSE IN FAMING

For each case, FAMING takes as input a structural model of an existing device, represented as a metric diagram, and a qualitative model of its function, represented as a set of device functions. The first step in reusing the case consists of understanding how it implements the function and, consequently, what can be changed without affecting it. FAMING constructs this understanding by using the symbolic mapping provided in the theory of qualitative kinematics (Faltings, 1992).

Based on the information in the metric diagram, FAMING first computes the place vocabulary, which defines all possible behaviors of the device. These behaviors are then automatically matched to the specified device function. For example, assume that the functional specification of a device contains the condition that there exists a blocking-place x:

$$(\exists z)(\textbf{blocking - place}(x)$$

and that the place vocabulary of the corresponding case contains a place P that is such a blocking-place. Unification of the functional specification with the place vocabulary substitutes P for x, thus transforming $(\exists z)$ **blocking-place**(x) into **blocking-place**(P). Assume that the device environment allows the qualitative motions $\{(-,-),(-,0,(-,+)\}$; these are thus the motions that must be blocked in P. Replacing the blocking-place predicate by the full expression in its definition and expanding the quantification over all motions, I obtain the following conjunction of predicates:

$$\neg\textbf{allowed - motion}(P,(-,-)) \wedge$$
$$\neg\textbf{allowed - motion}(P,(-,0)) \wedge$$
$$\neg\textbf{allowed - motion}(P,(-,+))$$

Next, FAMING translates this understanding into the shape features responsible for implementing the device function. Each predicate in the conjunction is implemented by particular aspects of the object shapes. Using a trace of their computation, it is possible to determine the constraints under which the behavior predicates remain valid. The behavior predicate $\neg\textbf{allowed - motion}(P,(-,-))$ is then mapped into shape features; that is, particular object vertices and constraints on their positions. FAMING provides such mappings for all kinematic properties modelled in the place vocabulary. Reversing the causal chain of the analysis thus establishes a mapping from functional features to shape features, which I call *structure-behavior inversion.* More details on the mapping between shape and qualitative behavior can be found in Sun (1994) and Faltings and Sun (1996).

The structure given by the case and the constraints defined in the interpretation form an intelligent object. Adaption is completed by choosing suitable dimensions to satisfy the set of constraints. Because there is a very large number of constraints and variables, complete methods for solving the constraint system (as described later in this chapter) are still too slow for use in a real-time design environment. Instead, I use local repair operators similar to those reported by Pu and Purvis (1994), Minton Johnston, Phillips, and Laird (1992), and Selman Levesque, and Mitchell (1992). The details of this procedure are described in Sun (1994), and Faltings and Sun (1996).

3.3. EXAMPLES OF FAMING

Being a research program, FAMING only treats devices from a limited domain, namely two-dimensional fixed-axis kinematic pairs with polygonal part shapes. This domain covers a large set of practical mechanisms, such as ratchets or escapements.

Figure 3.5 shows an example of case modification: a single case of a ratchet device (A) is modified into an escapement. An escapement, the central element of a mechanical clock, is a device where an oscillating motion of a pallet regulates the motion of a scape wheel, which is driven by a spring. This function requires alternatively blocking counterclockwise motion of the scape wheel, depending on the position of the pallet. FAMING first attempts to satisfy the functional constraints by changing the position of vertex v3 (B). It then discovers additional constraints that make the constraint system unsolvable, and solves the problem by introducing vertex v6, which makes the constraint system satisfiable and results in a working mechanism (C).

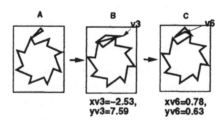

Figure 3.5. Incremental design of an escapement by fitting a new interpretation to a ratchet case.

Figure 3.6 shows an example of case combination. Here, an escapement is designed by combining part shapes from two ratchet devices. Ratchet (a) is interpreted as a normal ratchet with a blocking state for counterclockwise motion. Ratchet (b) is interpreted differently: The state shown provides in fact a partial blocking state that blocks motion of the wheel in the counterclockwise direction, but also transmits motion and, thus, energy from the wheel to the lever. All these functions combine into the correct escapement function. Version (c) is the raw combination of the shapes, version (d) is obtained after satisfying the constraints given by the interpretations and constitutes a working escapement.

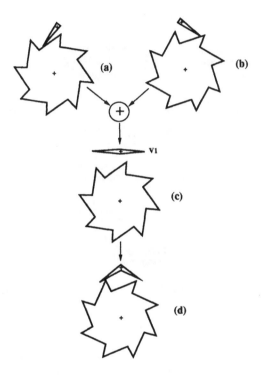

Figure 3.6. Design of an escapement by combining two ratchet devices.

Both examples are described in full detail in Sun (1994). FAMING has also been used to design entirely novel devices and thus has shown its potential for creativity. In Sun and Faltings (1994), we showed how reinterpretation of a ratchet structure and combination of two reinterpreted devices are used to create the novel forward-reverse mechanism already shown in Figure 3.2, which is much simpler than the solution proposed in the literature. FAMING has also been successfully applied to actual devices used in the watch industry.

4. CADRE: A Case Study in Architecture

CADRE is a prototype system for constraint-based adaptation of building designs
(Hua, 1994; Hua and Faltings, 1993). CADRE stands for Case Adaptation by
Dimensionality REeasoning, but also means framework in French. CADRE fixes
a framework for the designer that consists of the library of earlier designs which
can be used to construct new ones. Figure 3.7 shows the structure of CADRE.

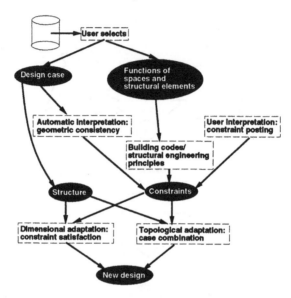

Figure 3.7. Data flow (ovals) and processes (boxes) in CADRE.

4.1. STRUCTURE, BEHAVIOR, AND FUNCTION IN CADRE

Like FAMING, CADRE uses separate models of structure, behavior, and function
to represent cases and their interpretation. However, due to the fact that the
domain is less formalized, their separation is less clear than in FAMING.

4.1.1. Structure: AutoCAD models

The structure of existing buildings is modeled using the commercial tool
AutoCAD. The structural model is similar to the metric diagram in FAMING and
consists of:

- objects; that is, the vertices, lines, and planes of the AutoCAD model;
- variables for the positions or dimensions of these objects; and
- a set of values currently assigned to the variables.

4.1.2. Behavior and Function: Constraints

The mechanical aspects of a building, in particular its stability, can be assigned mechanical behavior and function in a similar way as was done in FAMING: Movements have to be restricted by structural elements. In CADRE, I focused on architectural functions having to do with the use that occupants make of the spaces. For example, a space can be used as an office by putting desks and chairs in it, or as a kitchen by installing a stove and a sink, and this defines its function. The space then manifests a certain behavior: for example, by providing sufficient space and lighting to allow the occupant to carry out an activity. In contrast, if there is not enough space in an office to access the desk, or not enough light to work at it, then the office behavior is not satisfied.

To avoid the complexity of modeling behavior at this level of detail, in CADRE, both behavior and functional aspects are modeled by constraints formulated directly on the structure. This, in fact, corresponds well to current practice in the building industry, as building codes fix constraints for each particular use to ensure that the behavior of the spaces makes this use possible. Constraints fall in three different categories:

- *Definitions*, such as $area(x) = width(x) * length(x)$.
- *Integrity constraints*, such as $end(x) = beginning(y)$.
- *Restrictions*, such as $area(bedroom) > 8$.

Definitions and integrity constraints are instantiated automatically based on the structure. A user assigns an interpretation to a case by identifying its spaces and assigning each space functions from a library. An example of this assignment is shown in Figure 3.8. Each function has a model consisting of a set of constraints that the system automatically instantiates when the function is assigned to a space. These mostly automatic processes handle almost all of the necessary constraints, but the user can specify additional constraints where this is necessary.

4.2. CASE REUSE IN CADRE

By assigning an interpretation in terms of space usage to the AutoCAD model of an existing building in the case base, the user constructs an intelligent object where constraints restrict the dimensions in the CAD model. Additionally, an expert system adds constraints on the structural elements to ensure stability of the building.

When a case is reused in a different context, the context often causes conflicts with these constraints. These conflicts must be resolved by the two forms of adaptation provided in CADRE:

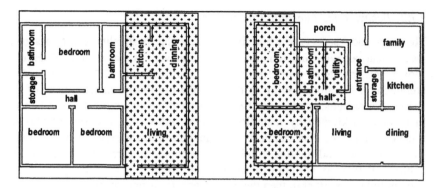

Figure 3.8. The unshaded parts show case fragments to be combined and adapted by
CADRE.

- *Dimensional adaptation*, where only dimensions of the case are changed.
- *Topological adaptation*, where the arrangement and number of spaces and
  walls are also modified.

We have developed a general solution for dimensional adaptation, based on the
notions of dimensionality expansion to make conflicts resolvable and subsequent
dimensionality reduction to limit the complexity of modifications.

In dimensionality expansion, additional degrees of freedom are added by
turning constants into variables. This process uses the constraint violations to
identify which variables must be introduced. For example, when a space does not
have the required minimal dimensions, the positions of its corners are turned into
variables.

Dimensionality reduction makes use of the fact that many variables are linked
by equations to eliminate dependent variables. For example, if we have three
variables $x_1 x_2$, and x_2, and two equalities $x_1 + 2x_2 - 3x_3 = 0$ and $3x_1 - 2x_2 +$,
$x_3 = 0$, only one variable can be changed independently; the remaining two will
be dependent and can be eliminated. Eliminating all dependent variables
simplifies the subsequent solution of the set of inequalities. Dimensionality
reduction applies particularly well to geometric structures, where the apparently
large number of variables is quickly reduced to a very small set. Dimensionality
reduction has been applied to reduce the complexity of shape matching in model-
based computer vision (Saund, 1988). The idea of separating dependent and
independent variables has also been proposed in Serrano and Gossard (1988).
Because a geometric structure like a building implies a very large number of
definitions and integrity constraints, dimensionality reduction usually reduces the
number of parameters and thus the complexity of case adaptation dramatically;
for example, from 112 to 2 parameters.

In some cases, it is not possible to adapt a case to a new environment using only changes to its dimensions; its topology has to be modified as well. Certain structures can be varied in a regular manner: for example, a string of rooms can be shortened by adding or removing one of them. However, in most cases, a topological change is likely to destroy the qualities the user sees in the case. CADRE provides two mechanisms for topological adaptation. For regular changes such as removing one of a set of identical rooms, it is possible to formulate rules that operate on a hierarchical object structure constructed on top of the CAD model (Hua, 1994). However, more general changes in topology are possible only when another case provides the knowledge required for the new layout. Significant parts of the new case are selected at the appropriate level of abstraction and combined with the existing one. This process is illustrated in the example shown next, and described in detail in Hua (1994).

4.3. EXAMPLE OF CADRE

My prototype system, CADRE, has been tested on examples of realistic complexity. Several of them are discussed in Schmitt, Dave, and Shih (1996). Figures 3.8 and 3.9 show an example of an adaptation of a layout carried out by the program.

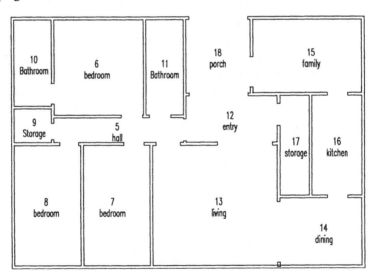

Figure 3.9. Result of adaptation by CADRE.

The user has specified the combination of the nonshaded parts of the two shown cases. The case on the left is called the *host case*, meaning that it dominates in case of conflicts, and the case on the right is a *guest case* that is adapted to fit the host case. One of the solutions proposed by CADRE is shown in Figure 3.9. This solution was obtained by connecting the unshaded parts of the two structures as well as the constraints which had been instantiated based on the assigned functions. The walls to connect have been indicated interactively by the user of the system. By using the constraint manipulation techniques described above, CADRE proposes the solution shown in Figure 3.9. Note that the solution involves substantial changes to the dimensions of the spaces, and would have been quite difficult to obtain for a human designer. This shows how CADRE can take over the 99% of perspiration associated with design.

5. Constraint Satisfaction Techniques

Both FAMING and CADRE translate case interpretations into constraints on the structures. This defines a CSP whose solution is the adaptation of the case that respects the interpretation that was attached to it. This constraint satisfaction problem involves many constraints on continuous variables, and there are no general and reliable methods for solving it available in the literature. Iterative refinement methods such as blackboard structures suffer from infinite cycling problems and are not guaranteed to ever find a solution.

Figure 3.10 illustrates how cycling problems arise: Assume that constraint C_1 is associated with parameter P_1 and that both are controlled by a blackboard agent A_1, while C_2 and P_2 are part of another agent A_2. Because the two agents act in isolation, A_1 will try to satisfy C_1 by adjusting P_1, and likewise A_2 will act on P_2 to satisfy C_2. In the example of Figure 3.10, these adjustments are indicated by arrows. Note that although there is a consistent solution satisfying both constraints, in the situation of Figure 3.10 the blackboard process actually diverges!

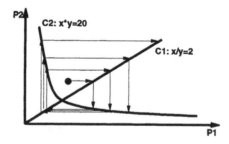

Figure 3.10. Blackboard control for constraint satisfaction may lead to infinite cycles.

Another possibility is the use of optimization techniques developed in operations research. However, these techniques require many implicit assumptions about the nature of constraints or the shape of the solution spaces that are often not satisfied in design.

For the purpose of the techniques I describe here, I have developed a comprehensive framework that allows efficient and complete solution of the constraint networks encountered in case adaptation. It relies on two concepts:

- *Equality* constraints are subjected to a process called *dimensionality reduction*: In each constraint, one parameter becomes a dependent parameter that cannot be chosen during adaptation. It is thus eliminated from consideration, and the dimensionality of the problem is thus reduced.

- In the remaining system of *inequalities*, all parameters eliminated during dimensionality reduction are replaced by the expression obtained through solving the equality. The resulting system is then solved using a novel propagation algorithm developed in this project and described later in this chapter.

Dimensionality reduction is implemented using Gaussian elimination for linear constraints, the REDUCE software package for certain nonlinear constraints, and special heuristics for other types of nonlinear constraints. This is described in detail by Hua and coworkers (Hua, 1994; Hua, Faltings, and Smith, 1995).

After dimensionality reduction, the task is to solve a system containing only inequalities. I solve such systems in two steps:

1. I find the consistent solution regions.
2. I instantiate particular solutions within the regions, either automatically or through user interaction.

Existing propagation techniques for solving systems of continuous variables are unsatisfactory in several respects:

1. Known local propagation rules fail to achieve the desired arc-consistent result in many practical cases.
2. Propagation rules based on interval bounds fail to terminate.
3. Many practical constraint networks contain cycles and require propagation algorithms that achieve more than local consistency.

Problem (1) is due to the fact that multiple constraints between the same pair of variables are propagated individually. Faltings (1994) showed that arc-consistency is guaranteed when constraints are propagated as a single total constraint, and gives a simple algorithm for carrying out such propagation. In Faltings (1994), the method is defined for binary constraints only. It has been extended to multiple variables in a straightforward manner.

Local propagation of interval bounds in constraint networks with cycles amounts to solving a system of simultaneous equations. Propagating constraints individually means that the system is solved by a numerically unstable fixed-point iteration, and can cause infinite cycling. A method that is both reliable and guaranteed to converge rapidly on such problems is that of binary search. Binary search recursively computes finer and finer approximations of the solution.

Haroud has developed a method for propagating total constraints, as shown necessary in Faltings (1994) using such a recursive decomposition (Haroud, 1995; Haroud and Faltings, 1994). Total constraints between any pair of variables are approximated using a quadtree decomposition, similar to that used in computer vision—see Figure 3.11, for an example of the quadtree decomposition constructed for a set of constraints (left), and the feasible regions (shown in white) after computing global consistency with the rest of the constraint network (right). The minimum granularity of the approximation determines the precision with which intervals of feasible variable values will be computed and depends on the requirements of the application. It can be shown that local consistency algorithms based on this approximation always converge rapidly even when the constraint network contains cycles.

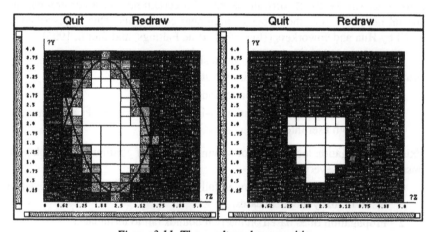

Figure 3.11. The quadtree decomposition.

Local consistency is not always enough for solving design problems. Computing higher degrees of consistency results in exponential time complexity and is not feasible in practice. However, research on the temporal reasoning problem has shown that in cases where constraints only admit single convex intervals, path-consistency (which can be computed in low-order polynomial time) is equivalent to global consistency. I have generalized this idea to general constraint satisfaction problems where total constraints are unions of convex regions and, thus, obtained an algorithm that determines globally consistent solutions for many classes of continuous CSPs in polynomial time (Haroud, 1995; Haroud and Faltings, 1994).

6. Importance of Cases

Many issues, such as representing function and its mapping to structure, are common to any intelligent design system. However, when geometric structures are involved, such principles by themselves are not enough to construct practical design systems. The translation from a qualitative functional specification to a physical structure is an abductive problem involving quantified variables that at the current state of the art, can only be solved by blind search. But blind search is not possible in a domain involving continuous variables because they cannot be enumerated.

FAMING and CADRE show how the use of cases can provide the missing element that makes the principles work on intelligent design of structures with geometry. By adapting cases, it is no longer necessary to address the problem of how to generate the infinite set of possible geometric structures. At the current state of the art, it would not be possible to construct systems as powerful as FAMING and CADRE without using cases.

In CADRE, another motivation is that cases are the communication medium where a designer can express the desired structure. Because there is no generally agreed-on functional language in architecture, in CADRE, the designer can indicate his desires by selecting buildings or parts of buildings that satisfy the intentions (see Schmitt et al. (1996) for a more detailed discussion of this issue). CADRE also would not have been possible without using cases.

The fact that case reuse is such an important condition for successful intelligent design systems might point to an explanation of why human designers base most of their activity, including creative design, on the reuse of existing cases.

7. Conclusions

Human intelligence has evolved to help people survive in natural environments: It is very good at handling natural, rounded shapes, reasoning with approximate information, and similar tasks. Modern engineering operates in a highly constrained world of artificial shapes with sharp edges, precise and well-controlled interactions, and many constraints to be respected. Human intuition is not well-suited to this environment, and its creativity cannot be exploited to its fullest extent.

By automating the low-level details, FAMING provides the designer with a mechanical intuition that he does not normally have and that makes it much easier for novel devices to be created. Using its numerical precision, the program provides the designer with the capability to envision and, thus, design devices whose behavior depends on precise shapes and interactions. Using FAMING, it took only one afternoon to produce and verify a watch escapement design that a team of four people had not yet completed after 6 months of work!

In building design, architects often produce designs that are costly or even expensive to build. Even worse, in complex design projects, there are many inconsistencies that are only discovered late in the construction process and cause tremendous cost overruns. A tool such as CADRE frees an architect from having to worry about low-level details, ranging from geometric consistency of drawings to the feasibility of integrating a suitable structure. He can now concentrate on composing spaces to implement the function he desires.

In collaboration with Schmitt of the architecture department of ETH Zürich, I am integrating CADRE with the virtual reality environment SCULPTOR. The increased interaction bandwith made possible by virtual reality makes it possible for users to really integrate the intelligence of the artificial provided by the computer with their own perception of form and style: Virtual reality is needed to make knowledge-based systems useful. On the other hand, in order to be convincing, virtual reality systems require complex models of behavior that can only be created using large amounts of knowledge: Knowledge-based systems are required to make virtual reality useful. Further interesting synergies can be expected from the combination of the two technologies.

Acknowledgements

The author would like to acknowledge for their contributions to the results reported in this chapter: Kefeng Hua, Djamila Haroud, Ian Smith and Kun Sun of the EPFL Artificial Intelligence Laboratory; Shen-Guan Shih, Bharat Dave and Gerhard Schmitt of the Chair for Computer-aided Architectural Design at the ETHZ. The work reported in this chapter was sponsored by the Swiss Fonds National de Recherche Scientifique under the national research programme 23 on Artificial Intelligence and Robotics as well as the special measures for research in computer science.

References

Davis, R.: 1984, Diagnostic reasoning based on structure and behavior, *Artificial Intelligence*, 24, 347–410.

DeKleer, J., and Brown, J. S.: 1984, A qualitative physics based on confluences, *Artificial Intelligence*, 24, 7–84.

Faltings, B.: 1990, Qualitative kinematics in mechanisms, *Artificial Intelligence*, 44(1), 89–119.

Faltings, B.: 1992, A symbolic approach to qualitative kinematics, *Artificial Intelligence*, 56(2), 139–170.

Faltings, B.: 1994, Arc-consistency for continuous variables, *Artificial Intelligence*, 65(2), 363–376.

Faltings, B., and Sun, K.: 1994, Computer-aided creative mechanism design, *Proceedings of the IFIP International Conference on Feature Modeling in Advanced CAD/CAM Systems*, Valenciennes, France, May.

Faltings, B., and Sun, K.: 1996, FAMING: supporting innovative mechanism shape design, *Computer-Aided Design*, 28(3), 207–216.

Gero, J. S.: 1990, Design prototypes: A knowledge representation schema for design, *AI Magazine*, 11(4), 26–36.

Gero, J. S., Lee, H. S., and Tham, K. W.: 1992, Behavior: A link between function and structure in design, *in* D. C. Brown, M. Waldron and H. Yoshikawa (eds), *Intelligent Computer-Aided Design*, North Holland, Amsterdam, pp. 193–220.

Goel, A. K.: 1991, A model-based approach to case adaptation, *Proceedings of the 13th Annual Conference of the Cognitive Science Society*, Chicago, pp. 143-148.

Haroud, D.: 1995, *Consistency for Continuous Constraints*, Doctoral Dissertation No. 1423, École Polytechnique Fédérale de Lausanne, Switzerland.

Haroud, D., and Faltings, B.: 1994, Global consistency for continuous constraints, *Proceedings of the 11th European Conference on Artificial Intelligence*, Wiley, Chichester, UK, pp. 115–119.

Hua, K.: 1994, *Case-Based Design of Geometric Structures*, Doctoral Dissertation No. 1270, École Polytechnique Fédérale de Lausanne, Switzerland.

Hua, K., and Faltings, B.: 1993, Exploring case-based building design—CADRE, *Artificial Intelligence in Engineering Design, Analysis and Manufacturing*, 7(2), 135-143.

Hua, K. Faltings, B., and Smith, I.: 1995, CADRE: case-based geometric design, *Artificial Intelligence in Engineering*, 10, 171–183.

Kolodner, J. L.: 1993, *Case-based Reasoning*, Kaufmann, San Mateo, CA.

Minton, S., Johnston, M., Phillips, A., and Laird, P.: 1992, Minimizing conflicts: A heuristic repair method for constraint satisfaction and scheduling problems, *Artificial Intelligence*, 58(1-3), 161–206.

Pahl, G., and Beitz, G.: 1988, Engineering Design: A Systematic Approach, *in* K. Wallace (ed.), Springer-Verlag, Berlin, Germany.

Pu, P., and Purvis, L.: 1994, Formalizing case adaptation in a case-based design system, *in* J. S. Gero and F. Sudweeks (eds), *Artificial Intelligence in Design '94*, Kluwer Academic, Dordrecht, NL, pp. 77–91.

Saund, E.: 1988, Configurations of shape primitives specified by dimensionality-reduction through energy minimization, *IEEE Spring Symposium on Physical and Biological Approaches to Computational Vision*, pp. 100–104.

Schmitt, G., Dave, B., and Shih, S.-G.: 1996, Case-based architectural design (this volume).

Selman, B., Levesque, H., and Mitchell, D.: 1992, A new method for solving hard satisfiability problems, *Proceedings of the 10th National Conference of the AAAI*, Kaufmann, San Mateo, CA, pp. 440–446.

Sembugamoorthy, V., and Chandrasekaran, B.: 1986, Functional representation of devices and compilation of diagnostic problem-solving systems, *in* J. L. Kolodner and C. Riesbeck (eds), *Experience, Memory and Reasoning*, Lawrence Earlbaum Associates, Hillsdale, NJ, pp. 47–74.

Serrano, D., and Gossard, D.: 1988, Constraint management in MCAE, *in* J. S. Gero (ed.), *Artificial Intelligence in Engineering Design*, Elsevier Science, Amsterdam, NL, pp. 217–240.

Sun, K.: 1994, *Computer-Aided Creative Mechanism Design*, Doctoral Dissertation No. 1271, École Polytechnique Fédérale de Lausanne, Switzerland.

Sun, K., and Faltings, B.: 1994, Supporting creative mechanical design, *in* J. S. Gero and F. Sudweeks (eds), *Artificial Intelligence in Design '94*, Kluwer Academic, Dordrecht, NL, pp. 39–56.

Umeda, Y., Takeda, H., Tomiyama, T., and Yoshikawa, Y.: 1990, Function, behavior and structure, *in* J. S. Gero (ed.), *Applications of Artificial Intelligence in Engineering V*, vol. 1, Springer-Verlag, Berlin, pp. 177–194.

Wagner, M. R.: 1990, *Understanding the ICAD system*, ICAD Inc, Cambridge, MA.

Wills, L. M., and Kolodner, J. L.: 1994, Towards more creative case-based design systems, *Proceedings of the 12th National Conference of the AAAI*, Kaufmann, San Mateo, CA, pp. 50–55.

chapter four

CASE-BASED DESIGN IN A SOFTWARE ENVIRONMENT THAT SUPPORTS THE EARLY PHASES IN BUILDING DESIGN

ULRICH FLEMMING, ZEYNO AYGEN,
ROBERT COYNE, JAMES SNYDER
Carnegie Mellon University

SEED is a software environment to support the early phases in building design currently under development at CMU. The environment is intended to eventually support the early design of buildings in all aspects that may benefit from computer support. This includes the reuse of past solutions or cases that have been generated with the help of the environment. We give a brief overview of SEED, describe the requirements for case indexing, retrieval, and adaptation as they arise in SEED, and describe how the requirements are met by the approach toward CBD taken in SEED. We outline the current implementation and conclude with putting CBD into the larger context of information management in team-based design.

1. Introduction

The SEED project intends to develop a software environment that supports the early phases in building design (Flemming and Woodbury, 1995). The goal is to provide support, in principle, for the preliminary design of buildings in all aspects that can gain from computer support. This includes using the computer not only for visualization, analysis and other forms of evaluation, but also more actively for the generation of designs, or more accurately, for the rapid generation of computable design representations describing conceptual design alternatives and variants of such alternatives with a sufficient level of detail that enables sophisticated evaluation tools to receive all of the needed input data from the representation. The creation of such representations constitutes a major bottle-neck in current CAD systems. They are therefore unable to support early design exploration, that is, the fast generation of alternative design concepts and variants of such concepts and their rapid evaluation against a broad spectrum of relevant and possibly conflicting criteria, where the criteria themselves may evolve dynamically through this process. SEED intends to encourage precisely this exploratory mode of designing.

A major stimulus for the development of SEED was the experience gained at the EDRC with two multigenerational research efforts focusing on generative design systems: LOOS/ABLOOS, a generative system for the synthesis of layouts of rectangles (Coyne, 1991; Coyne and Flemming, 1990; Flemming, 1990; Flemming Coyne, Glavin, and Rychener, 1988); and GENESIS, a rule-based system that supports the generation of assemblies of 3-dimensional solids (Heisserman, 1991; Heisserman and Woodbury, 1993).

The rapid generation of design representations can take advantage of special opportunities when it deals with a recurring building type; that is, a building type dealt with frequently by the users of the system. Design firms—from hous-ing manufacturers to government agencies—accumulate considerable experience with recurring building types. But current CAD systems capture this experience and support its reuse only marginally. SEED intends to provide systematic support for storing and retrieval of past solutions and their adaptation to similar problem situations. This motivation aligns aspects of SEED closely with current work in AI that focuses on CBD (see, for example, Domeshek and Kolodner, 1992; Kolodner, 1991; Hua, Smith, Faltings, Shih, and Schmitt, 1992).

The present chapter starts with a brief overview of SEED, followed by an outline of the requirements for CBD in SEED. We then introduce our general approach toward CBD in SEED. The next section deals with indexing and retrieval, and the section that follows with case adaptation. The middle of the chapter elaborates ideas first formulated in Flemming (1994). We then discuss implementation issues that arise from this approach, and the end of the chapter places CBD in the larger context of information management in design.

2. Overview of SEED

We have set SEED up as a collection of modules. This allows us to make local use of various pieces of existing and possibly heterogeneous software and to distribute the development efforts among several teams and over time. On the other hand, each module should appear to the user as part of a unified whole. We attempt to achieve these multiple objectives by basing each module on a common logic, which allows us also to develop a common style for their interfaces that goes beyond a common feel and look.

In order to arrive at this common logic, we divide the overall design process into distinct tasks or phases, where a phase is defined by the type of problem it addresses and the type of solution it generates. A module supports work in an entire phase. A common architecture and interface can then be developed for the modules based on this uniform problem-solving view.

Each SEED module attempts to relieve designers especially from more routine tasks. For example, if a designer creates a design variant by changing the size of a room, the adjacent rooms may also have to be resized in order to maintain proper sizes and dimensions across all rooms influenced by this change, and these changes may have to be propagated through an entire section of a building, if not an entire floor. Furthermore, internal walls may have become exterior or exterior walls may have become interior through any one of these modifications and may have to be resized, too. Designers using a current CAD system have to do most of these updates manually; that is, they are responsible for managing the requirements a design has to satisfy without support from the system. A SEED module, in contrast, attempts to take over the management of requirements to the largest possible degree.

A prerequisite is that the requirements currently at work are explicitly represented in the module. A SEED module therefore contains as one of its generic components a problem specification component that allows designers to specify and modify dynamic and interactive design requirements. A module can manage requirements, of course, only to the extent to which they are represented.

Given explicit requirements, a module can be asked not only to propagate design changes after some interactive modification by a designer, but also to show a designer one (or all) feasible ways of shaping and placing a certain building component or to generate alternative configurations of a set of components that satisfy the requirements. We call the different ways in which a SEED module may participate actively in the creation of design representations generation modes. A SEED module offers designers a range of generation modes to chose from and easy transitions between modes during a design session. These modes extend from interactive construction that is completely under the designer's control through various forms of semiautomatic or fully automated construction and include explicitly the retrieval and adaptation of cases as introduced in Section 1. These generative capabilities, taken together, comprise the generation component of a SEED module.

In addition to a problem specification and generation component, each SEED module contains an evaluation component able to evaluate an emerging design against currently specified requirements and thus to provide feedback to designers. A database supports work in the individual modules in multiple ways; for example, by storing temporary design versions and design variants within a specific project or by storing cases that can be reused across projects. Figure 4.1 depicts the resulting generic architecture of a SEED module. The three modules in Table 4.1 are planned for the first SEED prototype based on this generic architecture and currently under development.

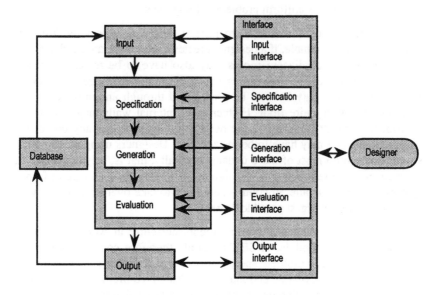

Figure 4.1. Generic architecture of a SEED module.

Table 4.1. Three modules planned for the first SEED prototype

SEED-Pro (SP): Architectural Programming	*Problem:* A project description as it is typically given at the start of a building project: context (including the site); the overall function and size of the building (e.g., an elementary school for 300 pupils); budget, etc. *Solution:* An architectural program or design brief.
SEED-Layout (SL): Schematic Layout Design	*Problem:* A specification of programmatic spatial components, a context, budget, and other parts of an architectural program *Solution:* A schematic layout of the spatial components that determines the overall building organization, zones (including the distribution of units on different floors), and form subject to the specifications of the program

SEED-Config (SC): Schematic Configuration Design	*Problem:* A schematic layout and programmatic requirements *Solution:* A three-dimensional configuration of spatial and physical building components that realizes the given organization subject to the programmatic requirements

3. Requirements for CBD in SEED

The reuse capabilities offered by SEED aim at aiding designers in two general ways. First, they provide access to a large memory of past solutions that is likely to contain instances designers will not recall on their own, either because there are too many of them or because they were generated by different designers. This motivation clearly differs from the motivation behind the system described in Hua et al. (1992), which relies solely on the designers' memories for the recall of solutions. A second aim is to quickly provide designers with an initial solution that is immediately available for editing and modifications under either the system's or the designer's control. This motivation differentiates SEED, for example, clearly from Archie-II (Domeshek and Kolodner, 1992), which retrieves pictures of design solutions that cannot be turned automatically into the representation of a solution to the current design problem with which the designer or the system are able to work.

The reuse of solutions is ubiquitous in building design and extends across all phases and many tasks, from programming to the design of construction details. A designer should therefore be able to call on and reuse past solutions to problems similar to a current one in any SEED module. The retrieval and adaptation of such solutions are therefore capabilities to be offered across modules.

Furthermore, the problem addressed in a module may be decomposed into a hierarchy of (sub)problems. For example, the layout of a building may be decomposed into the layouts of individual floors, of zones on a floor, of rooms within a zone, and of equipment or furniture in a room. Standard solutions may exist for problems at any level in such a hierarchy. As a result, retrieval capabilities for past solutions should also be available in SEED across hierarchical problem decomposition levels within a module.

An added requirement is that a solution to any subproblem in a problem hierarchy should be retrievable by itself. For example, the layout of public restrooms developed for an office building may be perfectly reusable in an educational facility, whereas the overall organization of the two buildings may be very different. When a designer works on the layout of the ancillary spaces in the educational facility, SEED should therefore be able to retrieve the restroom layout from the office design without being distracted by the overall differences between the two cases.

Furthermore, the indexing and retrieval mechanisms should be uniform across modules and problem decompositions within a module. This makes not only the development effort more effective because it can be shared between modules, but allows modules to share cases. When, for example, SEED-Pro attempts to find the programmatic components for a radiology department in a clinic, it may derive these from the layout of such a department developed with the aid of SEED-Layout.

The amount of work required to prepare a case for storage, retrieval, and adaptation becomes a crucial issue for a case memory of the size envisioned for SEED. The system is intended for use by architectural and other design firms, which cannot be expected to command the resources needed to support substantial preparation efforts. CBD in SEED therefore starts from the premise that its case memory accumulates as a side effect of a firm's normal design activities. Any indexing and other types of processing that need to be done must occur in the background and remain hidden from designers to the largest possible degree (although explicit personalized indexing of cases will also be eventually supported). This requirement distinguishes SEED from many approaches that rely on considerable efforts to build a memory of cases (Domeshek and Kolodner, 1992; Hua et al., 1992; Rosenman, Gero, and Oxman, 1991).

We believe that these requirements, taken together, reflect a realistic application context and that the approach by which we attempt to meet these requirements is therefore of practical interest.

4. Overall Approach

The SEED modules under development are not meant to be activated in a linear sequence that starts with programming and ends with a 3-dimensional building model. For example, a designer working with SEED-Pro should be able to start SEED-Layout on the side to experiment with the consequences of some programmatic requirements and, possibly, import results generated with SEED-Layout back into SEED-Pro. That is, it should be easy to share problem specifications and solutions between SEED-Pro and SEED-Layout in either direction. The same holds for the interactions between SEED-Config and the other modules in SEED and extends to yet unspecified modules that may be added in the future.

Every module uses an internal representation that is particularly suited to the tasks addressed in the module; thus, the sharing of information between modules necessarily involves translations. But information sharing becomes particularly easy to implement and unify if the module-internal representations of problems and solutions are based on the same conceptualization of a design task. Such a shared conceptualization will also greatly reduce the cognitive load placed on designers who are expected to switch easily between modules in pursuit of specific design ideas; that is, designers do not have to change their view of what a problem specification or a solution is when they move between modules. In fact, the interfaces through which they work with this information may have important features in common across modules.

A side effect is that this shared conceptualization provides the basis for a uniform indexing and retrieval mechanism to support CBD across modules and problem decompositions within a module. If a solution has been developed with the aid of a module, the associated problem specification can be used, on the designer's request, to compute an index that will be stored together with the solution to form a case so that at a later time, when the same or a different designer defines a similar problem, the resulting problem specification can be compared with the stored indices to retrieve solutions to similar problems.

The shared conceptualization of problem specifications and solutions in SEED relies on three central constructs: design units, functional units, and specification units. *Design units* are the basic spatial or physical entities that make up the representation of a design; examples are a room and a wall. Design units are the primary focus of attention during form generation in SEED-Layout and SEED-Config, which concentrate on specifying the shape, location, and non-geometric attributes of spatial and physical design units, respectively.

A design unit is generally multifunctional; that is, has to accomplish more than one purpose. A *functional unit* collects all of the requirements that a design unit has to satisfy in a single construct. For example, a wall may have to provide certain load-bearing capacities, sound insulation, thermal resistance, visual privacy, and light reflectance. All of these requirements are collected in SEED in a single location, the functional unit associated with that wall. Functional requirements are normally expressed in the form of constraints and criteria; examples are the lateral and vertical loads a wall has to be able to resist, its minimum thermal resistance, sound absorption, and so forth.

A functional unit can contain constituent functional units as indicated: A functional unit building may contain constituents floors, a floor may contain constituent zones a zone rooms, and so forth. Similarly, a structural system may contain bays; a bay orthogonal planes; and a plane, physical structural elements like slabs, columns, and so on. That is, constituent relations establish part-of hierarchies through several abstraction levels (see also the General AEC Reference Model (GARM), which uses functional units in our sense and technical solutions that are equivalent to our design units (Gielingh, 1988).

Any functional unit hierarchy is based on assumptions about the envisioned form or shape of the building. This becomes obvious when we look at the spatial hierarchies that distribute the required spatial units over several floors, zones on a floor, and so forth. SEED intends to encourage designers to experiment with alternative hierarchies and the formal concepts on which they are based. On the other hand, any such hierarchy may have to take general project requirements that hold for any building concept into account. We capture these general project requirements in a third type of unit, which we call a *specification unit*. A specification unit captures functional requirements in a manner that is form-independent. For example, one such unit may express general requirements of physical comfort; from this specification, specific requirements for functional spatial units can be derived when these functional units are created.

SEED-Pro accepts a problem specification in the form of specification units that reflect general project requirements. Its specification component allows designers to expand on these initial requirements. Its generation component supports the generation of alternative hierarchies of spatial functional units and the specification of a physical context in which these units have to be allocated. During this process, functional requirements are redistributed over functional units; that is, they become localized within a specific formal concept.

Spatial hierarchies and an associated design context are the problem specifications accepted by SEED-Layout. Its specification component again allows designers to modify such a specification as they learn more about the specifics of the problem at hand or the implications of a specific spatial decomposition. This explicitly includes the generation of additional functional units, the need for which was initially not obvious. The generation component of SEED-Layout supports the generation of schematic spatial layouts as collections of spatial design units, each of which is associated with a specific functional unit and attempts to satisfy the associated requirements in the given context. At the present time, all spatial design units are assumed to be rectangles.

SEED-Config accepts a schematic layout of design units: the associated functional units as well as specification units that deal with physical building systems as a problem specification. It supports the generation of design units that represent the physical components of a building within the context of the layout subject to the requirements captured in the functional and specification units. This may involve the generation of new functional units that collect the requirements associated with the physical building components being generated. At the present time, SEED-Config is restricted to the generation of enclosure and structural components.

There is no assumption that a problem specification is complete at any time when a SEED module is used in the design of a building. The specification is formally restricted to requirements that can be evaluated by the module and taken into account during interactive construction, automated form generation, and case retrieval. It is restricted in its content to requirements that appear currently important to the designer. In general, design in SEED proceeds in an open world (Hinrichs, 1992).

We have found it useful to add a fourth construct, technology, to the concepts shared between modules in SEED. An example of a technology as used in SEED-Config is a set of production rules that generate the representation of external walls between specific rooms and the outside, where the wall consists of appropriately spaced metal studs, insulation, gypsum board on the inside and brick veneer, and so forth on the outside, and satisfies certain load-bearing and performance requirements. In general, a technology is a collection of computational mechanisms to create solutions from a problem specification, which consists of a collection of requirements and a design context. In the previous example, the wall is the solution (in the form of a design unit), the associated functional unit collects the requirements it has to satisfy, and the surface shared between the room and the outside is the context into which the wall has to fit. It is easy to see how a production rule that belongs to a technology available in SEED-Config can match on this context and these requirements and create the representation of a corresponding design unit in the form of a wall sized and placed to fit its context. We must stress, however, that there is more to the implementation of technologies in SEED-Config and the other SEED modules than this simple example suggests.

The triad design unit, functional unit, and specification unit—with the addition of technologies—is sufficient to indicate how the requirements for CBD specified in the preceding section can be met, in principle, in SEED. A case consists generally of:

- a solution generated by a module;
- an associated index in the form of a problem specification consisting of a context and functional requirements;
- the technology that was used to create the solution in the context, given the functional requirements; and
- (possibly) an explicit evaluation of the solution against the requirements, which may be used, for example, to break ties between alternative cases during retrieval or to exclude solutions from consideration.

These definitions hold across modules and reflect the general problem-solving architecture on which they are based. Modules furthermore share the underlying constructs of design unit, functional unit, specification unit, and technology (when applicable), and how they are used in constructing problem specifications and solutions. A conceptually uniform indexing and retrieval mechanism across modules becomes thus possible, in principle at least (subject to translations in both directions between a module and the case library). The same mechanism is applicable across problem decompositions within a module because the representations of problem specifications and of solutions are formally identical across levels. This makes it possible to index subproblems and retrieve them independently using a uniform mechanism.

Conversely, the explicit problem specification that exists in a module can be used to automatically compute an index when a designer decides that a solution generated with the help of the module is worth entering into the case library and tells the module to do this. The computation of the index itself and the translation of the solution into the schema required by the case library can then happen in the background. This does not prevent, of course, the designer from adding comments to the case or embellishing it in other ways. We plan to offer designers opportunities of this kind in order to facilitate, among other things, communication about cases between different designers and to give designers at the receiving end the opportunity to trace the history of a case within the organization, for example, to uncover intentions not captured in the formal problem specification associated with the case.

Finally, a solution is retrieved in a form that makes it immediately amenable to manual or automatic adaptation using any one of the generation modes available in the given module, although the technology retrieved together with the case offers a set of generative mechanisms that are particularly promising because they were used originally in the generation of the solution.

The following sections indicate how the general approach outlined in the present section is being implemented in the first SEED prototype. They use illustrations mainly from SEED-Layout, which is currently the best understood and most fully implemented module.

5. Indexing and Retrieval

A generic matching and retrieval mechanism as outlined in the preceding section becomes conceivable, in principle, for the first SEED prototype because it will be implemented based on an object-oriented approach in which all major entities handled by a module are objects with attributes that can be compared with the attributes of other objects. We use the term *object* here in a conceptual, generic sense (independent of a specific programming language or implementation environment) to denote an entity characterized by attributes with values. An object may belong to a type or class hierarchy through which it inherits attributes and values from other objects. For example, a room may inherit attributes from a superunit spatial functional unit. We call an object structured if some of its attributes are collections of objects of the same type. An example is the constituents of a functional unit, which define a spatial or physical hierarchy as described previously.

The attributes of a structured object typically fall into two categories: *value attributes*, where the values belong to a specific domain or type, and *relational attribute*, containing links to one or several other associated objects. An example of a structured object is the problem specification shown in Figure 4.2 (more accurately, the figure shows the problem specification window (PSW) of SEED-Layout displaying a current problem specification).

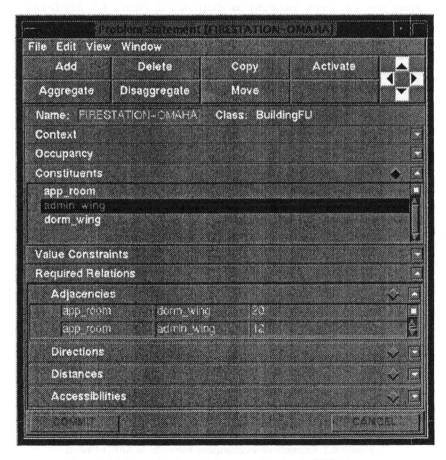

Figure 4.2. Example of a problem specification in SEED-Layout.

It describes a firestation named FIRESTATION-OMAHA, the context for its design collected in an associated context object, links to functional unit constituents collected in a constituents list, and constraints of various types, each of which is expressed by an associated object of the appropriate class; an example is an adjacency object whose value attributes are the names of the functional units that must be adjacent and the minimum required overlap between the two units. In the PSW, all of this information is collected into folders that can be opened to show their contents. In Figure 4.2, this is demonstrated for the constituents and adjacency constraints folders.

The administrative and dormitory wings of the sample firestation have constituents of their own, which in turn have constituents, and so on, creating a spatial functional unit hierarchy as illustrated in Figure 4.3. SEED-Layout interprets constituent relations strictly as spatial containment relations: The constituents of a functional unit will always be allocated within the design unit associated with that functional unit. SEED-Config interprets constituent relations more loosely as part-of relations that may include spatial containment as a special case.

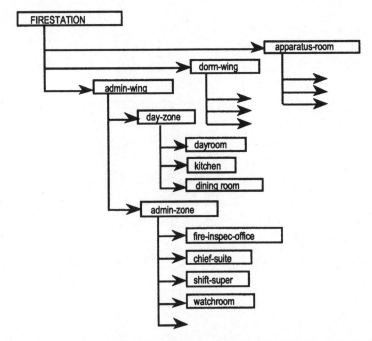

Figure 4.3. Example of a constituent hierarchy in SEED-Layout.

We use the term *structure* in the following to refer solely to hierarchical constituent or part-of structures and the hierarchical problem structures they imply. These hierarchies have to be distinguished from the inheritance hierarchies to which individual objects may belong through their class membership. Constituent relations are considered transitive; that is, if B is a constituent of A and C a constituent of B, C is also a constituent of A.

Given this type of structured object representation, comparisons of a current problem specification, which we call a *target index* or *target* for short, with a case index can proceed, in principle, object-by-object and attribute-by-attribute. In the simplest case, only objects of the same class or type and attributes with the same names and values of the same type are compared. But this would be too rigid in certain instances. For example, if the target contains the requirement that an open space be adjacent to a lounge, a case in which a courtyard (a special type of open space) is adjacent to a lounge would certainly satisfy this requirement. In order to extend the allowed matches, JULIA uses several schemes including subtype, subrange, and subset matching (Hinrichs 1992). A similar approach suggests itself for SEED.

Specifically, an object A is comparable to an object, B, if B belongs to the same class or to a subclass of A. Similarly, an attribute, a, is comparable to an attribute, b, if a is implied by b.

Comparability of attributes implies that the attributes have values of the same type. For example, a minimum x-dimension attribute is implied by a minimum dimension attribute. The converse is generally not desirable; that is, an object in a subclass does not match on an object belonging to a superclass of it. An important exception is mentioned in Section 6.

Comparisons can become complex when the structure of the target matches the structure of a case index only partially. Details are given in Flemming (1994); we restrict ourselves here to some general points.

The degree to which the structure of the target and that of a retrieved case index match determines largely the degree to which a module can actively support the refinement or adaptation of a retrieved case because this indicates also how closely the retrieved solution solves the current problem. We are particularly interested in cases whose index refines the target; that is, it transitively preserves the hierarchical dependencies between the constituents of the target, but adds constituents at certain levels, thus expanding the hierarchy in a way that is compatible with the target. For instance, if we take the constituent hierarchy in Figure 4.3 as an example, the problem specifications in Figures 4.4 and 4.5 should both match the constituent relation between the firestation and the shift supervisor office in the target despite the fact that this relation is not direct in one case: In Figure 4.4, the office is a constituent of a distinct administrative wing, which in turn is a constituent of the firestation.

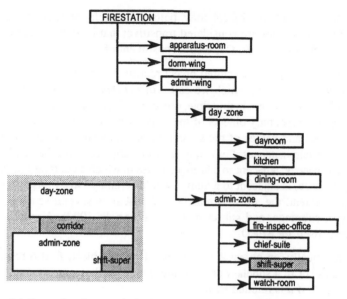

Figure 4.4. Example of a case index matching problem specification in Figure 4.3.

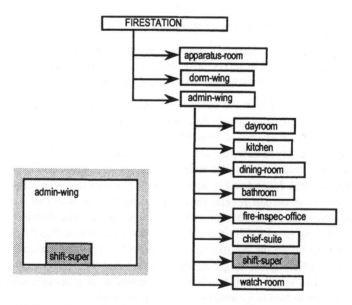

Figure 4.5. Second example of a case index for the problem specification in Figure 4.3.

Everything else being equal, we want to retrieve both cases for the target because they demonstrate two contrasting ways of handling offices and recreational units in the administrative wing of a firestation: In Figure 4.5, they are combined in an otherwise undifferentiated administrative wing, whereas in Figure 4.4, a deliberate attempt has been made to formally differentiate these two functions and to express this differentiation. Each scheme is based on a distinct expressive intent, none of which is in any way indicated in the target. An important role of CBD is to bring such additional aspects to the designer's attention. If we call the constituent relations that connect one object to a constituent deeper down in the constituent hierarchy a constituent path, we want to match the constituent relations in a target on constituent paths of arbitrary lengths in a case index.

Refinement may be a desired side effect of the retrieval of a case. It may be an important means of bringing interesting design alternatives to a designer's attention. In addition, it may save time in terms of refining the problem specification itself. As a consequence, the comparisons made during search through the case library should not discriminate against a case when its index refines the current problem structure; on the contrary, they may favor it for that very reason. That is, a case with a compatible index may be preferred over another case if it has more structure, everything else being equal. The latter restriction is important because a designer dealing with a one-bedroom apartment, for example, may not be interested in a 3-bedroom apartment, let alone an apartment building. Problem attributes like size restrictions, budget, and so forth, will prevent cases with such over-refinements from being retrieved.

6. Case Adaptation

When the designer asks a module to find good candidate solutions in the case library to solve the problem currently specified, the module tries to find solutions that satisfy as many requirements as possible. In SEED-Layout, for example, it tries to find layouts that allocate at least all of the functional units currently specified. But in the case of refinement, such solutions may contain design units associated with functional units that are not yet specified. After retrieval, the new design units become part of the current solution and the associated functional units (which are preserved in the index and retrieved with the solution) become part of the current problem specification, where they are available for inspection and editing. That is, case adaptation may include adaptation of the problem specification, a situation also encountered in other domains.

A SEED module supports the interactive editing and expansion of problem specifications. The operations underlying these capabilities are immediately available, after a case has been retrieved, to incorporate refinements in the retrieved problem structure into the current one. That is, they form a base from which automatic or interactive adaptation mechanisms can be constructed.

SEED-Layout, for example, offers designers operations to:
- add an object to a list attribute;
- delete an object in a list attribute;
- aggregate units in a constituents list into a new constituent;
- disaggregate units in a constituents list;
- move a functional unit to a different constituents list; and
- edit other types of attributes of an object.

These operations are available through the horizontal command bar at the top of the PSW shown in Figure 4.2.

An object present in the target, but not matched in the case index, requires no adaptation. But the designer should be informed because this object may also be missing from the solution in some form (a functional unit not allocated, a constraint not satisfied). An object present in the target and matched in the case index to an object in an equivalent location in the constituent hierarchy also requires no adaptation, except when the values of certain corresponding attributes differ. In this case, the editing capabilities of the module can be invoked to change the attributes. A functional unit present in the case index, but not matched in the target, that refines its structure can be inserted with these commands. In each case, the designer's agreement is sought before execution of the adaptation.

The trickiest situation occurs when an object present in the target matches an object in the case index, but not in an equivalent location in the constituent hierarchy. The evaluation component of a SEED module allows designers to evaluate a solution with respect to the requirements of an associated problem specification. The solution retrieved from a case can be evaluated in this way before, during, or after adaptation of the current problem specification. This will bring out all existing discrepancies, and the generation commands available in a module are immediately executable to adapt the solution so that these discrepancies are eliminated; alternatively, the problem specification can be modified to achieve the same effect.

We mentioned before that the present version of SEED-Layout handles design units only in the form of rectangles. Figure 4.6 shows an example of a configuration of such design units that represents a solution to a layout problem. In order to support the allocation of design units, SEED-Layout offers designers a range of commands, some of which are listed here:

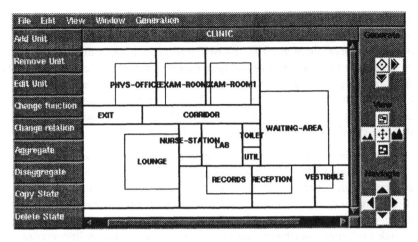

Figure 4.6. A collection of design units forming a solution in SEED-Layout.

- add a design unit in a location specified by the designer and associate with it a functional unit not yet allocated;
- remove a design unit;
- edit the dimensional attributes of a design unit;
- change the functional unit associated with a design unit; and
- generate the next or all alternatives to allocate selected functional units in the current solution.

These commands can again be used as building blocks to implement interactive or automated adaptation procedures. For example, the Remove operation can be used to eliminate functional units that do not exist in the target or that are incorrectly allocated, or the Edit operations can be used to adapt the dimensional attributes of a design unit to satisfy certain constraints. At any time, a design unit may have no functional unit associated with it, in which case all constraints on its shape and location are relaxed. This suggests an interesting extension of the retrieval procedure outlined in the preceding section. If we allow functional units to be comparable—on an optional basis—not only with subclasses, but also with superclasses, we may be able to retrieve layouts based on size and dimensional constraints alone; for example, we may retrieve a narrow, linear scheme for a narrow site from a project dealing with building functions that differ from the ones currently under consideration.

7. Implementation

The following requirements for the case library in SEED have fundamental implications for its implementation: The case library is expected to grow over time via designer interaction; it is to be used by multiple modules and across module sessions; and it is to support the rapid generation and sharing of problem or solution representations. The first two requirements imply that the case library be stored in a persistent format and have a common module access interface. The third requirement implies that the representation of cases should be closely aligned with the general SEED modeling concepts, especially the basic constructs design unit, functional unit, specification unit, and technology, so that cases can be easily moved to and from the case library.

A case-based system in general must be supported by a reasoning and a storage system. The reasoning system performs indexing, matching, and adaptation, and is responsible for the transfer of information to and from the SEED environment. The storage system manages the persistency of information, which comprises collections of attribute-value pairs aggregated as objects and includes relational attributes linking objects to each other. A first version of a reasoning and storage system has been implemented for SEED using the object database UniSQL (UniSQL, 1995), which we selected as the general database for SEED for the following basic reasons: the database object model is independent of a programming language, which is extremely important in a multi-agent environment like SEED, where agents can be expected to be written in different languages; UniSQL supports a query language incorporating object-oriented constructs; and it can integrate traditional relational databases into a unified database.

In this first implementation, the problem specifications available within a module are used as indices and associated with a solution saved in the database as a case. The technologies retrieved with a case serve as the initial mechanisms to support interactive adaptation. The capability that has to be added to these existing functionalities is a matching and retrieval mechanism.

If we take SEED-Layout as an example, a case is typically composed of a problem specification containing a spatial functional unit along with a context object, a solution in the form of a layout of the constituents of the functional unit, and an outcome. To initiate case matching and retrieval, the designer defines and submits to the case retriever a problem specification of this type, which serves as target index into the case-base. Suppose, for example, that the target contains a building functional unit classified as a firestation, which contains, among other constituents, a room functional unit classified as a shift supervisor office as shown in Figure 4.7.

The case retriever matches the target to the case indices residing in the case library to find object configurations that match as closely as possible; these matches have to take, at the minimum, four criteria into account, which are introduced next.

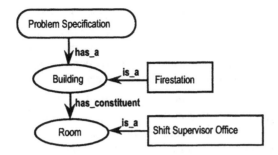

Figure 4.7. Example target in SEED-Layout (simplified)

Buildings and rooms—as well as additional subclasses such as floors or zones—are subclasses of spatial functional units that have distinct behaviors when it comes to placement. A building knows, for example, that it may contain different floor constituents that have to be allocated vertically rather than horizontally. Similarly, a room knows that it cannot contain other spatial functional units as constituents, only physical functional units such as furniture or equipment. These classes therefore have a very important function in structuring the generation process, especially in SEED-Layout, and are therefore used as the primary classification for spatial functional units. The first important matching criterion therefore are subclass matches for any functional unit in the target. In the current example, any object belonging to a subclass of building or room would match the objects belonging to these respective classes in the target, or more succinctly, any object in the target that is a building (room) will match an object in a case index that is a building (room). This criterion extends to other target objects, like its context.

But the shift supervisor office, aside from being a room, may also belong to the class office and inherit specific requirements through this subclass relation, like public access. Furthermore, it may be classified as a private spatial unit; that is, public circulation cannot pass through it, as opposed to public functional units. All of these classifications are essentially orthogonal: An office may conceivably be public or a zone (like a secretarial pool); a public functional unit may also be a floor or a zone on a floor, and so forth. In an object-oriented approach, these multiple classifications have traditionally been handled by multiple inheritance. There are, however, strong reasons why this technique should not be used in a multiagent environment like SEED. Chief among them are the well-known anomalies and ambiguities that arise with multiple inheritance and cannot be consistently resolved across agents using different programming languages. SEED circumvents this problem through an application of the delegation principle (Gamma, Helm, Johnson, and Vlissides, 1995): Any object can be linked to an arbitrary number of classifiers. Classifiers are objects in themselves that can be attached to other objects (through a relational classifier attribute), thereby allowing these objects to belong to multiple classifications. In this way, the shift supervisor office in our example can be a room, an office, and a private functional unit at the same time. Classifier matches therefore provide a second matching criterion for any classified object in the target.

A third matching criterion is structural similarity with respect to the constituent relations specified in the target objects. These matches have to take the transitivity of the constituent relation into account. The fourth and last matching criterion is the similarity between comparable value attributes as outlined in Section 4.

We next outline briefly how these four matching criteria are implemented in a first prototype, starting with the last criteria. To compare the value attributes of a target object[*OBJ1*] against those of a case object [*OBJ2*], we use the procedure **base_match** given below in pseudo-code. It uses predicates *is_subclass_of* and *is_of_same-_class_as,* which query the database in two ways. First, the database class memberships of the objects are compared. Second, the classifiers of the objects are compared. **base_match** returns a number between 0 and 100, which is the weighted sum of the individual attribute matches; it can be interpreted as an expression of the closeness of fit in percentage. The reasons for using such a weighted measure in our first prototype are given in Flemming (1994). The procedure takes only three possible types of value attributes into account and must be expanded if additional ones are needed.

```
base_match  (OBJ1,  OBJ2)
 1     if OBJ1 is_subclass_of OBJ2 or OBJ1 is_of_same_class_as OBJ2
 2         then total_match_value  0
 3               construct attribute couple set P such that
                     p (a1, a2) and
                     a1 is an attribute of OBJ1, a2 is an attribute of OBJ2 and
                     domain[a1] is comparable with domain[a2]
 4               for I  0 to |P |
 5                   do dt dataType (domain[a1],domain[a2])
 6                   if dt =LOWER_BOUND_TYPE
 7                       then if val[a1] < val[a2]
 8                               then match_value  100val[a2]val[a1]
 9                               else match_value  100
10                   else
11                           if dt = UPPER_BOUND_TYPE
12                               then if val[a2] < val[a1]
13                                       then match_value
                                                100val[a1]val[a2]
14                                       else match_value  100
15                               else
16                                       if dt = STRING_TYPE
16                                           then if val[a1] = val[a2]
17                                                   then match_value  100
```

```
18                              else match_value  0
19                  total_match_value total_match_value + match_value
20            return total_match_value  nAttribute[OBJ1]
21  else
22      return 0
```

The following is the pseudocode for the procedure **traverse_and_match**, which combines criteria 3 and 4; that is, it determines the match between a target object and case object by first calling **base_match** and then traversing the target object's constituents and matching these transitively against the constituents of the case object. It also returns a weighted measure of fit between 0 and 100.

```
traverse_and_match  (OBJ1,  OBJ2,  matchLimit)
1     matchValue base_match (OBJ1, OBJ2)
2     if matchValue > matchLimit      objects match; check the constituents
3        then if nConstituents[OBJ1] = 0 Leaf node
4                then return matchValue
5             for each constituent v of OBJ2
6                do visited[v]  false
7             sumValue  0
8             for each constituent u of OBJ1
9                for each constituent v of OBJ2
10                  do Value traverse_and_match(u, v, matchLimit)
11                     if Value > matchLimit and visited[v] = false
12                        then sumValue sumValue + Value
13                             visited[v]  true
14                             break
15             normValue  sumValue  nConstituents[OBJ1]
16             return
                  (nAttribute[OBJ1] matchValue + normValue)
                  (nAttribute[OBJ1] + 1)
17    else find matching object deeper in the hierarchy
18        if nConstituents[OBJ2] = 0
19           then  return 0
20        else
21             for each constituent v of OBJ2
22                do Value  traverse_and_match(OBJ1, v, matchLimit)
23                   if Value > matchLimit
24                      then return Value
25             return 0
```

As given, this algorithm can be viewed as a transitive directed subgraph matching process. As a result, it suffers from the same performance problems that other subgraph matching algorithms have. In our case, we want to avoid having to retrieve all cases from the case library before their indices can be explicitly compared. To remedy this, we make use of two database-indexing mechanisms, which are not to be confused with a case index. The first index is known as a class-division index that indexes a class hierarchy (Ramaswamy and Kanellakis, 1995). We use this technique to reduce the number of cases to be retrieved by matching on both the target classes and the associated classifiers (criteria 1 and 2). Part of this indexing is supported by UniSQL; the remaining part has been built on top of this and incorporates the indexing of classifiers.

The second indexing mechanism of interest for SEED are R-trees (Guttman, 1984). This index is geometrically based and can index any number of spatial dimensions. It allows us to retrieve cases based on geometrical or topological properties as envisaged at the end of the preceding section. R-trees are easy to implement in UniSQL because of its object-oriented structure.

8. The Larger Context

We believe that CBD, as envisioned here, should be viewed in the larger context of information management in team-based design. Empirical studies reveal a broad range of problems and bottlenecks in everyday work in such domains as bridge construction (Grønbæk, King, and Mogensen, 1993) and in a variety of engineering design and manufacturing contexts (Levy et al., 1993). Problems have been identified in archiving and retrieving information, in interrelating information from multiple and diverse sources and media, and in searching for and finding the right information at the right time. They typically occur because there is a discrepancy between large, monolithic, vertical systems (applications) and daily work. This leads to costly overhead in information management, to communication breakdowns and errors of interpretation unless the related problems of information structuring and management are addressed together with usability issues.

Since usefulness and usability are primary goals of the SEED project—bringing research design methods and technology closer to practice was one of its initial motivations—these observations are relevant to SEED or any of its modules in general and apply particularly to the creation, elaboration, adaptation, and reuse of cases. For instance, a designer may ask: "What was the case Fred was working on yesterday that he said would be a good starting place?" or, "What were the cases that I considered six months ago when I was faced with a similar design problem, and how did I select from the alternative matches and adapt the one chosen?" These examples suggest that the content of cases should be enlarged, for example with annotations, that retrieval should also be possible based on clues that are less explicit and structured than the problem specifications in a module, or that it should be possible to link cases to project information outside of SEED itself. It is also true that a CAD system like SEED should not and pragmatically cannot encompass all general information management dimensions within or across design projects because tools exist in a continuum of tools and activities, and it would be counter-productive to extend any one tool to manage these issues for all the others; and it is not possible to foresee all types of information and tools that should be cross-referenced in a project: They are dynamically dependent on project-specific issues and phases, on the participants, tools, work process, design-office context, and so on.

The studies cited in this chapter suggest that CBD capabilities as planned for SEED become part of a uniform information management environment that makes it possible to link heterogeneous information types and allows tools (like SEED) to be used and tracked within the environment. Because tools that are open and provide hooks for external manipulation are more easily embedded in such an environment, these features should be taken into account in the system design from the start. Aside from a variety of approaches and technologies known under loose categories such as CSCW, hypermedia and concurrent engineering that may bear on these issues, we are aware of a few research efforts that specifically address information modeling and design projects, for instance the SHARE project (Kumar, Glicksman, and Kramer, 1994; Toye, Cutkosky, Leifer, Tenenbaum, and Glicksman, 1993) and the *n*-dim project (Coyne and Ehrenberger, 1994; Levy et al., 1993; Robertson, Subrahmanian, Thomas, and Westerberg, 1994; Subrahmanian et al., 1993).

We must admit that resource limitations prevented us from making these concerns a main focus in the development of SEED. However, we implemented the interaction between modules in a way that gives us extensibility in a very fundamental way. We constructed software tools that give us the ability to incorporate new applications that were initially not intended to work with SEED (see Snyder, Aygen, Flemming, and Tsai, 1995, for details).

Acknowledgments

The development of SEED is sponsored by Battelle Pacific Northwest Laboratories, the US Army Corps of Engineers Construction Engineering Research Laboratory, the National Institute of Standards and Technology, the Engineering Design Research Center at Carnegie Mellon University, an NSF-supported Engineering Research Center, under grant EEC-8943164NSF, the Australian Research Council, and the University of Adelaide.

References

Coyne, R. F.: 1991, *ABLOOS, An Evolving Hierarchical Design Framework*, Doctoral Dissertation, Carnegie Mellon University, Pittsburgh, PA.

Coyne, R. F., and Flemming, U.: 1990, Planning in design synthesis: Abstraction-based LOOS, *in* J. S. Gero (ed.), *Artificial Intelligence in Engineering V, Vol. 1: Design*, Springer-Verlag, Berlin, pp. 91–111.

Coyne, R. F., and Ehrenberger, M.: 1994, Information modeling for software engineering: An illustrative project history, *Technical Report, EDRC-05-88-94*, Engineering Design Research Center, Carnegie Mellon University.

Domeshek, E. A., and Kolodner J. L.: 1992, A case-based design aid for architecture, *in* J. S. Gero (ed.), *Artificial Intelligence in Design '92*, Kluwer Academic, Dordrecht, NL, pp. 497–516.

Flemming, U.: 1989, More on the representation and generation of loosely packed arrangements of rectangles, *Environment and Planning B. Planning and Design*, 16, 327–359.

Flemming, U.: 1990, Knowledge representation and acquisition in the LOOS system, *Building and Environment*, 25, 209–219.

Flemming, U.: 1994, Case-based design in the SEED system, *in* G. Carrara and Y. E. Kalay (eds), *Knowledge-Based Computer-Aided Architectural Design*, Elsevier, New York, pp. 69–91.

Flemming, U., Coyne, R., Glavin, T., and Rychener, M.: 1988, A generative expert system for the design of building layouts—Version 2, *in* J. S. Gero (ed.) *Artificial Intelligence in Engineering: Design*, Elsevier, New York, pp. 445–464.

Flemming, U., and Woodbury, R.: 1995, A software environment to support the early phases in building design: Overview, *Journal of Architecural Engineering*, 1(4), 147–152.

Gamma, E., Helm, R., Johnson, R., and Vlissides, J.: 1995, *Design Patterns: Elements of Reusable Object-Oriented Software*, Addison Wesley, Reading, MA.

Gantt, M., and Nardi, B. A.: 1992, Gardeners and Gurus: Patterns of cooperation among CAD users, *in* P. Bauersfeld, J. Bennett and G. Lynch (eds), *CHI '92 Conference Proceedings: Striking a Balance*, Addison-Wesley, Reading, MA.

Gielingh, W.: 1988, General AEC Reference Model. ISO TC 184/SC4/WG1 doc 3.2.2.1, TNO Report BI-88-150.

Grønbæk, K., Kyng, M., and Mogensen, P.: 1993, CSCW challenges: Cooperative design in engineering projects, *Communication ACM*, 36, 67–77.

Guttman, A.: 1984, R-trees: A dynamic index structure for spatial searching, *Proceedings of ACM-SIGMOD Conference*, ACM Press, San Jose, CA, pp. 47–57.

Heisserman, J.: 1991, *Generative Geometric Design and Boundary Solid Grammars*, Doctoral Dissertation, Carnegie Mellon University, Pittsburgh, PA.

Heisserman, J., and Woodbury, R.: 1993, Generating languages of solid models, *in* J. Rossignac, J. Turner, and G. Allen (eds), *Proceedings Second ACM/IEEE Conf. on Solid Modeling and Applications*, ACM Press, New York, pp. 103–111.

Hinrichs, T. R.: 1992, *Problem Solving in Open Worlds. A Case Study in Design*, Lawrence Erlbaum Associates, Hillsdale, NJ.

Hua, K., Smith, I., Faltings, B., Shih, S., and Schmitt, G.: 1992, Adaptation of spatial design cases, *in* J. S. Gero (ed.), *Artificial Intelligence in Design '92*, Kluwer Academic, Dordrecht, NL, pp. 559–575.

Kolodner, J. L.: 1991, Improving human decision making through case-based decision aiding, *AI Magazine*, 12(2), 52–68.

Kumar, V., Glicksman, J., and Kramer, G.: 1994, A SHARED web to support design teams, *Proceedings of Third IEEE Workshop on Enabling Technologies: Infrastructure for Collaborative Enterprises*, IEEE Computer Society Press, Los Alamitos, CA, pp. 178–182.

Levy, S., Subrahmanian, E., Konda, S., Coyne, R., Westerberg, A., and Reich, Y.: 1993, An overview of the n-dim environment, *Engineering Design Research*

Center Technical Report EDRC-05-65093, Carnegie Mellon University, Pittsburgh, PA.

Ramaswamy, S., and Kanellakis, P.: 1995, OODB indexing by class-division, *in* D. Schneider (ed.), *Proceedings of ACM SIGMOD*, ACM Press, San Jose, CA, pp. 139–150.

Robertson, J., Subrahmanian, E., Thomas, M., and Westerberg, A.: 1994, Management of the design process: The impact of information modeling, *in* L. T. Biegler and M. F. Doherty (eds), *Proceedings of Foundations of Computer-Aided Process Design*, American Institute of Chemical Engineers, New York, NY.

Rosenman, M. A., Gero, J. S., and Oxman, R. E.: 1991, What's in a case: The use of case bases, knowledge bases, and databases in design *in* G. N. Schmitt (ed.), *CAAD Futures '91*, Vieweg, Wiesbaden, Germany, pp. 285–300.

Snyder, J., Aygen, Z., Flemming, U., and Tsai, W.: 1995, SPROUT—A modeling language for SEED, *Journal of Architectural Engineering*, 1(4), 195–203.

Subrahmanian, S., Coyne, R. F., Konda, S., Levy, S., Martin, R., Monarch, I., Reich, Y., and Westerberg, A.: 1993, Support system for different-time different place collaboration for concurrent engineering, *Proceedings of the Second IEEE Workshop on Enabling Technologies: Infrastructure for Collaborative Enterprises*, IEEE Computer Society Press, Los Alamitos, CA, pp. 187–191.

Toye, G., Cutkosky, M. R., Leifer, L. J., Tenenbaum, J. M., and Glicksman, J.: 1993, SHARE: A methodology and environment for collaborative product development, *Proceedings of the Second Workshop on Enabling Technologies: Infrastructure for Collaborative Enterprises*, IEEE Computer Society Press, Los Alamitos, CA, pp. 33–47.

UniSQL: 1995, *UniSQL Documentation*, UniSQL, Inc, Austin, TX.

chapter five

KRITIK: AN EARLY CASE-BASED DESIGN SYSTEM

ASHOK K. GOEL, SAMBASIVA R. BHATTA,
ELENI STROULIA
Georgia Institute of Technology

In the late 1980s, we developed one of the early CBD systems called Kritik. Kritik autonomously generated preliminary (conceptual, qualitative) designs for physical devices by retrieving and adapting past designs stored in its case memory. Each case in the system had an associated SBF device model that explained how the structure of the device accomplished its functions. These case-specific device models guided the process of modifying a past design to meet the functional specification of a new design problem. The device models also enabled verification of the design modifications. Kritik2 is a new and more complete implementation of Kritik. In this chapter, we take a retrospective view on Kritik. In earlier publications we had described Kritik as integrating CBR and MBR. In this integration, Kritik also grounds the computational process of CBR in the SBF content theory of device comprehension. The SBF models not only provide methods for many specific tasks in CBD, such as design adaptation and verification, but they also provide the vocabulary for the whole process of CBD, from retrieval of old cases to storage of new ones. This grounding, we believe, is essential for building well-constrained theories of CBD.

1. Introduction

Design is a very common, wide-ranging and open-ended activity. It includes not only the design of physical artifacts but also abstract artifacts, such as software interfaces, and conceptual artifacts, such as causal explanations. It can vary from everyday to specialized, naive to expert, and routine to creative design. Although design sometimes is original, even revolutionary, much of design is evolutionary in that new designs are generated by adapting old ones. Evolutionary design includes both variant design, in which new designs locally differ from old in the values of specific parameters of the design elements, and adaptive design, in which new designs locally differ from old in the specific design elements.

CBR is a cognitively inspired computational theory in which new decisions are made by retrieving and modifying the decisions made in similar situations encountered in the past, and new problems are solved by retrieving and modifying the solutions to similar, previously encountered, problems. CBR thus views decision-making and problem-solving as memory tasks in that the memory supplies an answer in the neighborhood of the right answer, an almost right answer that need only be tweaked to get to the right answer (Riesbeck and Schank, 1989). The memory is not only rich but also dynamic because new cases with potential for future use may enter the memory.

In the late 1980s, Goel and Chandrasekaran at the Ohio State University developed one of the earliest CBD systems called Kritik (Kritik in Sanskrit roughly means *designer*) (Goel, 1989; Goel and Chandrasekaran, 1989a, 1989b, 1992). Kritik was an autonomous system that addressed Function–to–Structure design tasks in engineering domains. In particular, it generated, adapted, and evaluated preliminary (conceptual, qualitative) designs for physical devices, such as simple electrical circuits and heat exchange devices. The Kritik experiment showed that CBR provides a good process account of the variant and adaptive aspects of preliminary design. But it also raised a number of content and strategic issues that appear to occur in all case-based systems:

1. What might be the content, representation, and organization of a case?
2. How might a case be indexed? What might be the indexing vocabulary? How might the case memory be organized?
3. How might a new problem be specified? What might be the problem specification language?
4. Given a new problem, how might a similar case be retrieved from the case memory? How might a probe for exploring the case memory be prepared? What kinds of features in the new problem determine the similarity?
5. Once a case has been retrieved from memory, how might it be modified to address the new problem? What knowledge might guide the modification?
6. How might the candidate solution for the new problem be evaluated? What knowledge might enable the verification of the candidate solution for the new problem?
7. What might happen if the verification fails?

8. If the verification succeeds, how might the new case be stored in memory for potential use in future? How might it be indexed in memory and how might the indices be acquired dynamically?

In their work on Kritik, Goel and Chandrasekaran (1989a) developed a model-based framework for addressing some of these issues. The key idea was that evolutionary design involves not only how designs work through past design experiences (i.e., cases) but also through comprehension (i.e., models). whereas the high-level processes of variant and adaptive design are largely case-based, the design models give rise to both the vocabulary and the strategies for addressing the different tasks in the case-based process. The specific hypothesis was that because preliminary design is a Function–to–Structure mapping, the inverse Structure–to–Function map of old designs may provide guidance in adapting an old design to achieve a new functional specification. The Structure–to–Function map of a device design in Kritik is specified as a Structure–Behavior–Function model. The SBF model of a device explicitly specifies the structure and the functions of the device as well as its internal causal behaviors that explain how the structure delivers the functions, and how the device functions are composed from the functions of its structural components.

Kritik was one of the earliest systems to integrate CBR and MBR. Experiments with Kritik showed that the SBF models not only give rise to model-based adaptation strategies for making local modifications to old designs (Goel, 1991a), but that they also give rise to model-based simulation strategies for verifying whether the new design achieves the functions desired of it (Goel, 1991b; Goel and Prabhakar, 1991) and, in addition, provide the vocabulary for indexing the design cases (Goel, 1992). In the early 1990s at Georgia Institute of Technology, we reimplemented Kritik's theory in a new system called Kritik2 (from InterLisp-D/Loops on Xerox Lisp to Symbolics CommonLisp/CLOS on Symbolics Lisp machines) and reproduced the earlier experiments for a larger class of devices (Bhatta and Goel, 1992; Stroulia and Goel, 1992; Stroulia Shankar, Goel, and Penberthy, 1992). Whereas Kritik designed simple electrical circuits and heat exchange devices, Kritik2 also designs electromagnetic devices and electronic circuits containing operational amplifiers. Also, whereas Kritik's case memory was nonhierarchical (or flat), Kritik2's design cases are organized into multiple hierarchies. Experiments with Kritik2 show that the SBF device models not only provide the vocabulary for indexing design cases, but that they also enable the learning of new indices in order to better index new designs in the case memory (Bhatta and Goel, 1995). This chapter describes Kritik2's integrated theory of adaptive design, using examples inherited from Kritik.

2. An Illustrative Example

Let us consider the problem of designing an electrical circuit that will produce light of intensity 20 lumens, when a circuit known to produce light of intensity 10 lumens is available in the case memory. The following two subsections use this illustrative example to introduce Kritik2's device models and its process model for CBD.

2.1. DEVICE MODELS

Kritik2's SBF model of a device explicitly represents the function(s) of the device (i.e., the problem), the structure of the device (i.e., the solution), and the internal causal behaviors of the device. The internal causal behaviors express Kritik2's comprehension of how the device works: They specify how the functions of the structural components of the device are composed into the device functions.

2.1.1. Structure

The structure of a device in the SBF language is expressed in terms of its constituent components and substances and the interactions between them. Figure 5.1b shows the specification of the structure of the red light bulb circuit in Figure 5.1a. Components and substances can interact with each other structurally and behaviorally. For example, electricity can flow from battery to bulb only if they are structurally connected, and, due to the function, allow electricity of the switch that connects the battery and the bulb. For simplicity, we ignore the wires in the circuit in the rest of our discussion, assuming that the other components are connected directly.

2.1.2. Function

The function of a device in the SBF language is represented as a schema that specifies the input behavioral state of the device, the behavioral state it produces as output, and a pointer to the internal causal behavior of the design that achieves this transformation. Figure 5.1c illustrates the function of the electrical circuit. Both the input state and the output state are represented as substance schemas. The input state specifies that the substance electricity at location battery in the topography of the device (Figure 5.1a) has the property voltage and the corresponding parameter 2 volts. The output state specifies the properties intensity and color, and the corresponding parameters 10 lumens and red, of a different substance, light, at location bulb. Finally, the slot by-behavior points to the causal behavior that achieves the function of producing light.

In Kritik2's memory, the design cases and their associated SBF models are indexed by the functions delivered by the devices. Thus the existing electric circuit is indexed by the function illustrated in Figure 5.1c. The functions, in turn, act as indices into the internal causal behaviors of the SBF model through their by-behavior slot.

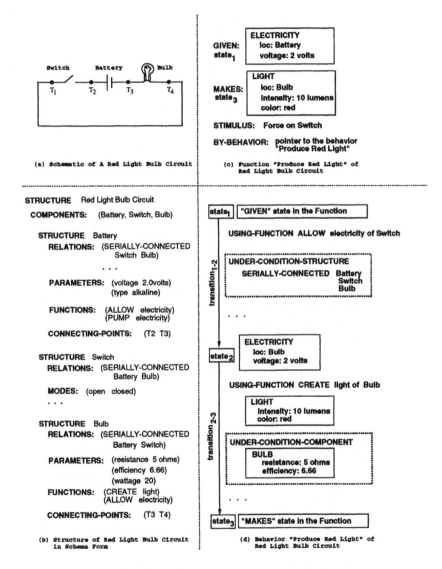

Figure 5.1. Design of a red light bulb circuit.

2.1.3. Behavior

The SBF model of a device also specifies the internal causal behaviors that compose the functions of device substructures into the functions of the device as a whole. In the SBF language, the internal causal behaviors of a device are represented as sequences of transitions between behavioral states. The annotations on the state transitions express the causal, structural, and functional contexts in which the state transitions occur and the state variables get transformed. The causal context specifies causal relations between the variables in preceding and succeeding states. The structural context specifies different structural relations among the components, the substances, and the different spatial locations of the device. The functional context indicates which functions of which components in the device are responsible for the transition. Figure 5.1d shows the causal behavior that explains how electricity in the battery is transformed into light in the bulb. *State*-1 describes the state of electricity at location battery and *state*-2 specifies the state of the same substance at location bulb; *state*-3 describes the state of a different substance, light, at location bulb. The annotation *using-function* on *transition2→3* between *state*-2 and *state*-3 indicates that the transition occurs due to the primitive function create light of bulb. Similarly, the annotation *under-condition-structure* in *transition1→2* specifies that the components battery, switch, and bulb need to be serially connected in order for the transition to occur.

Before we end this introduction to Kritik2's device models, it is useful to note that new problems are presented to Kritik2 in the SBF language. The specification of the new problem of designing an electric circuit producing light of higher intensity is shown in Figure 5.3. Note that of the two functions, the function of the known circuit (Figure 5.2) and the function of the desired one (Figure 5.3) are similar except for the value of the property intensity of the substance light at the output behavioral state.

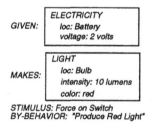

Figure 5.2. Function of the know red-light circuit.

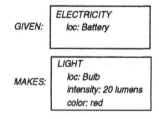

Figure 5.3. Desired function of a higher-intensity red-light circuit.

2.2. COMPUTATIONAL PROCESS

Figure 5.4 illustrates Kritik2's processing. Given the problem of designing an electric circuit that will produce light of a specific intensity, the first step is to retrieve a relevant design case from memory.

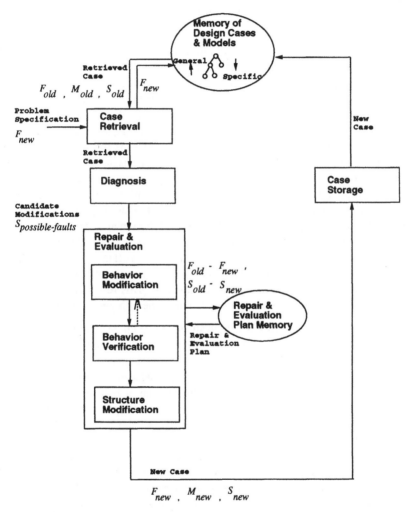

Figure 5.4. Kritik2's process model of design.

One issue here is how to index the design cases in memory and what features in the new problem to use to probe the case memory. New problems for Kritik2 are specified by the functions desired of a device; for example, the desired function of the new circuit in Figure 5.3. The cases are indexed by the functions delivered by the known designs; for example, the function delivered by the existing low-intensity circuit illustrated in Figures 5.1c and 5.2. The functional specification of the new problem is used as a probe into the case memory, and the cases whose functional specifications at least partially match the probe are selected. If more than one design is selected, they are heuristically ordered by their ease of adaptation.

The second step in this process is to adapt the relevant parts of the design solution in the retrieved case to fit the new problem; the third step is to evaluate the modified design. Kritik2 interleaves these two steps. (The dotted lines between different steps in Figure 5.4 indicate that they are interleaved.) It first diagnoses the faulty parts in the retrieved design so that the modified design satisfies the requirements of the new problem. That is, it views the retrieved design as having failed to satisfy the requirements of the new problem and diagnoses and repairs the failure. The important issue then becomes the identification of what to modify; for example, the diagnosis of the faulty parts in the retrieved design that need to be repaired in order to meet the functional specification of the new problem. In Kritik2's model-based approach, the device model indexed off the design case guides the localization and identification of the faulty parts that need to be repaired. In our example, the SBF model of the existing circuit (Figure 5.1d) suggests that the voltage of the battery is responsible for the difference in the functions of the known and the desired device (i.e., light intensity 10 lumens versus 20 lumens). This results in the candidate modification of replacing the battery with a new one of higher voltage.

The next step in this process is to evaluate the candidate solution for the new problem, that is, to verify whether the proposed design satisfies the functional requirements of the new problem. In Kritik2, the changes first due to the proposed modification of battery replacement are propagated to the other parts of the SBF model of the existing circuit (i.e., the substep of behavior modification). This results in a revised SBF model for the candidate design for the desired circuit (but without any structural changes as yet). Next, the revised SBF model is qualitatively simulated to verify if its causal processes result in the functions specified in the new problem (i.e., the substep of behavior verification). In our example, the simulation of the revised circuit model indeed results in the achievement of the function specified in the new problem. If the evaluation succeeds, then in the repair step, the candidate modification is actually executed on the structure of the candidate design (i.e., the substep of structure modification). If the evaluation fails, an alternative modification can be generated if possible. If an alternative candidate modification is not available, then an alternative candidate design (i.e., a different retrieved case) can be selected for adaptation. In this way, Kritik2 interweaves the diagnosis, repair, and evaluation steps.

In the final step, the design that satisfies the requirements of the new problem is stored in the case memory for potential reuse in future problem solving. In order for the new case to be useful in the future, it needs to be stored in the right place in memory; that is, its indices need to be selected appropriately. The device model of the new design case indicates what features of the problem specification are crucial in the functioning of the new design and thus the model helps learn the right indices for the new case.

3. Structure-Behavior-Function Models

In this section, we specify the SBF language for representing design cases and device models using as examples the earlier electric circuit and a nitric acid cooler (Figure 5.5), a simple device that cools nitric acid by exposing the pipes through which it flows to contact with cold water. The schema for representing a design case in the SBF language (shown in Figure 5.6) consists of three slots: function, structure, and behaviors. The fillers for these slots are coherent in that the behaviors specifies internal causal behaviors that explain how the structure delivers the function. Each slot in any SBF schema may be filled with one of three entities: an element from an enumerated set of primitive entities in the SBF language, another schema, or a list of other schemas.

3.1. STRUCTURE

Figure 5.7 shows the schema for representing a design structure in the SBF language. The structure of the device is described hierarchically in terms of its constituent structural elements. The constituent elements of a device may be primitive components (i.e., the components assumed by Kritik2 to be primitives of the design domain), such as a battery. Alternatively, they may be substructures, such as an operational amplifier in an electronic circuit, which can be further described in terms of smaller constituent elements. Each structural element in this hierarchy (except for the overall structure of the device) points to the structural elements of which it is a part. In addition to the part-of relation, the structure schema can also specify the following structural relations: containment of a substance in a component or in another substance, inclusion of a component within another component, and connection between two components. Consider the example of the low-acidity NAC schematically shown in Figure 5.5a. In this design, heat can flow from the nitric acid to the water only when the nitric-acid pipe is included in the heat-exchange chamber. The connection between two components can be of two types: serial and parallel. The two connectivity relations differ in that the former specifies a relation between

two components such that the output of one component becomes the input to
the other, whereas the latter specifies that the two components share the same
input and same output.

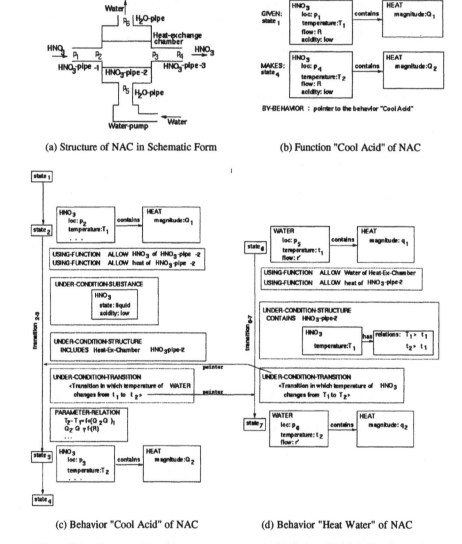

(a) Structure of NAC in Schematic Form   (b) Function "Cool Acid" of NAC

(c) Behavior "Cool Acid" of NAC   (d) Behavior "Heat Water" of NAC

Note: All locations are with reference to components in this design. All labels for states and
transitions are local to this desgn.

Figure 5.5. Design case of low-acidity nitric acid cooler.

design:
    function: the intended output behavior of the device
    behaviors: the internal causal behaviors of the device
    structure: the device components and their structural relations

Figure 5.6. Design case schema.

structure:
    components: a set of structural elements into which the element under description can be
        decomposed
    structural-relations: a set of relations between the subelements of the structure under
        description

Figure 5.7. Structure schema.

3.2. BEHAVIORAL STATE

In the component-substance ontology of SBF device models, a behavioral state
(input, output, or intermediate state) can be of two types: component state,
which concerns the state of a component; and substance state, which concerns the
state of a substance in the device. The component and substance behavioral states
are characterized by the variables characteristic of the respective component and
substance specified in the states. Figure 5.8 shows the schema for a behavioral
state in the SBF language.

behavioral state:
    previous: previous state
    next: next state
    enabled-by: preceding state-transition
    enabling: succeeding state-transition
    substance-state-schema: substance description at this state:
        location: the location of the substance in the device
        main-substance: the schema for the substance:
                                is-a : pointer to a prototype substance
                                (property value unit)*
        {contained-substances: their description at the state }
    OR
    component-state-schema: component description at this state:
        component: the schema for the component:
                                is-a : pointer to prototype component
                                (parameter value unit)*
        mode: the mode of the component's operation at this state

Figure 5.8. Behavioral state schema.

The behavioral state schema contains links to previous and next states, preceding and succeeding state transitions, and either a component-state schema or a substance-state schema. The schema for a component state (partially) specifies the component under description, its mode of operation in the state, and points to the component schema. An example of a component state is the state of the switch in the electrical circuit when its mode is closed. The component schema itself specifies the type of component with the *is-a* slot, and a partial list of the component parameters along with their values. Similarly, the schema for a substance state (partially) specifies the state of the substance under description at a particular point in the device topology. It contains the slots for the location of the substance and other substances contained in the main substance under description, and it points to the schema for the main substance. Again, the schema for a substance itself specifies the type of substance with the *is-a* slot, and a partial list of substance properties along with their values. We explain the representation of components and substances in detail a little later.

3.3. FUNCTION

Functions of devices can be of different kinds, such as transformation functions, control functions, maintenance functions, and prevention functions. Kritik2 currently deals with transformation functions only, in which the device transforms an input behavioral state into a different behavioral output state. Figure 5.9 shows the schema for the representation of transformation functions in the SBF language.

functional specification:
    makes: output behavioral state
    {given: input behavioral state }
    by: causal behavioral-state sequence
    {stimulus: event in the external environment triggering the functioning of the device }
    {provided: external to the device conditions necessary for the functioning of the device }*

Figure 5.9. Functional specification schema.

In addition to the input and output behavioral states (*given* and *makes* respectively), the function schema contains the *by-behavior* slot for specifying the internal causal behavior that transforms the input state into the output state, the *stimulus* slot for specifying the interaction of the device with its environment that triggers its functioning, and the *provided* slot for specifying the environmental conditions necessary for the functioning of the device. An example of stimulus is a force on a switch, shown in the functional specification of the electric circuit in Figure 5.1c. In the specification of a desired function in a new design problem, the slot *by-behavior* would not be filled, and the slots *given, stimulus, provided* too may not be filled (see for example the specification of the new desired electric circuit in Figure 5.3). This schema for representing device functions is borrowed from Sembugamoorthy and Chandrasekaran (1986).

Figure 5.5b shows the function Cool Nitric Acid of the low-acidity NAC. Both the *given* and *makes* behavioral states of this function are substance states. The former specifies the state of in-flowing nitric acid, whereas the latter specifies the state of the nitric acid as it flows out of the device. In addition, the *by-behavior* slot points to the Cool Acid internal causal behavior that explains the previous transformation.

Note that the function of a device in SBF models is an abstraction of the internal causal behaviors of the device. For transformation functions, the initial state and final state in an internal causal behavior are respectively the input state and output state in the function. For instance, the given and make states of the function of nitric acid cooler (Figure 5.5b) are respectively the same as the initial state (*state*-1) and the final state (*state*-4) in the internal causal behavior Cool Acid of the nitric acid cooler (Figure 5.5c). Note also that the functions of a device in SBF models are a subset of the set of its observable, output behaviors. In particular, a function is an output behavior of the device intended by the designer. For instance, the abstraction of the internal causal behavior Heat Water of the nitric acid cooler (Figure 5.5d) is an output behavior of the device. But in SBF models, this output behavior is included under the device functions only if it was actually intended by the designer.

3.4. BEHAVIORAL STATE TRANSITION

A behavioral state transition is a partial description of a transformation of one behavioral state into another during the functioning of the device. Figure 5.10 shows the schema for representing such a transition in the SBF language. In addition to the links to the previous and next states, the behavioral state transition schema contains the slots *by-behavior, using-function, as-per-domain-principle, parameter-relations,* and *conditions* of different kinds that have to be true in order for the transition to occur.

state-transition:
    previous-state: preceding state
    next-state: succeeding state
    { by-behavior: pointer to a more detailed behavior explaining the transition }
    { using-function: component's function }*
    { as-per-domain-principle }*
    { parameter-relations }*
    { condition }*

Figure 5.10. Behavioral state transition schema.

A behavioral transformation of a device element may be explained at several levels of causal abstraction and structural aggregation. Thus, the specification of a state transition may include a pointer to another behavior (through the *by-behavior* slot) that explains in greater detail the transformation described by that transition. The *by-behavior* pointer results in a hierarchical organization of the device internal behaviors. In addition to pointing to a more detailed behavior, a state transition may be explained in terms of the functions of structural elements of the device (i.e., *using-function* slot), or in terms of a domain principle (i.e., *as-per-domain-principle* slot) such as physics laws (e.g., the law of conservation of momentum). The *using-function* slot of a behavioral state transition schema is filled with a list of schemas, each of which refers to a component in the device and a primitive function of that component.

Moreover, the transition schema may be annotated with qualitative equations (i.e., *parameter-relations* slot) describing the changes to the values of different substance properties and component parameters because of the transition. Qualitative equations may be based on physics principles but are specific to the device parameters. The *parameter-relations* slot of the state-transition schema is filled with a list of qualitative equations, where each qualitative equation itself consists of a qualitative relation between values of two substance properties or between values of a substance property and a component parameter. A qualitative relation is an enumerated type and can have one of the two values: *directly-proportional-to* and *inversely-proportional-to*.

Often, the occurrence of a state transition is conditioned on the co-occurrence of other behavioral states in the device (the representation of this condition by a pointer to the state via *under-condition-state*), or the co-occurrence of other state transitions (a pointer to the transition via *under-condition-transition*), or specific structural relations among the device elements (a list of structural relations via *under-condition-structure*), or specific property values of a substance (a pointer to the partial description of the substance via *under-condition-substance*), or specific parameter values of a component (a pointer to partial description of the component via under-condition-component). The SBF language provides the vocabulary for specifying all five different types of conditions in a state transition.

For instance, in *transition2→3* (Figure 5.5c), the annotation *under-condition-substance* specifies that the behavior *allow* of nitric-acid-pipe-2 can allow the flow of only some substances: The substance should be in liquid state and should have low acidity (i.e., behavioral or causal context). Further, the annotation *under-condition-structure* specifies the structural relation that Heat-Exchange-Chamber includes nitric-acid-pipe-2 in order for the transition to occur (i.e., structural context). Annotations may also include conditions on other transitions as indicated by *under-condition-transition*. For example, *transition2→3* refers to *transition6→7* in another behavior (the behavior Heat Water) of NAC shown in Figure 5.5d. In addition, a transition may be annotated by knowledge of deeper domain principles and qualitative equations as indicated in Figure 5.5c.

3.5. BEHAVIOR

An internal causal behavior is a sequence of alternating behavioral states and behavioral state transitions. Figure 5.5c shows a fragment of the causal behavior that explains how nitric acid is cooled from temperature T1 to T2. *State-2* is the preceding state of *transition2→3* and state-3 is its succeeding state. *State-2* describes the state of nitric acid at location p2, and so does *state-3* at location p3. The different types of annotations on *transition2→3* indicate the different types of causal contexts under which the transition can occur. For example, the annotation *using-function* in *transition2→3* indicates that the transition occurs due to the primitive function *allow* of nitric-acid-pipe-2.

3.6. OTHER KNOWLEDGE

In addition to design cases and their associated device models, Kritik2 has knowledge of the primitive functions, and the generic components and substances of the design domain. Although Kritik2's SBF models are case-specific, its knowledge of components and substances is generic; that is, case-independent. But all domain knowledge, from case-specific SBF models to generic components and substances, is represented in the same SBF language. In addition, the different types of knowledge are cross-indexed in Kritik2 as indicated in Figure 5.11.

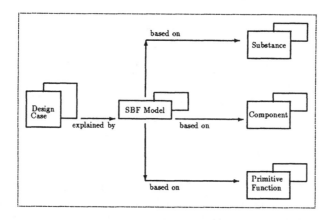

Figure 5.11. Types of knowledge in Kritik2.

For instance, design cases index into their SBF device models, and a SBF device model is described in terms of the participating substances, components, and primitive functions. The partial specification of a substance or a component in the SBF model contains pointers to the more complete specifications of generic substances and components as indicated in the earlier discussion of the behavioral state schema.

A primitive function in the component-substance ontology of SBF models can be one of: *allow, pump, create,* and *destroy.* This typology of primitive functions is directly borrowed from Bylander (1991).

Unlike a device, a primitive component is a structure assumed to be non-decomposable by Kritik2. A component is represented as a schema consisting of *is-a, structural-relations, parameters, modes, functions,* and *connecting-points.* Figure 5.12 shows a portion of Kritik2's memory of primitive components organized in a taxonomic hierarchy. The schema for a specific component, battery-1, is shown in the dashed box. *Is-a* is a pointer through which a specific component is linked to a prototypical component in Kritik2's conceptual memory of components. For instance, battery-1 *is-a* battery in Figure 5.12. The *structural-relations* slot specifies a list of structural relations between this component and the others in the device. The *modes* slot in a component schema specifies one or more modes of operation of the component. The *parameters* slot contains a list of characteristic parameters of the component and their corresponding values and units. For example, the volume of a heat-exchange chamber has a value of 1 cubic foot. The *functions* slot of a component contains the set of primitive functions that the component delivers and the *connecting-points* slot specifies the structural points in the component where the other components can be connected.

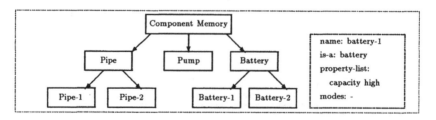

Figure 5.12. A Snapshot of Kritik2's component memory.

Figure 5.13 shows a portion of Kritik2's conceptual memory of substances organized in a generalization-specialization hierarchy. The schema for representing a specific substance nitric acid is shown in the dashed box. *Is-a* is a pointer through which a specific substance is linked to a more general substance.

For instance, nitric-acid *is-a* liquid in Figure 5.13. *PropertyList* contains a list of characteristic properties of the substance and the corresponding values and units. For example, the temperature of nitric acid in a specific behavioral state of a given device may have a value of T1 degrees. In the description of a substance in a behavioral state of a specific device, only some of these characteristic properties are of interest, and thus only their values are specified. Note that in Figure 5.13 many properties for a substance nitric acid are shown as "–," which means that Kritik2 knows that these properties are relevant to this substance but in its generic knowledge, there are no values specified for these properties. However, a specific substance in a specific device, for instance, nitric acid in low-acidity NAC may have additional values specified (i.e., acidity: low; temperature: T1) as shown in Figure 5.5b.

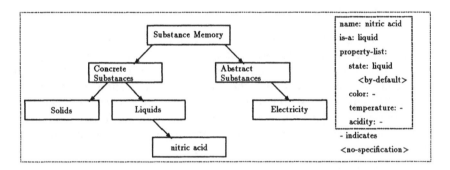

Figure 5.13. A snapshot of Kritik2's substance memory.

4. Case-Based Adaptive Design

Figure 5.4 illustrates Kritik2's computational process for case-based adaptive design. In this section, we describe how the SBF models give rise to the vocabulary and strategies for addressing the different subtasks of case-based adaptive design.

In the domain of physical devices, a typical problem in preliminary design is to design a device that achieves specific functions. This Function–to–Structure design task takes, as input, a specification of the functions desired of a device, and has the goal of giving, as output, a specification of a structure that delivers the desired functions. Consider, for instance, the task of designing a sulfuric acid cooler, a device that delivers the function of cooling sulfuric acid of high acidity. Kritik2 accepts representations of new problems in the SBF language. The specification of the desired function in the SBF language is shown in Figure 5.14.

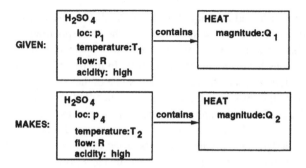

Figure 5.14. Function of cooling high-acidity sulfuric acid.

4.1. CASE RETRIEVAL

The task of case retrieval takes the functional specification of a desired design; and the functional specifications of design cases stored in memory as input. It has the goal of giving, as output, an ordered set of known design cases that can potentially be adapted to satisfy the functional specifications of the desired design. The retrieved cases are ordered by a qualitative estimate of their ease of adaptation for satisfying the functional specification of the desired design. The computational advantage of retrieving and ordering a set of known designs is that if the adaptation of one design fails, another design can be selected without again probing the case memory.

4.1.1. Organization and Indexing of the Case Memory

The retrieval of appropriate design cases raises the issues of indexing the design cases, matching the design problem with the problems in past design cases, selecting a set of candidate design cases (when there are many partial matches), and finally ordering the selected designs. The case indexing in Kritik2 is task-specific: because Function–to–Structure design problems are specified by the functions desired of the new device, the stored design cases in Kritik2 are indexed by their functions. The SBF language provides the vocabulary for representing the functions delivered by the stored designs.

The design cases are organized in a generalization-specialization hierarchy. The properties of the substances specified in the device functions are used as dimensions along which the designs are generalized/specialized. For example, designs of acid coolers are organized along the dimension of property acidity and discriminated on the corresponding parameters low versus high, as shown in Figure 5.15. The property acidity is important because the choice of pipe in the design depends on whether it has to allow a low-acidity substance or a high-acidity substance. The exact dimensions of generalization depend on the past design experiences of Kritik2. The NIC case (see Figure 5.15) is the design of the low-acidity NIC that we described in the last section and it is stored under the category of low-acidity coolers.

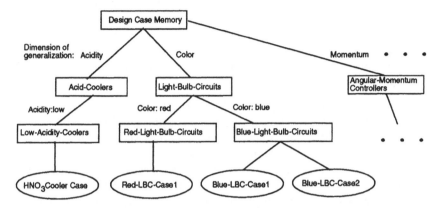

Figure 5.15. A snapshot of Kritik2's functionally organized case memory.

The functions at the higher-level nodes in this hierarchy are more general than those at the lower-level nodes of the hierarchy. That is, along a single dimension defined by a particular property, the values of this property in the functions of designs associated with a higher-level node subsume the values of this property in the functions of cases associated with a lower-level node. For instance, the higher-level node acid-coolers in Figure 5.15 has both classes of designs, low-acidity coolers and high-acidity coolers, associated with it. In contrast, the lower-level node low-acidity-coolers has only the designs of acid coolers with low acidity. Formally, the set of cases associated with a node in the hierarchy is a superset of the set of cases associated with any of its immediate child nodes.

4.1.2. Case Retrieval: Selection of Known Designs

The task of case retrieval is decomposed into the subtasks of selection and ordering. The selection subtask takes the functions specified in the new problem and the functions delivered by the stored cases as input. It has the goal of giving, as output, a set of known design cases that can be potentially modified to satisfy the requirements of the new problem specification.

The selected cases are such that the differences between their functions and the functions in the new problem are of a type that Kritik2 knows how to reduce. The SBF vocabulary for representing device functions gives rise to a taxonomy of functional differences; that is, a taxonomy of differences between two functions. For example, two functions may differ only in their input states, or only in their output states, or in both. Further, two substance states (input or output) from two different functions may differ in several ways: Their substances can differ (i.e., substance difference), the values of a common substance-property can differ (i.e., substance-property-value difference), or a substance property may be specified only in one of the states (i.e., substance-property-unspecified difference and substance-property-additionally-specified difference). Kritik2 knows how to reduce substance and substance-property-value (for single or multiple properties) differences between the output behavioral states of two designs. Thus, it selects only these designs whose functions differ from the function in the new problem in these ways.

Figure 5.16 shows the algorithm that Kritik2 uses for selecting design cases. It searches through the functionally organized case memory along the dimensions of generalization that correspond to the properties specified in the desired function. Along each dimension of generalization, it goes as far specific as possible in comparing the value of that property specified in either the input state or the output state of the desired function. It collects the design case associated with the most specific value it could reach along each dimension. Note that in this and subsequent algorithms, the notation slot-name(schema) denotes the value of a slot in a schema. For example, PropertyList(State-IN(F)) denotes the value of the slot PropertyList in the schema for State-IN, which in itself is a slot of the schema for function F.

For example, the matching of the functional specification of the high-acidity sulfuric acid cooler (Figure 5.14) with the functions of the designs stored in the case memory (Figure 5.15) results in the selection of the design for the low-acidity NAC (Figure 5.5). Consider a hypothetical situation where the memory contained both the low-acidity NAC and a neutral-acidity motor-oil cooler (i.e., a design for cooling motor oil that has neutral acidity). In such a situation, Kritik2 would have selected both of these cases because they both match partially the desired function on the property of acidity.

4.1.3. Case Retrieval: Ordering of Selected Designs

Several situations are possible on the retrieval of a set of stored cases relevant to a given problem:

1. *Exact Match*: The set of selected design cases includes a design whose functional specification exactly matches that of the desired design. In this situation, the structure of the exactly matching design is the solution, and problem solving is terminated.

2. *No Match*: The set of selected design cases is empty. In this situation, there is no solution to the design problem by the case-based method, and problem solving can be terminated (or, in principle, some other method for the design task can be selected).

Input: • Desired function, $F_{desired}$.

Output: • A set of design cases Set_{Cases}, whose functions partially match $F_{desired}$.
Assumptions: • root-list contains the root nodes of all the hierarchies
                    along with the dimensions of generalizations, and
                    dimension-list contains all the dimensions of generalization.
Procedure:
SELECT($F_{desired}$);
  begin
     Set_{Cases} = {};
     selected-nodes = {};
     tobe-seen-nodes = {$node_i$ | $node_i \in root\text{-}list\wedge$
                         function associated with $node_i$ and $F_{desired}$
                         have at least one common property specified. }
     while not-empty(tobe-seen-nodes) do
        begin
        child-nodes = MATCHING-CHILDREN ($F_{desired}$, first(tobe-seen-nodes));
        if empty(child-nodes)
           then selected-nodes = first(tobe-seen-nodes) $\cup$ selected-nodes;
           else tobe-seen-nodes = tobe-seen-nodes $\cup$ child-nodes;
           tobe-seen-nodes = rest (tobe-seen-nodes);
        end;
     Set_{Cases} = {$case_i$ | $node_i \in selected\text{-}nodes\wedge case_i$ is associated with $node_i$, };
     return (Set_{Cases});
  end.

MATCHING-CHILDREN($F_{desired}$, node-in-hierarchy);
  begin
     child-nodes = {};
     foreach (dimension $\in$ dimension-list) do
        begin
        child = DISCRIMINATE (dimension, $F_{desired}$, get-children(dimension, node-in-hierarchy));
        if not-empty (associated-cases(child))
           then child-nodes = {child} $\cup$ child-nodes;
        end;
     return (child-nodes);
  end.

DISCRIMINATE(property, $F_{desired}$, children);
  begin
     foreach (child $\in$ children) do
        begin
        if (value-of(property, input-state($F_{desired}$)) = value-of(property, input-state(F(child))))
           $\vee$ (value-of(property, output-state($F_{desired}$)) = value-of(property, output-state(child)))
           then return(child);
        end;
     return (nil); /* as failure */
  end.

Figure 5.16. The selection algorithm.

3. *Single Partial Match*: The set of selected design cases contains no exactly matching design and exactly one partially matching design. In this situation, there is no need for ordering the selected design cases.

4. *Multiple Partial Matches*: The set of selected design cases contains no exactly matching design and more than one partially matching designs. In this situation, there is a need for ordering the selected design cases for further processing.

As mentioned, for the sulfuric-acid cooler example, the selection subtask results in a single partial match because the design of the NAC is the only stored design whose functional specification partially matches with the desired function of a high-acidity sulfuric-acid cooler. But, for the purpose of illustrating Kritik2's method for ordering cases, consider a hypothetical situation where two low-acidity cooler designs, the low-acidity NAC and a low-acidity sulfuric-acid cooler were selected.

The ordering subtask takes, as input, the desired design specification and a set of selected design cases, and has the goal of giving, as output, the same set of cases ordered according to some measure of their ease of adaptation. In Kritik2, the ease of adaptation of a partially matching design is measured by the qualitative distance between the function it delivers (which represents the current state in the design adaptation space) and the function desired of it (which is the goal state). There are two aspects to the estimation of this distance between the goal state from the current state:

1. *Behavioral States*: The distance of the goal state from the current state depends on the degree of match between the functional specification of the desired design and that of the candidate design case.

    For instance, if the input behavioral state in the function of the desired design exactly matches the input behavioral state in the function of the retrieved design, whereas the output behavioral states match only partially, then the distance between the goal state and the current state is smaller than if both the input and output states were to match only partially. Similarly, if both the input and output behavioral states in the function of the desired design partially match with the input and output behavioral states in the function of the retrieved design respectively, then the current state is closer to the goal state than if only the input states match partially or if only the output states match partially.

2. *Behavioral State Features*: The distance of the goal state from the current state depends on which features in the function of the candidate design case match with the corresponding features in the function of the desired design. That is, the distance depends on which features in the input and output behavioral states in the function specification of the candidate design need to be transformed to match with the corresponding features in the input and output behavioral states in the functional specification of the desired design.

    For example, it is, in general, easier to transform the value of a property of a substance into another value than to transform one substance into another. Thus, if the function of one partially matching design differs from that of the desired design in the value of some property only, while the function of another partially matching design differs in the substance itself, then the former design is probably closer to the desired design than the latter. Similarly, it is, in general, easier to transform the value of one property of a substance into another value than to transform values of two properties, and so on. Of course, these heuristics for determining the distance between the goal state and the current state can only provide an estimate, and not an accurate measure, of the distance between them. Also, these heuristics can be domain specific.

In sum, Kritik2's heuristic estimate for case ordering is based on how many of the input and output behavioral states, and which state features and how many of them, match in the functional specification of the new problem and the function delivered by the candidate design. In the hypothetical situation where both a low-acidity NAC and a low-acidity sulfuric-acid cooler were selected, Kritik2 would order the latter as a better match than the former because the sulfuric acid cooler matches with desired function on the substance also.

4.2. DESIGN ADAPTATION

The task of design adaptation involves, first, the mapping of the differences between the desired function of the new problem and the function delivered by the candidate design into potential modifications to the structure of the candidate design (*functional differences*⇒*structural modifications*), and second, the evaluation and execution of the candidate modifications. The generation of useful candidate structural modifications is computationally complex because the differences between the function desired of and delivered by the retrieved design can be large and many, the needed structural modifications can be large and many, there may be no simple correspondence between the functional differences and the structural modifications, and the needed structural modifications can interact with one another and with the components in the structure of the known design.

Kritik2 decomposes the adaptation into the subtasks of diagnosis and repair. It views the retrieved design as a faulty solution to the new problem and repairs it appropriately. Solving the diagnosis and repair tasks effectively and efficiently requires knowledge that constrains and focuses the processes of identifying possible faults and generating potentially useful modifications. In this section, we discuss how the SBF model of the retrieved design provides Kritik2 with the needed knowledge.

4.2.1. Diagnosis

The task of diagnosis in the context of adaptive design is to identify possible faults in the known design that, if fixed, can help to deliver a solution to the new problem. The diagnosis task takes the new desired function, a retrieved design, and the differences between the desired function and the function delivered by the retrieved design as input. It has the goal of giving, as output, a set of plausible faults in the retrieved design. Each possible fault is described as a three-tuple, consisting of either a substance or a component in the retrieved design, a property of that substance or component, and a relation between that property and some substance or component property in the output state of the desired function.

The SBF model of the known design specifies how the internal causal mechanisms of the device compose the functional abstractions of its structural components into the functions of the device as a whole. Thus, Kritik2 uses that knowledge to identify the causes that prevent the solution of the retrieved case to satisfy the new problem. In particular, it uses the algorithm shown in Figure 5.17, which, given the functional differences and the SBF model of the known design, traces through the model and identifies specific structural elements (components or substances) that can potentially be modified in a way that will result in the accomplishment of the function desired of the new design.

In our example, because the substance-property-value difference *low-acidity* ⇒ *high-acidity* occurs in the function of cooling low-acidity nitric acid, Kritik2 uses this function to access the internal causal behavior responsible for it, a fragment of which is shown in Figure 5.5c (recall that in the SBF model, functions act as indices to the behaviors responsible for them). Then, it traces through the retrieved case, starting from the final state of the behavior and checking each state transition in the behavior to determine whether reducing the substance-property-value difference *low-acidity*⇒*high-acidity* requires any component in the transition to be modified (or replaced). If so, it identifies a potential fault that could be eliminated by the corresponding structure modification.

For example, when Kritik2 arrives at the transition *transition2→3* shown in Figure 5.5c, it finds that nitric-acid-pipe2 allows the flow of only low-acidity substances (i.e., some property of this component is related to the property *acidity* of the substances that it can allow). It therefore generates the structure modifications of component-parameter adjustment (in case nitric-acid-pipe2 can allow the flow of high-acidity substances in a different parameter setting), component-modality change (in case nitric-acid-pipe2 can allow the flow of high-acidity substances in a different mode of operation), and component replacement (in case the first two modifications are not possible and nitric-acid-pipe2 has to be replaced with some sulfuric-acid-pipe2 that can allow the flow of high-acidity substances).

In this way, Kritik2 uses the SBF model for NAC to generate structural modifications that can help reduce the functional difference *low-acidity*⇒*high-*

acidity. Similarly, given the functional difference of *substance1⇒substance2* (nitric acid⇒sulfuric acid), Kritik2's diagnosis results in the generation of the structure modification of substance substitution *nitric acid⇒sulfuric acid*.

```
Input:    • Desired function, F_new.
          • Source design case, C.
          • Functional difference, FD = F_new - F_old, where F_old is the function in C.
Output:   • A set of possible faults (or candidate modifications), S_possible-faults.
Procedure:
initialize
    F_old = functional-spec(C);
    S_possible-faults = {(E, P_i, Relation) where
                    E ∈ {Sub, Comp}, P_i ∈ PropertyList(E), and
                    ∃P' ∈ PropertyList(State_OUT(F_new))s.t.P'RelationP_i
                    and P' is the property whose value needs to be changed,
                    and Relation ∈ {directly-proportional-to, inversely-proportional-to}};
    B_old = function-by-behavior(F_old);
begin
    S_possible-faults = BACKTRACE(behavior-final-state(B_old), S_possible-faults);
end.
BACKTRACE (state, S_possible-faults)
    current-state = state
    LOOP
        previous-state = state-previous-state (current-state);
        IF previous-state = NIL, THEN Exit LOOP
        CASE :
        (1)    IF there is a qualitative equation in state-previous-transition(current-state),
               and property P_i ∈ S_possible-faults such that P_i^old RelationP_l , where
               P_l is a parameter of a component or a property of another substance E, and
               P_i^old is a property in the current design,
               THEN S_possible-faults = S_possible-faults ∪ {(E, P_l, Relation)}
                            where P_l.value^new Relation^{-1}(P_i.value^new), and
                            P_l.value^new is the value of property P_l in the desired design,
        (2)    IF there is a functional abstraction of a component E (i.e., Comp in using-function)
               and a condition on the substance properties on which E operates
               (i.e., Condition_SUB) in state-previous-transition(current-state),
               and property P_i ∈ S_possible-faults such that P_i^old = P_l, where
               P_l is a property of the substance in Condition_SUB, and
               P_i^old is a property in the current design,
               THEN S_possible-faults = S_possible-faults ∪ {(E, P_l, directly - proportional - to)}
                            where P_l.value^new determinesthetypeofcomponentE, and
                            P_l.value^new is the value of property P_l in the desired design,
        (3)    IF there is a pointer to a new behavior sequence B' such that
               the transition state-previous-transition(current-state)
               depends on a transition, trans, of B'
               THEN spawn
                        BACKTRACE (transition-next-state(trans),S_possible-faults)
        END-CASE
        current-state = previous-state
        goto LOOP
    END-LOOP
```

Figure 5.17. The diagnosis algorithm.

4.2.2. Repair

The task of repair is to execute a candidate modification given a set of possible modifications. In the context of adaptive design, this involves modifying the old design so that the possible faults are eliminated. It takes, as input, the desired function, the retrieved design, the functional difference between the desired and the retrieved, and a set of possible faults as identified by the diagnosis task; and gives, as output, a modified model and its corresponding function.

As mentioned in Section 4.1.2, the SBF language provides a vocabulary for expressing certain types of functional differences between design cases, such as substance difference, substance-property-value difference, substance-location difference, component difference, component-modality difference, and component-parameter difference. In addition, it provides the vocabulary for expressing certain types of modifications to the structure of a design, such as substance substitution (including substance generalization and specialization), component modification (including component replacement, component-modality change, and component-parameter adjustment), relation modification (for example, series-to-parallel and parallel-to-series conversion), substructure deletion (for example, component deletion), and substructure insertion (for example, substructure replication).

Given the function desired of a design (e.g., to cool high-acidity sulfuric acid) and the function delivered by the selected design case (e.g., to cool low-acidity nitric acid), Kritik2 classifies the differences between the two functions into its typology of functional differences. If the desired and the delivered functions differ in more than one feature, then it heuristically ranks the differences in order of the difficulty of reducing them. In the NAC example, for instance, the desired function and the delivered function differ in two features: *substance1⇒substance2* (*nitric acid⇒sulfuric acid*), and *value1⇒value2* of property *acidity* (*low-acidity⇒high-acidity*). Because, in the domain of physical devices that can be modeled in terms of flow of substances between components, reducing the difference *substance1⇒substance2* is, in general, less difficult than reducing *value1⇒value2* of a property, Kritik2 reduces the latter before the former.

Given the substance-property-value difference between the retrieved design of low-acidity NAC and the desired function of cooling high-acidity sulfuric acid, Kritik2's ontology suggests that such a difference can potentially be reduced by the structural modifications of component-parameter adjustment, component-modality change, and component replacement. Kritik2, prior to diagnosis, however, does not know what components in the given design need to be modified. This is determined by the diagnosis of the NAC SBF model, which we have already seen.

In Kritik2, the repair step is interleaved with the evaluation step. This interleaving includes two further subtasks: repair-and-evaluation plan selection and repair-and-evaluation plan instantiation. During the former, the functional difference and the structure modification are used to retrieve an applicable repair and evaluation plan from Kritik2's repair and evaluation plan memory. During the latter, the selected plan is applied first to the behavior of the known case. The structure of the known design is modified only after verifying (by simulation of the SBF model) that the modification will result in the achievement of the desired function.

4.3. EVALUATION OF THE CANDIDATE MODIFICATIONS

Because modifications in general are done to some localized parts of the solution in the known design case, it is essential to evaluate whether each initial modification, and the subsequent ones it may invoke in other parts of the device, are leading toward the satisfaction of the requirements of the new problem. An important element in Kritik2's integrated theory is that the SBF model of the known design can be modified and simulated to verify if the proposed modifications indeed result in a solution for the new problem without actually making modifications to the solution (i.e., the device structure in design problem solving). The task of repair and evaluation in Kritik2 takes, as input, the functional specification of a desired design; the functional and structural specification of a candidate design; the SBF model of the candidate design; and the specification of a candidate modification to the structure of the candidate design. It has the goal of modifying the behavior of the retrieved design and giving, as output, an evaluation of whether the candidate modification, upon execution, would result in satisfying the functional specification of the desired design.

4.3.1. A Model-Based Method for Repair and Evaluation

The evaluation of a candidate modification—such as component replacement for example—involves two subtasks. The first task is to determine whether a design that satisfies the functional specification of the needed component (e.g., the functional specification of the sulfuric-acid-pipe; that is, a pipe that can allow high acidity substances) is available in memory. Recall that in the previous section, we described how Kritik2 determines that one candidate modification in adapting a low-acidity NAC to cool high-acidity sulfuric acid is the component replacement of nitric-acid-pipe2 with a component that allows high-acidity substances. If the needed design is not available in memory, the candidate modification of component replacement is not feasible. Thus, one subtask of repair and evaluation is to determine the feasibility of the candidate modification.

Let us suppose that there exists such a component as the one required by the modification plan. Then, the second subtask of repair and evaluation is to determine whether, on execution, the candidate modification would result in satisfying the functional specification of the desired design. This involves the simulation of the effects of (the execution of) the candidate modifications on the output behaviors of the candidate design. The availability of the SBF model for the known design and the localization of the candidate modification gives rise to the method of model revision. In this method, the causal and output behaviors of the modified design are obtained by revising the causal and output behaviors of the known design (i.e., behavior modification). If the revision succeeds; that is, if the revised causal behavior results in the desired output behavior of the desired design, then the candidate modification may be executed on the candidate design (i.e., structure modification). If the revision fails, an alternative candidate modification may be evaluated.

The types of knowledge required for revising the SBF model of the known design depend on the type of candidate modification to be executed on it. For instance, the method for model revision corresponding to the candidate modification of component replacement requires knowledge of how to compose causal behaviors. More specifically, it requires knowledge about how to compose the causal behavior of the new component with causal behavior segments from the known design. For adaptation problems in which the distance between the known and the desired design is small, the candidate modifications are local, and knowledge is available for revising the model for the candidate design, the method of model revision is a computationally attractive method for evaluating whether the behavioral effects of a structure modification would result in satisfying the behavioral specification of a given desired design (i.e., behavior verification).

Kritik2 uses a plan- and model-based method for the task of modification evaluation; that is, it uses repair and evaluation plans that, in turn, make use of the SBF model of the candidate design to perform the interleaved steps of repair and evaluation. A skeletal repair and evaluation plan embodies knowledge of how the causal and output behaviors of the new design can be composed from the causal and output behaviors of the known design and the causal and output behaviors of other substructures such as components. The operations specified by such a plan are at two levels. At the first level, it specifies the tasks of design retrieval and model revision. At the second level, the subplan for model revision specifies the operations for modifying the causal and output behaviors of the known design.

The relation between the types of knowledge required for model revision and the types of candidate modification implies a family of model-revision plans, and, hence, a family of repair and evaluation plans, with particular methods applicable to specific candidate modifications. The need for a set of stored skeletal plans for the modification-evaluation task implies yet another subtask of the task, namely, the task of selection of the particular plan applicable to a given candidate modification.

Thus, in general, the plan-based method decomposes the task of repair and evaluation into three subtasks: plan selection, design case retrieval, and simulation of behavioral effects. The task of design case retrieval has been discussed in Section 4.1. The other two tasks can be characterized:

1. *Plan Selection*: The task of plan selection takes, as input, the specification of a candidate modification, and has the goal of giving, as output, a specific repair and evaluation plan applicable to the given candidate modification. (Note again that the repair and evaluation are interleaved in our computational model.)

2. *Simulation of Behavioral Effects*: The task of simulation of behavioral effects takes, as input, the function of the desired design; the SBF model of a candidate design; and the specification of a candidate modification. It has the goal of giving, as output, an evaluation of whether the effects of (the execution of) the candidate modification on the output behaviors of the known design result in satisfying the function of the desired design.

4.3.2. Selection of Repair and Evaluation Plans

The repair and evaluation plan memory contains a plan for each type of structural difference that corresponds to a structural modification. The stored plans are indexed by the types of structural modifications to which they are applicable, as well as the functional differences they can reduce. The retrieval of a plan applicable to a given structure modification is performed by the associative method. In this method, elementary structure modifications are directly mapped onto the stored plans.

Once a repair and evaluation plan corresponding to an elementary structure modification is retrieved, it can be instantiated and executed. This section describes one type of repair and evaluation plans that corresponds to substructure modification; that is, substance-modification plans. The other types are component-modification, relation-modification, and substructure-deletion plans. The discussion assumes the availability of the causal behaviors of the known design, and, in particular, the specific causal behavior to be revised (as determined by the task of localization of structure modifications, a subtask of diagnosis.)

In substance-modification plans, a substance in the known design case is substituted by another substance. The substance-substitution plan does not involve design case retrieval as a subtask. Instead, model revision is performed directly. For instance, if the design problem is to modify the design of the low-acidity NAC to cool high-acidity sulfuric acid (Figure 5.18), the substitution of nitric acid by high-acidity sulfuric acid is generated as a candidate modification. Then the causal behavior for the SAC is obtained by a substitution of nitric acid by high-acidity sulfuric acid in the causal behavior segments, one of which was shown in Figure 5.5c.

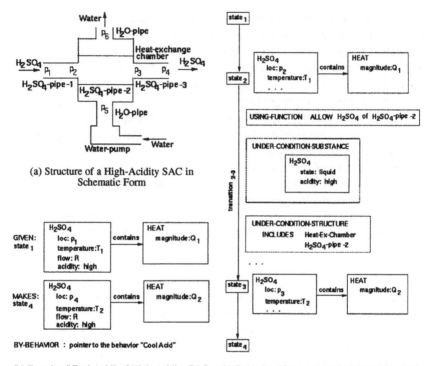

(a) Structure of a High-Acidity SAC in Schematic Form

(b) Function "Cool Acid" of High-Acidity SAC   (c) Behavior "Cool Acid" of High-Acidity SAC

Note: All locations are with reference to components in this design.
All labels for states and transitions are local to this design.

Figure 5.18. Design case of high-acidity sulfuric acid cooler.

Also, in the example of designing a high-acidity SAC, the *under-condition-transition* pointer in *transition* 2→3 is used to retrieve the causal behavior Heat Water of the NAC. This behavior is traced to find the pointer to the behavior segment of cooling nitric acid (Figure 5.5). The pointers are modified to point to the corresponding behavioral states and state transitions in the behavior segments of the behavior, Cool Sulfuric Acid.

Finally, the schema for the desired output behavior (i.e., the function) of the high-acidity SAC (shown in Figure 5.18) is revised. A pointer to the causal behavior Cool Sulfuric Acid composed is placed in the *by-behavior* slot of the function. The other slots are filled by copying their values from the schema for the function of the NAC shown in Figure 5.5.

4.3.3. Simulation of Behavioral Effects

This task involves instantiating a repair and evaluation plan in the localized behavior, propagating the changes to the other parts of the same behavior and to the dependent behaviors, and finally simulating the behavior (from the input state to the output state) to determine if the revised model results in the achievement of the desired function. Kritik2 instantiates the retrieved plan in the context of the SBF model of the known case and executes it to produce an SBF model for the new design.

The model-revision process (pointed to by the retrieved repair and evaluation plan) specifies a compiled sequence of abstract operations. Figure 5.19 shows the algorithm that Kritik2 uses for revising the model of an old design and evaluating the proposed modifications by simulating the behavioral effects (i.e., the substeps of behavior modification and behavior verification). The function *update* in the algorithm updates the value of a given property in a given state or a given qualitative equation. At the end of *simulate*, comparing the initial and final states of the new modified behavior with those in the desired function verifies whether the modifications worked.

To illustrate the model-revision, we consider the NAC and SAC devices, where the two devices differ in that although SAC cools high-acidity sulfuric acid, NAC cools low-acidity nitric acid, and although the pipes through which sulfuric acid flows in SAC need to allow high-acidity liquids, the pipes through which nitric acid flows in NAC allow only low-acidity liquids. The first of these two differences, *nitric acid ⇒ sulfuric acid*, is an instance of the substance substitution type of structural differences; the second, *pipe(allow low-acidity substances) ⇒ pipe(allow high-acidity substances)*, is an instance of the component replacement type of structural differences. The structures of SAC and NAC differ in more than one way, and, in the class of domains of interest, revising a SBF model to accommodate the structural difference of component replacement is in general more difficult than revising it to accommodate the difference of substance substitution. Therefore, Kritik2 ranks the two differences between the structures of SAC and NAC so that the model for NAC is first revised for the difference of *pipe(allow low-acidity substances) ⇒ pipe(allow high-acidity substances)*, and then for the difference of *nitric acid ⇒ sulfuric acid*.

Let us consider the revision of the model for NAC, given the structure difference of *pipe(allow low-acidity substances) ⇒ pipe(allow high-acidity substances)* between the structures of NAC and SAC. This structural difference can suggest as one of the candidate repair and evaluation plans, the one that corresponds to *component-replacement*. The model-revision process for component-replacement revises the SBF model for NAC in several steps.

Input: • Behavior in new design, B_{new}, in which a chosen property from the diagnosis
                  has been changed.
             • Model of the old design, M_{old}.
Output: • Model of the new design, M_{new}, modified to be consistent with the changes in B_{new}.
Procedure:
initialize
$\quad S_{diff_s} = \{ (P_i, P_{i.value}^{old}, P_{i.value}^{new}),$ where
$\qquad\qquad P_i$ is a property whose value $P_{i.value}^{old}$ in state $state_i^{old}$
$\qquad\qquad$ has changed to $P_{i.value}^{new}$ in $state_i^{new}$ and
$\qquad\qquad state_i^{old}$ and $state_i^{new}$ are respectively from B_{old} and B_{new}.}
$\quad$ SIMULATE $(state_i^{new}, S_{diff_s})$

SIMULATE $(state, S_{diff_s})$
$\quad$ current-state $=$ state
$\quad$ LOOP
$\qquad$ next-state $=$ next-state (current-state);
$\qquad$ IF next-state $=$ NIL, THEN Exit LOOP
$\qquad$ CASE :
$\qquad$ (1)$\quad$ IF P_i is mentioned in next-state
$\qquad\qquad$ THEN update(P_i, next-state, current-state)
$\qquad$ (2)$\quad$ IF there is a qualitative equation qe in state-next-transition(current-state),
$\qquad\qquad$ such that $P_l = f(P_i)$ where $(P_i, P_{i.value}^{old}, P_{i.value}^{new}) \in S_{diff_s}$
$\qquad\qquad$ and P_l is mentioned in next-state
$\qquad\qquad$ THEN update(P_l, qe)
$\qquad\qquad\qquad S_{diff_s} = S_{diff_s} \cup \{(P_l, P_{l.value}^{old}, P_{l.value}^{new})\}$
$\qquad$ (3)$\quad$ IF there is a functional abstraction of a component E (i.e., Comp in using-function)
$\qquad\qquad$ and a condition on the substance properties on which E operates
$\qquad\qquad$ (i.e., $Condition_{SUB}$) in state-previous-transition(current-state)
$\qquad\qquad$ such that $P_i = P_l$, where
$\qquad\qquad P_l$ is a property of the substance in $Condition_{SUB}$, and
$\qquad\qquad (P_i, P_{i.value}^{old}, P_{i.value}^{new}) \in S_{diff_s}$
$\qquad\qquad$ THEN update(P_l, $Condition_{SUB}$)
$\qquad\qquad\qquad S_{diff_s} = S_{diff_s} \cup \{(P_l, P_{l.value}^{old}, P_{l.value}^{new})\}$
$\qquad$ (4)$\quad$ IF there is a pointer to a new behavior sequence B' such that
$\qquad\qquad$ the transition state-next-transition(current-state)
$\qquad\qquad$ affects a transition $trans$ of B'
$\qquad\qquad$ THEN spawn
$\qquad\qquad\qquad$ SIMULATE (transition-prev-state($trans$), S_{diff_s})
$\qquad$ END-CASE
$\qquad$ current-state $=$ next-state
$\qquad$ goto LOOP
$\quad$ END-LOOP

Figure 5.19. The model revision algorithm.

First, from the specification of the old pipe (nitric-acid-pipe2) in NAC, it determines that the nitric-acid-pipe2 plays a functional role in *transition2→3* of the behavior Cool Nitric Acid of NAC. Then, it decomposes the behavior into three segments: the transition in which the old component (nitric-acid-pipe2) plays a functional role (in the present example, *transition2→3* in the behavior Cool Nitric Acid shown in Figure 5.5c, the sequence of state transitions preceding it (not fully shown here), and the sequence of state transitions succeeding it (also not fully shown here). Next, the transition in which the old component (nitric-acid-pipe2) plays a role is revised by replacing the functional abstraction of nitric-acid-pipe2 (which allows the flow of low-acidity liquids) by the behavioral abstraction of the new pipe (sulfuric-acid-pipe2) in SAC (which allows the flow of high-acidity liquids). Then, the revised transition is composed with the preceding and succeeding segments of the original behavior to obtain the revised behavior. Finally, the constraints introduced by the new component, represented by changes in the values of the parameters characterizing the old and new components (nitric-acid-pipe2 and sulfuric-acid-pipe2), are propagated forward through the newly composed behavior to obtain the revised internal behavior and function. Also, the schema for the function is revised by associating with it a pointer to the revised internal causal behavior.

Similarly, the structural difference *nitric acid⇒sulfuric acid* between the structures of NAC and SAC is used to access the repair and evaluation plan for *substance-substitution*. The model-revision process for substance substitution further revises the (already revised) internal behaviors and functions in the model for NAC by replacing the old substance (low-acidity nitric acid) by the new substance (high-acidity sulfuric acid). This produces an SBF model for the SAC as shown in Figure 5.18 (only partial behaviors are shown). Then, the revised model is simulated (i.e., traced forward from the input state to the output state) to verify if it indeed results in the output behavior (i.e., the function) desired.

4.4. STORAGE OF NEW CASES

The final task in Kritik2's computational process is to store the new case in the case memory for later use. In order for a new design case to be recalled in later problem solving, Kritik2 needs to store it in the right place. That is, it has to index the new design by its functions because Kritik2 solves *Function–to–Structure* mapping types of design tasks. Because the design case points to the SBF model of the design, the newly learned case-specific SBF model is also stored in Kritik2's memory.

4.4.1. Learning Indices to New Cases

In general, there are two different issues pertaining to the selection of functional indices for the new design case. First, if a new design is stored only along the substance properties specified in its function, case retrieval would not be able to make use of knowledge of other substance properties relevant to the design. Second, if the new design is indexed by all the properties of the substance in its functional specification, case retrieval may result in a design based on a match with an unimportant property, which can make adaptation hard or even impossible. So the issue becomes how to determine the substance properties that are relevant to the functioning of the design.

Kritik2 capitalizes on the knowledge of the causal behavior in the SBF models to address these issues. In particular, it uses the behavioral requirements on the substance expressed in *under-condition-substance* to identify the substance properties relevant to the functioning of the design. These behavioral requirements of a substance specify that, in order for the transition to take place, the properties of the specified substance should satisfy certain conditions and hence are important to the design.

Kritik2's algorithm for selecting useful indices to a new case is shown in Figure 5.20. Given a new design case and the knowledge that functions are used to index the case, this method traverses through the causal behaviors in the SBF model of the design to identify substance properties on which the working of the design is predicated.

Input:
- Design case, C, that needs to be stored.
- Functional specification of the design, F.
- Type of indexing, T, that is, functional.
- One causal behavior (subset of model), M, corresponding to F.

Output: Exact vocabulary for indexing C, i.e., the set of useful features from F.

Procedure :

initialize
> containing-substance-props P = get-containing-substance-properties(F);
> indices = alternative-indices = plausible-sources-of-indices = {};

while true do
> 1. **foreach** causal behavior B ∈ M **do**
>
>   - **foreach** transition t ∈ B **do**
>   - conditions-on-features = get-under-conditions-from-transition(T, t);
>   - indices = indices ∪ {f | feature f ∈ conditions-on-features ∧ f ∈ P};
>   - alternative-indices = alternative-indices ∪ {f | feature f ∈ conditions-on-features ∧ f ∉ P};
>   - **if** indices = P **then** exit(indices);
>   - **if** conditions-on-features = {} **then** plausible-sources-of-indices = plausible-sources-of-indices ∪ get-detailed-behavior(t);
>
>   end
>
>   end
>
> 2. **if** plausible-sources-of-indices = {} **then**
>
>   - **if** indices ≠ {} **then** exit(indices);
>   - **if** alternative-indices ≠ {} **then** exit(alternative-indices);
>   - indices = {p | p ∈ P ∧ input-state-value(p) ≠ output-state-value(p)};
>   **if** indices ≠ {} **then** exit(indices);
>   - indices = {p | p ∈ get-contained-substance-properties(F) ∧ input-state-value(p) ≠ output-state-value(p)};
>   **if** indices ≠ {} **then** exit(indices);
>   - exit(P);
>
> 3. M = plausible-sources-of-indices;
> 4. plausible-sources-of-indices = {};
>
> end

Figure 5.20. A model-based method to obtain functional indices for design cases.

Because the SBF model can specify multiple behaviors, the outer loop (in step 1) in the algorithm analyzes each causal behavior in the model. The second loop is for analyzing the transitions within a causal behavior. If a substance property is a part of the causal context of a transition, the algorithm adds it to the set of indexing features if it is a property of the containing substance in the functional specification, and to the set of alternative indexing features if it is a property of a contained substance. This results in using the properties of a contained substance (e.g., heat in Figure 5.18b) in the function as indexing features only when none of the properties of the containing substance (e.g., sulfuric acid in Figure 5.18b) are central to the design. Because the causal behaviors in Kritik2's SBF model are specified at different levels of detail, the algorithm searches the space of behaviors in a breadth-first manner. If a higher level behavior does not lead to the identification of any useful substance properties, the more detailed behavior, indicated as *by-behavior*, is added to the list of plausible sources of indexing features.

For the purpose of illustrating how Kritik2's model-based index-learning method addresses these issues, let us now consider the task of identifying indices in our example, namely, the newly designed high-acidity SAC (Figure 5.18), before storing it in memory. Although the case memory presently has the designs of acid coolers organized only along the dimension of property *acidity* (as shown in Figures 5.15 and 5.21a), the new design case may better be indexed along other dimensions also, so that it is more useful in later design problem solving. So an important aspect of the index learning task is to learn new indexing features. This results in the introduction of new dimensions of generalization/ specialization of cases in the memory, and, thus, in a reorganization of the case memory.

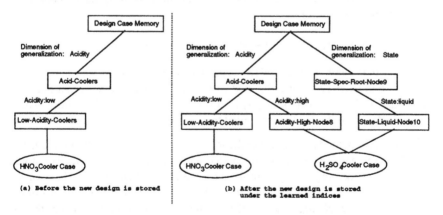

(a) Before the new design is stored

(b) After the new design is stored under the learned indices

Figure 5.21. Snapshots of Kritik2's functionally organized case memory.

Given the functional specification of high-acidity SAC (Figure 5.18b) and its causal behavior (Figure 5.18c), this method results in acidity and state as the indexing features for storing this case in memory. This is because the annotation on *transition* 2→3 specifies that the transition can occur only under certain conditions related to the state and acidity of the substance flowing through sulfuric-acid-pipe-2. The initial case memory (Figure 5.21a) did not have the property state as part of its indexing vocabulary. The SBF model, however, suggests that *state* is a useful index to the new case, and so Kritik2 indexes the new case by state also. The case memory after storing this design is shown in Figure 5.21b. Once the indexing features are selected, Kritik2 uses similarity-based learning to generalize the indices to the design cases. It uses the differences in parameters of a given property that constitute a type of functional difference between two designs to determine whether the two designs belong to the same or to different categories. For example, the design of high-acidity SAC is stored under the category of acidity-high-node8 that is different from that of low-acidity coolers (Figure 5.21b). The level to which the indices are generalized depends on the similarity of the corresponding parameters in the new and old cases in memory.

5. Evaluation of the Integrated Theory

In principle, Kritik2's integration of case-based and model-based reasoning can be evaluated in a number of dimensions such as computational feasibility and efficacy, computational efficiency and scalability, generality in terms of domain independence, generality in terms of addressing different issues and tasks in CBD, and generality in terms of supporting CBR in the context of different tasks. We have built a growing family of systems for evaluating the integrated theory along many of these dimensions.

5.1. COMPUTATIONAL FEASIBILITY AND EFFICACY

Kritik (Goel, 1989, 1991a, 1991b, 1992) and Kritik2 (Bhatta and Goel, 1992; Stroulia and Goel 1992; Stroulia et al., 1992) are working systems that integrate CBR and MBR for designing physical devices just as described here. These systems demonstrate that the integrated theory is computationally feasible.

They also demonstrate that the theory is quite effective in solving a range of problems in adaptive design. Kritik started with the designs of six devices stored in a flat case memory, along with their corresponding SBF models. Four of the initial designs were from the domain of electric circuits and two were from the domain of heat exchange devices. Kritik autonomously used the known designs and their models to solve four new design problems. Two of the new problems were in the domain of electric circuits including the one described here, and two in the domain of heat exchangers again including the one discussed. For each of these four new problems, Kritik not only solved the new problems presented to it, but it also automatically acquired new designs and the associated SBF models for potential reuse. In one of these four experiments, Kritik reused its newly acquired design and SBF model for solving another problem.

Kritik2 is a newer, bigger, and more complete implementation of Kritik. It incorporates both the theoretical and practical lessons we learned from Kritik. It presently contains some 25 design cases and associated SBF models, and organizes them in a multidimensional hierarchy as outlined earlier. These cases are from five engineering domains, including the domains of electric circuits and heat exchange devices in which Kritik operates. It also contains more repair plans than Kritik (such as the structure replication plan). Our experiments with Kritik2 indicate that the integrated theory is effective because the case-specific SBF models explicitly represent the internal behaviors of the known device, which specify not only the behavioral states and the state transitions, but also the functional role played by each structural component in these states and state transitions. In addition, it shows that SBF models also address the tasks of case retrieval and storage, and provide answers to the related issues of index learning and memory reorganization.

5.2. COMPUTATIONAL EFFICIENCY AND SCALABILITY

Our experiments with Kritik2 also indicate that the integrated theory is quite efficient due mainly to two reasons. First, the organization of the case memory and the functional indexing scheme enable the retrieval of cases relevant to the current problem, and second, the organization of the SBF models enable rapid localization of the search for faults in the known case to a small portion of the SBF model. For instance, in the example of the low-acidity NAC, the substance-property-value difference plan needs to search only the internal causal behavior responsible for the function of cooling low-acidity nitric acid and can ignore all structural components that do not play any functional role in this behavior. This becomes possible because the functions in an SBF model act as indices to the causal behaviors responsible for them.

As we mentioned, Kritik2 contains about 25 design cases and device models. Therefore, although bigger than Kritik and many other CBR systems, it is a relatively small system. The scalability of the integrated theory thus remains an open issue. The main problem is in obtaining a large number of real designs, building SBF models for each of them, and entering them into Kritik2's case memory to bootstrap the design process. This is possible in principle but very expensive in practice—the building of Kritik and Kritik2 has taken some 6 to 7 years. A massive infusion of knowledge into these systems could be justified only after the feasibility of systems like Kritik2 had been demonstrated.

5.3. GENERALITY IN TERMS OF DOMAIN INDEPENDENCE

As mentioned , Kritik designs simple electric circuits and heat exchange devices of the kind described here. Kritik2 operates in the additional domains of simple mechanical assemblies such as reaction wheels and electromagnetic devices, and electronic circuits such as operational amplifiers and computer networks. This suggests that the integrated theory is not limited to any specific device domain. Our experiments with Kritik2, however, also indicate that the current version of the SBF language is inadequate for covering certain kinds of engineering devices. For example, the SBF language presently is well suited for representing devices whose function is to transform a behavioral state but needs additional primitives for representing devices whose function is to prevent the occurrence of a given behavioral state (e.g., a steam release valve in a steam chamber whose function is to prevent the pressure from becoming too high). Similarly, because the SBF language is based on a component-substance ontology, it presently does not provide primitives for drawing the needed inferences about fields such as the magnetic field (but see Goel, Stroulia, and Luk, 1994).

5.4. GENERALITY IN TERMS OF ADDRESSING DIFFERENT TASKS OF CASE-BASED REASONING

Kritik2 addresses all major tasks of CBR, not just the tasks of case retrieval and adaptation. This is important because each stage imposes constraints on the others. For example, the memory processes impose constraints on the kinds of problem-solving that can be supported, problem-solving processes impose constraints on the kinds of learning that are needed, and the learning processes impose constraints on what is available in memory. We believe that simultaneously satisfying the constraints of memory, problem-solving and learning is a critical aspect of the evaluation of any case-based system.

Note that Kritik2 uses the same representations of cases and their models for supporting the different tasks of CBR. Of course the inferences drawn, and therefore the role of the models, change from one stage of processing to another. The functional part of SBF models acts as index into the cases, and this enables Kritik2 to establish the similarity between the new problem and the cases in the retrieval stage. The language of the SBF models, that of the functional part in particular, provides a typology of functional differences between a known case and a new problem. The SBF models provide the functional and causal explanations of how the retrieved design works and this enables Kritik2 to infer the parts that need to be repaired in the adaptation stage. For instance, our experiments with Kritik2 indicate that SBF models are effective in solving the class of adaptation problems that can be characterized by the types of functional differences, such as substance difference (i.e., the substances being transformed by the known design function and the new desired function are different), single substance-property-value difference, and multiple substance-property-value differences. The SBF models also enable the verification of the new design (i.e., behavior verification) by qualitative simulation in the evaluation stage. In addition, they provide the functional and causal explanations of how the candidate design works and this enables Kritik2 to learn new indices while storing the new case, and so on.

5.5. GENERALITY IN TERMS OF SUPPORTING CASE-BASED REASONING IN THE CONTEXT OF DIFFERENT TASKS

Recently we have started experimenting with the integration of CBR and MBR in different tasks and domains. In the Router project, for example, we are investigating the integration of CBR and MBR for navigation and planning (Goel, Ali, Donnellan, Gomez de Silva Garza, and Callantine, 1994). Although the results from this project are still preliminary, they indicate that the benefits of integrating CBR and MBR are not limited to design.

6. Related Research

Our work on the Kritik and Kritik2 systems is related to several lines of research in design and problem solving, CBR and learning, and qualitative models and model-based reasoning. The following discussion focuses on AI research on these topics.

6.1. DESIGN AND PROBLEM SOLVING

AI research on design has led to the development, use, and application of a number of knowledge-based problem-solving methods ranging from heuristic association (McDermott, 1982) to constraint satisfaction (Sussman and Steele, 1980) to plan instantiation (Brown and Chandrasekaran, 1989; Mittal and Araya, 1992; Mittal, Dym, and Morjaria, 1986), to reasoning from first principles (Williams, 1991). Tong and Sriram (1992) provided a useful anthology of many important papers on knowledge-based design. The adaptive approach of CBR is fundamentally different from these synthetic methods. Although the synthetic methods can and do play an important role in design adaptation, the adaptive approach views design in terms of evolution, in which new designs are created by modifying, perhaps combining, earlier designs.

AI research on CBD has taken two distinct although related branches. In one branch, the emphasis has been on the theoretical development of CBR. This work has focused on developing and analyzing vocabularies and strategies for case representation, indexing, retrieval, adaptation, evaluation, and storage. Kritik and Kritik2 are examples of this line of research; Hinrichs and Kolodner's (1991) Julia system is another prominent example. In the other, more popular branch, the emphasis has been on development and exploitation of case-based technology for aiding human designers in their tasks. This work has focused on developing and analyzing vocabularies and strategies for case representation, indexing, retrieval, and presentation. CADSYN and CASECAD (Maher, Balachandran, and Zhang, 1995), CADET (Sycara Navin-Chandra, Guttal, Koning, and Narasimhan, 1991), CADRE (Hua and Faltings, 1993), and FABEL (Voss et al., 1994) are some examples of this work. In our own work along this line, we have explored the use of case-based technology for aiding architects in the preliminary design of office buildings (Pearce et al., 1992) and for aiding software engineers in the task of interface design (Barber et al., 1992).

6.2. CASE-BASED REASONING AND LEARNING

Several researchers (Ashley and Rissland, 1988; Hammond, 1989; Kolodner and Simpson, 1989) have developed computational models for CBR that posit different methods for adapting previous cases for solving new problems. The adaptation methods include heuristic search (Stallman and Sussman, 1977) and heuristic association (Hammond, 1989). The case-based method itself has been recursively used to adapt cases (Goel, Ali, Donnellan, Gomez de Silva Garza, and Callantine, 1994; Kolodner and Simpson, 1989).

Research on case adaptation has generally followed the two main computational models of CBR, namely, transformational approach and derivational approach. Some CBD systems (e.g., Barletta and Mark, 1988; Dyer, Flowers, and Hodges, 1986; Hinrichs, 1992; Maher and Zhao, 1987; Navin-Chandra, 1991) generally follow the first computational model of CBR (Kolodner, 1993) in which the solutions to previous, similar problems are tweaked to solve new problems. Some other CBD systems (e.g., Kambhampati and Hendler 1992; Mostow, 1989) closely follow the second computational model (Carbonell, 1983) in which the derivational trace of the problem-solving in a previous design situation guides the adaptation process in the current situation.

Kritik and Kritik2 offer an alternative and complementary approach to case adaptation. A design case contains the specification of the design problem, the design solution, and an SBF model of how the design delivers the functions desired of the device. The SBF model gives rise to adaptation strategies and guides the adaptation process. This choice is due to both pragmatic and theoretical reasons. In real design situations, the design outcome, and especially the derivational record, often are not available and are hard to encode when available. But a case-specific model of how the device works often is available, or can be reconstructed from the functional and structural specifications of its design, and Kritik2 provides a language for encoding it. From a theoretical perspective, Kritik2 provides an alternative account of how to automate CBD in which much of the design reasoning is in terms of the internal causal processes of physical devices.

Some other researchers too have explored model-based methods for case adaptation. For example, Koton (1988) has used causal domain models for comprehending diagnostic problems in internal medicine and retrieving appropriate diagnostic cases from memory, and Sycara and Navin-Chandra (1989) have proposed the use of causal domain models for elaborating engineering design problems, retrieving appropriate cases from memory, and adapting them. Simmons and Davis (1987), too, have used causal domain models for debugging plans but only for testing modifications to a plan, not for generating the modifications. In contrast, Kritik2 uses the model-based approach for all subtasks of CBR: case indexing and retrieval of similar cases from memory, generation of modifications to the retrieved design, evaluation and execution of the generated modifications, and index learning and storage of new cases in memory. In addition, Kritik2's SBF models are different from the causal models of Simmons and Davis, Koton, and Sycara and Navin-Chandra. The behavioral states and the state transitions in their models are grounded neither in the function nor in the structure of the system. In contrast, the SBF model explicitly relates the internal causal behaviors to both the function and the structure of a device, and thus constrains them both from the top and the bottom.

Interestingly, recent work on CBD aiding (e.g., Hua and Faltings, 1993; Maher et al., 1995; Sycara et al., 1991; Voss et al., 1994) has also been moving toward the use of case-specific models to support the tasks of case retrieval and adaptation. Maher et al. (1995) use case-specific FBS models that were very similar to SBF models.

6.3. QUALITATIVE MODELS AND MODEL-BASED REASONING

Because our work uses a model-based approach, we will briefly compare it to some related research on device qualitative models and MBR. Research on naive physics and qualitative reasoning, (e.g., DeKleer and Brown, 1984; Forbus, 1984; Kuipers, 1984), has focused on qualitative modeling and simulation of the physical world. The emphasis of this work has been on the content, representation, and use of qualitative models of physical systems, and the focus has been on the derivation of the system's behaviors at problem-solving time. In contrast, our work seeks to address the issues of organization, indexing, and acquisition of the qualitative models in addition to their content, representation and use. This has led us to the SBF models of physical devices.

Our memory-based view of device models is related to other work on memory-based approaches to comprehension (e.g., Minsky, 1975, and especially Schank1982). Schank described Memory Organization Packets (MOPs) for representing and organizing certain kinds of information in a compiled form; for example, the goals of volitional actors and the sequences of actions performed to achieve the goals. He also described how MOPs can facilitate story interpretation and enable generalization and learning from past experiences. We adopt a similar view towards device models: SBF models organize functional, causal, and structural information underlying the functioning of devices. They facilitate tasks such as interpretation of design descriptions, design generation and evaluation, and learning from design experiences. They also provide the indexing vocabulary for organizing design cases in memory and enable automatic learning of the indices to new cases.

As mentioned earlier, SBF models are based on a component-substance ontology. They integrate and generalize two earlier device representations: the functional representation scheme (Chandrasekaran, Goel and Iwasaki, 1993; Sembugamoorthy and Chandrasekaran, 1986) and the behavioral primitives of the consolidation method (Bylander, 1991; Bylander and Chandrasekaran, 1985). In addition, the SBF models are related to the commonsense algorithms of Rieger and Grinberg (1978). The representation of behavioral states and state transitions in our scheme is similar to their representation. The internal organization, the indexing scheme, and the typology of structural, causal, and behavioral relations in SBF models complement those used in the commonsense algorithms.

7. Conclusions

The Kritik and Kritik2 experiments lead us to the following four conclusions:
1. The computational process of CBR provides a good account of the variant and adaptive aspects of preliminary conceptual design of physical devices.
2. Although CBR provides a high-level computational process, it also raises a number of issues pertaining to case content, representation, indexing, organization, retrieval, adaptation, evaluation, and storage. The different issues and tasks in the CBR process impose constraints on one another. It is important to address all the different tasks and issues in order to develop a well-constrained theory of CBD.
3. SBF device models capture a reasoner's comprehension of how a device works; that is, how the structure of the device delivers its functions and

how the internal behaviors of the device compose the functions of the structural components into the functions of the device as a whole. The SBF language is expressive enough to cover a large domain of physical devices and precise enough to support the inferences needed to address a large range of design tasks and subtasks.

4. The SBF theory provides a grounding for CBD. In particular, the SBF theory provides an account of the case content and vocabularies for case representation, indexing, and organization. In addition, it provides strategies for the tasks for case retrieval, adaptation, evaluation, and storage, including index learning and memory reorganization.

Acknowledgments

This research has benefited from contributions by B. Chandrasekaran and S. Prabhakar. This work started when the first author was at the Ohio State University and after 1989 continued at Georgia Institute of Technology. At Georgia Tech, it has been supported by research grants from the National Science Foundation (grant C36-688), Office of Naval Research (contract N00014-92-J-1234), Northern Telecom, Georgia Tech Research Corporation, and a CER grant from NSF (grant CCR-86-19886), and equipment grants and donations from IBM, Symbolics, and NCR.

References

Ashley, K., and Rissland, E.: 1988, A case-based approach to modeling legal expertise, *IEEE Expert*, 3(3), 70–77.

Barber, J., Bhatta, S., Goel, A., Jacobson, M., Pearce, M., Penberthy, L., Shankar, M., Simpson, R., and Stroulia, E.: 1992, AskJef: Integrating case-based and multimedia technologies for interface design advising, *in* J. S. Gero (ed.), *Artificial Intelligence in Design '92*, Kluwer Academic, Dordrecht, NL, pp. 457–476.

Barletta, R., and Mark, W.: 1988, Breaking cases into pieces, *Proceedings of the AAAI Workshop on Case-Based Reasoning*, Kaufmann, San Mateo, CA, pp. 12–17.

Bhatta, S., and Goel, A.: 1992, Use of mental models for constraining index learning in experience-based design, *Proceedings of the AAAI workshop on Constraining Learning with Prior Knowledge*, AAAI Press, San Jose, CA, pp. 1–10.

Bhatta, S., and Goel, A.: 1995, Model-based indexing and index learning in analogical design, *Proceedings of the Seventeenth Annual Conference of the Cognitive Science Society*, Lawrence Erlbaum Associates, Hillsdale, NJ, pp. 527–532.

Brown, D. C., and Chandrasekaran, B.: 1989, *Design Problem Solving: Knowledge Structures and Control Strategies*, Pitman, London, UK.

Bylander, T.: 1991, A theory of consolidation for reasoning about devices, *International Journal of Man-Machine Studies*, 35(4), 467–489.

Bylander, T., and Chandrasekaran, B.: 1985, Understanding behavior using consolidation, *Proceedings of the Ninth International Joint Conference on Artificial Intelligence*, Los Angeles, CA, pp. 450–454.

Carbonell, J.: 1983, Learning by analogy: Formulating and generalizing plans from past experience, *in* R. Michalski, J. Carbonell, and T. Mitchell (eds), *Machine Learning: An Artificial Intelligence Approach*, Tioga, Palo Alto, CA, pp. 137–161.

Chandrasekaran, B., Goel, A., and Iwasaki, Y.: 1993, Functional representation as design rationale, *IEEE Computer*, 26(1), 48–56.

DeKleer, J., and Brown, J.: 1984, A qualitative physics based on confluences, *Artificial Intelligence*, 24, 7–83.

Dyer, M., Flowers, M., and Hodges, J.: 1986, Edison: An engineering design system operating naively, *in* D. Sriram and R. Adey (eds), *Proceedings of Applications of AI to Engineering Problems*, Springer-Verlag, Berlin, pp. 327–342.

Forbus,. K.: 1984, Qualitative process theory, *Artificial Intelligence*, 24: 85–168.

Goel, A.: 1989, *Integration of Case-Based Reasoning and Model-Based Reasoning for Adaptive Design Problem Solving*, PhD Thesis, The Ohio State University, Department of Computer and Information Science, Columbus, Ohio.

Goel, A.: 1991a, A model-based approach to case adaptation, *Proceedings of the Thirteenth Annual Conference of the Cognitive Science Society*, Chicago, pp. 143–148.

Goel, A.: 1991b, Model revision: A theory of incremental model learning, *Proceedings of the Eighth International Workshop on Machine Learning*, pp. 605–609.

Goel, A.: 1992, Representation of design functions in experience-based design, *in* D. Brown, M. Waldron, and H. Yoshikawa (eds), *Intelligent Computer Aided Design*, North-Holland, Amsterdam, pp. 283–308.

Goel, A., Ali, K., Donnellan, M., Gomez de Silva Garza, A., and Callantine, T.: 1994, Multistrategy adaptive navigational path planning, *IEEE Expert*, 9(6), 57–65.

Goel, A., and Chandrasekaran, B.: 1989a, Use of device models in adaptation of design cases, *Proceedings of the Second DARPA Case-Based Reasoning Workshop*, Kaufmann, Los Altos, CA, pp. 100–109.

Goel, A., and Chandrasekaran, B.: 1989b, Functional representation of designs and redesign problem solving, *Proceedings of IJCAI-89*, pp. 1388–1394.

Goel, A., and Chandrasekaran, B.: 1992, Case-based design: A task analysis, *in* C. Tong and D. Sriram (eds), *Artificial Intelligence Approaches to Engineering Design, Volume II: Innovative Design*, Academic Press, San Diego, pp. 165–184.

Goel, A., and Prabhakar, S.: 1991, A control architecture for model-based redesign problem solving, *Proceedings of the IJCAI-91 Workshop on AI in Design*, Sydney, Australia.

Goel, A., Stroulia, E., and Luk, K. Y.: 1994, Functional reasoning about devices with fields and cycles, *Proceedings of the AAAI-94 Workshop on Representation and Reasoning about Function*, Seattle, Washington, pp. 48–55.

Hammond, K.: 1989, *Case-Based Planning: Viewing Planning as a Memory Task*. Academic Press, Boston, MA.

Hinrichs, T. R., and Kolodner, J. L.: 1991, The roles of adaptation in case-based design, *Proceedings of the Ninth National Conference on AI*, MIT Press, Cambridge, MA, pp. 28–33.

Hinrichs, T. R.: 1992, *Problem Solving in Open Worlds: A Case Study in Design*, Lawrence Erlbaum Associates, Hillsdale, NJ.

Hua, K., and Faltings, B.: 1993, Exploring case-based building design—CADRE, *AI(EDAM)*, 7(2), 135–143.

Kambhampati, S., and Hendler, J.: 1992, A validation structure based theory of plan modification and reuse, *Artificial Intelligence*, 55, 193–258.

Kolodner, J. L.: 1993, *Case-Based Reasoning*, Kaufmann, San Mateo, CA.

Kolodner, J. L., and Simpson, R. L.: 1989, The mediator: Analysis of an early case-based problem solver, *Cognitive Science*, 13(4), 507–549.

Koton, P.: 1988, Integrating case-based and causal reasoning, *Proceedings of the Tenth Annual Conference of the Cognitive Science Society*, Lawrence Erlbaum Associates, Hillsdale, NJ, pp. 167–173.

Kuipers, B.: 1984, Commonsense reasoning about causality, *Artificial Intelligence*, 24, 169–203.

Maher, M. L., and Zhao, F.: 1987, Using experiences to plan the synthesis of new designs, in J. S. Gero (ed.), *Expert System in Computer-Aided Design*, North-Holland, Amsterdam, pp. 349–369.

Maher, M. L., Balachandran, M. B., and Zhang, D.: 1995, *Case-Based Reasoning in Design*, Lawrence Erlbaum Associates, Hillsdale, NJ.

McDermott, J.: 1992, R1: A rule-based configurer of computer systems, *Artificial Intelligence*, 19, 39–88.

Minsky, M.: 1975, A framework for representing knowledge, in P. Winston (ed.), *The Psychology of Computer Vision*, McGraw-Hill, New York, pp. 211–277.

Mittal, S., and Araya, A.: 1992, A knowledge-based framework for design, *Proceedings of the Fifth National Conference on Artificial Intelligence*, MIT Press, Cambridge, MA, pp. 856–865.

Mittal, S., Dym, C., and Morjaria, M.: 1986, Pride: An expert system for the design of paper handling systems, *Computer*, 19(7), 102–114.

Mostow, J.: 1989, Design by derivational analogy: Issues in the automated replay of design plans, *Artificial Intelligence*, 40, 119–184.

Navin-Chandra, D.: 1991, *Exploration and Innovation in Design: Towards a Computational Model*, Springer-Verlag, New York.

Pearce, M., Goel, A., Kolodner, J. L., Zimring, C., Sentosa, L., and Billington, R.: 1992, Case-based decision support: A case study in architectural design, *IEEE Expert*, 7(5), 14–20.

Rieger, C., and Grinberg, M.: 1978, A system for cause-effect representation and simulation for computer-aided design, in J. Latombe (ed.), *Artificial Intelligence and Pattern Recognition in Computer-Aided Design*, North-Holland, Amsterdam, pp. 299–334.

Riesbeck, C., and Schank, R.: 1989, *Inside Case-Based Reasoning*, Lawrence Erlbaum Associates, Hillsdale, NJ.

Schank, R.: 1982, *Dynamic Memory: A Theory of Reminding and Learning in Computers and People*, Cambridge University Press, Cambridge, UK.

Sembugamoorthy, V., and Chandrasekaran, B.: 1986, Functional representation of devices and compilation of diagnostic problem-solving systems, in J. Kolodner and C. Riesbeck (eds), *Experience, Memory and Reasoning*, Lawrence Erlbaum Associates, Hillsdale, NJ, pp. 47–73.

Simmons, R., and Davis, R.: 1987, Generate, test and debug: Combining associational rules and causal models, *Proceedings of the IJCAI-87*, Kaufmann, San Mateo, CA, pp. 1071–1079.

Stallman, R., and Sussman, G.: 1977, Forward reasoning and dependency-directed backtracking in a system for computer-aided circuit analysis, *Artificial Intelligence*, 9, 135–196.

Stroulia, E., and Goel, A.: 1992, Generic teleological mechanisms and their use in case adaptation, *Proceedings of the Fourteenth Annual Conference of the Cognitive Science Society*, Lawrence Erlbaum Associates, Hillsdale, NJ, pp. 319–324.

Stroulia, E., Shankar, M., Goel, A., and Penberthy, L.: 1992, A model-based approach to blame-assignment in design, in J. S. Gero (ed.), *Artificial Intelligence in Design '92*, Kluwer Academic, Dordrecht, NL, pp. 519–537.

Sussman, G., and Steele, G.: 1980, Constraints: A language for expressing almost-hierarchical descriptions, *Artificial Intelligence*, 14, 1–39.

Sycara, K., and Navin-Chandra, D.: 1989, Integrating case-based reasoning and qualitative reasoning in engineering design, in J. S. Gero (ed.), *Artificial Intelligence in Engineering*, Springer-Verlag, Berlin, pp. 232–250.

Sycara, K., Navin-Chandra, D., Guttal, R., Koning, J., and Narasimhan, S.: 1991, CADET: A case-based synthesis tool for engineering design, *International Journal of Expert Systems*, 4(2), 157–188.

Tong, V., and Sriram, D. (eds): 1992, *Artificial Intelligence in Design, Volumes I, II, and III*, Academic Press, Boston.

Voss, A., Coulon, C-H., Gräther, W., Linowski, B., Schaaf, J., Bartsch-Spörl, B., Börner, K., Tammer, E., Dürschke, H., and Knauff, M.: 1994, Retrieval of similar layouts—about a very hybrid approach in FABEL, in J. S. Gero and F. Sudweeks (eds), *Artificial Intelligence in Design '94*, Kluwer Academic, Dordrecht, NL, pp. 625–640.

Williams, B.: 1991, A theory of interactions: Unifying qualitative and quantitative algebraic reasoning, *Artificial Intelligence*, 51(1–3), 39–94.

chapter six

PLAUSIBLE DESIGN ADVICE THROUGH CASE-BASED REASONING

THOMAS R. HINRICHS
Northwestern University

Many common design tasks involve reasoning with incomplete domain theories and imprecise or dynamically changing problem specifications. We refer to such tasks as plausible design. A system for providing plausible design advice should be able to help elaborate a design problem, propose plausible values and solutions, create variations on a design, and guide the design process. The challenge for any computational model is that the problem spaces are not easily enumerable, problems may entail tradeoffs and compromises, and advisory systems must flexibly respond to users, rather than follow a single rigid strategy for control. We describe a model of plausible design and its implementation in JULIA, a program that designs the menu and presentation of a meal.

1. What is Plausible Design?

Many design tasks are specified informally and admit solutions of varying degrees of adequacy. For example, everyday problems such as arranging furniture or writing a conference paper often serve goals that are aesthetic and partially satisfiable. Even engineering problems typically have preliminary or conceptual design phases that are underspecified or incompletely understood. These problems require making tradeoffs and compromises, reasonable assumptions and best guesses. The primary challenge for automating or aiding such tasks is that they entail reasoning with incomplete information. We refer to such tasks as plausible design tasks.

Plausible design means that a problem solver should accept specifications that may be incomplete, it should be capable of producing satisfying solutions to those problems, and its behavior should be sufficiently flexible to accommodate revisions and additions to the problem specification late in the design process. Moreover, plausible design should not assume a deep model or complete domain theory. We believe these criteria suggest a multiparadigm model of problem solving, in which:

- The designer pursues design goals. Goals focus attention on parts of the design; they address the control problem.

- The designer works with constraints. Constraints may be specified as part of the problem, or they may be background knowledge about the domain.

- The designer re-uses past experience. The source of ideas lies ultimately in previous cases. Cases serve as an implicit domain theory.

Because plausible design implies a weak domain theory, an implementation may be best suited to be an advisor rather than a fully automated system. An advisor can help elaborate a problem, make assumptions, suggest design structure and contents, warn of relevant failures, and narrow down decisions to manageable sets of alternatives. But in an advisory system, the ultimate evaluation of adequacy comes from the client. It turns out that implementing a design system as an advisor both simplifies and complicates the task. On the one hand, it permits some assumptions about correctness of results to be relaxed because there is a human client checking results. On the other hand, interactive advisory systems demand greater flexibility of control. An advisory system must be able to dynamically respond to changes in specification and to flexibly use what it knows.

In this chapter, we describe a computational model of plausible design as implemented in JULIA, a program that interactively designs the menu and presentation of meals to satisfy multiple, interacting constraints (Hinrichs, 1992). We examine the key features of the model and discuss how they help and hinder the implementation of plausible design in other domains.

2. A Computational Model of Plausible Design

Our model of plausible design is implemented in JULIA, a computer program that advises a client on the design of a meal to satisfy multiple, interacting constraints (Hinrichs, 1992). JULIA takes a partial description of a desired meal as input in the form of constraints and partial commitments. Through a dialogue with a user, it evolves a solution by retrieving previous cases with similar constraints and features, and proposes parts of those cases to progressively elaborate the design. The user accepts or rejects proposals, sometimes chooses among small sets of alternatives, and may suggest other alternatives and constraints. The program must accommodate these suggestions and resolve ambiguous or conflicting suggestions and oversubscribed decisions.

For example, a client might request a meal that would satisfy Richard (a known vegetarian) and Mike (a meat and potatoes eater), was inexpensive, and contained eggplant. JULIA takes these constraints, along with the more general domain constraints it knows about, and retrieves partially matching cases from memory. It then attempts to transfer the menu and presentation from these cases to the new problem. Because the problem constraints on the main dish are fundamentally incompatible, JULIA fails to find a case that satisfies all the constraints and is unable to adapt a dish to make it acceptable. It then decomposes the problem further and decides to serve two main dishes, skewered lamb and eggplant for Mike and baba-ghanouj for Richard. In order to do this, it must synthesize the meal design from two previous cases.

As this example shows, JULIA is a case-based designer that uses previous cases to propose plausible solutions, adapts those solutions to fit the current situation, and evaluates the result. Roughly characterized, this is a propose-critique-modify method of design (Chandrasekaran, 1990) that implements the propose phase using CBR (Hammond, 1989; Kolodner, Simpson, and Sycara, 1985). What makes JULIA an implementation of plausible design is that it solves under-specified problems by using similar cases to elaborate the problem. It can solve problems despite a weak domain theory by synthesizing solutions from multiple cases, plausibly adapting components of those cases under the guidance of domain constraints and domain-independent heuristics, and relaxing its evaluation criteria when necessary to produce satisfying solutions. It is flexible in its dynamic behavior because it is able to adapt (or patch) the current solution in response to the addition of new constraints, rather than backtracking to a previous state.

The four key features of our model that support plausible design are:

1. The integration of CBR and constraint posting to propose plausible designs.

2. The synthesis of solutions from multiple cases.

3. The adaptation of designs and design components through a process of constraint-driven transformation.

4. The production of satisfying solutions by relaxing constraints and abandoning some unsatisfiable subgoals.

In this section, we discuss these features of the model and describe how they support the task of plausible design.

2.1. INTEGRATING CBR AND CONSTRAINT POSTING

Plausible designs come from experience. What form this experience takes and how it is employed can be modeled in many different ways, but, ultimately, experience is the source of design ideas and the basis of their plausibility. In our model, experience takes the form of previous design cases that are adapted and combined to form new, plausible solutions. The need to adapt and combine cases suggests that an explicit domain theory is required to guide this process, although it need not be a complete model of the domain. JULIA uses constraints and constraint posting (Stefik, 1981) to serve this function.

CBR is an important part of plausible design because it permits solutions to be proposed when the problem constraints are not generative. It is an effective means for surmounting incomplete specifications because it enables a problem solver to elaborate a problem based on experience with similar problems. This means that cases themselves form a large part of JULIA's domain theory, rather than simply serving as a heuristic shortcut to solutions that could otherwise be generated from scratch. To use cases in this way means that the cases are not plans or procedures that can be simulated or replayed, but are instead representations of actual artifacts or events.

Constraint posting is also an important part of plausible design because some design knowledge really is rule-like, because constraint propagation can serve as an automatic inference method, and because constraints can guide or restrict adaptation. Constraints can be thought of as representing a partial model of a design, and in case-based design, constraints on the design can serve as indices into case memory.

The integration of CBR and constraint posting is especially suited to plausible design problems because constraints are satisfied using associative knowledge in the form of indexed cases, rather than by enumerating and intersecting equivalence classes of design components. Here, associative indexing is seen as a weak form of plausible inference rather than as a way to shortcut search. Another benefit of this scheme is that the integration of CBR and constraint satisfaction yields a more flexible control strategy for underspecified problems. JULIA uses cases to propose plausible solutions early and constraints to allow the system to defer commitment until more information is available.

2.1.1. Generation: Design in the Small

This synergy of CBR and constraint posting is best understood in the context of the design process as a whole because the language of constraint satisfaction is only partly adequate for describing design. Whereas constraint satisfaction is concerned with relationships that fix values on sets of variables, in design it is not always apparent what constitutes a variable, which relationships are relevant and which must be satisfied. Consequently, we think in terms of constraint satisfaction only for problems in the small, and only at particular moments in time. The context for treating a portion of a design problem as constraint satisfaction is determined by the current design goal being pursued.

In JULIA, CBR and constraint posting are invoked when the problem solver is trying to satisfy a goal to choose values for a set of features of the problem. The method to achieve this first formulates constraints on those features by inheriting them from the abstraction of the problem (e.g., from the concept of a meal.) It then attempts to propose plausible values for the features using a variety of associative indexing techniques, the primary method being CBR. The CBR process attempts to retrieve similar cases using the overall problem as an initial query and progressively narrowing the scope of the query if necessary (e.g., to retrieve appetizers rather than entire meals.) When cases are retrieved, they are ranked in order of similarity (by a weighted feature sum of matching features) and examined in order.

The process that applies a case first examines the outcome of the case to determine if it was a failure or a success. If the case was a failure and heuristic rules show it to be relevant to the current problem, JULIA warns the user and volunteers to transfer the repair from the previous case (a constraint recorded in the explanation of the failure). If the case was successful, the CBR process examines the values of the features of the case that are to be transferred. The proposed values are checked against the constraints on the features of the problem and if a value violates any mandatory constraints, the problem solver attempts to adapt the value to make it acceptable. If this fails the value is rejected. Values that are accepted are added to a list of suggested values for that feature, along with an indication of the case they came from and the constraints they satisfy and any preference constraints they might violate.

If the CBR process returns with suggested values for all the features in the scope of the goal, the problem solver proceeds to try to select the best value for each feature or to reduce the set of choices to a small set (≤ 3) and ask the user for his preference. Choice sets are reduced in two ways: by weeding out alternatives that violate more preference constraints than others, and by abstracting alternatives until there is a small mutually exclusive set of prototypes (e.g., soup or salad). JULIA presents the suggestions to the user who either accepts a suggestion, chooses among alternatives, suggests his own alternative, or rejects the suggestions. When a suggested value is accepted, it is added to the problem description and the constraints on that feature are propagated.

Constraint propagation is a forward-chaining inference that asserts values, constraints, or structure based on commitments in the design. For example, a decision to serve Italian cuisine will transfer the structure of the prototypical Italian meal to the current problem, thereby replacing a salad course with a pasta course. Other decisions in the design, such as who the guests will be, can cause constraints to be propagated from the eating preferences of the individuals to the ingredients of the current problem. Whenever new constraints, structures, or values are propagated in this way, the propagation process is repeated until no further changes are made.

Combining CBR with constraint posting in this way is a critical part of plausible design because it puts reasoning on a firmer footing than is possible with associative knowledge alone. Constraints make synthesis and adaptation possible. However, JULIA is not a hybrid system (Rissland and Skalak, 1989). The different types of reasoning do not compete with each other to solve the same task, but instead play complementary roles in an integrated model of design.

2.2. SYNTHESIZING SOLUTIONS FROM MULTIPLE CASES

A designer that could only repeat similar cases would be extremely limited in the kinds of solutions it could generate. To go beyond extending the old to creating something new requires synthesis—the ability to create new combinations of components. In plausible design where the domain theory may be weak, it makes sense to avoid synthesizing from multiple cases whenever possible because decomposition can be arbitrarily hard, and because the problem solver may not know what components work well together and why. But when a problem cannot be solved from a single case, it should be possible to synthesize a solution from multiple cases by decomposing the problem and transferring parts of different cases. Conceptually, this looks like:

$$\{Decompose\}^* \rightarrow Transfer \rightarrow \{Synthesize\}^*$$

When JULIA solves a problem, it first attempts to retrieve and transfer design components from a single complete case. For example, it tries to adopt the entire menu or the overall cuisine and presentation of a previous meal. If this fails, it breaks the problem down under the guidance of design plans (e.g., by dividing the meal into separate courses or to individual dishes). It then recursively solves for each part, typically by retrieving and using different cases for each. In this way, it attempts to avoid the synthesis problem whenever possible. When it must synthesize, it first attempts to adapt the components to make them compatible with each other, and if that fails, it falls back on its search with dependency-directed backtracking.

2.2.1. Decomposition through Plan Instantiation

JULIA's primary method of decomposing a problem is to retrieve design plans from memory that instantiate and reduce design goals to subgoals. For example, it has a couple of alternative plans for refining a meal into courses. One plan schedules goals that elaborate the problem by determining more descriptive features and then recursively refining typical courses of a meal in order of salience (i.e., main course first.) The rationale for this is that the descriptive features (such as cuisine or cost) provide hooks for more accurately retrieving cases and also provide constraints on the dishes of the meal. The alternative plan decomposes a meal in temporal order, starting with an appetizer and ending with dessert. This is appropriate when descriptive features are already known.

One problem that stems from this type of plan instantiation is that it makes assumptions about the structure of the design. It is quite possible that the problem could specify a different structure altogether, either directly (e.g., by requiring an appetizer course) or indirectly (e.g., by specifying a presentation or cuisine that traditionally has a different structure, such as a buffet, or Middle Eastern cuisine in which many small dishes are typically served all at once).

JULIA recovers from such assumption violations by verifying that the objective of a goal is still part of the problem before scheduling it for execution or refinement (i.e., it ignores phantom goals) and by automatically posting new refinement goals whenever new structures are asserted. This entails determining how a new goal relates to the network of goals already in place, so, for example, if a goal to refine a second main dish is posted, it is made a subgoal of the goal to refine the main course. These goal relationships are necessary to ensure that goals that are abandoned will also abandon their subgoals, but will not propagate and cause the entire problem to be abandoned.

2.2.2. Failure-Driven Decomposition

In addition to plan instantiation, the problem may also be decomposed in response to goals that are partially satisfied. If the problem solver proposes values that are too abstract (e.g., soup), or fails to propose enough values to satisfy a goal (e.g., it suggests a main dish but no side dishes), the goal may be reduced to subgoals that focus on the specific part of the design that needs to be refined. Here, decomposition is guided by the hierarchy of features present in the design, rather than by design plans.

Decomposition is also driven by impasses in the problem-solving process. If JULIA is unable to choose a value for some attribute from among several competing alternatives, one of its adaptation strategies is to examine the constraints on that attribute to determine if they are incompatible. In other words, it determines if the difficulty lies in JULIA's inability to generate a good solution, or if the problem constraints themselves are mutually exclusive. If the constraints are mutually exclusive and they come from different sources, and the attribute can take on multiple values, then JULIA decomposes the problem further by splitting the feature into two features, partitioning the constraints into two internally compatible sets, and posting new goals to solve for each feature separately. In practice, this typically means serving two main dishes to satisfy different guests. In its fullest generality, knowing whether a feature is splittable and knowing the criteria by which to partition constraints is a type of plausible knowledge that might be domain dependent. In JULIA, such knowledge is not represented explicitly, although it probably should be.

2.2.3. Mapping and Transfer

Supporting synthesis through decomposition can raise problems for transfer: What happens if cases do not have the same structure as the problem? As we have seen, JULIA does make some assumptions about the structure of the problem through its use of design plans, but it does not prespecify the exact mappings between the problem and retrieved cases. In order to transfer values, the problem solver must first establish the best correspondence mappings. If features do not correspond directly, the problem solver traverses up the hierarchy of features until a common feature is found. It then disambiguates the mappings between subfeatures using heuristics that prefer mappings between features whose values achieve the same function, or satisfy the same constraints. This approach can be thought of as lazy abstraction.

Another problem raised by synthesizing from multiple cases is how to assess the plausibility of transfer. When an entire solution is transferred from a single case, it is a good bet that the components of that solution will be compatible with each other and that they will result in the same outcome. When design components are transferred from different cases, that assurance is gone. A case-based reasoner can only rely on its explicit domain theory and on the assumption that if the different cases are all sufficiently similar to the problem, that their components are likely to be compatible.

An alternative to this would be to rely on inductive transfer, in which statistical or coherence information about the population of cases would determine the plausibility of an attribute being acceptable or possible. Strictly speaking, JULIA does not perform induction, except for the purposes of storing and retrieving cases. In designing a meal, it only looks at one case at a time, never at the distribution of properties over a category.

In fact, the one place where JULIA does look at collections of cases is in generalizing MOPs for constructing the redundant discrimination network

(Kolodner, 1984; Schank, 1982). In practice, these MOPs turn out to be almost useless for reasoning because the only regularities (normative features, or norms) that tend to get represented are the values of the predictive features by which the MOPs are indexed. It would be nice if the retrieval of a generalization were to permit a plausible inference (e.g., if a MOP were retrieved based on its cuisine being Middle Eastern, it would supply the generalization that they tend to be vegetarian), but that seldom happens. The generalization facilities are nevertheless critical because they permit cases to be stored based on specializations of norms. In other words, as JULIA stores a number of cases that include different kinds of poultry, it creates a poultry MOP. If it then starts to store a preponderance of chicken meals, it will further discriminate that MOP into chicken and other types of poultry. To do this, JULIA has to be able to generalize the norms of its MOPs to different levels of abstraction. Although this aspect of generalization works well, it is less effective for plausible transfer.

The ability to synthesize solutions from multiple cases is important because it relaxes the requirement for the case-base to completely cover the domain and increases the generative capacity of a problem solver. Some of the earliest CBR programs were able to synthesize from multiple cases, such as PERSUADER (Sycara, 1987). PERSUADER synthesized quantitative parameters and consequently was able to avoid problems of decomposition and mapping. Later related work has addressed decomposition using influence graphs, an innovative representation of behavior and function (Sycara and Navin-Chandra, 1991, and this volume). Issues of mapping and transfer have long been active topics in the field of analogical reasoning, but have received little attention in design.

2.3. ADAPTING CASES AND PATCHING SOLUTIONS

Transferring parts of previous solutions is not always sufficient to solve a new problem. Sometimes, the parts themselves must be modified. For example, if JULIA does not know about a vegetarian version of lasagne, it may need to create one by modifying the recipe. This transformation of designs is what we refer to as *adaptation*. Adaptation can reduce the reliance on a primitive vocabulary of design components by transforming or adapting the components themselves. To do this requires a type of plausible reasoning to which three main observations pertain:

- *Adaptation is not analogy.* The criteria for what makes a good analogy is a deep conceptual similarity. However, just because two concepts are analogous does not mean that one can be substituted for the other. Electrical current may be a lot like water flowing through a pipe, but you cannot use water to power a light bulb.

- *Adaptation is not debugging.* Whereas a problem solver that debugs a faulty design must know about different ways that a design can fail in the world, one that adapts a previous design starts with a working design and transforms it into a different design. Adaptation must be concerned with different ways that transformations of designs can fail.

- *Adaptation can serve multiple functions.* In addition to adapting parts of cases in the case-based generation process, it is also useful for adapting or patching a partial solution in response to constraints that may be added late in the design process. This can help to avoid backtracking and undoing large parts of the design.

In our model of plausible design, adaptation is a feature-based transformation that seeks to eliminate constraint violations in a design component. Conceptually, it can be thought of as decomposing the source concept, substituting a subfeature, and resynthesizing to create a new concept:

$$\{Decompose\}* \rightarrow Substitute \rightarrow \{Synthesize\}*$$

JULIA can adapt a design by directly applying a transformation method to find a substitute, or it may decompose the design (arbitrarily deeply), replace a component or ingredient of the design, and then resynthesize to create a new design. For example, it might attempt to transform a lasagne recipe into a vegetarian version by substituting a known recipe, such as spinach lasagne, or if no such recipe is known, it would create one by decomposing the lasagne recipe to its ingredients and deleting beef (the null substitution). A benefit of this approach is that it permits designs to be adapted at different granularities, resulting in a greater range of solutions that can be achieved.

There are four requirements for this process: a vocabulary of primitive, domain-independent substitutions; a defined mapping between constraint violation types and applicable transformations; an algorithm that can compose multiple transformations; and heuristics for searching through multiple transformations. JULIA's ability to adapt designs is partly determined by the vocabulary of substitution methods at its disposal. These methods are purposely very simple; complex adaptations result from combining primitive substitutions. JULIA's substitution methods include specialize, generalize, substitute-sibling, substitute-by-function, delete, insert, increase-quantity, decrease-quantity, invert, share-function, and split-function. These methods, although domain-independent, nevertheless rely on the taxonomic organization of concepts in memory and on a hierarchy of representational features. The mapping between constraint violations and substitutions methods is defined primarily by using both the concept to be adapted and the constraint that is violated to index substitution methods in memory.

Because JULIA's domain theory is weak, its adaptation algorithm takes a relatively conservative approach to decomposing and synthesizing design components. First, it applies negative heuristics to guide it away from bad adaptations. For example, it attempts to repair the most salient features of a design first (as indicated by a distinguished feature called the maincon), and gives up if this does not succeed, rather than possibly relaxing the constraint.

JULIA's second strategy for decomposition and synthesis is to use constraints on the internal structure to regress to the independent features of the design. In other words, if a recipe violates a constraint that it be low calorie, the recipe is repaired by regressing from the calories feature to the ingredients feature by traversing the constraint that relates those two features. JULIA uses a hierarchy of features to represent the idea that calories is a type of descriptive feature (i.e., an epiphenomena) and cannot be directly manipulated. If there are internal constraints on the recipe (i.e., a partial model), then it uses that information to regress. If there is no such information, then it fails to adapt the recipe.

2.3.1. Context and Granularity

Adaptation inevitably occurs in some larger context. The context is the set of constraints that determine the adequacy or correctness of the adaptation. In JULIA, designs are adapted first in the local context of a specific constraint violation and then evaluated in progressively more global contexts until they are finally accepted or rejected by the human user in the real world. For example, in designing a meal, a proposed dish such as lasagne might be rejected because it violates a specific constraint; for example, that it be vegetarian. The local adaptation problem is to find or create a viable lasagne dish that is vegetarian. When one is found, that dish is evaluated with respect to its compatibility with other dishes already on the menu. If the adaptation passes these explicit constraints, it may be proposed to the user, who may evaluate it in the context of adequacy in the world, where constraints may not be explicit or formulated beforehand. Whenever a proposed adaptation fails for some reason, the adaptation engine picks up and continues generating solutions where it left off.

There are several reasons for adapting at progressively more global contexts. The main reason is that all the constraints on a design, taken together, are not generative. However, by starting with a particular constraint violation and a particular feature, it is possible to retrieve substitutions that are likely to repair the violation. When a proposed adaptation is evaluated in a more global context, these substitutions can be incrementally weeded out if they violate other constraints on the design.

2.3.2. Make or Buy Decisions

One of the key features of the adaptation algorithm is that it does not rely on having a complete repertoire of design components. If a proposed component is inadequate, JULIA has the option of constructing a new component as an alternative. Of course, this is possible only if the component is not representationally opaque. If it has some sort of internal structure and the constraint violation is traceable to an independent variable, some internal substitution or modification may result in an acceptable variant. In other words, design components are just designs writ small. We can think of this as making a new concept, rather than buying one off the shelf.

The problem with making a new concept is always that it is a plausible inference. The problem solver must assume that a modified concept that is sufficiently similar to the original will be viable. The more a modification deviates from the original, the less likely it is to be acceptable. This suggests that it is better to use existing concepts off the shelf whenever possible. On the other hand, although an existing concept is more likely to be a viable component in its own right (e.g., a dish that would taste good), it may be less compatible with the rest of the design into which it is supposed to fit. In other words, plausibility in the local context can be at odds with plausibility in the global context. Consequently, the adaptation engine provides two policies for the make-or-buy decision: the Minimal Effort Policy, and the Minimal Change Policy. Minimal Effort always prefers to select an existing concept before resorting to something new, although Minimal Change prefers to create a new concept as similar to the source concept as possible. The former is used when adapting parts of a case before transferring them. The latter is used to repair constraint violations that are imposed by new constraints being added to the design.

Adaptation is one of the critical processes in plausible design. Some previous design programs, such as the Redesign System and BOGART (Mostow, 1989), implemented adaptation as replay rather than reuse. This can be very effective for routine design tasks, but makes it virtually impossible to synthesize solutions from multiple cases. In CBR, problem solvers have often used catalogues of modification strategies (e.g., CHEF (Hammond, 1989) and COACH (Collins, 1987), but these strategies did not decompose components and apply transformations at different granularities, and were therefore more limited in their generative capacity. KRITIK (Goel, 1989, and chapter 5, this volume) models design as a re-design problem and emphasizes the importance of deep models of function, structure and behavior in transforming designs. This achieves broad generative capacity at the expense of requiring a stronger domain theory. Ideally, the domain theory in a plausible design system should be additive, such that as more constraints are added, its accuracy and generative capacity improve monotonically.

2.4. ACHIEVING SATISFICING SOLUTIONS

Herb Simon coined the term *satisficing* to denote solutions that are good enough in the real world, as opposed to optimal. By its very nature, plausible design implies that solutions will be satisficing. What is less obvious is that there are two fundamentally different ways that a design can be satisficing. The first is the degree to which the designed artifact fulfills its intended purpose. The second is the adequacy of the design itself as a description of an artifact to be produced. A description may be too ambiguous or incomplete to adequately convey the design. This is a lot like the distinction between accuracy and precision. In our model, we refer to these criteria as the integrity of a design and its completeness.

2.4.1. Integrity

The problem of maintaining integrity in plausible design is that solutions will inevitably entail tradeoffs and open-ended criteria. Operationally, this means that some constraints will be violated and some goals may not be achieved. How can a problem solver decide which solutions are better than others and which are good enough? Our approach is that the problem solver does not try to assess the adequacy of an entire design. Instead, we take a more derivational approach such that if any design is produced, it is satisficing by virtue of the explicit set of preferences used to resolve contradictions and the set of invariants that are enforced between the problem solver's goals, the design structure, and the constraints on the design. This means that the primary way that JULIA achieves satisficing solutions is through its method of resolving local integrity violations.

Integrity violations can arise in several ways. The user might suggest a design component or constraint that conflicts with the rest of the design, or its role in the design might be ambiguous. More commonly, integrity violations are discovered during the process of constraint propagation. Either a value may be asserted for a feature that is oversubscribed or a constraint may be propagated to a feature with which it is inconsistent. JULIA is constantly resolving such contradictions by deciding how to minimally alter the design and by propagating integrity invariants.

The problem solver tries to decide how to minimally alter the design to resolve a contradiction: either by adapting a component, choosing a value to retract, or relaxing the constraint. This is the most critical decision in the entire design process. The decision-making process uses explicit preferences to recursively compare reasons for and against different alternatives. These reasons are automatically recorded by a reason-maintenance system (RMS) that keeps an audit trail of the source of suggested values (e.g., the user, a case, a default, or inferred from a constraint) and records the constraints that are satisfied and violated by the suggestion. JULIA represents explicit preferences between these and other criteria, so that for example, everything else being equal, it will prefer alternatives that are justified by the user or by explicit constraints over default suggestions.

When a resolution is chosen, the problem solver propagates integrity invariants, which are essentially metaconstraints that ensure consistency across the problem solver's constraints, structured representation, and goals. This can cause a ripple effect that can ultimately lead to a design goal being posted or abandoned. In particular, relaxing a constraint may cause a representational inconsistency that could require a piece of the structure of the design to be ruled out, which might in turn cause a design goal to be abandoned. For example, if a decision is made to serve Italian cuisine, this will trigger the constraint that the structure of the meal be the same as the cuisine's default structure. This constraint would be violated if the existing meal structure includes a salad course. The salad course would then be ruled out and a pasta course would be ruled in. This in turn would require the goal to refine the salad course to be abandoned along with all of its subgoals, and a new goal to refine a pasta course would be posted.

The implication of this process is that if a critical piece of a design cannot be solved, then integrity maintenance ensures that the corresponding design goals are abandoned and that this propagates up to the top-level design goal. Thus, design is halted as soon as it is clear that no satisficing solution can be found. In the case of JULIA, a critical piece of a design is defined by one of the integrity invariants as its most salient feature (represented explicitly in the domain theory). For a different domain, the notion of what is critical might be quite different.

2.4.2. Completeness

The other aspect of evaluation assesses the completeness of a design solution. Unlike integrity maintenance, completeness is evaluated retrospectively to determine whether a goal has succeeded although, as we have seen, completeness also plays a role in at least one integrity invariant. In JULIA, design goals to choose a set of values indicate their satisfaction criteria by prescribing the required specificity of the values and scope of the goal in terms of the set of features being determined. These are effectively stopping rules that permit partially satisfied design goals to be iteratively refined. Although somewhat crude, the representation of completeness criteria allows a problem solver to evaluate its goals when there is no goal state to match against, as in most puzzle-type problems.

3. Designing with JULIA: An Example

To put the described features into context, we look at an example session of designing a meal with JULIA. The flavor of the process is a lot different from working with a CAD tool or a spreadsheet. JULIA asks questions and permits the user to ask it questions and/or add new requirements as the design progresses. The process begins with a sketchy description of the desired features of a meal, and this problem specification is interactively elaborated until the problem solver can propose specific dishes that are potentially acceptable.

Our initial problem specification is essentially to plan a meal that is inexpensive, easy to prepare, and includes eggplant in its main dish:

```
How can I help you?
   (host tom)
   (guests (richard mike))
   (cost inexpensive-meal)
   (ease-of-prep easy)
   (ingredients (eggplant))
```

Some additional constraints are available indirectly, based on what the program knows about the food preferences of individual people. In this case, JULIA knows that Richard is a strict vegetarian and Mike is a meat-and-potatoes eater (i.e., he requires meat in his meal). These incompatible constraints are what make this problem hard. Other constraints on the solution are inherited from default knowledge about meals in general. These constraints form a major part of JULIA's domain theory of meal planning.

Because the initial problem is so underspecified, it must be elaborated in order to retrieve possible solutions. To do this, JULIA decomposes the problem into features that are descriptive of the overall meal and features that represent individual courses. This decomposition is guided by plans that direct the problem solver to focus its attention on the cuisine of the meal, because that can provide strong constraints on the rest of the design.

JULIA generates possible cuisines by directly discriminating the features of the meal. The requirement of being inexpensive and including eggplant suggests a possibility:

```
What do you think about mid-eastern-cuisine?
   Ok.
```

The focus of attention now shifts to finding dishes for a main course. Because the main course is represented as the most salient component of a meal, it is addressed first. JULIA retrieves several inexpensive mid-eastern meals but fails to find any with dishes that can be adapted to satisfy all the constraints. At an impasse, JULIA relaxes the assumption that there be a single main dish. It applies the split-function adaptation strategy to achieve the function of a main dish with two different dishes and partitions the constraints on the dishes into two mutually exclusive sets based on their source:

```
There appear to be incompatible constraints between {Tom and
    Richard}, and {Mike}.
We will try to solve this by increasing choice in main-dishes.
```

It now proceeds to focus on finding a dish that will satisfy Tom and Richard. This is a much easier problem and it comes up with two suggestions:

```
Which main dish would you prefer, baba-ghanouj or vegetarian-
    casserole?
Baba-ghanouj
```

For choices between two or three acceptable alternatives, JULIA allows the client to decide. For larger choice sets, it tries to reduce the number of alternatives by generalizing them to a smaller set of mutually exclusive alternatives, and failing that, by choosing among alternatives based on its own preference structure. It now proceeds to look for a Middle Eastern dish for Mike that contains meat and eggplant:

```
Would you like skewered-lamb&eggplant for a main dish?
    Why?
Skewered-lamb&eggplant was suggested by Mid-East Lamb Feast to
satisfy Mike's constraints.
Baba-Ghanouj is not it.
It contains meat-or-poultry.
Its main-ingredients contains eggplant.
Its cuisine is mid-eastern-cuisine.
Ok
```

JULIA justifies its suggestion by explaining where it came from and what constraints it satisfies. The somewhat stilted phrasing "Baba-Ghanouj is not it" refers to a constraint that meals should have variety by not repeating a dish in the same meal.

After transferring the dishes to the new problem, the problem solver re-evaluates its goal to design a main course and determines that it is still incomplete. It further decomposes the problem to look for a vegetable side dish.

```
Which vegetable side dish would you prefer, zucchini-stuffed-
with-                        spinach or hummus?
    hummus.
```

It continues to fill in the rest of the menu with dishes from the same case:

```
Would you like lemon-potatoes for a starch side dish?
    Ok
How about pita-bread for a bread?
    Yes
```

```
How about retsina for a drink?
   Ok
```

At this point, the main course is complete and JULIA starts to work on finding an appetizer. It fails to find a case with an appetizer that satisfies constraints, so it relaxes constraints on the appetizer dish. When it again reaches an impasse, JULIA abandons the goal to design an appetizer altogether and proceeds to work on the salad course:

```
What do you think about greek-salad for a salad?
   Good
```

The problem solver now focuses its attention on the dessert. From the first case retrieved, it proposes a hot drink and a dessert dish:

```
Would you like baklava and turkish-coffee for dessert?
   Yes
```

The last step is to summarize the design and allow the client to make any desired changes:

```
The proposed menu is to have:
greek-salad for a salad-course
skewered-lamb&eggplant, baba-ghanouj, hummus, lemon-potatoes,
retsina, and pita-bread for a main-course,
baklava and turkish-coffee for a dessert-course.
Is this acceptable?
   yes.
```

If the design were not acceptable, the client could enter deletions and additions to the design in the same form as the initial specification. Any contradictions would be detected, and the design process would resume. Otherwise, JULIA says goodbye:

```
Bon Appetit!
```

This example shows some of the types of reasoning that must take place to solve even a simple problem. The fact that problems tend to be underspecified can actually make them harder to solve because the problem must be elaborated. JULIA's interactive nature raises control issues that are seldom addressed in programs that solve design problems autonomously. The ability to modify the structure of the problem and to accept constraints late means that JULIA needs sophisticated methods for maintaining the integrity of the design.

4. JULIA's Software Architecture

JULIA implements the process model described using eight main functional units, as shown in Figure 6.1.

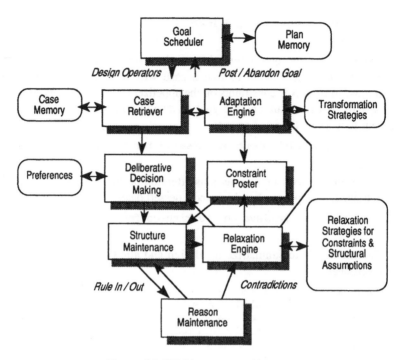

Figure 6.1. JULIA system architecture.

These modules can be loosely grouped into three conceptual units: focusing attention and establishing completeness, generating plausible designs, and maintaining integrity. Together, they implement two nested cycles of control: a problem-reduction cycle and a constraint satisfaction cycle.

The Goal Scheduler implements the problem-reduction cycle of the design process. It builds and maintains a network of design goals and schedules active goals on an agenda (see Figure 6.2). These design goals are primarily of three types: Advise, Refine, and Choose. Advise elicits an initial problem statement from the user; Refine instantiates its objective and packages subgoals to recursively refine and choose values for parts of the design; Choose generates possible design components and/or chooses among them. The scheduler selects a goal to pursue and retrieves from memory plans and primitive methods to achieve the goal. It decomposes problematic plans (such as refine meal-1) into subgoals and executes primitive methods. When methods return, it evaluates whether or not the goal is achieved. It maintains the consistency of the goal net by either rescheduling goals that are partially satisfied, decomposing them to subgoals, abandoning unsatisfiable goals, or posting new goals as structures are added to the design.

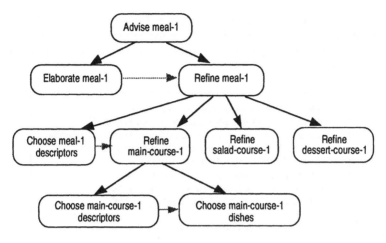

Figure 6.2. A portion of JULIA's goal network.

The primitive methods that the scheduler executes are design operators. The operator for choosing values implements the constraint satisfaction cycle to find consistent values for the feature or features that are the objective of the design goal. This operator first formulates constraints on the feature, then applies associative routines to generate values. It then uses deliberative decision making to either choose a best value or coalesce the values into a manageable set of mutually exclusive alternatives and queries the user. Finally, when a decision is made, it revises the design and propagates constraints forward.

The generation routines include direct discrimination from an abstract concept such as a cuisine, the determination of mutually exclusive competitor sets, and CBR. The main components of CBR are a case-retriever and an adaptation engine. The case-retriever searches a dynamic memory (Kolodner, 1984; Schank, 1982) for similar cases, ranks them, suggests constraints to avoid previous failures, identifies the mapping of features between the case and problem, and adapts and adopts pieces from successful cases (with the help of the adaptation engine). A case-storer adds new cases to memory and inductively generalizes MOPs and indices.

The adaptation engine transforms cases and design components to eliminate constraint violations. The constraint violations are used to guide the decomposition of the component, to guide blame assignment, and to retrieve primitive adaptation transformations.

The constraint poster (Stefik, 1981) implements the constraint formulation and propagation, and the evaluation of constraint satisfaction. The constraint poster supports second-order constraints such as Boolean connectives and constraints that propagate other constraints. Figure 6.3 shows some of the constraints on one of the main dishes from the earlier example. Some of these constraints are problem-specific and some are part of JULIA's meal-planning domain theory.

```
(different (?main-dishes-1) (?main-dishes-2) required)
(doesnt-contain (?dishes ingredients) meat-or-poultry required)
(contains (?main-dishes main-ingredients) (part-of ?ingredients) relaxable)
(at-most (?dishes ease-of-prep) (part-of ?ease-of-prep) required)
(instance (?dishes functions) edible-dish required)
(instance (?dishes cuisine) (part-of ?cuisine) preferred)
(or (instance (?dishes cuisine) (part-of ?cuisine) required)
    (instance (part-of ?cuisine) (?dishes cuisine) required)
    required)
```

Figure 6.3. Some of the constraints on main-dishes-1.

The deliberative decision-making component compares alternatives and chooses one based on an explicit preferences. This is used both to choose among design components and to choose the best way to resolve contradictions. The comparison algorithm is described in more detail in Hinrichs (1992).

The Structure Maintenance System (SMS) ensures that the representation of the solution is internally consistent and consistent with the goals of the problem solver. All changes to the design pass through the SMS, which rules in or out design components, constraints, and structural variables (e.g., whether or not there will be an appetizer course or a vegetable side dish). As it updates the structure of the design, it detects violations of structural assumptions, such as the assumption that there will only be one main dish, or that there will be an appetizer course. When structures are added or removed from the design, it posts or removes the corresponding design goals via the goal scheduler. Part of the structured representation of the example problem is shown in Figure 6.4.

The relaxation engine is invoked whenever constraint propagation reveals a constraint violation and whenever a structural assumption is violated. The relaxation engine tries to find the smallest change to the design that will resolve the violation. Sometimes this is as simple as realizing that the user has merely changed his mind about a design component. Other strategies include adapting the design component that violates constraints, or choosing the least important preference constraint that leads to the violation and weakening it just enough so that the contradiction goes away. Finally, the relaxation engine can traverse the dependency structure to choose a design commitment to retract, thereby implementing dependency-directed backtracking.

```
name: meal-1
isa: (m-meal)
agents:
  eaters:
    host: *tom*
    guests: (*mike* *richard*)
descriptors:
  primary-descriptors:
    cost: inexpensive-meal
    cuisine: mid-eastern-cuisine
components:
  events:
    salad-course: salad-1
    main-course:main-course-1
    dishes:
      main-dishes:
        main-dishes-1: baba-ghanouj
        main-dishes-2: skewered-lamb&eggplant
      side-dishes:
        veg-dish: hummus
        bread: pita-bread
        drink: retsina
    dessert-course: dessert-1
```

Figure 6.4. A portion of the structured design representation.

Structural assumptions are typically variants of the uniqueness assumption, in which a feature is assumed to have a single value. The relaxation engine must decide whether or not an apparent structural violation is in fact a contradiction. For example, if JULIA decides to serve pasta for a starch dish, and later another case (or the user) suggests spaghetti, it must realize that spaghetti is just a specialization of pasta. However, if the user demands a baked-potato, then this really is a violation. If the user requires both spaghetti and a baked potato for some perverse reason, the system must relax the structural assumption and permit two starch dishes.

The RMS (Doyle, 1979) maintains justifications for and against candidate decisions and records the consequences of decisions and the sources of values. As candidate decisions are ruled in and out, it invokes the SMS to update the structured representation. When primitive contradictions are discovered, it invokes the relaxation engine to choose the best way to resolve them.

5. Lessons Learned

Implementing and experimenting with JULIA has taught us a number of lessons about CBR and design. For the purposes of this chapter, we divide these into representational and control lessons.

5.1. REPRESENTATION

What sort of representation is needed to support the retrieval, adaptation, and evaluation of design cases? Although this surely depends on the domain and type of design being pursued, we believe the following observations are generally applicable:

- *A hierarchy of features facilitates case mapping.* JULIA's structured representation includes a hierarchy of features. For example, every episode has primitive feature objects. In a meal, the objects are further broken down into dishes and utensils. Dishes may be further divided into the subfeatures main-dish and side-dishes, and for traditional-cuisine meals, still further into green-vegetable and starch-dish. This sort of hierarchy helps when mapping and transferring components from a case with a different structure, as for example, from a middle-eastern meal.

- *Structured design categories aid adaptation.* A case-based designer that adapts designs by searching for plausible substitutes needs heuristics to tell it where to look first. This is simplified if the representation captures the notion of typicality or centrality within a category. JULIA does this by distinguishing between classes and prototypes. The subclass relationship is an abstraction relationship, whereas the subtype relation–ship is a typicality relationship. For example, because chicken and duck are subtypes of poultry, JULIA is likely to try substituting one for the other. On the other hand, because poultry and fish are both subclasses of food, JULIA's heuristics will not permit it to substitute one for the other.

- *A common vocabulary for matching rules, constraint types, and transformation methods is critical.* If a case-based design system is to adapt its cases, then there must be some sort of impedance match between the matching rules that are used to index and retrieve a case, the constraint types that establish the acceptability of the case, and the transformation methods that are used to adapt it. This makes it possible to tailor the indexing to retrieve cases that are likely to be adaptable.

5.2. CONTROL

What sort of control strategy should be used for case-based design? JULIA uses a variety of strategies in different phases of design. This is partly because our model of design combines approaches that are typically considered distinct, such as decomposition, CBR, and transformation (Maher, 1990).

- *Plan instantiation guides problem decomposition.* The benefit of plan instantiation is that it provides guidance on how to decompose a problem and in what order to attack the subproblems. As it turns out our domain has relatively few strategic plans of this sort (e.g., refine-main-course, refine-in-temporal-order, etc.) If most problems are solved in roughly the same manner, why bother to instantiate plans? We found that it was important to instantiate these plans (or more precisely, their subgoals) because it is sometimes necessary to abandon unattainable subgoals. To decide whether or not a subgoal may be abandoned, JULIA must reason about its criticality and relationship to the rest of the plan.

- *Constraint satisfaction is an appropriate strategy for well-structured subproblems.* We chose to model individual decisions as constraint satisfaction problems because design problems are typically specified in terms of constraints and because constraints can easily represent incomplete information, such as a partial domain model. The problem with constraint satisfaction is that many constraints are open-ended (e.g., minimize cost), and most design constraints are not constructive; that is, they cannot be used to deduce a unique solution. We address open-ended constraints through constraint relaxation and preference-based deliberation in the contradiction-resolution phase. We satisfy nonconstructive constraints by using CBR to propose plausible solutions, rather than trying to deduce solutions or exhaustively generate and test.

- *CBR can be an effective means of proposing values to satisfy constraints.* Rather than using CBR in competition with from-scratch methods, we use it in complementary roles. Cases supply a partial domain theory, augment inference, and support decomposition and synthesis. Constraints supplement the domain theory by expressing rule-like regularities that can be tested, propagated, and if necessary, relaxed. Rather than using CBR to replay previous inference (inference that could, in principle, be performed from scratch), we use it as a form of plausible reasoning. For example, if a previous case suggests that turkey and white wine are complementary, then in the absence of knowledge to the contrary, JULIA will use them together again. Notice that the previous case does not have to be a problem that JULIA solved previously; it could (in theory) be simply an observation of someone else's solution or of a solution that occurs in Nature. There need not be any reasoning trace at all.

6. Issues in Applying Plausible Design to Other Domains

Although the meal planning domain has been an effective illustration of plausible design, it is not what most people would consider a practical problem in the real world. To what extent are the principles of plausible design applicable to other domains? Ultimately, we believe that plausible design advice can play a role in most types of design, regardless of the degree to which the domain is formalizable and quantifiable. In this section, we try to define that role and to distinguish theoretical limitations from weaknesses in the existing implementation.

The primary role of plausible design is to propose plausible design solutions. In informal domains, this can take the form of advice to a user, as we have seen in JULIA. In domains with a stronger theory and correctness criteria, this can be used as a starting point for more detailed design, or as a heuristic for searching the problem space. How effective this can be is determined by several factors: the density of the solution space, the coverage of the case base, and whether or not previous solutions can be reused as opposed to replaying their derivations. Plausible design works best when the solution space is dense (i.e., similar problems have similar solutions), when the case-base largely covers the classes of problems of interest, and when solutions can be directly reused. If solutions are to be replayed, it is unlikely that they can be synthesized from multiple cases or adapted with any likelihood of success.

Probably the most formalizable and quantifiable design domains are engineering domains. In many ways, engineering design is diametrically opposite the meal planning domain we have been investigating. Engineering usually entails a strong quantitative domain theory with definite criteria for correctness. And yet, engineers certainly do not reinvent the wheel every time they design something, and they often do combine and adapt previous solutions and occasionally have to revise solutions based on new constraints. Where does plausible reasoning fit into this?

Consider an example. In electronic circuit design, there are many different topological structures for amplifiers. In designing an amplifier, the choice of which structure to use is often a judgment call, as is the choice of the particular components to implement it with (e.g., the particular type of op-amp, etc.) Where the quantitative domain theory comes in is in the parametric part of the design, where particular values of resistances and capacitances are selected. Here, the equations are reused, effectively replaying the calculations from the original paradigmatic case. It seems reasonable that plausible design could help in choosing the structure and implementation of an amplifier while leaving the parametric decisions to other processes. The benefit this provides over, for example, a rule-based expert system, is the flexibility it provides. Whereas an expert system might derive an implementation based directly on desired output parameters, it typically would not be able to suggest alternatives if that implementation were ruled out for some reason (e.g., part discontinued.) This is an intrinsic part of plausible design.

To support this, engineering representations need to be augmented such that they capture some notion of similarity (through structured categories), an indication of centrality or typicality of cases within a category, and a way to describe the relative salience of features with respect to the typicality assessment. These plausible associations help a reasoner not only retrieve similar cases, but also determine what constitutes useful decompositions and minimal adaptations.

Conversely, to support engineering design, our plausible design system must be augmented with other types of reasoning such as reasoning about function and structure, reasoning about shape, time, and causality. Moreover, any given domain may require additional problem-solving knowledge about problem reduction, decompositions and decision-making preferences, and design-specific knowledge such as knowledge about design integrity. This turns out to be a big impediment in applying an existing system such as JULIA to engineering design.

JULIA is fundamentally a meal-planning system, but the problem-solving architecture is not intrinsically domain dependent. We have made tentative efforts to apply JULIA to other domains, such as circuit design and simple machine design. Many of the problems we have encountered have been representational:

- *Vocabulary:* In applying JULIA to engineering design, its domain representation would have to be extended to deal more adequately with geometry, time, causality, and function (staples of engineering representations).

- *Quantitative reasoning:* JULIA tends to be geared toward discrete values rather than continuous values. It treats continuous quantities by translating them into ordinal neighborhoods such as cool or cheap. This simplifies retrieval and matching at the cost of flexibility and precision. It would be preferable to dynamically characterize values.

- *Compositionality of constraints:* JULIA's constraint representation is impoverished in that its only facility for composing constraints is through Boolean connectives. For physical domains, equations compose constraints through arithmetic and geometric operations, among others.

- *Reliance on symbolic features:* Feature-based recognition may be insufficient for domains in which design is primarily structural. For example, to use CBR to solve problems in resistive networks would be difficult at best because it is not possible to retrieve only relevant cases based on the set of features.

One of our efforts at the Institute for the Learning Sciences has been to construct a library of alternative case-retrieval modules and knowledge acquisition tools. This has afforded us the opportunity to examine other retrieval algorithms, such as spreading activation and PROTOS-style retrieval. Although all such algorithms have their advantages and disadvantages, they all effectively perform feature-based recognition. None can retrieve concepts based on relationships implicit in the representation.

To extend JULIA to support case retrieval and adaptation on the basis of topological structure requires a fundamentally different approach. We have recently developed a structural recognition algorithm that uses principles of grouping and similarity to decompose an input, recognize abstract configurations, and re-represent the input in terms of higher-level domain concepts (Hinrichs, 1995). We expect this algorithm to greatly extend the utility of the case retrieval and adaptation components.

Although JULIA is no longer an active project, some aspects of its design architecture continue to evolve:

1. The representational expressiveness has been improved by representing slots and numbers as frames to facilitate reasoning about features and quantities.

2. New modularities have been developed that separate inference from side-effect in constraint posting, and that more fully develop integrity maintenance as an abstraction of which goal scheduling, constraint posting, structure maintenance, and reason maintenance are special cases.

3. The beginnings of some new domain vocabularies have been added for shape, physical laws and their effects, and simple machines.

7. Conclusions

In this chapter, we have described plausible design as implemented in JULIA, a meal-planning program. The basic premises of plausible design are that domain theories are seldom (if ever) complete, that problems are usually under-specified, and that satisficing solutions are often acceptable. The computational model we have explored integrates CBR with constraint posting, synthesizes solutions from multiple cases, adapts designs and design components, and is able to relax constraints, abandon unsatisfiable subgoals, and accept new constraints late in the design process.

One of the important ramifications of plausible design is that it requires taking category structure seriously. Family resemblance can be a critical plausible inference in design because it enables a design problem solver to retrieve similar designs, suggest variations, help decompose the problem, and anticipate subsequent problems. Supporting such inference means that a problem solver cannot be limited to the traditional physics model of design representation involving sets of equations, equivalence classes, and fixed sets of parameters.

Plausible design also suggests that it is possible to perform adaptation, decomposition, and synthesis despite a weak or informal domain theory by using what knowledge is available both in the form of associations, heuristics, and explicit constraints. Recent trends in interactive CBR have tended to emphasize the retrieval of representationally opaque multimedia cases at the expense of adaptation and synthesis. We would argue that to provide truly useful design advice, sophisticated indexing and retrieval are not enough. To use cases more creatively, we must put the *reasoning* back into CBR.

References

Chandrasekaran, B.: 1990, Design problem solving: A task analysis, *AI Magazine*, 11(4), 59–71.

Collins, G.: 1987, *Plan Creation: Using Strategies as Blueprints*, Doctoral Dissertation, YALE/CSD/RR–559, Yale University.

Doyle, J.: 1979. A truth maintenance system, *Artificial Intelligence*, 12, 231–272.

Goel, A.: 1989, *Integration of Case-Based Reasoning and Model-Based Reasoning for Adaptive Design Problem Solving*, Doctoral Dissertation, Ohio State University.

Hammond, K.: 1989, *Case-Based Planning: Viewing Planning as a Memory Task*, Academic Press, New York.

Hinrichs, T.: 1992, *Problem Solving in Open Worlds: A Case Study in Design*, Lawrence Erlbaum Associates, Hillsdale, NJ.

Hinrichs, T.: 1995, Some limitations of feature-based recognition in case-based design, *Proceedings of the First International Conference on Case-Based Reasoning*, Springer-Verlag, New York, pp. 471–480.

Kolodner, J.: 1984, *Retrieval and Organizational Strategies in a Conceptual Memory: A Computer Model*, Lawrence Erlbaum Associates, Hillsdale, NJ.

Kolodner, J., Simpson, R., and Sycara, K.: 1985, A process model of case-based reasoning in problem solving, *Proceedings of the International Joint Conference on Artificial Intelligence*, Los Angeles, CA, pp. 248–290.

Maher, M.: 1990, Process models for design synthesis, *AI Magazine*, 11(4), 49-58.

Mostow, J.: 1989, Design by derivational analogy: Issues in the automated replay of design plans, *Artificial Intelligence*, 40, 119–184.

Rissland, E., and Skalak, D.: 1989, Combining case-based reasoning and rule-based reasoning: A heuristic approach, *Proceedings of the International Joint Conference on Artificial Intelligence*, Detroit, Michigan, pp. 524–530.

Schank, R.: 1982, *Dynamic Memory: A Theory of Reminding and Learning in Computers and People*, Cambridge University Press, Cambridge, UK.

Stefik, M.: 1981, Planning with constraints, *Artificial Intelligence*, 16(2), 111–140.

Sycara, K.: 1987, *Resolving Adversarial Conflicts: An Approach Integrating Case-Based and Analytical Methods*, Doctoral Dissertation, GIT-ICS-87/26, Georgia Institute of Technology.

Sycara, K., and Navin-Chandra, D.: 1991, Influences: A thematic abstraction for creative use of multiple cases, *in* R. Bareiss (ed.), *Proceedings: Case-Based Reasoning Workshop*, Kaufmann, San Mateo, CA, pp. 133–144.

chapter seven

CASECAD AND CADSYN:

Implementing case retrieval and case adaptation

MARY LOU MAHER
University of Sydney

The success of CBR for design applications is dependent on the recognition of design as an ill-structured process in which design goals change and shift as the designer considers different alternatives. In addition to the opportunistic or explorative aspect of design, the nature of design is such that each new design must be different to previous designs. This chapter focuses on the strategies for retrieving design cases in the context of a changing design problem and the strategies for adapting a selected design case for the new design context. This focus is developed through a presentation of the implementation of two case-based design systems, CASECAD and CADSYN. The issues raised by the application of CBR to design are discussed in light of the experience of implementing CASECAD and CADSYN.

1. Introduction

Case-based design is a paradigm for generating design alternatives that uses previous design cases as the basis for a new design solution. Case-based design can be considered an application area of CBR, however, some of the considerations in implementing case-based design introduces new concepts to CBR. The development of a case-based design system requires the interaction of two major concerns in CBR: memory organization to enable memory-based reasoning and the formalization of analogical reasoning. The first concern has to do with reminding and memory structures. The second has to do with reasoning and knowledge to support the reasoning. The purpose of this chapter is to show how these two concerns lead to memory structures that support specific types of design reasoning.

The implementations of case-based design systems have been done in a relatively intuitive manner. The reason for this lack of formalism or uniformity in implementation is that the field of CBR is not mature enough to have produced a wide range of system building tools and because design does not easily fit within the confines of goal-directed problem solving. Design introduces difficulties in finding a map between the design requirements and a design solution as, often, the design requirements are vague and need to be refined before a solution can be generated. Design also introduces difficulties in the concept of solution reuse because each design situation is unique or the problem would not be a design problem.

The issues in developing case-based design systems include:

- The acquisition of design cases.
- The development of a representation and organization of design case memory.
- The development of an indexing structure for recalling design cases.
- The development of strategies for flexible retrieval of design cases.
- The development of a metric for selecting a design case or subcase.
- The formalization of design case adaptation.
- The representation of knowledge to support design case adaptation.
- A model for verifying the results of design case adaptation.

These issues need to be addressed at some stage in the application of CBR to design. Rather than assume that there is a simple solution to each of these issues, the focus of a particular design domain and the identification of alternative ways of addressing the issues can lead to formalization. Given a sufficient number of examples of case-based design systems, it is possible to use these systems as a starting point, with adaptation of course, to the development of another case-based design system.

This chapter addresses these issues through example, specifically through the examples of the implementations of two case-based design systems: CASECAD (Maher and Balachandran, 1994a; Maher and Balachandran, 1994b) and CADSYN (Maher and Zhang, 1993; Maher Balachandran, and Zhang, 1995). CASECAD is a CBR shell developed in coordination with the acquisition of cases of structural design of buildings. The focus of CASECAD is the multimedia representation of design cases to support flexible retrieval strategies. CADSYN is a CBR system developed as an implementation of design case adaptation using constraint satisfaction. The focus in CADSYN is the formalization of cases and design knowledge to support case adaptation. Both CASECAD and CADSYN were implemented in the context of the structural design of buildings.

The remainder of this chapter comprises a description of the implementation of CASECAD, then CADSYN, and then a discussion of the issues presented in light of the experience of implementing CASECAD and CADSYN.

2. CASECAD

CASECAD is a domain independent design system based on an integration of CBR and computer-aided design (CAD) techniques. CASECAD employs a memory organization scheme that partitions memory into model-based memory and case memory. Model-based memory provides generalized knowledge about the design domain as well as an organizational schema for case memory. Case memory is a multimedia representation of design episodes using an object-oriented representation of design variables and text descriptions, CAD drawings to illustrate the geometry of design cases, and graphical illustrations of behaviors of design cases.

CASECAD provides a multimedia design case library browser that allows designers to view and compare relevant past design cases in both symbolic and graphical modes. Case retrieval can be based on the required function, behavior, and/or structure of the new design. Once a set of suitable cases are retrieved from the case library, the designer can navigate the retrieved cases in the multimedia environment in order to select the most applicable case for the current situation. The designer can then modify the text and graphic descriptions of the selected case for the new design context if needed. This is possible using text editors for the object-oriented representation, a CAD system for the CAD drawings, and a drawing program for the graphic representation of behaviors. The current version of CASECAD is considered a design aiding system as opposed to an autonomous design system.

2.1. THE CASECAD SYSTEM

The architecture of CASECAD is illustrated in Figure 7.1. The main modules of the CASECAD system are the case memory module, the case base manager, the case-based reasoner, the CAD module, and the user interface.

The Case Memory Module (CMM) is made up of two components: model memory and case memory. Model memory includes generalized knowledge about the design domain as function-behavior-structure descriptions and provides an organizational schema for indexing case memory. Case memory is a multimedia representation of design episodes using an object-oriented representation of design attributes, CAD drawings, and graphical illustrations of behaviors of design cases. The graphically represented examples are indexed symbolically so that they can be retrieved if given a problem specification in symbolic form.

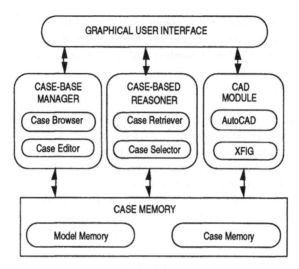

Figure 7.1. CASECAD system architecture.

The Case Base Manager (CBM) provides facilities for creating, browsing, modifying, displaying, and saving information associated with model memory and case memory. A mouse-based editing facility allows text and/or graphics to be modified. The CBM allows a user to modify an existing case and store the modified case as a new case. This supports user-based case adaptation.

The Case-Based Reasoner is made up of two modules: the Case Retriever and the Case Selector. The task of the Case Retriever is to retrieve relevant cases given a set of requirements of the current problem in terms of function, behavior and structure. Retrieval is based on a match between the attribute-value pairs in the new design requirements and the attribute-value pairs used in the case description. The Case Selector ranks the retrieved cases and presents the ranking to the user. Once a set of relevant cases is retrieved from the database of design cases, the designer can browse those retrieved cases in order to select the most applicable case for the current situation.

The CAD module provides the capability to supplement textual data about design cases with graphical data. The CAD package consists of two drafting/drawing programs: AutoCAD[1] and XFIG. AutoCAD is a general purpose CAD modelling system used to create 2-D drawings and 3-D models of design cases. XFIG is a general purpose 2-D drawing system used to represent abstractions of case behaviors as simple drawings.

---

[1]AutoCAD is a trademark of Autodesk, Ltd.

The Graphical User Interface (GUI) allows the designer access to the CBM, the case-based designer, AutoCAD and/or XFIG, and indirectly, the case memory. The GUI provides a window-based interface to each module of the system. The user of CASECAD can be either the case-base developer, adding models or cases to case memory; or a designer, browsing and retrieving cases and/or models from case memory.

2.2. REPRESENTATION OF CASE MEMORY IN CASECAD

In CASECAD, memory is partitioned into two modules: model memory and case memory. Generally speaking, design models cover normative situations and design cases cover specific instances. A design model represents a range of design solutions and contains relevant design knowledge from which a number of different abstractions can be derived. Integrating design models and design cases in case memory provides a rich source of knowledge to perform case-based design. Design models serve several purposes in CASECAD:

- Provide templates for organising information within a design case.
- Provide indices and functional groupings for design cases.
- Provide design knowledge for the elaboration of a new design problem.
- Provide design knowledge for guiding case adaptation.

Because design in many domains is composed of subproblems, it is feasible that design solutions to subproblems can come from different design cases. Organization of design case memory as a hierarchical decomposition allows for the generation of new designs using pieces of different cases. Design models serve both as a basis for decomposing design cases into subcases and for determining relevant or critical features to describe new design problems.

2.2.1. Representation of Design Models in CASECAD

Design models within a domain can be organized into a hierarchy. The hierarchy represents part-subpart relationships. The hierarchical organization of the design models provide templates for the organization of a design case. Figure 7.2 shows a hierarchical organization of the design models representing a structural system of a building. The structural system of a building can be based on models for different types of grid systems, alternatives and parameters for framing systems, simple or complex floor systems, and models to represent the core structure. This is not the only way to decompose the structural system into models, but represents a functional decomposition, where each submodel serves a primary structural design function.

To support flexibility in both indexing and retrieving design cases CASECAD represents design models according to function (F), behavior (B), and structure (S) properties distinctively. This representation is derived from the design prototype schema as introduced by Gero (1990), where each attribute of a prototype is categorized based on the role it plays in reasoning about a design artifact. Function properties describe the intended purpose of the design, behavior properties described the expected and actual performance features of the design, and structure properties describe the physical features and geometry of the design.

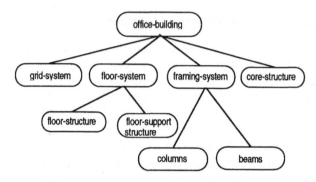

Figure 7.2. Design model hierarchy of a structural system for a building.

Attributes characterize the design instance through their labels and values. In the design model, additional information about an attribute can be represented as attributes of attributes, or the facets of an attribute. In CASECAD, the facets of an attribute include type, default, units, range, and dimension. Figure 7.3 shows an example of a model-based representation of a floor system in CASECAD.

2.2.2. *Representation of Design Cases in CASECAD*

Design cases represent previous situated design solutions individually. In order to store a design case, the salient features that describe it need to be identified. In CASECAD, design cases are described by a vocabulary and hierarchical organization derived from the definition of the design models. The representation of design models was also influenced by collecting design cases; however, the initial representation of design models was developed before the design cases. A design case is organized into a partonomic hierarchy in which each node is described by the most discriminating function, behavior, and structure attributes.

The case base currently contains about 20 partial building cases. The buildings are primarily medium-rise office or hotel buildings, each with a core structure used to resist wind load. The buildings are distinguishable by their geometric constraints, represented by the grid system, and the use of structural components to complement the core structure, represented through a different set of subcases for each building. Each case in the case memory is a single building design. A subcase is a structural component of the building, for example, a rigid frame or a floor system component. The cases and subcases are related to the design models stored in model memory. Figure 7.4 shows the relationship between design models and design cases in CASECAD.

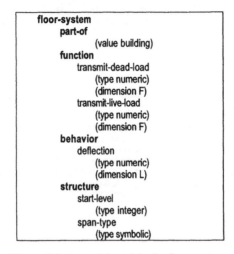

Figure 7.3. A partial model of a floor system.

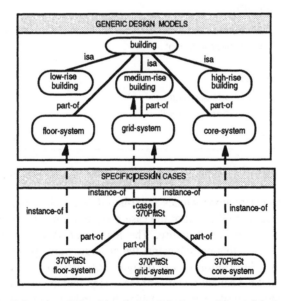

Figure 7.4. The relationships between design models and design cases.

The content of a design case/subcase is made up of attribute-value pairs, including symbolic and graphic attributes. The labels and facets of the symbolic attributes are derived from the relevant design model and the values are specific to the design project. The graphic attributes assume a value that points to a file in which the graphic representation is stored. Figure 7.5 shows the subcase representing the floor system of the building at 370 Pitt Street.

---

subcase1001

    part-of: 370-PIIT-ST

    instance-of: floor-system

  description

  "The floor system is a combination of standard Rescrete precast 'Formplank' panels supported by custom made precast beam shells and by facade wall panels. The ends of the 'Formplank' panels rested on either corbels on the facade wall units or the upturned edges of the precast beam shells. These precast elements were used to produce a one-way slab, one-way beam system with structural detailing providing continuity between beams, precast columns and facade panels."

function

  transmit-dead-load 3 kPa

    ...

behavior

  deflection 18 mm

  xfig-file "floor-system.fig"

    ...

structure

  material precast-cocncrete

  acad-file "floor-system.sld"

    ...

Figure 7.5. A partial case representation of a floor system.

The case representation includes a text-based description, relational attributes that link the subcase to the root of the case hierarchy, and attributes categorized as function, behavior, or structure. The text-based description provides an overview of the case that complements the attribute-value pairs by providing a more qualitative description of the design. The attribute-value pairs provide information about the salient features of the design that are used for indexing the case and provides a set of decision variables that can be modified when the design is adapted.

Graphical representations are traditionally used by designers to store and communicate information about their designs. They serve not only to communicate design ideas effectively but also to manage the complexity of design information. In the CASECAD system, graphical data is included to provide a visualization of the design case. The structure of each subcase is visualized as a CAD model. Some important behaviors of subcases are visualized by 2D abstract drawings. Behavior properties that are of particular interest to structural designers include stress distribution, deflection pattern, and bending moment variation.

2.3. CASE MEMORY ORGANIZATION

CASECAD employs a two-level indexing scheme. The first level of indices is called category indices. These are intended to support selection of a particular category of memory to perform the search procedure. Each node of a design case is indexed by three labels: function, behavior, and structure. The second level of indices is called attribute indices. These indices include the function, behavior, and structure attributes of all cases in case memory. One of the key aspects of this indexing approach is that it allows a case to be indexed by focusing on the function, the behavior, or the structure of the case. By focusing on one type of requirements, a different set of cases may be retrieved than if all requirements are used. The indexing scheme in CASECAD is illustrated in Figure 7.6.

FUNCTION INDICES

support-building-type: case 101, case103
support-live-load: case1206, case 1307
...

BEHAVIOR INDICES

deflection: case1555, case1543
shear-stress: case 1555, case1435
cost: case103, case104
....

STRUCTURE INDICES

building-shape: case 101, case103
number-of-stories: case101, case103
floor-system-type: case1102, case1203
...

Figure 7.6. Indexing scheme in CASECAD.

The indexing scheme focuses on the attributes in a case as the bases for retrieval. The text-based description and the graphical descriptions of the design cases are not indexed directly but are retrieved when a case is retrieved. In CASECAD, it was assumed that the text and graphics are available for the user to understand the case and that new design specifications would be described in terms of the function, behavior, and/or structure requirements.

2.4. RETRIEVING DESIGN CASES

The retrieval process begins when the designer specifies a new design problem. The new problem description is referred to as the *specifications* in CASECAD. The specifications are categorized as function, behavior, and structure and are specified as attribute name and value. An example of specifications for a new problem is given in Figure 7.7.

```
NEW DESIGN PROBLEM SPECIFICATIONS

FUNCTION REQUIREMENTS
support-building-type: office
support-grid-geometry: rectangular
maximum-span: 9 m

BEHAVIOR REQUIREMENTS
cost-of-construction: <= 20 $millions

STRUCTURE REQUIREMENTS
material:  reinforced concrete
```

Figure 7.7. Specifications for a new design problem.

CASECAD uses the problem specifications to search for relevant design models or design cases from case memory, where one specification is an attribute-value pair and the set of specifications is a set of attribute-value pairs. When searching case memory the case retriever finds all cases and/or models that match the given specifications perfectly or partially. The retrieved case can be used directly as a starting point for a new design, or can be the basis for revising the problem specifications.

Case retrieval is carried out in two steps. First, a category of attributes of the cases/subcases are retrieved, followed by an attribute-value matching process. The system only retrieves cases that have at least one match with the specifications. The system ranks the retrieved cases by their similarity to the problem specification. The similarity of a case to the problem is measured by the number of matching attribute-value pairs. Figure 7.8 shows the cases retrieved using the function attributes of the specifications.

SPECIFICATIONS

FUNCTION
   support-grid-geometry : (= rectangular)
   maximum-span: (= 9m)
   support-building-type: (= office)
BEHAVIOR
   cost-of-construction: (<= 20 $millions)
STRUCTURE
   material: (= reinforced-concrete)

CASE RETRIEVAL USING FUNCTION SPECIFICATIONS

subcase-node	case-name	number-of-matchings
SUBCASE401	THE-HUNTINGTON	3
SUBCASE301	THE-AMERICA-TOWER	3
SUBCASE101	130-ELIZABETH-ST	3
SUBCASE402	THE-HUNTINGTON	2
SUBCASE302	THE-AMERICA-TOWER	2
SUBCASE201	370-PITT-ST	2
SUBCASE103	130-ELIZABETH-ST	2
SUBCASE202	370-PITT-ST	1

Figure 7.8. The cases retrieved using the function attributes.

One advantage of the case retrieval in CASECAD is that the search for matching cases can be done using different categories of specifications independently. During the retrieval shown in Figure 7.8, the search was confined to one particular category of case attributes, thus minimizing the search time. If the same set of specifications were used to focus the search on the behavior attributes of the specifications, a different set of cases is retrieved. This highlights the effect of focusing on one category of the specifications and that there is no single best case for a particular design situation.

Once a set of cases is retrieved by the system, the designer may add more requirements about the problem to explore the case memory. The designer can browse the retrieved cases as a multimedia representation in order to select the most applicable, or best case to the current problem. The case retriever provides a list of cases or subcases after searching the case memory. The user can then display the contents of any of the retrieved cases, select one to adapt, or modify the specifications and initiate case retrieval again.

3. CADSYN

CADSYN is a domain independent case-based reasoner that retrieves and adapts design cases using a combination of a case memory and generalized design knowledge in the form of system definitions and constraints. Case retrieval is implemented as a closest match algorithm that finds and ranks cases according to the number of attributes that match the specifications of the new problem. If a sufficiently similar case is not found, CADSYN uses a knowledge-base of generalized systems to refine the problem specifications to include more detailed descriptions. If a sufficiently similar case is found, CADSYN implements case adaptation by constraint satisfaction. The constraint satisfaction process uses a knowledge-base of generalized systems, similar to the design models in CASECAD, and generalized constraints, representing heuristic and causal constraints on the composition of subcases. CADSYN was implemented using a case base of structural designs as the domain to illustrate the approach. CADSYN does not emphasise user interaction and graphic-based representations.

3.1. THE CADSYN SYSTEM

The conceptual architecture of CADSYN is shown in Figure 7.9. There are five process modules in the architecture of CADSYN. The retriever is used to identify a relevant design (sub)case based on the retrieval of a set of cases from case memory and selection of a relevant design case.

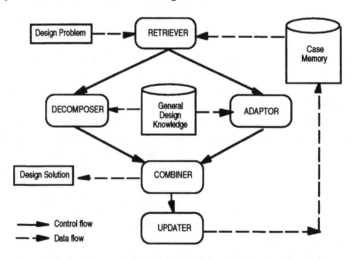

Figure 7.9. The conceptual architecture of CADSYN.

If a relevant (sub)case is found, case adaptation is performed; otherwise the problem is decomposed into a set of subproblems. Case adaptation uses a constraint satisfaction approach. Problem decomposition is based on EDESYN (Maher, 1987), a domain independent design synthesis shell. Case combination checks for consistency between the partial solutions developed through problem decomposition and those from case adaptation. Finally, the solution to the design problem is used to update case memory by adding the new design description into case memory for future use.

3.2. MEMORY REPRESENTATION IN CADSYN

There are two memory modules in CADSYN: case memory and general design knowledge-base. Case memory contains specific previous design situations and indexing information to serve as a starting point for a new problem. The generalized knowledge-base contains knowledge required to refine and expand the new design problem specifications. It is comprised of a hierarchy of design (sub)systems, constraints, and procedural functions. The design context is a representation of the new design problem and its current solution.

3.2.1. Representation of Specific Design Cases

A design case in CADSYN comprises design requirements and design descriptions of structural systems. The knowledge sources used to acquire the design cases include design drawings, design documents, and design experts. Several categories of information about buildings were derived from structural design drawings followed by discussions with designers. These categories include general information, geometric information, special architectural specifications, load information, and the functional subsystems: lateral systems, gravity systems, and transfer floor systems.

The following design information about a particular building design is stored as contents of a design case in CADSYN.

- *General description.* This includes building location, building type, building name, design construction date, occupancy category, wind exposure category, material, and total costs.
- *General geometric information.* This includes length, width, height, plan aspect ratio, height aspect ratio, overall shape, and gross floor area.
- *Other architectural specifications.* This includes the number of stories below and above grade, floor-to-floor height, floor-to-ceiling height, grid systems, number of architectural functions, and general description of their location in the plan.
- *Load information.* This includes dead load, live load, and wind load.
- *Lateral systems.* This includes the structural type of systems, the construction material and directions in which they are placed.
- *Gravity systems.* This includes types of floor systems, types of support systems and construction material of the support systems.

- *Transfer system.* This includes the structural details of transfer floors such as transfer type, material, crosssection, and so forth.
- *Beam information.* This includes the material and beam designation such as beam type, shape, width, and so forth.
- *Column information.* This includes material and column designation such as width, depth, and span.

Each design case is stored declaratively in a hierarchical structure where each node in the hierarchy is comprised of a label and a set of attribute-value pairs. The information recorded in a structural design case has three layers (Figure 7.10): problem specification as a global context, a grid representation for each geometric/functional use of the building, and descriptions of structural systems stored in a hierarchy of subcases as a design solution for each grid level. Each subcase describes the local context and the solution of a design (sub)system.

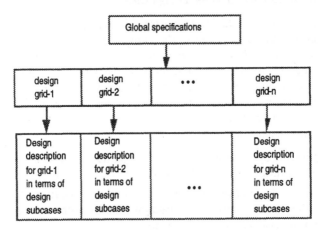

Figure 7.10. The layers of information in a structural design case.

CADSYN uses a feature-based indexing scheme. Structural design cases are indexed by a system list in terms of names of design subcases. The names of the subcases indicate their functionality. The system list in CADSYN consists of all structural (sub)system names used in the decomposition knowledge; for example, lateral-system, 2D-lateral-X-system, 2D-lateral-Y-system, gravity-system, transfer-system, core-system, and so forth. The system list provides pointers to all relevant design cases that contain the given subcase name.

3.2.2. Representation of Generalized Knowledge in CADSYN

The generalized knowledge of systems in CADSYN can be shown as a hierarchy. Figure 7.11 shows a hierarchy of (sub)systems used in CADSYN for the structural design of buildings. At the top level, the bldg-design system is broken into grid-systems based on the number of architectural functions of a building. Each grid-system is further decomposed into three subsystems: structural-system, core-system, and transfer-system. The structural-system leads the synthesis process to a further decomposition of the structural design solution.

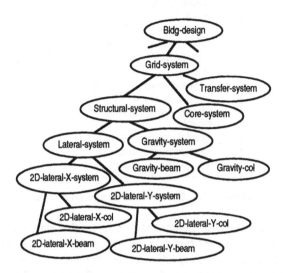

Figure 7.11. The hierarchy of structural (sub)systems in CADSYN.

The generalized knowledge describes how the design of a problem can be decomposed into the design of (sub)systems that are eventually represented by a set of relevant attributes and their alternative values. An attribute in a generalized system definition is described in terms of various items:

- name of the attribute that specifies the design feature of the system;
- identification of the attribute as a requirement specification or a descriptive feature of the solution;
- type of design method used to find the value for the attribute: either selection or procedure;
- a set of values or a procedural function corresponding to the design method; and
- name of the subsequent system if the attribute is specified as a subsystem.

Generalized knowledge as design constraints is used to identify inconsistencies in the potential design solution. Examples of design constraints are shown in Figure 7.12. Because attribute-value pairs are used to describe the design case, each constraint is expressed as a set of attribute-values pairs that indicate an invalid design when they occur together.

```
Constraint-1
    (bldg-type)  in  (hotel apartment)
    (gravity/floor-type)  = slab
Constraint-2
    (gravity/floor-type)  = flat-plate
    (gravity/action)   =  one-way
    (gravity/typical-span) <10 m
Constraint-3
    (gravity/floor-type) in (flat-plate slab)
    (gravity/typical-span) > 9 m
    (gravity/action)  =  two-way
Constraint4
    (gravity/support)  in (4-edges cols-only)
    (gravity/max-aspect-ratio) > 1.5
    (gravity/action)   =  two-way
```

Figure 7.12. Examples of design constraints.

For example, in Figure 7.12, Constraint-1 specifies that slab is not used as floor type in a hotel or apartment building, or, when the floor-type is slab and the building type is either hotel or apartment, then the design is invalid. Constraints 2, 3, and 4 indicate the conditions for when the flat-plate and flat-slab work as one-way or two-way floor systems.

3.3. CASE RETRIEVAL IN CADSYN

Case retrieval in CADSYN can be based on a set of specifications for an entire building or on the set of specifications for a specific structural (sub)system. If a relevant case is not found for the entire building or for a structural subsystem, the specifications are expanded into subproblems. When considering the entire building, the subproblems are defined as each of the grid specifications; for example, see Figure 7.13. When considering the specifications of a structural subsystem, the decomposition knowledge in the general knowledge-base is used to generate the specifications of the subproblems for the subsystem. Regardless of the level of abstraction of the design specifications, the specifications are represented as attribute-value pairs.

Case retrieval is achieved by finding cases or subcases in case memory that have one or more attribute-value pairs in common with the design specifications. A set of retrieved cases is presented to the user, who decides whether the cases are sufficiently close to the new design problem. If a case is selected, case adaptation begins. If a case is not selected, the new problem specifications are refined into a set of subsystem designs. Introducing the possibility of adaptation or refinement requires that the new problem context be represented and managed.

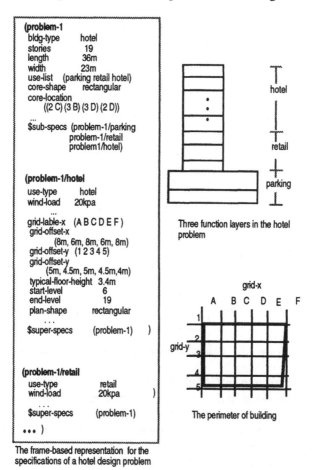

The frame-based representation for the specifications of a hotel design problem

Figure 7.13. Specifications for a hotel design.

The design context is a dynamic representation of the intermediate states of a design solution, as well as a complete solution to a given design problem. During problem solving, solutions to subproblems are generated by the adaptation of relevant (sub)cases or the synthesis of sets of design attributes and their values. These solutions are stored in a hierarchy in the design context. Once a subsolution is generated, it is attached to the set of specifications that were expanded into subproblems. Alternatively, the result of case adaptation can itself be a hierarchy of adapted subcases, where the solution to the design problem is a hierarchy.

Regardless of the level at which a case is retrieved and adapted, the resulting design solution is represented as a hierarchy of sets of attribute-value pairs.

3.4. DESIGN CASE ADAPTATION IN CADSYN

Design case adaptation in CADSYN is based on a propose-verify-modify cycle, as illustrated in Figure 7.14. The retrieved case or subcase is initially modified to match the attributes in the new design specifications. This modified case becomes the proposed design solution. The proposed design is verified and modified using a constraint satisfaction process.

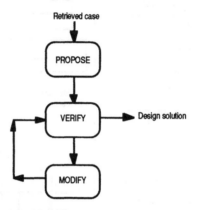

Figure 7.14. Case adaptation by propose-verify-modify.

Constraint satisfaction in CADSYN consists of six main steps as shown in Figure 7.15: checking and looking for constraint violations in the potential solution, finding design subsystems involved in the violated constraints, selecting one system to modify, generating all feasible combinations of values for the selected system, selecting a combination of values as a new description of the selected system, and propagating the effect of modifications by recomputing the associated procedures. The process iterates by identifying new constraint violations until all constraints are satisfied. The six basic tasks in the constraint satisfaction process are further described here.

Checking Constraints. The potential design that is produced, based on the structural adaptation of the retrieved (sub)case, provides an initial assignment for design attributes. The routine adaptation process then commences by comparing this assignment to the design constraints in the generalized knowledge. This process identifies the violated constraints and the attributes associated with the constraints. If no constraints are violated, the current assignment for design attributes is regarded as a feasible design solution, and adaptation is completed.

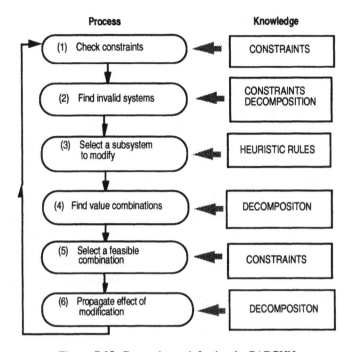

Figure 7.15. Constraint satisfaction in CADSYN.

Finding Invalid Systems. In order to repair constraint violations that have been detected, all adaptable systems related to those violations are listed. The attributes in a violated constraint are characterized as independent, which have discrete domains from which new values of attributes can be selected, or dependent, which have continuous domains. All systems corresponding to the independent design attributes in violated constraints are taken as invalid systems. For dependent attributes in violated constraints, the invalid systems are identified by the independent attributes associated with the dependent attributes. The systems corresponding to associated independent attributes with these dependent attributes are treated as invalid systems.

Selecting an Invalid System. After all invalid systems involved in constraint violations are identified, one system is selected for modification using a set of heuristic rules.

Finding Value Combinations. A value for an attribute can be determined from a discrete set of values or it can be computed using a procedure. The possible value combinations for the selected system are generated by assigning possible discrete attributes, then recomputing dependent attributes based on the value combinations of discrete attributes. All candidate value assignments are checked for local consistency. The constraints related to this system are regarded as local constraints. The result is a set of value combinations without local constraint violations. These value combinations are candidate descriptions of the selected system.

Selecting a Feasible Combination. Given a set of value combinations, one of them is identified as the new description of the selected invalid system. The determination of which value combination is used as a new system description is based on satisfaction of global constraints. The value combination that violates the least number of global constraints is regarded as a new design description.

Propagating the Effect of Modification. Repairing a constraint violation leads to a new value combination of a selected invalid system. As multiple systems are associated through constraints and dependent attributes, appropriate modification needs to be made concurrently on other systems associated with the selected system. This process propagates the effect of modification on the selected system to those relevant dependent attributes. To do so, all relevant attributes with continuous domains in the potential design description are updated by evaluating their corresponding procedures.

4. Comparing CASECAD and CADSYN

CASECAD and CADSYN were developed in parallel but with a different focus for each project. CASECAD focused on design case representation and the strategies for retrieval and selection, where CADSYN focused on design case adaptation. Each of the issues previously presented are considered here as the basis for reviewing the implementations of CASECAD and CADSYN.

4.1. ACQUISITION OF DESIGN CASES

Both CASECAD and CADSYN were implemented using project data from a collection of medium to high-rise buildings in Sydney. The design data for the building cases was collected through the cooperation of the engineers in Acer Wargon Chapman Associates. The engineers provided the CAD drawings and access to analysis results. The drawings included information about the design solution, but very little about the functional decomposition of the structural systems, and nothing about the original design specification. The analysis results provided some insight into the functional aggregation of structural components, but did not make this information explicit. Interviews with the engineers clarified the assumptions made about the intended function of the structural system and subsystems.

The acquisition of design cases occurred primarily through interviewing and handcrafting the representation of the design cases. The design drawings were not reused, they were redrawn. The design brief for the projects was not available so the intended function and behavior of the designs needed to be inferred through interviews. The decision variables for each design case had to developed specifically for CASECAD and CADSYN because the engineers did not understand their designs in terms of decision variables.

The case acquisition process was lengthy, approximately one year of one person's time, and produced a lot of data that was not used and did not produce some data that would have been useful. The implication of this experience is that case acquisition has proved to be as difficult as knowledge acquisition for an expert system. This is partly due to the lack of a formalism in describing conceptual design of structural systems and partly due to the lack of formalization in representing design project data.

The same cases were used for CASECAD and CADSYN. These cases lead to slightly different representations that do not contradict each other, but complement each other.

4.2. DEVELOPMENT OF A REPRESENTATION AND ORGANIZATION OF CASE MEMORY

The representation of case memory for CASECAD was more comprehensive than the representation in CADSYN. Because CASECAD was developed as an interactive case retrieval system, the representation included aspects of a design case that made the case understandable to the human designer. The use of text descriptions and graphical illustrations was necessary for browsing cases. Human designers do not easily comprehend a design by looking at a set of decision variables and their values. However, this information facilitated the indexing of cases and the modification of a set of design specifications. The decision variables were also useful to the designer in determining what features of the design could be changed as they made the variables in the design explicit.

The representation of design cases in CADSYN comprised decision variables only. This is due to the need to make explicit what can change in a design case during case adaptation. Regardless of whether all engineers would agree with our identification of the decision variables for the conceptual structural design of buildings, the important issue here is that the decision variables need to be made explicit before case adaptation can proceed.

Both CASECAD and CADSYN decomposed design memory into case memory and model-based memory. The generalized knowledge of models within the domain of the cases was needed in order to effectively organise case memory, to index and reason about case retrieval, and to adapt a design case with an understanding of the implications of the adaptation. In CASECAD, a hierarchy of design models represented through their FBS properties was sufficient. In CADSYN, in order to support design case adaptation, the additional knowledge of constraints was needed. The representation of constraints was considered as domain knowledge, rather than case-specific knowledge, primarily because many of the constraints in structural design can be generalized across several cases, and in fact are the result of the experience of several cases.

4.3. DEVELOPMENT OF AN INDEXING STRUCTURE FOR RECALLING DESIGN CASES

The indexing structure for recalling design cases was similar for both CASECAD and CADSYN, as both were based on a feature-based indexing system. Although CASECAD included drawings and text-based description of cases, these aspects of a case were recalled on the basis of their associated, explicitly defined features. The indexing structure in CASECAD was based on a mapping between the function, behavior, and structure labels to the feature labels on one level; and then a mapping from the feature labels to the cases/subcases that had those features at a second level. In effect, this allowed many paths to a case/subcase as well as provided an organization for the features used to describe a design.

The indexing structure in CADSYN is also a two-level structure. The first level of indices comprised the names of all the systems (or models) in the memory of CADSYN. The second level of indices comprised the name of all the features used to describe a particular case/subcase. The first level provided a pointer to all the cases that are instances of the model. The second level provided the basis for finding the instance that is most closely related to the new problem. Because CADSYN uses a functional decomposition of design cases and design models, the first level of indices provide a functional mapping from a design specification to a design case and assume the functional mapping is based on the primary function of the design case.

The effect of these different approaches to indexing cases is that CASECAD provided many paths to locating a design cases given a new design specification and CADSYN assumed that the specification would include the primary function of the design problem and therefore there was only one path to recalling a case. CASECAD allowed more flexible retrieval and CADSYN was more focused.

4.4. DEVELOPMENT AND IMPLEMENTATION OF STRATEGIES FOR RETRIEVAL OF DESIGN CASES

The development of strategies for flexible retrieval of design cases was important for CASECAD, but not for CADSYN. CASECAD provided a browsing environment so the retrieval strategies could be based on user interaction with the system, or directly supported in later implementations by iterative retrieval methods (Gomez de Silva Garza and Maher, 1996). The CASECAD system allowed the user to retrieve design cases based on one category of design specifications, required function, behavior, or structure; based on a combination of all categories; or could invoke the iterative retrieval methods that first retrieved relevant design models for situation assessment prior to case retrieval. The ability to model this in the implementation required a graphical user interface as well as formal methodologies for case retrieval. The result of implementing CASECAD was a better understanding of retrieval strategies for design case recall.

CADSYN assumed that the retrieved design case was sufficiently close to the new design specifications that a constraint-based approach to case adaptation would result in a feasible solution. Because of this assumption, flexible retrieval was not as important as defining a retrieval methodology based on a close match. CADSYN used a more conventional, weighted count of matching features for retrieval.

4.5. DEVELOPMENT OF A METRIC FOR SELECTING A DESIGN CASE

In CASECAD, the development of a metric for selecting a design case became a result of the retrieval process. A designer could choose among many metrics when retrieving cases or models from the memory representation. In fact, the metric became the focus of the search. Rather than assuming the metric can be inferred from the problem specifications, the metric was inferred from the result of case/model retrieval.

In CADSYN, the metric for selecting a case was based on a weighted count of the features in the design specifications. The closest match was assumed to be the best match, as it implied that fewer changes would be made to make the design case feasible in the new design context.

4.6. FORMALIZATION OF DESIGN CASE ADAPTATION

The formalization of design case adaptation depends on the intended use of the case-based design system. For example, in CASECAD, design case adaptation was not formalized at all even though it was supported; in CADSYN, design case adaptation was formalized to the point that the user interacted with the adaptation process by responding to suggestions made by the CADSYN system. CASECAD supported design case adaptation by providing the user with the design drawings in an environment in which they could be modified, by identifying the decision variables and their alternative values in an environment in which they could be edited, and by providing a mechanism for integrating the adapted design case as a new case in case memory. The entire adaptation process was directed and determined by the user but supported by the interface to CASECAD. The idea of a CBM made adaptation and integration possible. However, the modified case was not verified as a feasible case by CASECAD; it was assumed that the human designer would verify the result.

In CADSYN, the formalization of design case adaptation was essential. The development of an adaptation process required a formalization of the transition from a case representation to the representation of a proposed design solution, a formalization of the process in which the proposed design solution was verified, and a formal methodology for modifying a proposed solution that was not valid. This formalization in CADSYN is based on the propose-verify-modify cycle of case adaptation, and uses a constraint satisfaction approach to the verify-modify cycles. Through such a formalization, automated design case adaptation becomes possible in domains where the design constraints can be explicitly represented in terms of the design decision variables.

4.7. REPRESENTATION OF KNOWLEDGE TO SUPPORT DESIGN CASE ADAPTATION

Design case adaptation can be performed in an environment that provides feedback to the designer as he adapts the design case, or can be performed by the case-based reasoner. The representation of knowledge to support adaptation depends on whether it is done by the designer or the system. In CASECAD, adaptation is done by the designer. The knowledge available to support adaptation included model memory and the graphical representations of the design case. In CADSYN, adaptation is done by the system. The knowledge needed to support adaptation included the generalized system definitions to provide the domain of potential values for the attributes in the case and the generalized constraints to identify which aspects of the design case needed to be changed.

4.8. MODEL FOR VERIFYING THE RESULTS OF DESIGN CASE ADAPTATION

Verifying the results of design case adaptation is not trivial. A CBR system can provide constraints or heuristics that can partially verify the results, but, ultimately, other resources are needed for complete verification. In other words, the case-based reasoner does not necessarily have a complete model for verification. In CASECAD, there was no knowledge for verifying the results of adaptation. Adaptation is designer-centred, and the designer would identify the resources needed for verification. In CADSYN, constraints are used to verify adaptation. This constraint approach is convenient in a CBR system because it can be incorporated with the case representation by using a common set of variables to make design decisions. However, there is a need to link CBR with more complex models of the behavior of designs in order to fully verify the results of case adaptation.

5. Conclusions

Case-based design systems are implemented based on a complex convergence of design case data, generalized knowledge of the domain of the cases, and a set of CBR algorithms and techniques. The development of case-based design systems requires experience in developing such systems. This chapter reports on the experiences of CASECAD and CADSYN as a resource for identifying the relevant issues and their resolution. As shown in this chapter, the implementation of case-based design will vary from domain to domain and will be based on the focus of the resulting system and how it intends to support the designer.

Acknowledgments

The author acknowledges the contributions of the research group at the Key Centre of Design Computing, specifically, the contributions of Dong Mei Zhang, Bala Balachandran, Rita Villamayor, Stone Wang, and Andres Gomez de Silva Garza for their respective roles in implementing CASECAD, CADSYN, and their descendants. This project was supported by a grant from the Australian Research Council and the University of Sydney Overseas Postgraduate Research Awards.

References

Gero, J. S.: 1990, Design prototypes: A knowledge representation schema for design, *AI Magazine*, 11(4), 26–36.

Gomez de Silva Garza, A., and Maher, M. L.: 1996, Design by interactive exploration using memory-based techniques, *Knowledge-Based Systems*, 9(1), 151–161.

Kolodner, J. L.: 1993, *Case-Based Reasoning*, Kaufmann, Los Altos.

Maher, M. L.: 1987, Engineering design synthesis: A domain independent representation, *Artificial Intelligence for Engineering Design, Analysis, and Manufacturing*, 1(3), 207–213.

Maher, M. L., and Balachandran, B.: 1994, Multimedia approach to case-based structural design, *Journal of Computing in Civil Engineering*, 8(3), 359–376.

Maher, M. L., and Balachandran, B.: 1994, Flexible retrieval strategies for case-based design, *in* J. S. Gero and F. Sudweeks (eds), *Artificial Intelligence in Design '94*, Kluwer Academic, Dordrecht, NL, pp. 163–180.

Maher, M. L, Balachandran, B., and Zhang, D. M.: 1995, *Case Based Reasoning in Design*, Lawrence Erlbaum Associates, Hillsdale, NJ.

Maher, M. L., and Zhang, D. M.: 1993, CADSYN: A case-based design process model, *Artificial Intelligence for Engineering Design, Analysis, and Manufacturing*, 7(2), 97–110.

chapter eight

REPRESENTATION AND SYNTHESIS OF NON-MONOTONIC MECHANICAL DEVICES

S. NARASIMHAN
Lockheed AI center

KATIA P. SYCARA, D. NAVIN-CHANDRA
Carnegie Mellon University

This chapter describes an approach for behavorial synthesis of devices with dynamic behavior. The aim is to develop a computational mechanism that, given the behavior specification of the inputs and outputs of a dynamic device, will synthesize the device from a case library of previous designs. The behavior of a device is described by the observable parameters of the device and its components. The components in a library encapsulate fundamental device behaviors in terms of relevant parameters. There is no reference to the physical embodiment of these components. The result of the synthesis procedure is a behavorial layout diagram of the device identifying its inputs, outputs, the components, and the connections between the components. The device model refines and extends our influence graph-based device representation that was developed as part of the CADET project.

1. Introduction

Research in developing models for design computation has primarily focused on providing tools for analysis of designed artifacts and their computerized representation as solid models. This chapter describes an approach for behavioral synthesis of devices with dynamic behavior. The aim is to develop a computational mechanism that, given the behavior specification of the inputs and outputs of a dynamic device, will synthesize the device from a case library of previous designs. The behavior of a device is described by observable qualitative variables of the device and its components. The components in a library encapsulate fundamental device behaviors in terms of relevant device variables. There is no reference to the physical embodiment of these components. The result of the synthesis procedure is a behavioral layout diagram of the device identifying its inputs, outputs, the components, and the connections between the components.

Influence graphs, confluences, and other behavioral representations have primarily focused on the steady-state continuous behavior regions. Thus, using those representations, it is difficult to reason about state transitions and to analyze the effects of transitions in coupled-device models. The implemented device model refines and extends our influence graph-based device representation that was developed as part of the CADET project and enables representation and reasoning about multiple device states and state transitions. The multistate device representation language is Influence State Diagrams (ISDs). Using ISDs, we have been able to represent 80% of the devices in the six volumes of Artobolevsky (1979) (approximately 3800 devices). The extended representation and generalized index transformation algorithms allow CADET to expand the complexity of devices it can design. Currently, the system can perform conceptual design of mechanical devices that exhibit continuous, reciprocating, intermittent, and feedback behavior.

The system uses behavior-preserving transformation techniques to transform an abstract description of the desired behavior of the device into a description that can be used to find relevant designs in memory. This approach, in effect, decomposes given behavior specifications into sub-behaviors, making it possible to recognize parts of previous designs that can be synthesized to form a new device. The synthesis process proceeds through alternate steps of elaboration and retrieval of devices and device pieces from the case library. During the elaboration and retrieval process, the sequence of feasible connections between the components is also synthesized. Thus, the synthesis process generates a feasible behavioral layout diagram consisting of the components and respective couplings.

CBR is the problem-solving paradigm in which previous experiences are used to guide problem-solving (Carbonell, 1986; Hammond 1986; Simpson, 1985; Sycara, 1987). Cases similar to the current problem are retrieved from memory; the best case is selected from those retrieved and compared to the current problem. The retrieved case is adapted to fit the current problem context based on identified differences between the current problem and the retrieved case. Successful cases are stored so that they can be reused in the future. Failed cases are also stored so that they can warn the problem solver about potential pitfalls in the solution steps. Once the problem is solved, the case base is updated with the new experience and, thus, integrates learning in the problem solving process.

CBR is an appropriate problem-solving paradigm for conceptual mechanical design for several reasons. First, human designers rarely design from scratch. To solve a new design problem, they use components and assemblies from previous designs. Second, previous successful designs already contain efficient subassemblies that can be directly used in the current design without further optimization procedures. Third, because the conceptual design domain is an ill-structured domain, it is almost impossible to arrive at a set of prescriptive rules that can automatically generate the required design. Under such a situation in which a domain model is not available, past designs can aid in the design of the new artifact. Fourth, previous designs are more readily available in design catalogs and records in the industry than domain rules. Fifth, cases can be elicited from their sources independent of the underlying representations in the case base and can be potentially used for different domain viewpoints such as manufacturing, scheduling, and so forth. Hence, cases can serve as a central representation of the design in a concurrent engineering framework.

Motivated by the above mentioned considerations, we have developed a case-based computational model for conceptual design and have implemented it in the CADET (CAse-based DEsign Tool) system. In CADET, previous designs are stored as cases in a library called the case base. A set of relevant cases and their parts are retrieved from this case base and are synthesized together to generate solution alternatives for the current design problem. Relevant design cases are retrieved based on the match between their function (and behavior) and the index for case retrieval; the index being the required function or subfunction of the artifact to be designed. If there are no cases in the case base that match on the index, the index is subjected to transformation to generate a new index that can potentially retrieve a case. We have also developed a qualitative representation of function and behavior of engineering artifacts that we use in the index and case representation. In Sycara and Navin-Chandra (1991b), we described this representation (called the Influence Graphs) and showed how they can be used in generating conceptual design alternatives for devices that possess continuous and monotonic behavior.

In this chapter, our focus is a more generalized representation called the ISD that can represent the discontinuous and non-monotonic function and behaviors in cases. We also describe appropriate index transformation rules and case retrieval for these ISDs and illustrate the approach with a design example. Although we have emphasized on mechanical design as the domain of application in this chapter, the case-based computational model is applicable to other design domains as well.

2. Related Work

A variety of CBR techniques for case representation and reasoning in design have been suggested in the literature: Causal representation of prior design problems and solutions in the architecture domain was used in the CYCLOPS system (Navin-Chandra, 1988). Such causal networks have also been used in the medical domain (Koton, 1988). In the meal planning/design domain, JULIA (Hinrichs, 1992) uses plans and subplans represented as frames with slots for the different courses of the meal. In the engineering design domain, deep models have been used successfully. We will discuss and compare five systems: architectural design systems STRUPLE (Maher and Zhao, 1987) and ARCHIE (Domeshek and Kolodner, 1992); motion synthesis by connecting the inputs and outputs of primitive mechanisms; Ibis, a system that connects a given set of primitives to satisfy a given goal (Ibis goes beyond motion synthesis by including functional parameters such as pressures and flow rates); and the behavioral component-substance based modeling and reasoning in KRITIK.

In STRUPLE, experience is stored in the form of descriptions of building design solutions (Maher and Zhao, 1987). Matching is done using a similarity metric that compares significant common aspects of the matched buildings and the current building. A matching criteria is a requirement of similarity imposed on a feature of a matching building; for example, the number of stories, the intended use, the design wind load, and so forth. Each matching building is ranked to measure how well it resembles the current building according to both required and desired criteria. The method is similar to measuring the relative error of two function values. STRUPLE's similarity metric is based on a fixed set of criteria that does not consider the rationale involved in the decision process. Because it involves only specific domain features, STRUPLE's index mechanism is unable to find analogies across domains.

The ARCHIE system is an architectural design system for office buildings (Domeshek and Kolodner, 1992). It also uses a flat, frame-based representation of cases (there is no deep reasoning about shape and form). ARCHIE's contribution lies in its use of qualitative domain models for retrieving cases. For example, it has a model of how various features of an office space (e.g., wall color, lighting quality) affect the lighting quality of the built environment. Such a model can be used to evaluate a design concept and to retrieve all prior cases where a similar problem was encountered. This idea is similar to how causal models were used in the CYCLOPS system that retrieved cases to debug landscape architectural layouts. For example, a noise problem may be fixed by using trees or barriers from a prior case. CYCLOPS, however, used adhoc models for each case. ARCHIE, on the other hand, is able to work with several domain models. This makes the approach more general.

Mechanical designs can be viewed as being synthesized from conceptual building blocks that perform specific kinematic functions (Kota, 1990). The motion synthesis approach provides a method for recognizing a given behavior in terms of known primitive behaviors. This is one of the first formalized ways of viewing design as the synthesis of kinematic processes; however, the approach is limited to a fixed set of primitives. CADET, on the other hand, is able to reach into a large case base and select pieces of cases dynamically. The notion of synthesizing devices from known components is extended beyond basic kinematics in the Ibis system (Williams, 1989, 1990). In Ibis, components are represented as sets of interactions among behavioral parameters of the component. This approach allows one to use any aspect of a behavior, not restricting behavior descriptions to just one domain (e.g., qualitative motion synthesis). Ibis' major drawback is that its problem-solving ability depends on the syntactic form of the goal. Because the program suffers from a functional fixedness (Dunker, 1945; Maier, 1931), it cannot recognize behavioral equivalence between a given index and a case if they are not syntactically similar. CADET's transformation-based approach, on the other hand, adequately addresses this problem. If CADET cannot find a direct equivalence, it looks for behavioral similarities. Through the process of influence hypothesis and matching, the system is able to use physical laws and principles embedded in prior design cases to achieve its current goals. In this way, CADET is opportunistic about the principles it exploits in a design. This is unlike other approaches that assume that all the relevant principles have been identified *a priori*, as in the Ibis system. Because CADET hypothesizes influences, it does not limit itself to the given knowledge. Consequently, it can generate elaborations that represent designs that have never been conceived of before. Further, CADET's ability to recognize behavioral equivalences reduce its sensitivity to the form of the problem description.

KRITIK is another deep-model-based design system (Goel, 1989). It uses a component-substance model that captures the components (e.g., battery, pipe), substances (e.g., water, electricity) and relations (e.g., containment, connection). Behaviors of such systems are represented as graphs of states and transitions. When the system is given a design task, it retrieves the best case and deduces modifications that can be made. Modifications involve changes in relations, substitution of substances, parametric changes of components, and so forth. The CADET approach is quite different. We use a representation that has no structure in the behavior description. This allows us to transform behavior descriptions in a principled way. We believe that the space of elaboration of behaviors is complete (proving this is a whole dissertation in itself.) Another advantage of not committing to structure is CADET's ability to mix, match, and reuse the whole and parts of many prior cases to solve a given problem. The use of multiple cases has been shown to be important in advanced CBR systems (Redmond, 1990).

Before we describe our case-based computational model, we briefly discuss the domain of application of the model—conceptual mechanical design—in the next section.

3. Conceptual Mechanical Design

Figure 8.1 shows various phases and the information flow in the mechanical design process. The design process starts with the identification of the need for an artifact. In this phase, the overall use of the artifact is identified; the operating conditions and the environment are determined, and the user-artifact interaction is specified. At the end of this phase, the designer has a rough and qualitative description of what the artifact is intended to do.

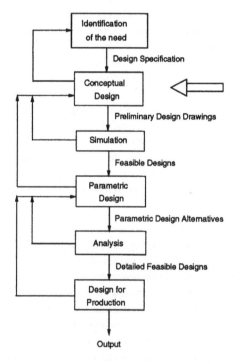

Figure 8.1. Mechanical design phases.

In the conceptual design phase, the designer starts from the identified need and the function of the required artifact and comes up with, possibly, a set of feasible design alternatives in terms of rough design sketches of the product. In the first simulation phase, the preliminary design sketches are checked for whether they can be physically realizable and whether they will work in reality as they were intended to. At the end of this phase, a set of feasible design alternatives is generated. In the parametric design phase, decisions regarding the physical dimensions of the artifact and its components are taken. In addition, initial design specification is also refined (made more specific). In the analysis stage, the parametric designs are analyzed using various engineering analysis programs (such as ANSYS) to verify whether the design satisfies the specified constraints in the refined design specifications. Finally, in the design for production phase, decisions on various manufacturing-related design parameters such as surface finish and tolerance are taken.

The conceptual design phase described can be further subdivided into the following four tasks:

- Concept generation
- Schematic synthesis
- Configuration design
- Shape design

In the concept generation phase, the designer brainstorms and comes up with different concepts that use various physical laws to achieve the given need. For instance, given that the need is to transport water, the designer comes up with different concepts such as the principle of liquid flow, the evaporation-condensation cycle, and transportation of water in storage tanks. In schematic synthesis, the designer generates a set of satisficing design alternatives in terms of schematic diagrams from a given concept generated during the concept-generation phase. Schematic diagrams identify various components in the design and their connectivity (topology). For example, given the concept of the principle of liquid flow, the designer comes up with various pipelines and valves for flow control. Configuration design refers to the process of generating various possible configurations; that is, spatial position and orientation of the components, given the schematic diagram of the design. Shape design deals with the creation and modification of component shapes based on design and assembly requirements.

The case-based computational model that we describe in this chapter is for the second stage of the conceptual design process; that is, schematic synthesis. The goal of the system is to generate feasible design alternatives in terms of schematic diagrams of the artifact given a qualitative description of its function. In the next section, we describe this model in more detail.

4. The Case-based Model in CADET

The case-based model used in CADET is given in Figure 8.2. The part of the model indicated in broken lines represents the traditional case-based model used in other systems.

Our model works as follows: Indices for case retrieval are generated from the input design specifications. Case retrieval is then attempted with these indices. If any case that exactly matches on the index already exists in the case base, it is directly retrieved. If not, the indices are subjected to an index transformation step. This index transformation step is behavior-preserving in that the overall specified function and behavior are left unchanged. The transformed index is then used to retrieve new cases from the case base. The index transformation step is performed as many times as specified by the system user (designer). The designer is also allowed to intervene to suggest a better case, if any. The retrieved cases, each of which may match only a part of the index, are synthesized together to result in the set of design solutions. Here we describe the solution steps in more detail:

Step 1. Problem Specifications (Input). The input to the system is the design specification that consists of a qualitative description of the required function of the device, the physical laws utilized by the concept (from the concept generation phase of the design process) and any constraints on the function. The specification language used is in terms of the Influence graphs and ISD, described later in this chapter.

Step 2. Case Retrieval. Cases are retrieved from the case base with the required behavior of the device as the index. The specified function of the device can be converted to a behavior specification by combining the function with the specified physical laws. The index representation being essentially a graph (described in the next section) with labeled edges, cases that match subgraphs of this graph are retrieved and synthesized together. Matching involves a direct literal matching of the nodes of the graph and the arc labels in the index and that of the function of a case in the case base.

Step 3. Index Transformation. Index transformation refers to the process of transforming the index according to certain rules if the original index fails to retrieve any case. In a traditional CBR approach, if an index fails to retrieve an exact matching case, a set of closest matching cases are retrieved and adapted for the new problem. Because it is difficult to define a suitable metric for the closeness of an index match in engineering design, index transformation offers an alternate and useful approach. Also, as done in other CBR systems, using a predefined set of indices is limiting in the domain of mechanical design because there is no one-to-one correspondence between the specified function and structure.

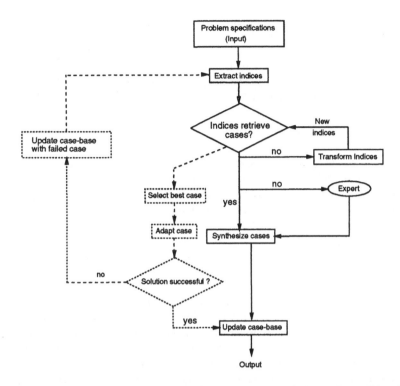

Figure 8.2. Case-based design process model (dotted lines indicate the traditional CBR model).

The index transformation technique that is dealt with in this chapter elaborates (expands) the index. The index transformation is preservative; that is, the transformed index is guaranteed to be equivalent to the original index. Preservative index transformation, followed by an exact matching of the index with features of a relevant case, eliminates the need to include a verification step of the resulting schematic diagram of the device. The elimination of the verification step is beneficial because its complexity has been reported as NP hard and incomplete even at the conceptual design phase (Williams, 1989).

Step 4. Synthesizing Cases. Because we view the schematic synthesis process as synthesizing components from previous cases, case retrieval is followed by synthesis instead of adaptation that occurs in the traditional CBR paradigm (Navin-Chandra, 1991a). Synthesis itself can, however, necessitate configuration and routine design decisions i.e., adaptation at a parametric level.

Step 5. Updating Case Base. Once the design has been successfully completed, the design is stored in the case base as a network of cases that were retrieved from the case base for the new problem. This network of cases is same as the schematic graph of the device.

In the model described, index transformation and case retrieval are the critical steps in the solution process. The next section describes the representation that we use for indexing and retrieval.

5. Case Index Representation

Because the main characteristic of an engineering artifact is its function (and behavior), the primary index for case retrieval is also the function of the device. Before developing a convenient representation for function and behavior of engineering artifacts, it is necessary to have clear definitions for them. In the next few subsections, we describe our notion of function and behavior and their interrelationship.

5.1. FUNCTION

The notion of function and behavior of engineering artifacts is also an issue of focus in design theory. Gero (1990b) defined the function of an engineering artifact as the use or purpose to which it can be put to, and distinguishes between intended function and unintended function. Intended function refers to the use that the designer intended the device to be used for whereas other uses are called unintended function. A common, agreed notion of function and behavior is still lacking and ranges from mathematical models at one end of the spectrum to something related to profit loss and teleology at the other (Hodges, 1992).

Following the popular Lagrangian view of the world as consisting of system and surrounding with a distinct boundary, we consider an engineering artifact as a system with a well-defined system boundary. Such an artifact does not function in isolation. It interacts with other physical systems in its surrounding to provide its function. In some cases, the interaction is due to a change in a property of the system. For example, the knob of a tap (system) moves (change in the property of knob position) and interacts with the flowing water to provide its function. In other cases, the mere existence of a property can give rise to an interaction. For example, a person enjoying a painting (due to its aesthetic property) results in the aesthetic function of the painting. These considerations lead to this definition:

Definition 1: The function of any physical system is defined as the description of its interaction with the surroundings assuming that the system has a well-defined system boundary.

The surrounding may consist of many systems (called surrounding systems) and the given system may interact with more than one surrounding system. Often only some of these interactions are of interest. We call such interactions the intended function whereas the other interactions between the system and the surrounding systems are the side effects (see Figure 8.3).

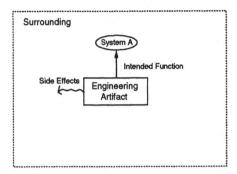

Figure 8.3. Artifact-surrounding interaction.

5.2. BEHAVIOR

The function of a physical system arises from the existence of some properties or the changes occurring in them. As illustrated, the artistic function of a painting results from its aesthetic property. Similarly, the changing colors of a red-amber-green traffic light enables its function to regulate traffic. Whenever a change in a set of properties of a physical system allows it to deliver a specific function, the system is said to possess a behavior. Because, strictly speaking, given an infinite time period, all systems change, one has to associate a convenient time frame for describing behavior. To illustrate, a rock that weathers with time may not be considered as possessing a behavior although its dimensions may change with time. Similarly, an object may have been moving sometime in the past but may be static in the given time frame and thus is not considered to possess a behavior.

Definition 2: Given a time frame, the behavior of any physical system is defined as a description of the change in a set of properties of the system with respect to time.

Functioning systems possess two basic kinds of behavior—behaviors that provide the intended function, and other incidental behaviors. The former can be called the dominant behavior and the latter can be called the dormant behaviors. Dormant behaviors do not participate in providing the intended function. From a design perspective, it is beneficial to suppress the dormant behaviors in a system so as to maximize the utilization of input energy. However, in practice, it is not always possible to suppress the dormant behaviors. This gives rise to side effects in the system. For example, a dominant behavior of the wheel in a slider-crank is its rotary motion. One of the side effects is its inertia. Because inertia cannot be removed from the system, often it is utilized to provide other functionalities such as energy storage thereby making it a dominant behavior. Thus, a good design will minimize the number of dormant behaviors in a system by either suppressing them or by making them a dominant behavior.

A complete behavior model of a physical system will include both the dominant behavior and the dormant behavior descriptions. Both the dominant and dormant behaviors can be expressed at different levels of abstraction—from a microscopic level to a system level. For our purposes, it is enough to describe them such that they are significant. To illustrate, the molecular motions in the rotating wheel are insignificant behaviors. Besides this, certain dormant behaviors themselves may be insignificant; that is, ignorable. In the rotary wheel example, rotary motion and inertia are significant behaviors whereas its heat dissipation (arising due to friction) may be an insignificant behavior.

To summarize, we have introduced three concepts on behavior here:
- Dominant Behavior (participate in delivering function)
- Dormant Behavior (suppressed behaviors but significant otherwise)
- Insignificant Behaviors

The distinction can be done easily by treating dominant behaviors as intended behaviors, dormant behaviors as side effects and insignificant behaviors as ignorable behaviors.

For example, in civil engineering domain, the changes in the lengths of each member of a truss are dominant behaviors, the rotation in each member due to end moments are dormant behaviors (made dormant using pin joints), and the stress variation across the cross-section of individual members are treated as insignificant behaviors during truss analysis.

As another example, in electrical circuits, the changes in voltages and currents may be dominant behaviors, the heat and other fields generated may be dormant behaviors whereas the changes in the dimension of a resistor, for example, are insignificant behavior.

5.3. FUNCTION-BEHAVIOR RELATION

Because function is a system-surrounding interaction and behavior is intrinsic to the system, there is no one-to-one correspondence between the behavior of a system and its function. The intended function for a given behavior depends on the surrounding conditions. For example, although a pump and a turbine may behave in the same manner (i.e., rotation of the blades) they serve different functions—to pump water with electricity input and to generate electricity with water flow input respectively. In the case of the pump, the static water in a reservoir is the intended surrounding system whereas in the case of the turbine, the flowing water (a river, for example) is the intended surrounding system.

Because function interaction occurs across the system boundary (which is arbitrary in the Lagrangian view) and the behavior interaction occurs at the subsystem level, it is possible to choose a system boundary such that the behavior under one system boundary appears as the function under another system boundary. In other words, function and behavior differ only at the level of abstraction of the system definition.

5.4. REQUIREMENTS ON THE REPRESENTATION

The index representation; that is, that of function and behavior, should be general enough that a wide variety of device behaviors can be represented. The representation should be explicit in that one should not have to derive the behavior from the representation. Differential equations is an example of an implicit representation. Design reasoning occurs at the functional, behavioral, and physical levels. Deriving behavior from implicit representations is not only time consuming, but also is not possible in some cases due to the resulting ambiguities in the interpretation of the simulation results (DeKleer and Brown, 1984). Because only qualitative information is available at the conceptual design stage, the representation should be qualitative in nature. Furthermore, the qualitative representation should be based on sound theoretical framework that allows for derivable assertions. Because devices and processes coexist, a canonical representation for both is preferred. In addition, as illustrated by the example comparing a water pump and a turbine given earlier, the direction of interaction is an important aspect of function. In the former, the pump moves the water and in the latter, the water moves the turbine blades. Hence any representation of function should include a direction of interaction between the system and its surrounding.

To describe the scope of the representation, we classify the mechanical devices into four broad categories based on the way they behave:

- Monotonic devices
- Reciprocating devices
- Intermittent devices
- Feedback devices

Monotonic devices are those that exhibit a strictly monotonic behavior; that is, the output function is monotonic with respect to the input. Examples of monotonic devices are a household water tap, a household warm water faucet, pumps, and so forth. In nonmonotonic devices (often called reciprocating devices), the output function is nonmonotonic with respect to the input. Examples of reciprocating devices are slider-crank mechanism, cam and follower, and so forth. In intermittent devices, there is a time lag between the input and the output. Examples are intermittent clocks, pawl and ratchet mechanism, and so forth. In feedback devices (that are in dynamic equilibrium), causality between the input and output is time varying. Examples are automatic flush-tanks, automatic pressure regulators, liquid level maintainers, and so forth.

In the next section we describe influence graphs, our representation for continuous device behaviors and in the following sections generalize it for other kinds of behaviors.

6. Influence Graphs

If A is the functioning system and is interacting with another system B, then the function (by *function* we mean intended function) of system A can be represented by the simple directed graph $A \rightarrow B$ where A and B are the descriptions of the system or its behavior. Because a changing system possesses changing subsystems, this representation can be recursively applied to represent the behavior of the system; that is, both A and B can be directed graphs with nodes as the changing system variables that characterize the system.

In general, the function and, hence, the behavior of any system can be represented as a directed graph with nodes as the state variables and the edges as the direction of interaction.

If the system state variables are quantifiable, the system function can be represented as an influence graph. An influence graph represents the interaction between two or more state variables as one causing the other to either increase (+), decrease (–), or remain constant. For instance, if state variable y increases with x, it is represented as the influence $x - [+] \rightarrow y$. We call the qualitative values +, –, 0. In this context, the influence values.

Definition 3: Influence graphs are directed graphs without loops where the nodes are the changing system variables, the directed edges indicate influence direction and variable dependence, and edge labels represent the kind of dependency.

From a qualitative reasoning perspective, we define an influence graph as the qualitative operation on the first order differential of a dependent variable with respect to an independent variable. Thus, the influence graph $x - [+] \rightarrow y$ represents:

$$[dy/dx] = [+]$$

where [.] is the qualitative operator (DeKleer and Brown, 1984).

The behavior of a simple valve shown in Figure 8.4 can be represented as the influence graph:

$$\theta - [+] \rightarrow Y - [+] \rightarrow A$$

where θ is the input rotary signal, Y is the Cartesian y-coordinate of the plunger and A is the area available for flow. Similarly, the function of the valve—control of flow rate Q (interaction between the valve and the flowing process)—can be represented as the influence graph:

$$\theta - [+] \rightarrow Y - [+] \rightarrow A - [+] \rightarrow Q$$

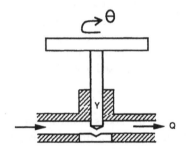

Figure 8.4. A simple valve.

Influence graphs possess some properties based on whether they can be subjected to many graph theoretic operations. These graph theoretic operations are based on a qualitative calculus and can be used to generate new expanded influence graphs (and hence new indices) that are behaviorally equivalent to the original influence graph. We have described these index transformation rules in other papers (Navin-Chandra et al., 1991a, 1991b). In this chapter, we extend the influence graph representation to general device behaviors in terms of ISD and describe the index transformation rules for these ISDs.

7. ISD–Representing General Device Behaviors Explicitly

Influences (or influence graphs) can be used to represent only the monotonic behavior of devices and processes at a qualitative level. However, system (devices and processes) behavior is often nonmonotonic in nature. Moreover, causal directions in the functioning system could potentially change with time, or new active parts of the system could be introduced with time. For example, consider the behavior of a see-saw shown in Figure 8.8. The left end and the right end displacements of the see-saw serve as inputs alternatively; that is, the influence direction changes alternatively between right to left and left to right. Such behaviors cannot be explicitly represented using one influence graph alone. Similarly, processes like the boiling process where the system attains a new phase and devices with feedback cannot be represented conveniently using unchanging influence graphs. In the following, we describe the ISD (distinct from the influence diagrams of Agogino and Almgren, (1987) as a canonical and explicit representation for the system behavior that allows us to model the changes occurring in a set of influence graphs.

7.1. ELEMENTS OF ISD

An ISD is a directed network with nodes representing influence states and the directed arcs representing the influence state transitions. The ISD is an explicit representation in that no further processing is required to realize the behavior or function of the artifact. The ISD diagram represents a specific instance of the system behavior and is not its complete behavior model. Thus, the qualitative values of the system variables are fixed in an ISD.

7.1.1. Influence States

System behavior states form the nodes in the ISD and represent the monotonic behavior of the system occurring in a finite interval of time. Each node in the ISD could potentially include multiple influence graphs, each representing the monotonic behavior of different parts of the system occurring in parallel. Each influence state also has associated state constraints that have to be true for the state to occur in the behavior of the system. These constraints are of the same form as the state transition label (discussed in the next subsection). In each state of the ISD, the set of dominant input and output parameters are identified explicitly.

7.1.2. Influence State Transitions

Arcs of the ISD are directed and represent the influence state transitions. State transitions are considered instantaneous (or spontaneous). Transition conditions are represented as edge labels. They consist of a set of ordered triplets of the form parameter, operator, value or parameter, operator, predicate where parameter is a quantifiable system parameter , operator is one of =, >, <, >=, <=, and value is a qualitative value (a landmark value). Valid predicates are maximum-value-of(variable), minimum-value-of(variable) and nth-landmark-value-of(variable, n).

7.2. ISD—EXAMPLES

Using the ISD representation, we have been able to represent the qualitative behavior of 80% of the devices (approximately 3,800 devices) given in Artobolevsky (1979) . Following are some examples that illustrate the use of ISD in representing system behavior and function.

A slider-crank is a simple reciprocating device as shown in Figure 8.5a. As the crank continues to rotate, the slider executes a to-and-fro motion along the x-axis. Its behavior can be represented in an ISD as shown in Figure 8.5b (t denotes time). Time has the unique property of ever-increasing and positive and hence can be used to unambiguously represent the direction of change of the independent variable. In the first state, as the crank rotates, Theta increases with time and X, the x-coordinate of the slider (its distance from the center of the crank wheel) increases while Y-coordinate remains constant. In the second state as Theta continues to increase with time, X decreases while Y-coordinate remains constant again. Thus, between the two states there is only a reversal of influence sign.

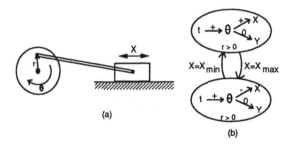

Figure 8.5. Slider-crank: A simple reciprocating device.

For the slider crank, the transition variable is the x-coordinate; that is, when X reaches X_{max} or X_{min}, the slider reverses its direction of motion.

An intermittent cam mechanism (Artobolevsky, 1979), the second example, is shown in Figure 8.6a. In the figure, the cam A is continuously rotated by the drive shaft a. When the cam tooth is in contact with pin 1 on disk B, there is a rotary output at the shaft b on which disk B is mounted. When the cam has rotated through π radians, the eccentricity between the shafts a and b causes the cam to disengage from the disk B. After the cam has rotated through 2π radians, it comes in contact with the pin 2 on the disk and rotates it again. Thus, there is an intermittent rotary output at the shaft b. This behavior can be represented as the ISD given in Figure 8.6b. The time-graph representation for the behavior is depicted in Figure 8.6c.

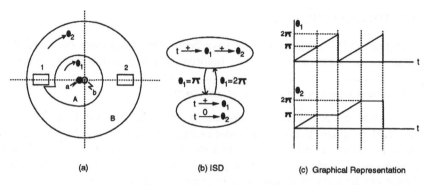

Figure 8.6. Intermittent cam mechanism.

In our third example, when water in a container is heated, the water temperature continues to increase until boiling point is reached. At the boiling point, there is a change of state from liquid to gas. Assuming an instantaneous state transition, the state diagram for the process is given in Figure 8.7.

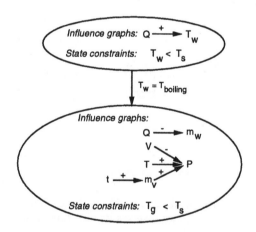

Figure 8.7. Influence state diagram for the boiling process.

State 1: The following relations hold:

$$Q = kA (T_s - T_w) \quad \text{with} \quad T_w < T_{boiling}$$

In this state, the water in the container behaves as a substance absorbing heat from the heat source. Q is the heat-flow rate, k the thermal conductivity, A is the heat flow area, and T_s, T_w are the source temperature and water temperature respectively.

State 2: The following relations hold:

$$Q = ml$$
$$PV = MrT$$

In this state water exists in two phases: liquid and vapor. Relation 1 holds for the liquid phase and relation 2 (assuming that the vapor behaves as an ideal gas) holds for the vapor phase. Note that in the second state, a new influence graph is introduced.

Consider a simple see-saw for our next example. The behavior of the see-saw can be represented as the ISD given in Figure 8.8. In the first state, Y_1 increases with time corresponding to the upward motion of the right-hand side of the seesaw. This upward motion causes the left-hand side to go down and, hence, Y_2 decreases. In the second state, Y_2 increases with time corresponding to the upward motion of the left-hand side of the seesaw. This causes the right-hand side to go down; that is, Y_1 decreases. The state transitions occur when Y_1 or Y_2 reach their minimum value.

Figure 8.8. Influence state diagram for a see-saw.

In the fifth example, a locked state in a device is represented in terms of zero influence value. Consider an indexing device (Figure 8.9) that indexes every 90 degrees. Indexing key 1 can move up and down due to the action of the spring 2. Disc 3 has four grooves at regular intervals and can rotate about axis B, when the indexing key is not in any of the grooves. The ISD is given in Figure 8.10.

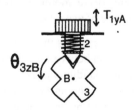

Figure 8.9. An indexing device.

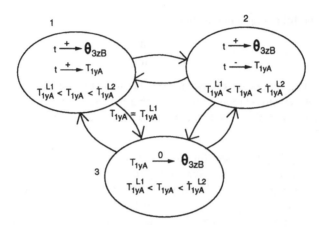

Figure 8.10. ISD for the indexing device.

In state 1, the indexing key 1 is moved up (increase in T_{1yA}). Because of this, the disc 3 is free to rotate. In the second state, the key moves down while disc 3 completes the rotation. In state 3, the key locks the disc. Each state also includes the ranges of the values of T_{1yA} in which the state occurs.

8. Index Transformation

The first step in the index transformation process is to convert the given functional specifications of the design to behavior specifications. Once this is done, cases can be retrieved from the case base, using the required behavior of the device as the index. In addition, it would also be possible to carry out further meaningful transformations.

According to our definition of function, the functional specification is given as an ISD relating the input to the device and the controlled variable of the intended surrounding system. Consider, for instance, the design specification of a device that regulates water flow. The functional specification of the device is: Given a continuously running drive motor, design a device to alternatively increase and decrease the flow-rate of water Q.

This functional specification specifies the input to the device (rotary motion of the drive motor) and the relation between the input and the controlled variable (flow rate Q) of the intended surrounding system (flowing water). Depending on the nature of the flow, the flow rate can be controlled by the drive motor in different ways. For example, if the flow is made possible by a pressure head (by a overhead tank, for instance), then the flow rate can be controlled by varying the pressure head (by moving the tank up and down). On the other hand, if the pressure head has to remain constant, the flow rate can be varied by changing the available flow area. Because this is situation-dependent, the user has to specify the constants and the controllable parameters along with the specification of the process involved. This information can be described as part of the design specification in terms of ISDs as given in Figure 8.11.

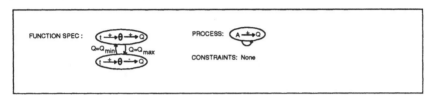

Figure 8.11. Functional specification for a flow regulator.

In the function specification given in Figure 8.11, the continuously increasing Theta represents the running drive motor. Because the process considered is a constant pressure, constant density flow process, the only controllable parameter in the flow process is the flow area.

Given the functional specification and the process specification, the behavior specification can be automatically derived by combining them. In the previous case, the process ISD is elaborated (expanded) into two states (in the next few sections, we describe this elaboration in more detail) and combined with each state of the functional specification (Figure 8.12). It can be inferred that if θ has to influence Q and given that A can influence Q then θ could influence A to control Q.

If there are more than one control variable, then Theta could control one or more of them in a design alternative. The resulting ISD is the behavior specification for the device (righthand side in Figure 8.12). This new derived behavior ISD is used as the index for retrieving cases from the case base. If no cases are retrieved, the behavior ISD is subjected to further transformations as described next.

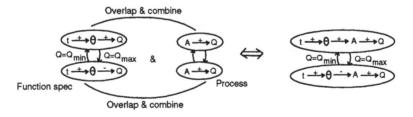

Figure 8.12. Converting functional requirements to behavior requirements.

8.1. INDEX TRANSFORMATION OF ISDS

Index transformation of ISDs can be effected based on equivalences of ISDs. Various possible ISD equivalences are given in Figures 8.13 and 8.14. The equivalences are shown for a typical influence graph $a \to b$ that occurs in two states with different influence values. a should be input variable and b the output variable.

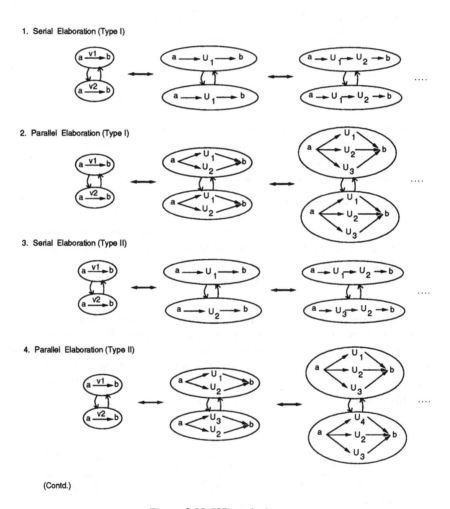

(Contd.)

Figure 8.13. ISD equivalences.

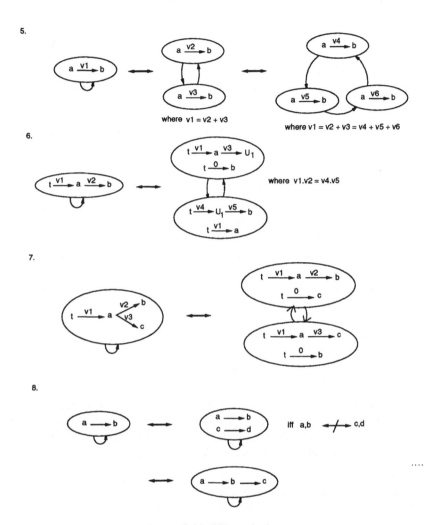

Figure 8.14. ISD equivalences.

1. Serial Elaboration (Type I): In this type of index elaboration, a given influence graph $a \rightarrow b$ is elaborated serially in all the states that it occurs. The same variables (U_1, U_2 etc.) occur as the hypothesized intermediate variables in all the states. The hypothesized variable(s) must be bound by the same variable from a case in all the states. Thus, Type I elaboration can be considered as a symmetric (elaboration of all occurrences of the influence graph in all the states) and homogeneous (a given intermediate variable bound to the same case variable in all the states) elaboration.

2. Parallel Elaboration (Type I): This is a symmetric and homogeneous parallel elaboration of the ISD.

3. Serial Elaboration (Type II): In this type of elaboration, a given influence graph $a \rightarrow b$ is elaborated serially in all the states that it occurs. Different variables occur as hypothesized intermediate variables. These intermediate variables are bound with different variables of the same case or from different cases. Thus, Type II elaboration can be considered as a symmetric and heterogenous elaboration.

4. Parallel Elaboration (Type II): This is a symmetric and heterogeneous parallel elaboration of the ISD.

5. In this type of elaboration, a new ISD state is introduced at each elaboration step. The influence values of the new influences obey the summation rule. Hence, this elaboration is analogous to the parallel elaboration in Rule 2 (occurring over space) but occurs over time.

6. In this type of elaboration, a new state and a new hypothesized variable U1 are introduced as shown. Because the influence values get multiplied, this elaboration is analogous to the serial elaboration given in Rule 1 (occurring over space), but occurs over time. This rule results in the design of devices that have an energy storage component such as fly-wheel and springs.

7. In this rule, the given influence graph on the left-hand side is split to result in the ISD given on the right-hand side.

8. Influence Introduction: According to this rule, influences can be introduced in a state if it is known that the new influence does not affect other parts of the influence graph (which can be typically ascertained from a case). This rule is useful in case-driven elaboration.

Consider the flow regulator design mentioned earlier. One in-state serial elaboration (Rule 2) of the behavior ISD results in the elaborated index given in Figure 8.15 where U_1 and U_2 are hypothesized variables.

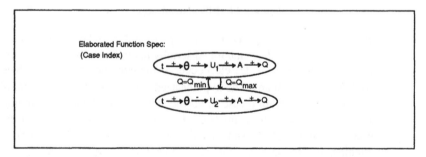

Figure 8.15. Design alternatives for in-state serial elaboration.

An inter-state elaboration (Rule 1) of the derived behavior ISD followed by one in-state serial elaboration results in the case index shown in Figure 8.16. Once the new indices have been generated by the index transformation rules, cases are retrieved from the case base as described in the next section.

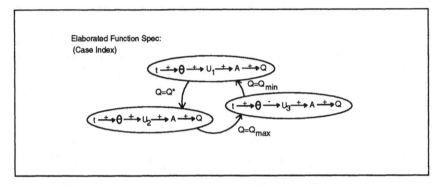

Figure 8.16. Design alternatives for interstate elaboration.

9. Case Retrieval for ISDs

Cases for the ISD index are retrieved based on what we call the index partitioning. Index partitioning groups the node variables in the influence graphs and the graph edges across the ISD states. Figure 8.17 gives an example of this kind of partitioning. The important aspect of the partitioning is that each partition shares at least one variable with its neighboring partitions. Depending on the grouping, each index ISD can give rise to many partitionings. Once the index has been partitioned, cases are retrieved using each partition as the new index. It can be shown that the connectivity between the partitions defines the device topology of the final design.

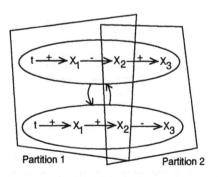

Figure 8.17. Index partitioning.

Given the index partitions, cases are retrieved by comparing the node variables and the signs on the edges. Only those cases that contain the partition in their respective function and behavior ISDs at least as a subset are retrieved. In other words, partial matching is allowed.

As an example, consider the transformed ISD (from the behavior ISD of the flow regulator described earlier). The ISD is partitioned and cases retrieved as shown in Figure 8.18. The first partition retrieves a slider crank and a cam-follower while the second partition retrieves the slider-tap. The corresponding synthesized design is also shown. In this particular situation, U_1 and U_2 are bound to the same parameter X (x-translation input of the slider tap) of the retrieved case.

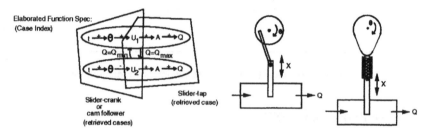

Figure 8.18. Design alternatives for interstate elaboration.

In Figure 8.19 retrieved cases for another elaboration is shown. The corresponding design is a time-synchronized device where each one-tooth gear acts on the slider to provide its up and down motion. In this particular instance the hypothesized variables U_1, U_2, U_3 are bound to θ_1, θ_2 and θ_3—the rotary input of the three single-tooth gears. Each influence state of the elaborated ISD corresponds to the behavior of each gear in succession.

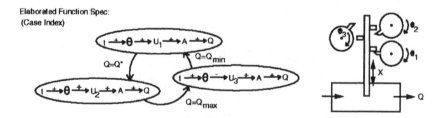

Figure 8.19. Inter-state elaboration.

During the inter-state elaboration a new transition condition $Q = Q^*$ where $Q_{min} < Q^* < Q_{max}$ is created. If the three transition conditions $Q = Q^*$, $Q = Q_{max}$, and $Q = Q_{min}$ correspond to the transitions occuring at time $t = t_1, t_2, t_3$ respectively, then the period of revolution of each gear is $t_1 + t_2 + t_3$.

10. Design Example

In this section we illustrate the previously mentioned approach with a design example. Consider the design of a manually operated flush tank. The flush tank setup is shown in Figure 8.20a. As shown in the setup, Q_1 is the input water flow rate into the tank and Q_2 is the output water flow rate. V is the volume of water in the tank and V_1 and V_2 are the volume of water entering and leaving the tank respectively. Hence,

$$Q_1 = \frac{dV_1}{dt} \text{ and } Q_2 = \frac{dV_2}{dt} .$$

The functional specification for the flush tank is: Given the setup mentioned, design appropriate devices such that the output water flow is controlled by a manually operated lever, which, when rotated through positive Theta, drains the water from the tank. And, the tank is automatically filled by the input water flow whenever the water level in the tank goes below a certain height. This functional specification is described as the ISD given in Figure 8.20b. The states taken in successively specify the sequence in which various behaviors of the flush tank are specified to occur.

State 1:

In this state, the tank is assumed to be filled and output is opened to drain the water. The state requires this to be achieved by the increasing external signal S0 (bound to θ_0) causing Q_2, the output water flow rate, to increase. Consequently, V_2 should increase, causing V to decrease (assuming $Q_2 > Q_1$). In addition, the state specifies that the decreasing V should cause Q_1 to increase via an appropriate mechanism (because V is input and Q_1 is an output).

State 2:

In state 2, Q_2 has already reached its maximum (corresponds to maximum opening) and is to be held constant. However, as the water continues to pour out (increasing V_2), the volume of water in the tank V continues to decrease and Q_1 is specified to increase with decreasing V. Because Q_1 is positive, V_1 is increasing. Transition to next state occurs when Q_1 reaches maximum (corresponds to maximum input water flow rate).

State 3:

In this state, both Q_1 and Q_2 have reached their maximum and are held constant. Because $Q_2 > Q_1$, V continues to decrease.

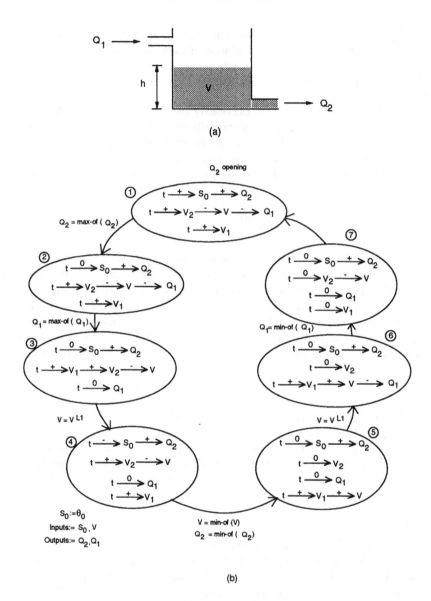

Figure 8.20. Flush tank setup.

State 4:

Once V reaches some landmark value V_{L1}, the output water flow has to be shut off. The rotation input S0 changes direction and starts to decrease and causes Q_2

to decrease. However, V_2 continues to increase (because Q_2 is positive) and causes V to decrease. Q_1 is held steady at its maximum value. Transition to the next state has to occur when the tank is empty.

State 5:

When the tank gets empty (minimum value of V), Q_1 has to reach its zero value, making the output water flow nil. However, Q_1 remains constant at its maximum value. This will make the volume of water in the tank increase.

State 6:

In this state, the output water flow remains zero. The input water flow rate is made to decrease by the increasing water level in the tank. Transition to the next state has to occur when the input water flow is zero and the water level in the tank reaches its maximum.

State 7:

This is the rest state; that is, all flows are held constant at zero. Transition to State 1 has to occur when the input rotary signal S0 starts to increase. Consider the design alternative shown in Figure 8.21. Figure 8.21a gives the synthesized design for the elaborated ISD shown in Figure 8.21b. In the synthesized design, 3 is a tap that controls the output water flow rate. Similarly, 4 is another tap that controls the input water flow rate. 6 is a floating device and is connected to the seesaw 5, which is in turn connected to the tap 4.

The design works as follows: When the external signal S_0 opens the tap 3, the water is drained from the tank. When S_0 closes tap 3, the output water flow stops. When the water is draining, the level of water inside the tank drops and float 6 moves down, causing tap 4 to open. This action causes the tank to be filled with water. As the water level increases, the float moves up causing the left arm of the seesaw to go down. This closes tap 4.

The elaborated index ISD of the design is shown in Figure 8.21b. This index is generated by applying the ISD transformation rule 1 given in Figure 8.13. Variables U_1, U_2, and U_3 are hypothesized as shown. The retrieved cases are a float (Figure 8.22), a see-saw, and two taps. Based on the retrieved cases, U_1 is bound to T_{3y} of the tap, U_2 is bound to T6y of the float and U_3 is bound to T_{4y} of the see-saw. Further elaboration results in the design shown in Figure 8.23.

In the alternative, another variable, U_4, is introduced in all the states as shown. The retrieved cases for the variable are a see-saw and a pulley that have the same conceptual behavior. This design works the same way as the previous alternative, except that the output water flow is controlled by the external signal S0, which moves see-saw 7 or pulley 7 that in turn closes or opens tap 3.

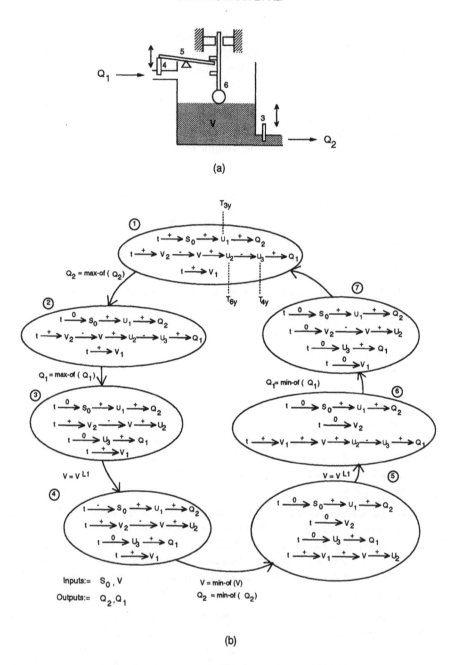

Figure 8.21. Design alternative for the flush-tank.

(a)   (b)

V_0 := Input

T_{1y} := Output

Figure 8.22. Retrieved case—a float and its behavior ISD.

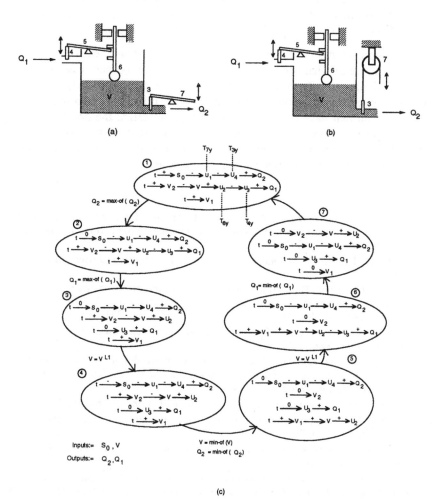

(c)

Figure 8.23. Other alternatives for the flush tank design.

11. Conclusion

We have presented a system, CADET, that aids in the conceptual design of multistate mechanical devices using a case base of previous designs. Devices are represented in a qualitative manner in terms of ISDs. Using ISDs, CADET is able to represent and reason about continuous, reciprocating, intermittent, and feedback electromechanical devices. In fact, we have represented the qualitative behavior of 80% of the devices given in Artobolevsky (1979) (approximately 3,800 devices). The approach allows retrieval of analogically related cases from other domains. If CADET does not finds an exact match, it transforms the index so that subassemblies that can fulfill part of the specified artifact behavior can be retrieved and synthesized to produce the overall device behavior.

Our approach has the following advantages: the system at each point in the search is aware of what behavior it is trying to achieve; because cases embody design optimizations, the accessed components correspond to already optimized physical structures; solutions may involve use of principles from outside the given domain that have been successful in a prior design; the problem solver does not have to re-solve problems from scratch. Current work concentrates on enhancing the qualitative representation to allow the system to seamlessly reason from conceptual to configuration and parametric design stages.

References

Agogino, A. M., and Almgren, A. S.: 1987, Techniques for integrating qualitative reasoning and symblic omputation in engineering optimization, *Engineering Optimization*, 12(2), 117–135.

Artobolevsky, I. I.: 1979, *Mechansims in Modern Engineering Design*, MIR Press, Moscow.

Carbonell, J.G.: 1986, Derivational analogy: A theory of reconstructive problem solving and expertise acquisition, *in* C. J. Michalski and T. Mitchell (eds), *Machine Learning, Vol II*, Kaufmann, Los Altos, CA, pp. 371–392.

DeKleer, J., and Brown, J.: 1984, A qualitative physics based on confluences, *Artificial Intelligence*, 24, 7–83.

Domeshek, E. A., and Kolodner, J. L.: 1992, A case-based design aid for architecture, *in* J. S. Gero (ed.), *Artificial Intelligence in Design '92*, Kluwer Academic, Dordrecht, NL, pp. 497–516.

Dunker, K.: 1945, On problem-solving, *Psychological Monographs*, 58(270).

Gero, J. S.: 1990, Design prototypes: A knowledge representation schema for design, *AI Magazine*, 11(4), 26–36.

Gero, J. S. (ed.): 1990, *Applications of Artificial Intelligence in Design*, Springer-Verlag and CMP, Berlin.

Goel, A: 1989, *Integration Of Case-Based Reasoning And Model Based Reasoning For Adaptive Design Problem Solving*, Doctoral dissertation, Ohio State University.

Hammond, K.: 1986, Chef: A model of case-based planning, *Proceedings of AAAI-86*, Philadelphia, PA, pp. 267–271.

Hinrichs, T.: 1995, Some limitations of feature-based recognition in case-based design, *Proceedings of the First International Conference on Case-Based Reasoning*, Springer-Verlag, New York, pp. 471–480.

Hodges, J: 1992, Naive mechanics: A computational model of device use and function in design improvisation, *IEEE Expert*, 7(1), 14–27.

Kota, S: 1990, A qualitative matrix representation scheme for the conceptual design of mechanisms, *Proceedings of the ASME Design Automation Conference (21st Biannual ASME Mechanisms Conference)*, pp. 217–230.

Koton, P.: 1988, *Using Experience in Learning and Problem Solving*, Doctoral dissertation, MIT, Cambridge, MA.

Maher, M. L., and Zhao, F.: 1987, Using experience to plan the synthesis of new designs, *in* J. S. Gero (ed), *Expert Systems in Computer Aided Design*, North-Holland, Amsterdam, pp. 349–369.

Maier, N.: 1931, Reasoning in humans: The solution of a provlem and its appearance in consciousness, *Journal of Comparative Psychology*, 12, 181–194.

Navin-Chandra, D.: 1988, Case-based reasoning in CYCLOPS, a design problem solver, *in* J. L. Kolodner (ed.), *Proceedings of the DARPA workshop on Case-Based Reasoning*, Kaufmann, San Mateo, CA, pp. 286–301.

Navin-Chandra, D., Sycara, K., and Narasimhan, S.: 1991a, Behavioral synthesis in CADET, a case-based design tool, *Proceedings of the Seventh Conference on Artificial Intelligence (IEEE)*, Miami, Florida, pp. 217–221.

Navin-Chandra, D., Sycara, K., and Narasimhan, S.: 1991b, A transformational approach to case-based synthesis, *AI EDAM*, 5(1), 31–46.

Redmond, M.:1990, Distributed cases for case-based reasoning facilitating use of multiple cases, *Proceedings of the Eighth National Conference on Artificial Intelligence, AAAI90*, Kaufmann, San Mateo, CA, pp. 304–309.

Simpson, R.: 1985, *A Computer Model For Case-Based Reasoning In Problem Solving: An Investigation In The Domain Of Dispute Mediation*, Doctoral dissertation, Georgia Institute of Technology, Atlanta, GA.

Sycara, K: 1987, *Resolving Adversarial Conflits: An Approach Integrating Case-Based And Analytical Methods*, Doctoral dissertation, Georgia Institute of Technology, Atlanta, GA.

Sycara, K., and Navin-Chandra, D.: 1991, Influences: A thematic abstraction for creative use of multiple cases, *in* R. Bareiss (ed.), *Proceedings: Case-Based Reasoning Workshop*, Kaufmann, San Mateo, CA, pp. 133–144.

Williams, B.: 1989, *Invention From First Principles Via Topologies Of Interaction*, Doctoral dissertation, MIT, Cambridge, MA.

Williams, B.: 1990, Interaction-based invention: Designing novel devices from first principles, *Proceedings of AAAI90*, MIT Press, Cambridge, MA, pp. 349–356.

chapter nine

FORMALIZING THE ADAPTATION PROCESS FOR CASE-BASED DESIGN

PEARL PU
Swiss Federal Institute of Technology (EPFL)

LISA PURVIS
University of Connecticut

In design, past experience is often used to guide and inspire new design solutions. Thus, CBR is a natural framework for an automated design system, as it allows prior designs to be stored in the case base to help solve new problems. The complexities of engineering design, however, rarely permit an existing solution to entirely solve a new design situation. Therefore, existing designs typically are used as a basis for the new design, but must be further adapted in order to properly address the characteristics and issues associated with the new problem situation. This adaptation process is difficult because it must consider many existing designs in conjunction to solve a new problem, each of which may be represented differently and also may not readily lead to a valid solution if not combined and adapted in a systematic way. In order to alleviate some of these difficulties, we investigate a methodology for adaptation that uses constraint satisfaction techniques. Each existing design case is formulated and stored in the case base as a CSP, and a repair-based CSP algorithm (Minton, Johnston, Phillips, and Laird, 1992) is then used to adapt these existing cases to solve new problems. In this way, we provide a general formalism for adaptation that can systematically find solutions to new problems and, because of its formalization as a CSP, it can be applied across a general class of design problems. We have implemented our methodology in COMPOSER, a case-based adaptation system, and tested it in two design domains: assembly sequence generation and configuration design.

1. Introduction

The domain of CBR has received much attention as a viable and natural formulation for design problems. That is because the complexities of the ill-defined design domain often require past design experience in order to create an effective new design. It is often the case that experienced designers recall past successful designs and can implement the same principles that worked in the past in a new design situation. Doing so reduces the amount of work that must be done to create the new design, and also helps to ensure the new design's viability and reliability. However, it is also often the case that a designer must adapt the old experience to properly fit the new situation because it is rare that an existing design exactly matches the demands of a new situation.

Therefore, adaptation is an important component of a case-based design system, and the methodology for adaptation must be both efficient and reliable in order to find effective new design solutions. Achieving an efficient and reliable adaptation mechanism is difficult, especially in complex domains such as design. The many interacting constraints, design components, and requirements may cause a chain of changes during adaptation that will not necessarily lead to a solution. For example Hua and Faltings (1993) pointed out that in a building, spaces define their functions of utility. At the same time, they also specify a circulation pattern. The adaptation triggered by allocation of spaces in a new context may destroy the circulation pattern of the case. Such a nonconvergent behavior is described by what they called *inadmissible generalization problem*. Therefore, without a systematic adaptation method, it is difficult to determine whether a solution is being converged on at all.

Another difficulty with adaptation in complex domains is that the compositional structure of such problems requires combining information from multiple existing cases in order to solve the new problem. Consider, for instance, the problem of designing a coloring scheme for a world map using four colors, so that no two neighboring countries or states have the same color. Perhaps we already have several separate smaller maps for which the coloring scheme has been designed. The solution to our new problem, then, results from merging the local colorings together to create a globally consistent coloring for the world map. However, the merging process is difficult because the local solutions typically exhibit conflicts when merged together. For example, consider combining the local colorings for the Eastern and Western portions of the United States into a coloring for the entire United States.

Although the two colorings are consistent when considered in isolation, it is apparent from Figure 9.1 that we do not obtain a globally consistent coloring for the entire United States simply by merging the two local solutions because of the conflicts that appear at the border of the two merged solutions. Therefore, the adaptation process must efficiently combine the local solutions to form a globally consistent solution for the new problem, and furthermore must do so systematically in order to ensure convergence on a solution.

To achieve this goal, we investigate a methodology in our system COMPOSER which formalizes the adaptation process using constraint satisfaction problem solving techniques. Traditional CSP techniques are prohibitive for practical problems because of their complexity: The general solution to the CSP has been proven to be NP-complete (Dechter and Pearl, 1988; Freuder, 1978; Mackworth, 1988; Mohr and Henderson, 1986). We have identified a repair-based CSP algorithm that has been shown to be quite efficient, especially when provided with an initial rough assignment of values (Minton et al., 1992). We investigate a technique in which cases are stored in the case base as individual CSPs, and are combined using the minimum-conflict algorithm to provide a solution to a new problem. We also incorporate dynamic constraints into the CSP formulation and the repair algorithm, allowing our adaptation process to be applied to any design problem that can be described as either a static or dynamic, discrete CSP. We have tested our methodology on two NP-hard problems: assembly sequence generation and configuration design.

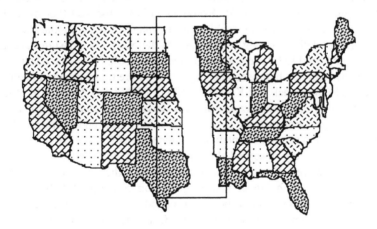

Figure 9.1. Eastern and western local solutions merged.

The rest of the chapter is organized as follows: Section 2 reviews related work on adaptation and CSP techniques. Section 3 details the CSP formulation of design problems and the representation of cases as CSPs, Section 4 describes the adaptation process itself, followed by two examples of the process in Section 5, and current results in Section 6. Finally, we conclude with a summary and review of the key issues in Section 7.

2. Related Work

Case-based adaptation can be described as the process of changing an old solution to meet the demands of a new situation (Kolodner, 1993). Three important, well known adaptation methods are substitution, transformation, and derivational analogy methods. Substitution methods are used in the existing CBDAs CHEF (Hammond, 1986), JUDGE (Bain, 1989), CLAVIER (Hennessy and Hinkle, 1992), and MEDIATOR (Kolodner and Simpson, 1989). These methods choose and install a replacement for some part of an old solution that does not fit the current situation requirements. Transformation methods use heuristics to replace, delete, or add components to an old solution in order to make the old solution work in the new situation. Transformation methods can be found in the case-based system CASEY (Koton, 1988), in which transformation is guided by a causal model, and JULIA (Hinrichs, 1992), which uses commonsense transformation heuristics to fix the old solution for the new problem context. Derivational analogy methods, found in ARIES (Carbonell, 1986) and PRODIGY/ANALOGY (Carbonell and Veloso, 1988), use the method of deriving the old solution in order to derive a solution in the new situation (Kolodner, 1993).

Recently, researchers have become interested in applying CBR techniques to the design domain (Pu, 1993). Kolodner (1993) observed that many design problems are hardly decomposable; that is, many of the components of a case have strong relations among each other. On the other hand, design cases tend to be large and need to be decomposed to facilitate reuse. Thus, the adaptation of a design case requires first decomposing a case before transformation methods can be applied (Domeshek and Kolodner, 1993). Maher and Zhang (1993) used an integration of case transformation and derivational analogies to tackle the adaptation problem in their system, CADSYN. Hua and Faltings combined multiple cases to achieve adaptation in their system, CADRE (Hua, Faltings, and Smith, 1993). They observed that cases achieve good balances for multiple features. However, changing one feature during the adaptation process may destroy this good balance, resulting in non-convergent behavior for the adaptation algorithm, which they have called the inadmissible generalization problem. Our work is closest to theirs from the point of view of problem formulation. However, they represent and process continuous variables and use a method called dimensionality reduction to tame the computational complexity, whereas we formulate problems as a discrete and dynamic constraint problem and use the minimum-conflict repair algorithm to resatisfy constraints.

A CSP can be defined as a problem consisting of variables, possible values for those variables, and constraints on the values. The solution to a CSP is an assignment of value to each variable, such that none of the constraints are violated. Detailed discussions of the technique will be given in Section 3.1.

Traditional CSP techniques either use a preprocessing strategy before beginning the search for a solution, or use lookahead and variable ordering schemes to guide the search. Preprocessing techniques such as arc and path consistency intend to eliminate as many inconsistencies as possible before the search begins in order to limit the search space, thus attempting to make the search itself more efficient (Mackworth, 1988). Nevertheless, the search space may still be prohibitive even after applying the preprocessing algorithm (Freuder, 1978; Nadel, 1988). Other CSP algorithms use lookahead or variable ordering schemes to guide the search (Dechter and Pearl, 1988; Nadel, 1988). Because the general solution to the CSP has been proven to be NP-complete, these techniques are generally not practical as the size of the problem grows.

The minimum-conflict repair algorithm has been shown to be more efficient than these traditional CSP techniques, a result that has been confirmed by our experiments, and is therefore used in our methodology to achieve adaptation. In the following sections, we describe how the CSP formulation can be used to represent cases as well as facilitate case adaptation.

3. Case Representation

The choice of a case representation language for Composer is strongly influenced by our adaptation method. Because we use a constraint satisfaction problem-solving method to combine cases, it requires that each case be formulated as a CSP. Additional information is included in case representation to facilitate retrieval and matching. To be more specific about our case representation, we describe how each of the two chosen domains are formulated as CSPs and how they are stored as cases.

The two domains are assembly sequence generation (ASG) problem and configuration design. We consider ASG as a design problem for two reasons. First, the typical formulation of the assembly sequence problem (ASP) as a planning problem requires extensive feasibility testing at each plan step in order to determine the valid subassemblies (Homem de Mello and Sanderson, 1991). We found that most assemblies are decomposable and thus lend themselves to a case combination process, which allows us to eliminate the costly feasibility computations necessary when the problem is formulated as a planning problem.

Second, by formulating the ASP as a design problem, we can more closely integrate the design decisions with the assembly sequence decisions, which traditionally are separated. The assembly sequence decision is usually made in isolation and does not have any influence on the design decisions, even though a modification of the design could very well simplify the assembly sequence.

3.1. CSP FORMULATION OF ASG CASES

An assembly case contains three main fields of information: variables, constraints, and solutions. Figure 9.2 shows the case representation of the receptacle assembly. The value assigned to each CSP variable is a mating connection between two parts, as shown in Figure 9.3, where V1 is the mating connection between the cap and the receptacle, V2 for the stick and the receptacle, V3 for the handle and the receptacle, and so forth. This method of labeling the connections is automatic once the relational model, provided by the designer, is given for the product.

```
((NAME (SIMPLE-CAP-STICK-RECEPTACLE-HANDLE) 0)
(PART (CAP) 5)
(PART (STICK) 5)
(PART (RECEPTACLE) 5)
(PART (HANDLE) 5)
(MATING-REL (INSIDE STICK RECEPTACLE V2) 50)
(MATING-REL (SHAFT-HOLE RECEPTACLE CAP V1)50)
(MATING-REL (SHAFT-HOLE HANDLE RECEPTACLE V3) 50)
(REL (TARGET-ATT CAP V1) 0.05)
(REL (TARGET-ATT RECEPT V3) 0.05)
(REL (AGENT-ATT RECEPT V1) 0.05)
(REL (AGENT-ATT HANDLE V3) 0.05)
(ATTACH (SCREW V1) 0.05)
(ATTACH (SCREW V3) 0.05)
(CHARACTERISTIC (THROUGH-ENDED-CYL RECEPTACLE) 50)
(CHARACTERISTIC (BLIND-HOLE CAP) 50)
(CHARACTERISTIC (CYLINDRICAL V2) 0.05)
(CHARACTERISTIC (THREADED-CYLINDRICAL V1) 0.05)
(CHARACTERISTIC (THREADED-CYLINDRICAL V3) 0.05)
(CONSTRAINT (C1 ((< V2 V3) (< V2 V1))) 0)
(SOLUTION (S1 ((V1 16) (V2 17) (V3 18))) 0))
```

Figure 9.2. Case representation of the receptacle.

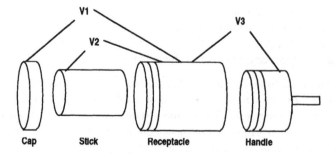

Figure 9.3. Receptacle assembly.

The constraints express the various feasibility constraints on the assembly. The example shown in Figure 9.3 has two feasibility constraints. C1: (< V2 V1) OR (< V2 V3) is a geometric feasibility constraint stating that the stick must be put inside the receptacle either before the cap or before the handle is attached to the receptacle, otherwise there is no collision-free path by which the stick can be properly added to the assembly. Constraint C2: (<> Vi Vj) is an operational constraint indicating that no two connections can be made at the same time.

The variable values in the ASP domain are integers representing step number in the assembly sequence. For example if we assign value 1 to variable V1, then this represents the fact that we will make the connection between the cap and the receptacle first in the assembly sequence. The solution to the ASP formulated as a CSP is a valid ordering of all mating connections so that none of the feasibility constraints are violated. In the case of the assembly shown in Figure 9.3, a valid solution would be: (V1 1) (V2 2) (V3 3), meaning that we connect the cap and the receptacle first, then insert the stick into the receptacle, and finally attach the handle to the receptacle. Thus the case representation for this particular assembly sequence problem is shown in Figure 9.2.

Further flexibility can be gained from the CSP formulation if dynamic constraints are allowed. Many design problems exhibit dynamic properties because the set of variables that are relevant to a solution changes dynamically in response to decisions made during the course of problem solving. These dynamic properties of design can be readily understood by examining a problem in the configuration design domain. In designing a computer configuration, selecting the type of hard disk controller is only relevant when a hard disk is chosen as the form of secondary storage. If a floppy disk drive were chosen instead of a hard disk, then a different set of variables and constraints would be effective in the problem. Dynamic properties are also common in assembly sequence problems, as shown by the 4-blocks assembly in Figure 9.4.

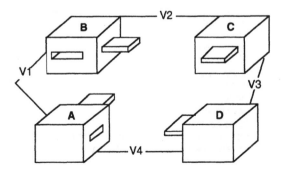

Figure 9.4. 4-blocks assembly.

In the 4-blocks assembly, if connections V1 and V3 have been made, and then we choose to make the connection V4, we no longer have to consider V2 because connection V2 will be made automatically when we make connection V4. Therefore, we can completely eliminate V2 from the problem, resulting in fewer problem variables and a smaller search space. Note from the 4-blocks feature-value pairs that along with the CSP variables, values, and constraints, a case also includes other characteristics in order to distinguish it during matching.

The work of Bessier (1991) described an algorithm for computing arc-consistency for dynamic constraint satisfaction problems, and Faltings, Haroud, and Smith (1992) explored dynamic constraint propagation in continuous domains. Mittal and Falkenhainer (1990) identified four types of dynamic constraints and implemented them within an ATMS framework. Our research has implemented all four types of dynamic constraints identified in Mittal and Falkenhainer (1990), within the minimum-conflicts CSP algorithm in order to extend the applicability of our adaptation methodology to all design problems that can be described as either static or dynamic CSPs.

3.2. CSP FORMULATION OF CONFIGURATION DESIGN CASES

A configuration design case, adapted from Mittal and Falkenhainer (1990) and formulated as a CSP is shown in Figure 9.5. Recall that the motivation behind representing existing cases as CSPs was to facilitate the use of CSP algorithms in order to do case adaptation. We describe the adaptation process next.

4. Adaptation

Case combination, a special form of adaptation, is the process of retrieving existing solved problems and combining them into a solution to solve a larger and a different problem. The general methodology for our approach is illustrated by Figure 9.6.

```
(model model-70)
(status standard)
(fuel-eff medium)
(aircond ac1)
(frame hatchback)
(engine    small)
(battery   large)
(sunroof sr1)
(glass not-tinted)
(constraint (and (status = standard) (aircond ≠ ac2)
(constraint (and (status = standard) (frame ≠convertible)))
```

Figure 9.5. Configuration design case represented as a CSP.

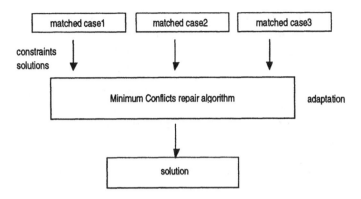

Figure 9.6. Adaptation methodology.

Existing cases are stored in the case base as primitive CSPs along with additional information to facilitate retrieval. The cases that match portions of the new problem are retrieved from the case base by first doing a structure mapping (Gentner, 1983), using the spatial and geometrical features of each case to determine correspondences between variables of the old and new case, and then applying the nearest-neighbor similarity metric (Kolodner, 1993) to compute which of the structural matches are most similar. The matched cases contribute their constraints and solutions to form the new problem into a CSP, which is subsequently adapted using the minimum-conflicts adaptation algorithm to find a solution for the new problem.

The important pieces of information that are contributed by the existing cases are the old solutions, and the constraints. These constraints are traditionally obtained by using path-planning methods or by posing a large set of questions to which users must painstakinly answer one by one. Once a case has been identified as a match with the new problem, its variables and values can be used to initialize the corresponding variables and values in the new case, thus providing guidance from past experience to help achieve a better CSP efficiency. In addition, the newly formed CSP obtains its constraints from the matched cases, thereby eliminating reliance on user input to determine the constraints and reducing the significant computational burden necessary in other approaches in order to calculate the constraints from first principles. For dynamic design problems such as configuration design, the old cases also contribute the essential information about what variables compose the new problem; information that would not be readily available without the existing cases.

Now that all contributing cases have been found, they are merged to form an initial solution to the new problem. If there are still missing pieces in the new problem to which old cases cannot be found, random values are assigned to these variables. Briefly speaking, this initial solution to the new problem is a complete assignment of values, but some of the values are inconsistent. At this point, the minimum-conflict repair heuristic from Minton et al. (1992) is used to gradually converge the inconsistent variables into a consistent solution.

A variable is called consistent if it does not conflict with any constraints. All variables of a problem are divided into two sets called VAR-DONE and VAR-LEFT, respectively. VAR-DONE contains consistent variables only. VAR-LEFT contains variables that are to be repaired. Initially all variables belong to VAR-LEFT and VAR-DONE is nil. If all variables (that is the union of VAR-DONE and VAR-LEFT) are consistent, the program stops and produces at least one solution. In principle, the program can continue to search for alternative solutions.

Figure 9.7 is our implemented version of the minimum-conflict repair CSP algorithm described in Minton et al. (1992).

```
Procedure informed-backtrack (VARS-LEFT VARS-DONE)

   if all variables in VARS-LEFT and VARES-DONE are consistent
      solution found, STOP.

   if VARS-LEFT is nil, NO-SOLUTION=true, STOP.

   Let VAR= a variable in VARS-LEFT that is in conflict.

   Remove VAR from VARS-LEFT

   Push VAR onto VARS-DONE

   Let VALUES = list of possible values for VAR ordered in
   ascending order according to number of conflicts with
   variables in VARS-LEFT

   For each VALUE in VALUES, until solution found:

      if VALUE does not conflict with any variable that is in
      VAR-DONE, then assign VALUE to VAR.

         Call informed-backtrack (VAR-LEFT VARS-DONE)

      endif
   endfor
end procedure
```

Figure 9.7. Minimum-conflict repair algorithm.

The effectiveness of the minimum-conflicts repair algorithm has been shown in the n-queens domain as well as in the complex Hubble Space Telescope scheduling domain (Minton et al., 1992), and has been confirmed by our results. The empirical results in Minton et al. (1992) showed that because the number of required repairs remains approximately constant as the number of problem variables grows, the program's empirical time is approximately linear, as opposed to the exponential complexity of traditional constructive backtracking techniques. The effectiveness of the algorithm stems from using information about the current assignment to guide the search that is not available to standard backtracking algorithms. Our methodology capitalizes on the efficiency of the algorithm by providing it with a good initial solution based on the already-solved cases in the case base.

5. Examples

This section clarifies further the methodology by going through the steps of Composer, as illustrated by two examples.

5.1. ASSEMBLY SEQUENCE EXAMPLE

Consider the problem of finding an assembly sequence for the motor shown in Figure 9.8. Recall that the first step in the adaptation methodology is to find the existing cases that match portions of the new problem. We look at the correspondence between a subassembly of this new problem and the existing case for the receptacle was shown in Figures 9.2 and 9.3.

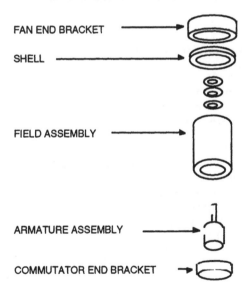

FAN END BRACKET

SHELL

FIELD ASSEMBLY

ARMATURE ASSEMBLY

COMMUTATOR END BRACKET

Figure 9.8. Motor assembly.

Recall that the constraints for the receptacle are such that the stick must be placed inside the receptacle either before the handle or before the cap is attached to the receptacle; otherwise, there is no geometrically feasible way to insert the stick into the receptacle. This same principle can be found in a subassembly of the motor case, in that the armature must be placed inside the field assembly before either the fan end bracket or before the commutator end bracket is attached to the field assembly; otherwise, there is no geometrically feasible way to insert the armature into the field assembly.

This correspondence is found in our system by doing a structure mapping on the mating-relationship feature-values of the old and new case. We find the case features that share a common structural tie (or, more generally, known as labels) in the old and the new case, as follows:

The new case's mating-relationship feature-values are asserted into a deductive database.

New case:

(MATING-REL (SHAFT-HOLE FAN-END-BRACKET FIELD-ASSEMBLY V19))
(MATING-REL (SHAFT-HOLE FIELD-ASSEMBLY COMMUTATOR-END-
    BRACKET V17))
(MATING-REL (INSIDE ARMATURE FIELD-ASSEMBLY V7))

The old case's mating-relationship feature-values are formed into a database query:

Old case:

(MATING-REL (SHAFT-HOLE CAP RECEPT V1))

Database query:

(AND (SHAFT-HOLE ?CAP ?RECEPT ?V1)
(SHAFT-HOLE ?RECEPT ?HANDLE ?V3)
(SHAFT-HOLE ?STICK ?RECEPT ?V2))

The database query determines whether the same pattern of structural ties exists in any component of the new case, thus giving us the following correspondences between the old and the new case:

HANDLE → COMMUTATOR-END-BRACKET
CAP → FAN-END-BRACKET
RECEPTACLE → FIELD-ASSEMBLY}
STICK → ARMATURE
V3 → V17
V1 → V19
V2 → V7

Now, the nearest-neighbor similarity metric is applied using the correspondence information and the features' weights to determine whether the match is close enough to warrant using the old case as part of our new CSP. At this point, all of the case's features are considered, not just the mating-relationship features used during the structure-mapping process. The more detailed case features allow a more accurate similarity score to be computed. In this example, additional case features of the receptacle case are:

(RECEPTACLE OPEN-CYLINDER 10)
(CAP BLIND-CYLINDER 10)
(HANDLE BLIND-CYLINDER 10)

Note that each of these detailed features has a weight of 10 out of a possible range from 1 to 10, indicating that each has significant importance to the case. In this example, the computed similarity measurement is large enough to warrant that the old case be used for the new CSP.

Now that we have found that the receptacle case is a match with part of our new problem, we take its solution and constraints to set up the new CSP. The correspondences found provide the mapping information between the old and new case.

Old case's solution: (V1 1) (V2 2) (V3 3)
Old case's constraint: (CONSTRAINT C1 (OR (< V2 V3) (<V2 V1)))

Because V3 from the old case corresponds to V17 from the new case, the initial value for V17 in the new problem is set to 3, which was V3's value in the old case. Similarly, the constraints for the new case are obtained by substituting the new variables for their corresponding variables in the old case's constraints.

(CONSTRAINT C1 (OR (< V7 V17) (< V7 V19)))
(V19 1)
(V7 2)
(V18 3)

Now consider the existing case shown in Figure 9.9, the pieced-stick case. One of its constraints indicates that the stick must be put together before it is inserted into the receptacle; otherwise, there is no way to attach part A to part B without disturbing the stability of the assembly.

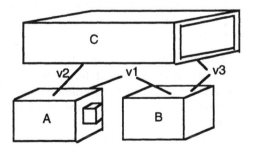

Figure 9.9. Pieced-stick case.

(CONSTRAINT C2 (OR ((< V1 V2) (RN V3)) ((< V1 V3) (RN V2))))

Its other constraint indicates that only one connection may be made at a time:

(CONSTRAINT C3 (<> Vi Vj))

We find, through our structure mapping and similarity assessment procedure, that this case also applies to the motor problem: The bearings and washers must be attached to the armature before the armature is placed into the field assembly because once the armature is inside the field assembly, the tight fit of the bearings does not permit them to be added to the subassembly without disturbing its stability. Thus, the correspondence between the old and the new case is:

C → FIELD-ASSEMBLY
A → ARMATURE
B → BEARING
V1 → V8
V2 → V7
V3 → V17

This correspondence information is substituted into the old constraint, producing the following constraints for the motor assembly:

(CONSTRAINT C2 (OR ((< V8 V7)(RN V17)) ((< V8 V17) (RN V7))))
(CONSTRAINT C3 = (<> Vi Vj))

The solution for the old pieced-stick case is: (V1 = 1) (V2 = 2). Therefore, using our correspondence information, we assign value 1 to V8, and because we find that there has already been an assignment to the new variable V7 from another case (the receptacle), we only use the value for variable V8 from the pieced-stick case. These two cases have resulted in the following initial assignment for the new case's variables:

(V17 = 1) (V7 = 2) (V19 = 3) (V8 = 1)

The following are the resulting constraints for the new case:

(CONSTRAINT C2 (OR ((< V8 V7)(RN V17)) ((< V8 V17) (RN V7))))
(CONSTRAINT C3 = (<> Vi Vj)).
(CONSTRAINT C1 (OR (< V7 V17) (< V7 V19)))

In this manner, each matching case contributes its constraints and solutions to the new CSP, providing an initial solution for the new problem that can then be fed into the minimum-conflicts repair algorithm for solving. The minimum-conflict algorithm begins by choosing one of the initial values that violates a problem constraint. Note that the choice of value 1 for variable V8, which was suggested by the existing pieced-stick case, is not consistent because it violates the constraint C3. Thus, the repair algorithm chooses a value for variable V8 that conflicts the least with the remaining values. Value 4 for variable V8 does not violate any of the constraints, and the algorithm continues this choose-and-repair process until no violations remain, giving us a solution to the problem.

5.2. CONFIGURATION EXAMPLE

Let us now examine how a configuration design problem can be solved using our adaptation methodology. We use the car configuration domain detailed in Mittal and Falkenheiner (1990). Consider two existing car configurations, represented in the case base as shown in Table 9.1.

Table 9.1. Car configuration cases.

FEATURES	CASE #1	CASE #2
MODEL	model-80	model-70
STATUS	luxury	standard
FUEL-EFF	high	medium
BODY	convertible	hatchback
ENGINE	large	small
BATTERY	large	large
CONVERTER	cv1	
AIRCOND	ac2	
CD-PLAYER	sony	
DOORS		dr222
INSTRUMENT-PANEL		ip228
STEREO		st2
SEATS		s536
CONSTRAINT C1	(and (MODEL = model-80) (FUEL-EFF = high))	(and (BATTERY = small) (ENGINE = small)(RN CONVERTER))
CONSTRAINT C2	(and (MODEL = model-80) (RV BODY))	(and (STATUS = standard) (BODY ≠ convertible))
CONSTRAINT C3	(and (MODEL = model-80) (RV ENGINE))	(and (MODEL = model-70) (RV BODY))
CONSTRAINT C4	(and (MODEL = model-80) (RV BATTERY)	(and (MODEL = model-70) (RV ENGINE)
CONSTRAINT C5	(and (MODEL = luxury) (RV AIRCOND))	(and (MODEL = model-70) (RV BATTERY)
CONSTRAINT C6	(and (MODEL = luxury) (RV CD-PLAYER))	(and (MODEL = model-70) (RV DOORS))
CONSTRAINT C7	(and (FUEL-EFF = high) (RV CONVERTER))	(and (MODEL = model-70) (RV INSTRUMENT-PANEL)
CONSTRAINT C8		(and (MODEL = model-70) (RV SEATS)
CONSTRAINT C9		(and (MODEL = standard) (RV STEREO))

Note that the cases include dynamic constraints: RV indicates a dynamic constraint meaning require variable, and RN indicates a dynamic constraint meaning require not variable. Our new configuration problem is to configure a STANDARD, MODEL-80 car. We search the case base for cases with the requested characteristics, finding the two existing cases shown. Case 1 matches the requested MODEL-80 feature, and Case 2 matches the STANDARD characteristic.

The variables and constraints related to the matched characteristics of the old case are used to set up the new CSP. Thus, from Case 1, all constraints having to do with MODEL-80 (C1, C2, C3, C4), and all variables encountered in those constraints (MODEL, FUEL-EFF, BODY, ENGINE, BATTERY) are added to the new CSP. Any constraints involving the added variables are also added (C7, because it involves FUEL-EFF). Any RV variables found in the added constraints are kept as reserve variables in case any of the dynamic constraints later involve their activation. Thus, CONVERTER is kept as a reserve variable for the new CSP. Therefore, from Case 1, we have:

```
(MODEL MODEL-80)
(BODY CONVERTIBLE)
(FUEL-EFF HIGH)
(ENGINE LARGE)
(BATTERY LARGE)
(CONSTRAINT (C1 (AND (MODEL = MODEL-80) (FUEL-EFF = HIGH))))
(CONSTRAINT (C2 (AND (MODEL = MODEL-80) (RV BODY))))
(CONSTRAINT (C3 (AND (MODEL = MODEL-80) (RV ENGINE))))
(CONSTRAINT (C4 (AND (MODEL = MODEL-80) (RV BATTERY))))
(CONSTRAINT (C7 (AND (FUEL-EFF = HIGH) (RV CONVERTER))))
(Reserve Variable: (CONVERTER CV1))
```

The same process extracts the appropriate variables and constraints from Case 2:

```
(STATUS STANDARD)
(STEREO ST2)
(CONSTRAINT (C2 (AND (STATUS = STANDARD) (BODY ≠ CONVERTIBLE))))
(CONSTRAINT (C9 (AND (STATUS = STANDARD) (RV STEREO))))
```

All of the extracted variables and constraints compose the initial solution to the new configuration design problem. The repair algorithm is now applied, finding that the dynamic constraint C7 from Case 1 is satisfied, and thus we add the reserve variable CONVERTER along with its value CV1 to the problem. Furthermore, the repair algorithm finds that the value for BODY violates the constraint C2 obtained from Case 2. Thus, that value is repaired by choosing a value for BODY that conflicts the least with the remaining values. A value of HATCHBACK is assigned to the variable BODY, resulting in a consistent final solution for the new configuration problem.

This example of a dynamic CSP illustrates how the existing cases not only provide the initial solution and constraints for the new problem, but also formulate the problem itself by identifying the necessary problem variables.

6. Analysis and Results

Both configuration design using backtracking and assembly sequence generation have been characterized as NP-hard problems. Our intuition was that if a problem is hard to solve, do not solve every one from scratch. In both domains, we found strong decompositional structure in the problems that allows application of old solutions to solve new problems. The computation time spent in adaptation is satisfactory compared to using conventional algorithms. Pu and Reschberger (1991) and Pu and Purvis (1994) discussed results of this framework applied in the domain of assembly sequence design. The work reported showed that this framework can be further generalized to discrete and static or dynamic configuration design problems. Response times for answering the question whether matched cases can be adapted to solve new problems are all within minutes.

Several dimensions are used to carry out our evaluations: efficiency for problems of large sizes, comparison of our case-based method versus non-case-based algorithms, and comparison of static versus dynamic constraint formulation. To test the algorithm's performance on large-scale problems, we have used the well known n-queens problem as well as the assembly sequence design problem. These tests gave us positive confirmation that the minimum-conflict algorithm outperforms constructive backtracking, as can be seen in Figure 9.9.

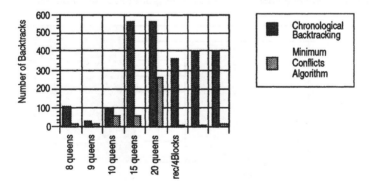

Figure 9.9. Difference between constructive BT and min-conflicts algorithm.

We tested whether the initial solutions taken from existing cases provide the minimum-conflict algorithm with more guidance than the minimum conflicts algorithm applied alone. As Figure 9.10 shows, the initial solutions do indeed provide more guidance and therefore less backtracks during the problem-solving process.

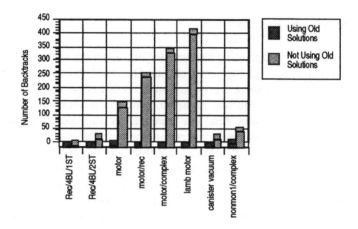

Figure 9.10. Comparison of using old cases vs. random initialization.

Finally, to test the hypothesis that dynamic CSP outperforms static CSP, we formulated our assembly sequence design problems in a dynamic representation as well as a static representation. We found that being able to remove variables from the problem dynamically improved performance significantly, as can be seen in Figure 9.11. This result corresponds to a similar result found by Mittal and Faulkenhainer (1990) in the configuration design domain.

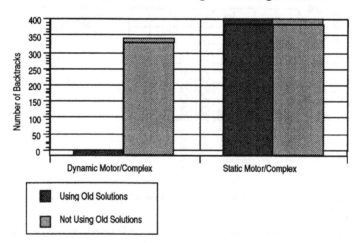

Figure 9.11. Difference between static and dynamic min-conflicts algorithm.

These experiments have confirmed the effectiveness of the minimum-conflict algorithm as a method by which to compose a global solution from several primitive solutions.

6. Conclusion

CBR is becoming widely recognized as a viable problem-solving methodology. It is being applied to a wide range of problem-solving domains such as design, diagnosis, planning, customer technical support, legal reasoning, and education. Our system COMPOSER formalizes the case adaptation process in the sense of combining multiple cases in order to make the process applicable across varied application domains.

Our methodology uses the existing cases in order to store important design information that will help to synthesize effective new designs. By formulating the cases as CSPs, we can combine many existing cases in a systematic way and ensure convergence on a solution. Together, the CBR and CSP formalisms combine to provide a methodology for adaptation that will help CBR systems for design achieve a wider applicability and a better efficiency.

References

Bain, W.: 1989, Judge, in R. C. Reisbeck, and R. Schank (eds), *Inside Case-Based Reasoning*, Lawrence Erlbaum Associates, Hillsdale, NJ, pp. 93–140.

Bessier, C.: 1991, Arc Consistency in dynamic constraint satisfaction problems, *Proceedings of the 9th National Conference of AAAI*, Anaheim, pp. 221–226.

Carbonell, J. G. 1986, Derivational analogy: A theory of reconstructive problem solving and expertise acquisition, in R. S. Michalski, J. G. Carbonell, and T. M. Mitchell (eds), *Machine Learning: An Artificial Intelligence Approach*, Kaufmann, San Mateo, CA, pp. 371–392.

Carbonell, J. G., and Veloso, M. M.: 1988, Integrating derivational analogy into a general problem solving architecture, *Proceedings of the Workshop on Case Based Reasoning Workshop*, Kaufmann, San Mateo, pp. 104–124.

Dechter, R., and Pearl, J.: 1988, Network-based heuristics for constraint satisfaction problems, *Artificial Intelligence*, 34, 1–38.

Domeshek, E., and Kolodner, J.: 1993, Finding the points of large cases, *Artificial Intelligence in Engineering Design, Analysis and Manufacturing (AI EDAM)*, 7(2), 87–96.

Faltings, B., Haroud, D., and Smith, I.: 1992, Dynamic constraint satisfaction with continuous variables, *Proceedings of the European Conference on AI*, Wien, Austria, pp. 754–758.

Freuder, E. C.: 1978, Synthesizing constraint expressions, *Communications of the ACM*, 21(11), 958–966.

Gentner, D.: 1983, Structure mapping: A theoretical framework for analogy, *Cognitive Science*, 7(2), 55–170.

Hammond, K.: 1986, Chef: A model of case-based planning, *Proceedings of AAAI-86*, Kaufmann, San Mateo, CA, pp. 237–258.

Hennessy, D. H., and Hinkle, D.: 1992, Applying case-based reasoning to autoclave loading, *IEEE Expert*, 7(5), 21–26.

Hinrichs, T. R.: 1992, *Problem solving in Open Worlds: A Case Study in Design*, Lawrence Erlbaum Associates, Hillsdale, NJ.

Homem de Mello, L. S., and Sanderson, A. C.: 1991, A correct and complete algorithm for the generation of mechanical assembly sequences, *IEEE Transactions on Robotics and Automation*, 7, 228–240.

Hua, K., and Faltings, B.: Exploring case-based building design—CADRE, *Artificial Intelligence in Engineering Design, Analysis and Manufacturing*, 7(2), 135–143.

Hua, K., Faltings, B., and Smith, I.: 1995, CADRE: Case-based geometric design, *Artificial Intelligence in Engineering*, 10, 171–183.

Kolodner, J. L.: 1993, *Case Based Reasoning*, Kaufmann, San Mateo, CA.

Kolodner, J. L., and Simpson, R. L.: 1989, The mediator: Analysis of an early case-based problem solver, *Cognitive Science*, 13, 507–549.

Koton, P.: 1988, Reasoning about evidence in causal explanation, *Proceedings of AAAI-88*, Kaufmann, San Mateo, CA, pp. 256–263.

Mackworth, A. K.: 1988, Consistency in networks of relations, *Artificial Intelligence*, 8, 99–118.

Maher, M. L., and Zhang, D. M.: 1993, CADSYN: A case-based design process model, *Artificial Intelligence in Engineering Design, Analysis and Manufacturing (AI EDAM)*, 7(2), 97–110.

Minton, S., Johnston, M., Phillips, A.,, and Laird, P.: 1992, Minimizing conflicts: A heuristic repair method for constraint satisfaction and scheduling problems, *Artificial Intelligence*, 58, 161–205.

Mittal, S., and Falkenhainer, B.: 1990, Dynamic constraint satisfaction, *Proceedings of the 8th National Conference of AAAI*, Kaufmann, San Mateo, CA, pp. 25–32.

Mohr, R., and Henderson, T. C.: 1986, Arc and path consistency revisited, *Artificial Intelligence*, 28, 225–233.

Nadel, B.: 1988, Tree search and arc consistency in constraint satisfaction problems, in L. Kanal and V. Kumar (eds), *Search in Artificial Intelligence*, Springer-Verlag, Berlin, pp. 287–342.

Pu, P.: 1993, Issues in case-based design systems, *Artificial Intelligence in Engineering Design, Analysis and Manufacturing (AI EDAM)*, 7(2), 79–85.

Pu, P., and Purvis, L.: 1994, Formalizing case adaptation in a case-based design system, in J. S. Gero, and F. Sudweeks (eds), *Artificial Intelligence in Design '94*, Kluwer Academic, Dordrecht, NL, pp. 77–92.

Pu, P., and Reschberger, M.: 1991, Case-based assembly planning, *Proceedings of DARPA's Case-based Reasoning Workshop*, Kaufmann, San Mateo, CA, pp. 245–254.

chapter ten

CASE-BASED ARCHITECTURAL DESIGN

The Experience of CADRE

GERHARD SCHMITT, BHARAT DAVE
Swiss Federal Institute of Technology, Zürich

SHEN-GUAN SHIH
National Taiwan Institute of Technology, Taipei

The discussion on CBR and case-based design (CBD) has primarily focused on technology and most research has explored in-depth one particular aspect of the activity of design. Artificial intelligence can learn much from the complex human activity of design, but the question remains to which degree a formalized and computer-based method such as CBD is able to support design and how it will change the human design process and the design products. This chapter focuses on representation of design and building cases, on the relation between CBD and creativity, on legal aspects, and on the integration of CBD in future design systems.

1. Introduction

Technological promise and practical application are two ends in the spectrum of Computer-Aided Architectural Design (CAAD). Although the implementation of research results has made computer support for Architectural, Engineering, and Construction (AEC) industries more feasible and attractive, the software instruments that architects use are still basic and often do not support the design process. Current CAAD programs support operations with points, lines, faces, volumes, and the associated attributes. Parametric design systems based on parameterized objects are slowly entering mainstream applications. Generative systems employing shape grammars are promising but have not shown commercial impact. Prototypes and intelligent objects evolve in various research programs. In the development of these instruments, CBD in architecture (CBD-A) is the next logical step.

Although CBD-A offers an attractive opportunity to overcome some of the problems associated with past approaches, it also raises challenging questions. A first question is to which extent a computer system can truly represent a case. A second question is whether CBD-A supports the creative design that is an absolute necessity for the improvement of the built environment, and how other techniques can coexist with CBD-A. The third question concerns the possible legal aspects of CBD-A, in that it might cause plagiarism and related problems. We address these aspects and end with a proposal for the form and extent to which CBD-A systems should become an integral part of future CAAD systems.

1.1. CBD IN THE CONTEXT OF OTHER COMPUTER-SUPPORTED DESIGN METHODS

We have explored and implemented a number of design support methods and instruments in the past for respective classes of design (Schmitt, 1993). The discovery of each new method was accompanied by the hope to finally solve previously difficult to tackle design problems, and each time this hope was disappointed. What remains is a collection of methods and instruments that are useful for particular design problems.

Methods describe general problem-solving techniques derived from models. Examples of methods are abstraction, representation, simulation, top-down, bottom-up, CBR, prototypes, and machine learning. The top-down and bottom-up methods are so basic that they are part of every decision-making process. The prototype method is related to the top-down approach and is helpful in routine design. Machine learning is a method that will rapidly increase in importance. CBR belongs in this context as a method to reason with entire cases.

Instruments are more specific tools that support the methods. The same instrument can assist in applying different methods. Examples of instruments are text, number, diagram, and geometry editors; parameterization; shape grammars and fractals; sequential, knowledge-based, and object-oriented programming techniques; as well as object-oriented modelling techniques. Instruments support the methods to arrive at design solutions. Using these methods and instruments, we have developed a set of hierarchical modelling tools (Schmitt, 1993).

2. CBD in Architectural History

Architectural design seeks to express simultaneously universals and particulars of a design context through formal compositions of design elements. As a result, architectural theories are in a state of flux and re-evaluation vis-a-vis a particular time and place. Given this state of affairs, education in architectural design relies heavily on the use of cases as a vehicle of discourse between teachers and students; the hope being that the particulars in a given case offer a holistic view of design issues that are difficult to articulate or view if they are taken up separately. This mode of example-based teaching and learning is perhaps not unique to the discipline of architecture, which entails developing a facility for making generalizations as a function of new examples that are encountered. Although these observations may have a number of interesting issues and implications for the development of CBD systems, we focus our work on generalising a particular case in response to a particular design problem (Dave, 1994).

Architectural history is full of examples for CBD. Buildings are not designed and built based on first principles. The knowledge necessary to create and construct a structure to successfully house people is so extensive that it cannot be taught in an ad-hoc manner. Even after a 5-year degree program, graduated architects need a number of years before they have accumulated sufficient experience to build professionally. This is not to say that first principles and formal methods are useless in teaching architectural design, but rather that they form a resource of growing importance to formalize the previously unstructured design knowledge. It is conceivable that the enormous knowledge base will slowly transfer into a set of formalized methods, including first principles knowledge. To achieve this, a new look at the architectural research and educational agenda is necessary. History as the discipline dealing with built structure and established theory is responsible mainly for built cases. Design theory must become an integral part of design, from which the models of design can be derived (Smithers, 1994). These models may later serve as cases.

2.1. INTERACTION WITH CASES: POSSIBLE USES

Architectural education and practice apply cases as generators of ideas. They are frequently selected for further adaptation or combination with other cases, based purely on the first visual impression. Seeing design as a rational decision-making activity, this appears to be a disadvantage, but with the rediscovery of the fact that design is also a social activity that requires more than just rationality, the intuitive use of existing cases, along with generative algorithms as a base for new design, becomes more interesting and convincing (Papamichel and Protzen, 1993).

Looking at a few examples in architectural history through the filter of CBD, there are three typical applications: null adaptation, dimensional and topological adaptation, and case combination. Once the description of a new project or problem is available, the designer can choose the appropriate strategy to select a case for adaptation or a number of cases for combination from the architectural case base to work with. This case base is most likely present in her or his memory, supported by external references in the form of magazines, drawings, or other descriptions.

2.2. STRAIGHT REVIVALISM OR NULL ADAPTATION

There is a type of case adaptation that we call null adaptation and that can be compared to straight revivalism in architecture. It means to find a case in the past and to apply it to the problem at hand without any or with only minimal changes. Even architecturally, this might not be a wrong decision because a different context or time changes the appearance of design solutions. Jencks (1982) posed the question: "does architecture have to be a creative art, or can it successfully be an applied craft? Cannot the architect, like the musician who performs a classical symphony, be intent on modestly rendering a previous score with maximum fidelity (even supposing that, for the architect, this score exists in a tradition rather than a simple manuscript)? Herein lies the modesty which is tied to the arrogance that overlooks cultural space" (p. 144). An example of null adaptation of the same design in a different context might serve van der Rohe's adaptation of the Bacardi Rum factory for the National Gallery in Berlin (Schulze, 1986).

2.3. DIMENSIONAL AND TOPOLOGICAL CASE ADAPTATION

Any change to the original case to fit it into a new situation can be considered a case adaptation. In general, the more radical the adaptation, the greater is the possibility of losing the quality of the original case. This is counterproductive because architectural quality was the reason for the selection of the original case. There is nothing wrong with case adaptation as long as the original is referenced appropriately and as long as this solves the problem at hand. Jencks (1982) remarked after discussing the death of the classical tradition: "historical styles are indeed dead. There are no first-class, creative talents pushing the extension of a traditional language, nor is there a significant craft-based organization capable of carrying out such work" (p. 142). Acknowledging that architectural case adaptation is different from reviving historical styles, the quote still poses a serious question: Can someone who uses case adaptation be a "first-class, creative talent"? The answer is yes, as most architects, even the ones considered to be creative and first-class, do acknowledge their use of case adaptation if asked. It appears that in the early days of their career, designers employ case adaptation only rarely, but later in their career they rely heavily on adapting their own, earlier cases. Oxman and Oxman (1992) have shown the processes of refinement and adaptation to be of significance in Palladio's, Kahn's, and Botta's work.

Another example is Burgee-Johnson's architecture school in Houston. The drawing from 1773 for a House of Education by Ledoux and the completed building by Burgee-Johnson and Morris-Aubry from 1967 show striking similarities, although on closer examination, differences in the facade and in the treatment of the roof become apparent. Here, some adaptation has occurred.

A second example for case combination is the Forstwerkhof in Turbenthal, Switzerland, by Sumi and Burkhalter (Burkhalter and Sumi, 1994). The architects received the commission to develop a prototype for forestry administration and storage buildings in remote areas. The program was simple: an open hall, a closed garage, and an administration building. The solution they invented is both strikingly simple and attractive. The open hall appears as a purified and elegant version of the primitive hut (Mitchell, Liggett, Pollalis, and Tan, 1992). The posts supporting the long-span roof were cut from the trees on the site and left untreated—as was the case with early wood constructions. Yet the flat roof, made from laminated, hollow wooden plates that span more than 30 feet, is supported in the middle by a thin steel construction. The garage is concrete on the inside for fire protection reasons and clad with horizontal wood on the outside. The office building is entirely constructed in wood, with the same flat roof construction as the other building parts. Although there are thousands of precedents or cases of this type, the combination of elements from these cases results in both an innovative solution and an example for architecture rather than building.

2.4. CASE COMBINATION

Case combination is the combination of parts of different cases to form a new case. Parts may or may not be adapted in the process. The architectural phenomena most closely related to case combination are historicism, eclecticism, and later Post-Modernism. Jencks (1982) wrote: "the Venturi team analysed the popular, commercial vernacular of architecture as a language or sign system. This work paralleled semiotic research in Italy and that carried out in England under George Baird, Geoffrey Broadbent, myself, and others. One important lesson in all this investigation was the simple, but previously disregarded, idea that architecture is a language perceived through a code" (p.115).

The notion of architecture as a language in which words are arranged according to syntax rules, thereby slightly declining or adapting a pure or primitive vocabulary, has a long tradition (Madrazo, 1993; Mitchell, 1990). In case combination, we combine parts of buildings rather than words. The problem arises that in case combination, we deal with compound objects that may have no meaning once they are taken out of their original context. The design skill lies in selecting appropriate elements and their reuse in a new design composition that is more than a mere collage. Such case combination is visible in Sir Edwin Lutyens' projects for the British Raj in India. For example, Lutyens combined elements from the traditional Indian chhatri and used them in the Guard House in the Viceroy's Court in New Delhi. Colonial architecture throughout the world relies on case combination: assembling traditional, local elements with imported architectural cases.

3. Case-Based Representation of Architecture

The term *architecture* includes both the process of architectural design as well as the resulting products in the form of buildings. The reason is that design and buildings are partial representations of the same discipline: architecture. Consequently, we distinguish between design cases and building cases. Designing we see as an activity within the paradigm of symbolic processes (Gero, 1994). Buildings are the semipermanent results of designing as well as of activities of other disciplines. Design may or may not be able to consider these external influences.

3.1. ARCHITECTURE: BUILDING CASES VERSUS DESIGN CASES

Buildings and designs are fundamentally different. A building has physical presence and is complete, in use, and real. A design is an abstraction of the building process and of the result that should be achieved. Therefore, in a case base, we must differentiate between the representation of buildings and the representation of designs. A building case base represents artifacts that really do exist, whereas a design case base contains descriptions of ideas that we call designs. Not only are representations of architectural designs often incomplete or even contradictory, they are also only one of a group of design descriptions that lead to the construction of the entire building. The building is thus a result of all disciplines that employ some kind of design process as well as of externally enforced constraints. Another differentiation is necessary between new buildings that are approximately in the state they were intended and older or used buildings that have undergone changes. This differentiation reduces our hope to define causal relations between the physical, behavioral, and atmospheric quality of buildings and design decisions. The representation of cases is, however, an excellent approach to discover causalities if they exist.

3.2. REPRESENTATION OF ARCHITECTURAL CASES

The technical description of case-based representation seems straightforward (Rosenman, 1992). Cases are stored in case bases, a special kind of database. To find and retrieve cases in a case base, they are indexed for special properties. Indexes are the attributes based on which we can immediately recall a specific object when someone mentions a prominent feature. As long as a case base is small, indexing is of less importance. Once the case base grows beyond several dozen objects with different functions, indexing and case retrieval become more important. Although this definition is constantly being expanded and refined, there is still the assumption that architectural cases should contain complete information about a building. In this sense, the best case representation is the building itself; any other representation is an abstraction with a number of disadvantages. But to achieve case adaptation, modification, and combination, we need to introduce structure and abstractions into cases.

3.3. ABSTRACTIONS AND STRUCTURE IN ARCHITECTURAL CASES

Case-based representations and abstractions seem to pose a contradiction. When we began research into CBD, one of the original intentions was to keep the description of architectural cases as unstructured and complete as possible to avoid adhoc definitions of parameters and other properties that could become detrimental in the later operations with cases. In thinking about parameters that could become necessary later, it is likely to overlook some parameters that evolve during case adaptation and combination. We assumed that in CBD, one deals with cases that are by definition as unstructured as possible to avoid adhoc pre-structuring and decision making, rather than dealing with highly structured representations used in other CAD methods.

The result of design is not abstract. It should be a physical building. If a physical structure is abstracted, for example in the understanding of structural design, there are important differences between the manner it is shown in the structural abstraction and the manner it behaves in reality. The advantage we found in working with cases was that we could begin with a minimum of pre-structuring (Hua, Smith, and Faltings, 1994). This differentiates cases from parametric objects and from prototypes, for which all parameters must be predefined. Our idea was to represent cases as close as possible to the original building to keep the quality of the design.

4. A CBD System

We attempted to translate the theory behind CBD into a model and to operationalize it to test both the theory and the model. The result is CADRE. Faltings and Smith (1996) describe other aspects of CADRE in this book. We began by implementing a modular system, the CAAD group using AutoCad, AutoLisp, and C on SUN workstations; the structural engineering team at EPFL (ICOM) using AutoCad and AutoLisp on SUN workstations; and the AI team at EPFL (LIA) team using CommonLisp and C on SUN workstations. This required communication over the network between various program modules residing on computers at ETH Zürich and EPF Lausanne, using a set of text files as the main mechanism of data exchange. Soon we realized the need for a more transparent interface that hides low-level communication details and identified Silicon Graphics (SGI) machines as the platform of choice for implementing the graphical interface. The advantages in favor of this platform include availability of fast graphics hardware and possibilities for software combination.

Initially, we implemented a prototype interface using the Inventor graphics tool kit in C++. Soon, we realized that the tool kit had certain limitations. Given this experience, we reevaluated available graphics software and decided to carry forth the implementation of the interface in OpenGL. All subsequent work on the interface was completed using OpenGL on SGI machines, and the results substantiate our expectations.

The final implementation of the program comprises the modules shown in Figure 10.1. Except for the case creation that is still supported through AutoCad and mod4, our own programming interface in AutoLisp, all other modules are accessible and invoked through the graphical interface. The boxes with dark grey shadows represent the modules in CADRE that are automated, whereas those with plain boxes represent the modules in CADRE where user interaction is required.

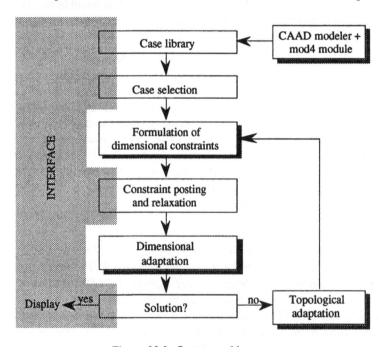

Figure 10.1. System architecture.

4.1. CASE REPRESENTATION

Building designs involve multiple abstractions; for example, architectural, structural, mechanical. It is possible to represent, view, and reason with each abstraction independently. At the same time, each abstraction is related to other abstractions and any change or proposal in one abstraction calls for propagation of such changes in all other abstractions (similar to how practitioners come together to resolve and negotiate design proposals). CADRE integrates two related abstractions of design cases: architectural and structural, both of which are specialized symbolic representations of a common 3-dimensional geometric model.

The architectural issues of a case are specified by elements such as partitioning walls, windows, doors, and spaces. Each element is described in terms of its properties such as location, size, and function, which is primitive information that can be directly derived from a raw model of the case. A graph-based data structure is used to make such information accessible and to simplify reasoning processes concerning spatial relationships. Using such information, some domain knowledge is applied to derive constraints that are crucial to the spatial quality of the case. The constraints are used to define a more generalized case model for processes of adaptation and combination.

The structural information in a case is primarily in the form of element dimensions. Constraints used during dimensional adaptation are generated automatically by generic processes within the CADRE system. For structural engineering design criteria, these constraints are valid for any structure of a given type. Structural information stored in a case is therefore limited to a minimum, and cases can be created from building plans.

A higher level representation of the geometric model is used during the topological structural adaptation process. The structure is represented by a grid and structural modules. A structural module is characterized by the type of structural system and contains domain knowledge for its instantiation as a function of the size of the grid. Different classes of structural modules comprise a different combination of columns, primary and secondary beams, and a slab.

The case library is a collection of design cases represented using the information described: geometric and symbolic pertaining to both architectural and structural issues. At present, the case library in CADRE contains a relatively small case base. Nevertheless, we have selected cases that are complex, large-scale, and diverse. The main focus is on developing a representation mechanism that will support incorporation of new cases without substantial, if any, changes in the future. A larger case base will certainly offer more and perhaps better opportunities for generating innovative designs as a result of case combination.

4.2. CONSTRAINT SPECIFICATION

Constraints are the fundamental element for building generalized models of cases on which the adaptation and combination of spatial layouts are based. In CADRE, constraints come into play during two phases. The LIA group has developed the constraint modelling mechanisms (Hua et al., 1994).

First, every case in the case base comes with its set of constraints on design elements as modeled. Some of these constraints are implicitly represented in each case, such as adjacency relations between spaces that may be derived based on the explicitly represented geometric information, such a' vertices of enclosed spaces. Some other constraints are explicitly represented, such as directional cardinality of exterior spaces. When a case is selected by the user for either adaptation, these constraints are retrieved from the case representation, displayed on the interface, and they are used for subsequent processing by CADRE.

Second, when the user edits or specifies constraints on a selected case using the graphical interface, each constraint introduces restrictions to one or more spaces regarding their geometric properties and relations. Using a set of constraints, it is possible to define spatial qualities that are important in the assessment of architectural designs. In CADRE, constraints are used to control case adaptation and combination so that the spatial integrity of the cases is not compromised. Each spatial constraint is defined with disjunctive and conjunctive combinations of mathematical equalities and inequalities on variables that define spaces. Primitive constraints, such as the minimum and maximum dimensions of a space, can be defined with one single or a conjunctive combination of some equalities and inequalities. More complex constraints can be defined by combining such primitive constraints. For example, a constraint that restricts two spaces from overlapping can be described as a disjunctive combination of four primitive constraints:

space1 does not overlap with space2 :=
        (space1 is on the east side of space2) or
        (space1 is on the west side of space2) or
        (space1 is on the south side of space2) or
        (space1 is on the north side of space2).

Using constraints, a case can be described according to various levels of generality. The most restricted level would be a set of constraints that completely fixes sizes and locations of all spaces in a case and disallows any modification. A more generalized case model may allow some changes on the sizes of spaces and an even more generalized model may allow topological permutations of spatial configurations.

A module integrated in the graphical interface supports direct manipulation and specification of constraints that was previously supported through text files only. Although this module required extensive programming efforts, it has made the use of the program more intuitive and easier. Once constraints are defined, the program invokes other relevant modules; for example, for dimensionality reduction, a process developed by Faltings and the LIA group (Hua et al., 1994), or for structural gridding and system design (Bailey and Smith, 1994). The results of all such processing are displayed graphically.

4.3. CASE ADAPTATION

Based on the given design problem and the constraints posted, CADRE carries out either dimensional adaptation or topological adaptation (followed by dimensional adaptation).

4.3.1. Dimensional Adaptation

Dimensional adaptation involves the solution of a set of linear and nonlinear constraints on the parameters used to describe the building. Because constraints from all abstractions are considered simultaneously, this kind of adaptation produces integrated solutions. Dimensionality reduction is used to identify key parameters for adaptation at run-time, which makes this process different from prototypical design.

Figure 10.2 illustrates an example of the case adaptation by CADRE. The original case—a U-shaped residential design on a rectangular site (Figure 10.2, left)—is inserted in a new site that is truncated on one side. The evaluation of the case in the new site context leads to the identification of constraints related to the corner of the case that now needs to be dimensionally adapted so that it lies inside the new site (Figure 10.2, middle).

Figure 10.2. Axonometric views: Original case (left), its parameterization in new site (middle), and dimensional adaptation (right) by CADRE.

Next, the process of dimensionality reduction identifies only those adaptation parameters that need to be changed and they are dimensionally varied by CADRE. Any changes are propagated to related variables inside relevant areas of the building (Figure 10.2, right). Once the dimensional adaptation process is complete, it may be necessary, as in this example, to also undertake topological adaptation; for example, to resolve problems caused by the shortened wing.

Because CADRE focuses on only what needs to be adapted, as in a local generalization of a case, it finds design solutions more efficiently than other approaches.

4.3.2. Topological Adaptation

Topological adaptation is attempted if a solution cannot be found by dimensional adaptation. Topological relations of spaces are expressed with disjunctive constraints that describe the necessary conditions for maintaining the spatial quality of the case. Valid topological variations of a given case are found by enumerating all possible ways to satisfy the system of disjunctive constraints. The enumeration is carried out by the branch-and-bound method in integer programming so that all possible design layouts are found.

Given a candidate design layout, the structural gridding process searches for possible grids to position columns such that no conflicts arise between structural elements and architectural spaces. The search begins with the grids used in the original case and iterates by alternatively increasing and decreasing the number of bays in each direction. For each candidate grid, a rule-based approach is used to identify suitable structural systems. These rules take into account the feasibility of certain systems for given grid sizes. Depending on the number of possible grids and suitable structural systems for each, more than one solution is generally found. Once the user makes a choice, the dimensional constraints generated during structural gridding and the relevant constraints governing the dimensions of structural elements are passed to the dimensional adaptation process.

Figure 10.3 illustrates the topological adaptation using the Computer Science Building at EPF Lausanne, as an example.

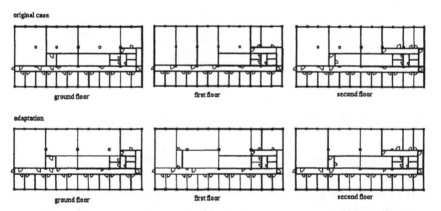

Figure 10.3. Case adaptation: original case (top) and its adaptation (bottom) by CADRE.

The building has a uniform column structure for all the floors but the room layout changes from floor to floor. The free-standing columns in the middle of some lecture rooms; for example, on the second floor, obstruct the proper usage of these spaces. CADRE was used to adapt this case so that the free-standing columns become coincident with the walls. Since the structural system is fixed, CADRE initially attempts to change the dimensions of spaces. This does not produce any solution that satisfies all the constraints. Next, CADRE attempts a topological adaptation of the structural system; for example, a new structural grid followed by a dimensional adaptation. This leads to an acceptable solution for the second floor, but creates a problem on the first floor where there is a free-standing column in the laboratory. Because no dimensional adaptation is possible to resolve this situation, CADRE carries out a topological adaptation of the first floor layout by making the walls and the columns coincident (Figure 10.3, bottom).

4.4. CASE COMBINATION

An alternative to the topological adaptation of one case is the combination of parts of several cases. At this stage, subsets of rooms may be selected from different cases to be combined during the adaptation process. A new room layout is produced by searching for new topologies that obey a set of constraints defining the desired room adjacencies. These constraints are derived from the original geometrical model and, in the event of combination, are also defined by the user. More than one alternative is generally found and the user chooses the layout with which to continue the adaptation. Dimensional constraints on the geometry of rooms for this layout are eventually passed to the dimensional adaptation process (Hua et al., 1994). A default geometric model of the chosen layout is generated using simplified linear architectural dimensional constraints, and is subsequently passed to the structural gridding process.

To illustrate the application of these ideas, the following describes an example of the use of case combination for generating a new design for an architectural school. From the case base comprising the architecture buildings at the University of Houston, Texas, Rice University, the University of Arizona, and Harvard University, we selected two for combination. From Houston, we decided to keep the floor plan with the atrium and the surrounding wings; from Harvard, we wanted the stepped-down design space that is known for its quality as a space for creativity and communication. The goal was to find a meaningful combination of the two. As shown in Figure 10.4 (left), two cases of the architectural schools have been selected for demonstrating case combination in CADRE. The design task is to combine the cruciform volume's atrium in the centre of the Houston building (Figure 10.4, bottom-left) with the terraced studio configuration of the Harvard building (Figure 10.4, top-left). In the process of combination, the four wings, the roof, the atrium, and the lantern of the Houston building are represented with rectangular volumes. Constraints are defined to maintain the proportion and the relation of these volumes so that important characteristics of the Houston building are preserved. These operations are supported by various options available in the constraint specification window in the graphical user interface. The spatial continuity of the terraced studios in the Harvard building is constrained by linking studios with adjacent open spaces. The studios are then inserted into the Houston building by asserting constraints that force the studios to fit in two of the four wings of the Houston building. Figure 10.4 (right) shows four alternatives, generated in one of our experiments for case combination. Constraints can be added or taken out for more restricted or more flexible results. Subsequently, CADRE also carries out the design of the structural system for each generated alternative.

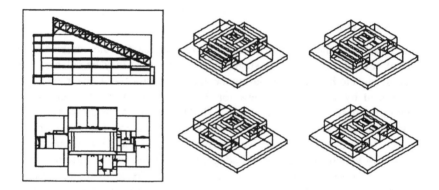

Figure 10.4. Some stages in the case combination process with two buildings as sources.

It was clear from the beginning that we needed to abstract the building to a high degree in order to combine important features. The abstraction we chose was that of bounding boxes of the individual spaces and zones that respected the proportions and the functional relations within these boundaries. The system then produced several alternatives to the floor plan of the Houston building that differed in the placement and orientation of the stepped-down wings for the design studios. The result was somewhat surprising in that it offered unexpected spatial qualities in the design spaces. We then manually inserted one of the proposed designs into the axonometric of the EPFL campus to evaluate the massing in relation to the surrounding buildings.

5. Discussion

5.1. CBD AND CREATIVITY

Can CBD be creative? Does the use of existing cases imply that no fundamentally new solutions are possible? These are serious questions that designers often ask when confronted with the computer method of CBR or CBD. Interestingly enough, they do not ask the same questions when looking at the human activity of CBD. In the latter case, they assume that through some nondefinable activity, even reasoning and designing from cases can lead to new, innovative, and creative solutions. The proof is that architects designing within the framework of a certain style can conceive a large number of innovative and creative solutions. If we use Schank's (1982) definition of creativity as the misapplication of explanation patterns, it will not be difficult to discover a large number of creative solutions from cases.

5.2. LEGAL ASPECTS: FROM QUOTES TO PLAGIARISM

How does one quote a building? How does one give reference to an architect in a design? Taking CBD seriously, these questions must be answered. The problem is not new nor solved, but has become more pressing with the arrival of CBD. If a designer uses a library of parameterized building elements, he knows and accepts the fact that the elements are produced by a manufacturer who guarantees their quality and that there is no possibility on the architect's side to drastically change the design of the element without losing the advantages of mass or parameterized production. This relates to the activity of quoting another author in a paper. The building part is labelled and can be reordered.

The situation is different when moving from components to building units or entire buildings. Kitchens and bathrooms can be produced like furniture. Fertighäuser, a type of prefabricated building, is common in Europe. The idea is to hide the signs of prefabrication as much as possible to make the product look more attractive and massive. In North America, the use of pattern books is common. Entire working drawing sets of buildings are available for very little money compared to the fees that architects must ask for. These books are the best examples for case bases in the traditional sense: The designs appeal to certain clients, the construction is not too difficult, and the buildings come in a price range from affordable to luxury. These are building designs that have proven their value in the past in many aspects.

The next level of complication arises when high class architecture appears in the case bases. World famous architects are known for reasons that are partly represented in their buildings. To quote forms from these buildings means to quote this architect. If the reference is not given, plagiarism is evident. But as it is not possible to label a building or its parts with quotes of the respective architects or buildings, an uneasy feeling remains if certain forms that seem to belong to a certain architect are reused.

The late- and mass-produced imitations of buildings with stylistic quotes from Modern Architecture are an expression of the inappropriate use of a case base. The icons of modern architecture, such as the Mies Pavilion in Barcelona or the Weissenhof Siedlung in Stuttgart, have found a large number of flat, syntactically and semantically incorrect followers. It is particularly annoying that these buildings originated in the name of Modern Architecture and have tarnished its name. This imitation of external stylistic features is even less than straight revivalism. On the other hand, starting from the same cases, there are architects who use these precedents (Oxman and Oxman, 1992) and previous cases correctly. Meier, who designs exquisite buildings in the tradition and style of modern architecture, or Campi, who does not reject modern roots, exemplify the innovative use of a case base.

The problem remains that with any use of a computer-based case base for adaptation, the question of copyright and other legal problems may arise. There is no copyright or patent for a building. If a designer uses the case base of well-known architects and adapts their masterpieces, a lawsuit could be the result. Lawsuits have been brought forward even when a design was to be changed. However, if case adaptation is applied to partial design solutions, the problem may not be as severe. Nobody can claim to be the patent holder of the rectangular room or the arched window, yet it is conceivable that mass production of slightly adapted Botta, Rossi, or Eisenman buildings will rightfully cause problems. It is therefore advisable that architects develop and use their own case base.

5.3. OTHER CHALLENGES FOR CBD

In spite of many positive aspects, there are a few critical drawbacks to CBD that emerge with the development of larger and more realistic systems. Two architectural examples are used here to demonstrate the potential drawbacks.

Case combination is an attempt to solve some of the problems posed by CBD. Case combination combines parts of different designs and thus allows for the creation of innovative products. Case combination poses new critical questions. For example, the quality of the original designs is not guaranteed to be maintained in the resulting new design. Case combination does not eliminate plagiarism caused by randomly combining parts of existing designs. And the deep understanding of design, required when a new product is developed from scratch, might disappear both with the exclusive use of adaptation and case combination.

Another problem not specific to CBD is the difficulty of making decisions on different levels of abstraction. The abstractions we introduce to structure cases and to enable useful operations have the disadvantage that they allow mappings only in one direction. It is easy to move from a more concrete representation toward a more abstract representation. Once on a more abstract representation, for example on that of a graph, and even more so after making changes at this level, it is impossible to return to a less abstract representation in a unique way without generating a large number of alternatives or without moving within very stringent constraints.

5.4. THE INTEGRATION OF CBD-A IN FUTURE DESIGN SYSTEMS

CBD is best explained and explored with small and well-working examples. Ideally, they should function within an environment that is known to the designer and that provides access to other methods and instruments of design as well. The desirable CBD-A environment is therefore to become part of the future CAD programs in which it can be called on at any time and at any level of abstraction. A few conditions must be fulfilled before this is possible:

- CAD representations must include the view as case ready for CBD, or there must be an easy translation from any CAD representation into a CBD representation.
- Cases must easily be added to the case base and indexed manually or automatically. The case base should be central with different designers being able to have individual views on it.
- Visual browsing through the case base, as well as search and selection based on criteria, must be possible.
- The system must support dimensional and topological adaptation as well as case combination.
- The system must check constraints and allow the fixing of free variables in real time.
- The final result must be compatible with other computer-based design methods.

If these conditions are met, CBD-A could become an important and useful component of all future design systems. Considering the time it took for parameterized design systems to become integrated into mainstream CAD systems, an integrated CBD-A system might still take 5 to 10 years for its realization.

6. Conclusions

The application of CBD in architecture offers a powerful opportunity to overcome some of the problems associated with traditional computer-based design methods.

- CBD has the potential to overcome the complexity barrier and allows for more than trivial computer-generated design solutions.
- CBD has the potential to eliminate the nondecompositionality problem of design.
- CBD offers an attractive opportunity to maintain the quality of a selected case with minimal search or adaptation.

Although CBD is mainly thought to solve routine design tasks, some of the techniques employed in case adaptation, such as automatic detection of conflicts and creation of new parameters, make it useful also for innovative and creative design.

Originally, we saw applications for CBD directly in architectural design for the development of entire building structures. We have learned since then that representation and manipulation issues are some formidable barriers to overcome. Therefore, the application of CBD to design elements up to the size of individual spaces seems to be more relevant. In routine design, CBD could be of significant use for entire buildings.

More advanced solutions to design need more complete representation and reasoning techniques. One problem is that many building designs that appear as a straight application of CBD were conceived differently. This is verifiable by asking the architect. Many architects are not aware of the term CBD and much less agree that they use it in their design process.

CADRE has been successfully tested on several practical examples. An advantage of the system is the support it provides for preliminary structural design, and the automatic resizing of structural elements and architectural spaces during dimensional adaptation. In spite of such advantages, there are a few important challenges to CBD that have emerged during the development of the system. These aspects are both in technical areas and within domains of design practice, considering legal and ethical issues.

Case combination combines parts of different designs and thus allows for the creation of innovative results. However, case combination poses a new set of challenges. For example, it does not guarantee that the quality of original designs will be maintained in new designs. Also, the issue of possible plagiarism caused by combining parts of existing designs may become critical. Furthermore, an exclusive use of CBD and case combination may retract from an original learning and understanding of design, and this capability is needed for the creation of any truly new product in the preliminary design stage.

Although the development of computational techniques to support both routine and innovative design tasks has been a long-standing agenda in the design circles, CBD in architecture is only now maturing as an approach that may address some of these issues. Our research in the development of CADRE and the work by other researchers demonstrate the feasibility and attractiveness of this approach and, at the same time, uncover new issues for future research agenda.

Acknowledgments

The authors want to thank their co-investigators, Boi Faltings and Ian Smith from the Laboratoire d'Intelligence Artificielle, who have developed crucial computational foundations for the project, as well as all the junior research faculty. The project was made possible by NFP 23, the Swiss Science Foundation program for Artificial Intelligence and Robotics.

References

Bailey, S. F., and Smith, I. F. C.: 1994, Case-based preliminary building design, *Journal of Computing in Civil Engineering*, 8(4), 454–468.

Burkhalter, M., and Sumi, C.: 1994, *Forstwerkhof, Turbenthal, Holz Bulletin 37*, Lignum, Zürich, pp. 1–5.

Dave, B.: 1994, Case based design: Issues for future agenda, *Workshop on Case-Based Design Systems*, Artificial Intelligence in Design'94 Conference, Lausanne, pp. 8–10.

Faltings, B., and Smith, I.: 1996, Model-based case adaptation, *in* M. L. Maher, and P. Pu (eds), *Issues and Applications of Case-Based Reasoning to Design*, Lawrence Erlbaum Associates, Hillsdale, NJ (this volume).

Gero, J.: 1994, Preface, *in* J. Gero, and F. Sudweeks (eds), *Artificial Intelligence in Design '94*, Kluwer Academic, Dordrecht, NL, ix–x.

Hua, K., Smith, I., and Faltings, B.: 1994, Integrated case-based building design: topics, *in* S. Wess, K. Althoff, and Richter, M. (eds), *Topics in Case-Based Reasoning, Lecture Notes in Artificial Intelligence 837*, Springer-Verlag, Berlin, pp. 436–445.

Jencks, C.: 1982, *Architecture Today*, Harry N. Abrams, New York.

Madrazo, L.:1993, *Key Words: Script*, Chair for Architecture and CAAD, ETH, Zürich.

Mitchell W. J.: 1990, *The Logic of Architecture*, MIT Press, Cambridge, MA.

Mitchell, W., Liggett, R., Pollalis, S., and Tan, M.: 1992, Integrating shape grammars and design analysis, *in* G. Schmitt (ed.), *CAAD Futures '91*, Vieweg, Wiesbaden, Germany, pp. 17–32.

Oechslin, W.: 1993, Computus et Historia, *in* G. Schmitt (ed.), *Architectura et Machina*, Vieweg, Wiesbaden, Germany, pp. 14–23.

Oxman, R. E., and Oxman, R. M.: 1992, Refinement and adaptation: Two paradigms of form generation in CAAD, *in* G. Schmitt (ed.), *CAAD futures '91*, Vieweg, Wiesbaden, Germany, pp. 313–328.

Papamichel, K., and Protzen, J.-P.: 1993, The limits of intelligence in design, *Proceedings of the Fourth International Symposium on System Research, Informatics and Cybernetics*, Baden-Baden, Germany, pp. 3–4.

Rosenman, M. A., Gero, J. S., and Oxman, R. E.: 1992, What's in a case: The use of case bases, knowledge basis, and databases in design, *in* G. Schmitt (ed.), *CAAD Futures '91*, Vieweg, Wiesbaden, Germany, pp. 285–300.

Schmitt, G.:1993, *Architectura et Machina*, Vieweg, Wiesbaden, Germany.

Schulze, F.: 1986, *Mies van der Rohe: Leben und Werk*, Ernst & Sohn, Berlin.

Smithers, T.: 1994, AI in design needs knowledge level theories, *in* J. S. Gero, and F. Sudweeks (eds), *Fourth Workshop on Research Directions for Artificial Intelligence in Design*, Key Centre of Design Computing, University of Sydney, pp. 73–79.

chapter eleven

INTEGRATING CASES, SUBCASES, AND GENERIC PROTOTYPES FOR DESIGN

COSTAS TSATSOULIS
The University of Kansas

PERRY ALEXANDER
The University of Cincinnati

We present a methodology for CBD that integrates whole design cases, pieces of cases (subcases), generic design prototypes, and skeletal design plans into a single framework. Each case is viewed as a collection of components. Viewing a case in this way allows adaptation through replacement of components by defining new problems based on the overall problem goal and the internal problem-solving state. Interconnections between components allow the reuse of solution substructures rather than entire components. We describe three systems, ASP-II, PANDA, and BENTON, that share the mentioned integrated methodological framework.

1. Introduction

Many CBR systems have been demonstrated in domains where case information can be represented at one level of abstraction. However, in design problem-solving a design can be extremely complex, necessitating the use of multiple levels of abstraction. The ability to represent design case information at different abstraction levels provides a wealth of information including problem modularization and organization of these modules. The systems described here generalize the idea of case representation (and, consequently, of CBR) by including other types of memories in addition to completely instantiated cases and taking advantage of the internal structure of cases. Cases, subcases, design prototypes, skeletal design plans, adaptation rules, and indices are stored, retrieved, and used during the design process. Each design system takes various actions based on the memories that are considered most applicable to the problem. How the retrieved memory is used depends on the problem and the type of information it contains.

In this work, we describe three CBR design systems. ASP-II, is a case-based system to design simulation plans for communication systems. PANDA is a system to assist novice designers in the component-level design of fire engines. BENTON is a distributed CBR system that designs software specifications (Alexander, 1992; Alexander and Tsatsoulis, 1991; Roderman, 1992).

The domain of ASP-II (Analysis Simulation Planner-II) is generating plans for automated computer analysis of electromagnetic compatibility (EMC) (Alexander et al., 1989). ASP-II generates simulation and analysis plans in a high-level language simulation language for COEDS (Alexander et al., 1989). The COEDS model for performing EMC analysis centers around the test plan, a declarative representation of what the user desires of an EMC analysis activity. The user specifies for COEDS what outputs are desired, and the test plan interpreter then determines how to obtain the specified information. The use of a declarative specification is a major step forward in performing such analysis because the burden of selection, configuration, and integration of analysis and presentation tools is removed from the user and assigned to the ASP-II reasoner.

ASP-II combines case-based and skeletal planning by viewing a case as a fully instantiated, skeletal plan. In doing so, a single plan memory representation applies to both fully instantiated plan memories (cases) and partially instantiated plan memories (skeletal plans). In either case, the structure of the plan memory is a partially ordered collection of submemories, or a procedural network (Sacerdoti, 1975) of submemories representing subplans or actions. ASP-II is not simply a skeletal planner with a collection of preinstantiated plans. The instantiated cases in ASP-II may or may not be associated with more abstract skeletal plans. Cases are not necessarily instantiations of skeletal plans already in the system. In addition, cases are adapted in ASP-II using traditional rule-based adaptation and subcase replacement as opposed to pure constraint posting in traditional skeletal planners. ASP-II is capable of both adapting fully instantiated plans and instantiating more abstract plans. Neither is ASP-II simply a CBR system with a specialized case representation. ASP-II has the capability of adding detail to a skeletal plan based on the constraints provided by the planning environment. Unlike classical constraint posting skeletal planners, ASP-II uses retrieval to apply constraints indicated by the planning environment. When retrieving memories, the similarity function indicates relative applicability. More detailed knowledge of a problem situation provides more constraints and thus reduces the number of memories deemed applicable to the current problem.

The second intelligent design system, PANDA, is an assistant for novice designers of fire engines. The domain of application was selected because the fire engine design is specified by the firefighters themselves, who are nonexperts. Design driven by nonexperts and potential users of a product has been mostly neglected by researchers. Slowly, however, such design may become widespread with the technologies of simulation-based design and scenario-driven design reaching new levels of maturity.

PANDA was developed based on our methodological approach of representing designs as cases, subcases, and generic prototypes. Additionally, PANDA is the implementation of a methodology that attempts to address the special needs of novice designers. PANDA uses CBR to generate a design, but, if it lacks expertise, it uses generic design prototypes to guide the novice user in completing the design. The prototypes constrain what the novice designer can do and form a template of acceptable design actions. PANDA users can also ask the system to evaluate design alternatives, and the system has an interactive mode that can advise the user about advantages and disadvantages of various components that can be used to achieve a desired function of the fire engine. PANDA allows the users to input specifications on different levels of detail and abstraction, from user wishes to concrete functional specifications to actual equipment required. So, the user may indicate that the fire engine should operate in humid weather, or that it should have a cab that holds 8 people, or that a herringbone structure should be used. The system then uses a rule-based system to translate all requirements into functional specifications, bringing all of them to the same level of detail and analyzing them for any constraint violations or inconsistencies. These specifications are used in the CBR component of PANDA to perform the actual design.

Design is performed in a manner similar to the one used in ASP-II, where cases, subcases, and generic design prototypes are combined to form a potential design. Domain knowledge and case histories are then use to adapt designs, to make components fit together, and to satisfy all design specifications. If PANDA is unable to finish a design, it allows the user to perform manual adaptations and provides advice about the suitability and quality of various design choices.

Finally, BENTON is a hybrid reasoning system that designs software specifications for Modula-3 programs. BENTON differs from the previous two systems in that it distributes its case base and design prototypes in a multi-agent, blackboard architecture, applying each knowledge part in an opportunistic fashion. In addition, BENTON uses cases not only to represent artifact solutions but also to represent solution methodologies, thus implementing both transformational and derivational analogy in the same system. Blackboard agents execute plans that organize and control other agents' problem-solving activities.

BENTON effectively combines techniques developed in the ASP-II and PANDA systems by using case-based planning to control the design process, and CBR to synthesize potential solutions.

BENTON's domain is transformation of informal specifications into the Larch/Modula-3 (LM3) specification language. It reuses specification fragments by applying the ASP-II reasoning methodology. Each specification is viewed as a collection of specification fragments. Unlike plans, these fragments are not partially ordered; however, each does play a specific role in the specification. This characteristic is required by the ASP-II approach. In addition to specification fragments, BENTON stores plans for constructing specifications. These design plans are treated exactly as plans are in ASP-II. Subcases are reused and replaced using the ASP-II approach. BENTON design plans allow representation of large, complex designs in a flexible, hierarchical fashion. By distributing the case base among several agents, specific indexing, retrieval, and adaptation processes are targeted to a specific problem class. These more specific systems are much easier to develop and manage than a single, monolithic case base.

2. Methodological Approach: The Structure of a Design Case

Our work is based on a simple premise: a design cannot be represented by a case. Although it is true that designs *have* been represented as a single case in previous research, it is also true that these designs were usually very simple. For example, CHEF (Hammond, 1989) and JULIA (Kolodner, 1987) are both considered design problem solvers, both represent finished designs as a case, but in both, the design produced is very simple. The design of a complex artifact cannot be represented by a case if we expect to use this representation for future reasoning. In our work, a complex system is represented by a number of memory structures, which are integrated in a reasoning framework. The structures we use are cases, subcases, and generic prototypes, sometimes also referred to as skeletal plans.

Most complex systems are collections of components where each component performs a subfunction within the system. In ASP-II, a component is a simulator run; in PANDA, a component is a fire engine subsystem; and in BENTON, a component is a specification fragment or design plan action. In each domain, a design case is a collection of subcases (or case fragments) representing the components of the system designed. Clearly, it is not enough simply to define what components constitute a system. For the collection to function correctly, components must be properly integrated. Plan actions must be ordered, fire engine components must be connected correctly, and software specifications must be composed properly. The structure of a case is the information used to integrate its components. In other words, the case structure contains reusable information. Knowing the organization of components in a system is as valuable as knowing what the components are. Case structure is used in ASP-II, PANDA and BENTON to replace components causing case failure, retrieve and reuse case components, and extract useful high level prototypes.

Each case component has a function in the overall system. Knowing the system's structure can help identify that function, allowing the component to be replaced or reused. ASP-II, for example, replaces case components by taking advantage of a plan's structure as a partial ordering of actions. By knowing the state of the world prior to an action and how that action changes the state of the world, the function of the action is determined. With this information, the action can be retrieved and reused, or it can be replaced by formulating and solving a new problem.

Designers often use prescriptive information to perform various design steps: They know the structure of the finished system without knowing the details of the individual components constituting the design. This prescriptive information is similar to design prototypes (Gero, 1990) and to skeletal plans. With the system's structure known, the missing component's function can be determined and used to retrieve and reuse components. ASP-II and PANDA use such structures as generic, high-level system prototypes. Each component definition is treated as a CBR problem, and the case-based reasoner retrieves and adapts components (or collections of components) for each system element.

BENTON uses case structures in the same manner as ASP-II and PANDA, but extends the technique to include the structure of problem-solving activities. BENTON is a multi-agent reasoning system within which each agent has specialized problem-solving knowledge. BENTON uses both derivational and transformational analogies by storing both design plans and designs in its agents' case bases. High-level agents execute design plans that send problems and instructions to other agents. These plans both organize the agents and represent skeletal solutions. The partial ordering of actions controls when agents are activated and in what order. The goals defined in the partial ordering represent the structure of the solution. Thus, the structure of the design plan represents both the agent organization and the solution structure.

In the rest of this chapter, we describe three CBR design systems that implement our methodology of integrating case contents, subcase structure, and generic prototypes to solve complex design problems.

3. ASP-II: A CBR System that Designs Simulation Plans

ASP-II generates plans for automated computer analysis of EMC (Alexander et al., 1989). ASP-II generates simulation and analysis plans in a high-level language interpreted by the COEDS (Alexander et al., 1989) analysis system.

ASP-II combines case-based and skeletal planning by viewing a case as a fully instantiated skeletal plan. In doing so, a single plan memory representation applies to both fully instantiated plan memories (cases) and partially instantiated plan memories (skeletal plans). In either case, the structure of the plan memory is a partially ordered collection of submemories or a procedural network (Sacerdoti, 1975) of submemories representing subplans or actions.

3.1. ASP-II MEMORY STRUCTURES

Cases and skeletal plan memories in ASP-II consist of a task environment associated with the plan memory, a set of features that describe the plan memory, and a case or skeletal plan. The task environment represents the global context of the plan memory. This structure situates the memory in an execution environment, constraining possible solutions. Features describe various aspects of the plan memory that may be useful in determining when the plan structure might be reused. The case or skeletal plan is either a single action or a partially ordered list of other memories.

One key element in ASP-II is the unified representation of skeletal plans and cases. The concepts of features and task environment are universal for skeletal plans and cases; the details of the plan are simply missing in a skeletal plan structure. Features still describe the skeletal plan in the same way that cases are described, allowing the skeletal plan to be retrieved when appropriate. In addition, features support the proper instantiation of a skeletal plan in a similar manner to the way that features can support the adaptation of a case. Thus, one memory structure is used to represent both an abstract skeletal plan and a specific, episodic memory.

The environment structure associated with each plan-memory structure situates the plan and provides a planning environment. This is termed as giving the memory a global context. *Environment* includes such information as the physical environment associated with the system, objects available for manipulation, available tools, and additional necessary information not a part of the plan itself. Generally, the goal of the planning process is expressed with respect to the planning environment.

The action list represents the plan associated with a memory structure. Either a completely instantiated plan or a skeletal plan, the structure of an action list resembles that of a procedural network. Each plan is a partially ordered set of independent memory structures, complete with features describing each. Both the partial ordering of the memory structures and the requirements features indicate how the memory structures together represent a more complex plan.

The lowest level action list is a single action. A memory structure whose action list consists of only a single action is called a base case. A *base case* corresponds to an atomic action or an instantiated operator—an action that cannot be viewed at a lower level of abstraction. Figure 11.1 gives an example of a base case in ASP-II. The environment consists of a set of collocated transmitters and receivers with certain power and frequency characteristics. The features define the goal of the simulation run and the special characteristics of the environment. In our example no-wb and no-fh indicate that there were no wideband and no frequency hopping transmitters in the environment. After the simulation run, the result was the calculation of SPS undesired power for transmitter rx1, which was -145 dB. The action list indicates the simulation designed and used.

```
(<mem-0>
  environment (<x-tx1 4.0 3.0 …> <tx1 3.0 3.0 …> <tx2 3.1 3.0 …>
    … <rx1 4.0 -120.0 …> …)
  features (no-wb no-fh
    (after (SPS-undesired-power rx1 -145)))
  action-list (COSAM rx1 tx1 tx2 … (SPS-undesired-power rx1 -145))
```

Figure 11.1. A base case representing a COSAM analysis run in an environment with several transmitting and receiving devices.

More complex plans are represented by action lists that order other memories. Each memory structure accessed by an action list is referred to as a submemory. The submemory is a free-standing memory structure and can be accessed as such. The inclusion of memory structures in action lists simply provides additional information about how the memory structure is used with others to accomplish a higher order goal. Such information forms a packaging hierarchy for the memory representation within the case itself.

Skeletal plans and cases differ in the content of their action lists. Cases have completely instantiated action lists. One can take a case and, without any modification, execute that case. In contrast, skeletal plans are not completely instantiated and cannot be executed prior to filling in missing details. At some level in a skeletal plans structure, the action list of one or more submemories is nil. Features describing such memories are present and are used to instantiate the null action list.

Figure 11.2 shows a skeletal plan structure for deriving maximum SPS transmit distance for a receiver. Structure <mem-1> consists of two substructures, <mem-2> and <mem-3>, indicating that calculating the value is performed in two sequential actions. First, find SPS-undesired-power and second, find SPS-distance. Because there is no action list for finding SPS-undesired-power in <mem-2>, both that memory and any memory referencing it are skeletal plans. Thus, both <mem-1> and <mem-2> are skeletal plan structures. In contrast, <mem-3> is a case because it has a specific action list associated with it.

```
(<mem-1>
 environment (<x-tx1 4.0 3.0 …> <tx1 3.0 3.0 …> <tx2 3.1 3.0 …>
   … <rx1 4.0 -120.0 …> …)
 features (no-wb no-fh
   (after (SPS-distance rx1 150)))
   action-list (:serial <mem-2> <mem-3>)

(<mem-2>
 environment (<x-tx1 4.0 3.0 …> <tx1 3.0 3.0 …> <tx2 3.1 3.0 …>
   … <rx1 4.0 -120.0 …> …)
 features (no-wb no-fh
   (after (SPS-undesired-power rx1 -145)))
 action-list nil)

(<mem-3>
 environment (<x-tx1 4.0 3.0 …> <tx1 3.0 3.0 …> <tx2 3.1 3.0 …>
   … <rx1 4.0 -120.0 …> …)
 features (no-wb no-fh
   (before (SPS-undesired-power rx1))
   (after (SPS-distance rx1 300)))
 action-list (LINCAL rx1 tx1 (SPS-undesired-power rx1 -145)))
```

Figure 11.2. Memory representing a skeletal plan for calculating SPS-distance.

ASP-II uses the *before* and *after* features to define the preconditions and postconditions of any simulation action. Thus, a simulation action can only happen if *before* is satisfied, while its successful completion will generate the *after* features (see <mem-3>, Figure 11.2). It is important to stress that the *before* feature is not exactly similar to the preconditions list of plan operators. *before* defines the environment; it also may include goals and constraints, thus defining both when an action is possible and when it is desirable.

3.2. ASP-II RETRIEVAL

The objective of retrieval in ASP-II is to collect and sort a number of memory structures appropriate to the current problem. Retrieval is performed using a weighted average of features matching between the current problem and all the memory structures in the system. Features may also match on an inheritance hierarchy (for example, receivers rx1 and rx2 will match because they are both receivers), but with weaker matching scores.

If ASP-II can identify a single memory structure that fits the problem well (i.e. higher than a user-defined threshold of acceptable similarity), it will proceed with adaptation. The structure may be a case, or instantiation, or contain skeletal plans. Most times, however, ASP-II will not be able to identify a single, complete, integrated memory structure, and it will attempt partial retrieval to find a collection of submemories that might be used to solve the problem.

Partial retrieval takes advantage of the partial ordering of submemories in an action list and the general tree structure formed by a memory and its submemories, to retrieve portions of existing, complex plans for reuse. The process starts by collecting two sets of memories, those that match the before feature and those that match the after feature of the current problem. Now the problem becomes finding a path from one memory that matches the before feature and one memory the matches the after feature using the partial ordering of the tree structure formed by submemories. What we are doing is using the internal context of memories, namely the partial time order, to retrieve parts of a memory as a potential solution. If such a path between memories is found, a possible solution is created from the collection of memories in the path. The system then proceeds to adaptation and testing.

3.3. ADAPTATION AND INSTANTIATION IN ASP-II

Adaptation and instantiation represent two methods that fit retrieved memories to a specific problem. Theoretically, adaptation and instantiation are quite different operations. Adaptation is applied to a fully instantiated case to apply it to a new problem. In most systems, adaptation is a process of applying adaptation rules to fix a case, or is an application of a domain theory to a case. In contrast, instantiation is a process of removing generality from a skeletal plan, constraining the solution to fit the current problem. The primary difference between adaptation and instantiation in this domain is the presence of variables in the skeletal structure. Instantiation is a configuration task of assigning values to skeletal plan variables. No such variables appear in a fully instantiated case; the specifics of the case are altered directly by the adaptation system. In ASP-II, adaptation and instantiation operate similarly.

Adaptation is viewed as the recursive process of modifying the features and action list of a case, using procedural rules. The features of a case are adapted. Then, if the action list is a partially ordered set of cases, each case is recursively adapted in the same manner. When the adaptation of a subcase fails, the subcase is replaced by replanning. The action list associated with the subcase is ignored and a new plan is generated based on the requirements and results of the failed subcase. If a subcase cannot be replanned, then the overall case must be rejected. Several attempts may be made to replan the subcase.

The principle behind adaptation by replanning is that rejecting the entire case because one aspect of it is not adapted by the adaptation knowledge is not wise. Adaptation by replanning is useful when the bulk of the case is correct and rule-based adaptation cannot correct problems in the failed part. Replanning is performed in a case-based fashion: ASP-II will search the case base for another subcase that performs a simulation function similar to the one of the failed subcase, and will replace the failed subcase action list with the newly retrieved one.

A skeletal plan memory is like a case memory with an incomplete action list. Instantiation is the process of assigning an action list to the memory. This process exactly parallels adaptation by replanning. Thus, when the action list of a memory needs to be instantiated, a planning process based on the before and after features of the memory is attempted. The null-action list can be instantiated either by finding a case or another skeletal plan that contain a similar problem solution. In the first case, the null action list is instantiated to the action list of the retrieved case or subcase, and then adaptation is performed to correct any dissimilarities. If the structure retrieved is a skeletal plan, its action list will contain a more detailed, but still not completely instantiated action list. Recursively, ASP-II will then attempt to instantiate the more detailed action plans.

3.4. FAILURE PREDICTION

Once a plan has been generated, failure prediction is performed. Failure prediction uses three techniques: rejection by adaptation processes; retrieval of similar failed cases; and simulation. If adaptation fails, ASP-II treats the plan as failed and makes no attempt to repair it. If a case passes through the adaptation process, the memory is searched for similar failed cases. If a failed case that is highly similar to the newly generated plan can be retrieved from memory, the newly generated plan may be repaired or rejected prior to evaluation. The failed case must be maximally similar (similarity value 1.0) to the new case to cause failure. In less tolerant domains, that threshold value could be changed to reduce the possibility of letting a plan destined to fail actually execute. In this way, ASP-II avoids making the same mistake twice by not repeating activities it can recall as failing. Finally, following retrieval of failed cases, the plan is simulated. Currently, the simulation model used is a causal network implemented using a Petri-net model.

Any plan that fails or is predicted to fail goes through a repair process. ASP-II repairs cases using the same approach to adaptation—a combination of rule application and replacement of failed subcases. The repair process first applies repair rules similar in nature to adaptation rules. Repair rules differ from adaptation rules as they generally access some aspect of the failure situation. In this way, domain specific debugging information is applied to the problem. Next, the system identifies subcases responsible for failure and replaces those subcases by replanning. This process is exactly the same as adaptation by replanning and may take the form of a skeletal or CBR process.

If failure is not predicted, the new plan is executed and stored in the memory base along with an indication of the success or failure of the plan. Failed cases help ASP-II avoid making the same mistake twice. Successful plans are currently used only to provide a richer set of cases for retrieval. We feel that a desirable enhancement would be using similar, successful cases and learning techniques to generate new general plans.

3.5. ASPECTS OF HYBRID REASONING IN ASP-II

Hybrid reasoning occurs because either case-based or skeletal planning may result from any planning or replanning activity. When performing adaptation by replanning, a skeletal plan structure may be retrieved and applied to the replanning problem. The result is a switch from case-based planning activities to skeletal planning activities. Alternately, when instantiating a null-action list, a case structure might be returned and adapted to fit the problem. The result here is a switch from skeletal planning activities to case-based planning activities.

In ASP-II, similarity is more general, measuring the relative applicability of a memory to a new problem. If a skeletal plan has the highest similarity value of a collection of memories, applying that memory requires a skeletal technique. Analogously, when a case has the highest similarity value, case-based techniques are required to apply the case to the current problem.

4. PANDA: A Case-Based System to Aid Novice Designers

The design of complex systems by nonexperts is an area of design that has been largely neglected by researchers in intelligent design methodologies. The implicit assumption is that all design activities are performed by highly skilled and experienced experts, and research in intelligent design aids is aimed at improving the performance of these experts (Kolodner, 1991). But there are many design activities performed by novices. Some are simple configuration problems (e.g., a customer putting together a computer system, or selecting features of a new car); others are true design problems of varying complexity (e.g., remote sensing scientists designing an antenna, a microwave transmitter, and a data collection system for an experiment). In these examples, the designers are not experts in the area in which they are asked to create a system and, often lacking the need to perform similar design activities, will never be more than novices. Novice designers may also be engineers who are experts in the field in which they design, but are new to a company or organizational environment. Such designers are knowledgeable in their domain but are novice in the design history of their environment. These novices have the motivation to become expert but need special assistance during their transition period. Both classes of novice designers lack the history associated with the activity they are performing. They need different kinds of assistance than the simple cognitive support needed by expert designers. Novice designers need an assistant system designed to work interactively to coach them through the design process. The reasoning behind each design decision needs to be revealed to the novice whenever this information is requested. The designer may also choose to make his or her own design decisions and the system must determine the repercussions of the design choice.

The Pumper Apparatus Novice Design Assistant (PANDA) is a design system to aid in the design of pumper apparatus. Fire engines[1] are an appropriate domain because the fire apparatus design is specified by the firefighters themselves who are nonexperts. Fire engines today in the United States are not simple utilitarian vehicles, but are also designed as a showpiece for the local community (NFPA, 1991). PANDA addresses only the first three design steps—formulation, synthesis, and analysis—and allows the designer to perform evaluation and reformulation. PANDA was developed based on our methodological approach of representing designs as cases, subcases, and generic prototypes or skeletal plans. Additionally, PANDA is the implementation of a methodology that attempts to address the special needs of novice designers. Our system was built to help firefighters to design pumper engines, and implements the following features:

- Allows design specifications to be given on multiple levels of abstraction, from general desires to requirements, to specific components. It also allows incomplete or inconsistent specifications.
- Uses parts of old design cases to construct possible solutions.
- Uses domain knowledge and case histories to adapt designs.
- Can evaluate its own designs and present justifications to the user.
- Can provide the user with alternative design decisions and can explain the advantages and disadvantages of each one.
- Allows browsing of the design space and can discuss design possibilities with the user.

4.1. PROBLEM FORMULATION IN PANDA

Formulation is the first step in the design process where the designer describes the desired artifact by specifying goals and constraints. These requirements are then transformed into a language used by the synthesis module. In PANDA, the designer is allowed to specify design constraints for the pumper on various levels. For instance, the user may want a fire engine that can operate as a command center. This high-level goal would translate into several lower-level structural constraints. The user may also specify a 500-gallon water tank for the pumper, which is a low-level, structural constraint.

PANDA decomposes all goals and constraints into a low-level requirements vocabulary using a traditional rule-based methodology. PANDA uses elementary structural components and their attributes as its requirements vocabulary because

---

[1]We will use the words *pumper engine, pumper apparatus, fire engine, fire apparatus* interchangeably to describe the type of fire engines PANDA designs.

higher-level goals translate into one or more specific structural constraints (e.g., the goal to operate a fire engine in a humid environment will translate into specific metals used to build the fire engine and specific constraints on the cab design, such as an enclosed crew compartment), and because studying consistency and completeness of specifications is simpler on the structural level. The result of applying the rule-based system to the initial specifications is a set of low-level structural requirements for the system being designed.

Next, PANDA studies the low-level requirements for inconsistencies. This is easy because all requirements exist at same level of representational abstraction, and inconsistent or conflicting requirements can be identified easily. PANDA displays the conflicting requirements and allows the user to reformulate the problem. Dealing automatically with conflicting constraints is avoided because that would require reasoning about design intent.

4.2. DESIGN SYNTHESIS IN PANDA

During synthesis, PANDA generates a potential solution based on formulation goals. Once the goals and constraints of the desired artifact have been specified and translated, PANDA's synthesis submodule uses CBR to generate one or more possible designs.

Design cases in PANDA, as in the other two systems described in this chapter, may contain a variety of structures, including completely instantiated cases, subcases, and generic prototypes[2]. As a result, PANDA allows the use of cases that are a combination of descriptive structures (fully instantiated descriptions of old designs or parts of designs) and prescriptive structures (skeletal prototypes of how some parts of a design should look).

4.2.1. Case Indexing and Organization

Cases in the case base are indexed according to their structural features. This simple indexing scheme is possible due to the rule-based preprocessor used in the formulation stage that translates all requirements into a common structural requirements vocabulary. To convey the most information to the designer, PANDA's designs contain some process information, knowledge about failure, drawbacks, or unexpected success of a design. The structural information is divided into hierachies. At the top of each hierarchy is the generic design prototype of the fire engine, shown in Figure 11.3.

---

[2]Here we do not imply the use of prototypes as defined by Gero (1990), but skeletal, prescriptive structural components.

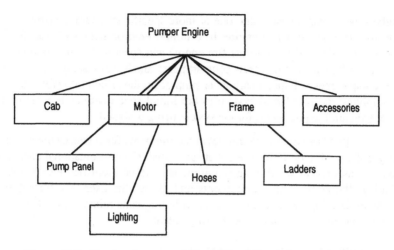

Figure 11.3. Top-level structural hierarchy of fire engine components.

Under each category is another partonomic hierarchy further defining these subparts. Under each upper-level partonomic hierarchy are instantiations of this category. In addition to the structural features, the case base stores information on the advantages and disadvantages of each structure. This information is gathered from design experts and from the experience of firefighters who use the equipment. The data is stored in cases as explanations for various structural features. Although PANDA currently cannot reason about these advantages and disadvantages, the explanations can be used by the user to make design decisions. An example of this is the following:

Feature: Enclosed Cab

Advantages: Low noise, climate control. Meets current NFPA standards.

Disadvantages: Higher cost, increased cab length.

4.2.2. Case Similarity and Retrieval

During case retrieval, similarity is assessed using a method of weighted sums. Each feature in PANDA is assigned a weight that indicates its importance in affecting the achievement of the overall design goals. For instance, a front-mount motor reduces the cab capacity whereas a rear-mount motor reduces the water tank capacity. Consequently, the location of the motor is weighted highly, and PANDA will first try to retrieve cases that require no adaptation of the motor location. Aesthetic decisions and structures that are easily modifiable, such as the types of compartment doors, have a lower weight value.

PANDA attempts to retrieve a case satisfying as many strongly weighted requirements as possible in the lowest level of abstractions to avoid extended adaptation. If a requirement cannot be satisfied at the lowest level, PANDA climbs the requirements hierarchy, and always returns at least an uninstantiated skeletal design prototype to suggest as a solution.

4.2.3. Case Adaptation

Once a case similar to the current situation is retrieved, it is adapted to handle all current constraints. Because PANDA targets novice designers, it attempts to produce a design that is as complete as possible. Whenever it cannot fully instantiate the design, it uses its generic prototypes as prescriptive structures to guide the novice designer in completing the design within the domain constraints.

PANDA uses one of three adaptation techniques: parametric adaptation (tweaking), reinstantiation, or generic prototype selection. Parametric adaptation (tweaking) is the simplest and most common adaptation technique. If a feature in the retrieved case does not exactly match the initial requirement, PANDA uses a set of procedural rules to see whether it can change the case and make it match the user's requirements. Tweaking is used most often in adapting numerical attributes, but it can also be used to change discrete symbolic values. If parametric adaptation cannot generate a perfect match between the retrieved case and the requirements, PANDA uses reinstantiation. Reinstantiation allows for a submodule from one case to be added or replace an existing submodule in another design solution. PANDA does not blindly pick pieces from one design and place them in a new one. The system uses constraints to be satisfied and changes to be made to other components to select a piece of an old case for adaptation by reinstantiation. Wherever possible, whole subsections of a component are kept intact to take advantage of any optimization performed by the original designer when creating that case solution. The generation and propagation of design changes due to reinstantiation of components is handled by critics implemented as rules.

Components whose values cannot be fully instantiated (due to incomplete or inconsistent initial constraints or incompleteness of knowledge) are presented to the designer as prescriptive prototypes. This helps the designer know what needs to be done, but makes him or her responsible for the appropriate instantiation. Prescriptive design prototypes are stored as generic cases that describe the general structure of a pumper, but give no details as to specific design decisions.

The initial design may also be instantiated by combining portions of several design solutions. This is often the case when no complete solution can be found to solve the current design problem. In the design of fire apparatuses, the cab from one fire engine in the case base may satisfy some of the given constraints while the body from another case satisfies the rest. This ability to take a portion of one design and combine it with another, rather than collecting specific components from different cases, allows for an optimized subassembly to be kept intact. Although critics must determine if these substitutions are compatible with one another, it is still more likely to obtain an optimized design using this method generating a design entirely from first principles.

4.3. DESIGN ANALYSIS IN PANDA

The designer may query the system for an explanation of design decisions. PANDA uses the explanations and annotations of retrieved cases to answer such questions. The user can also retrieve alternate solutions for various subassemblies from the case base. Because the user is allowed to design freely and receive suggestions from the system, the user can explore the design space. This form of iterative redesign is an effective teaching tool for the novice designer.

PANDA evaluates a design by comparing the constraints satisfied by the current solution with the initial goals specified by the designer. It also checks for any constraints violated by the current design and whether any component of the designed pumper engine is still represented by a prototype (i.e., it is not fully instantiated), and alerts the designer. By allowing the designer to instantiate prototypical structures or change an existing structure instantiation, designers can develop structures themselves, perhaps choosing a solution from the case base that is based on personal or aesthetic reasons. The system can then ensure that no goals or constraints are compromised by the designer's decisions.

4.4. AN EXAMPLE DESIGN BY PANDA

To illustrate how PANDA and a designer work together to generate a useful design solution, we present an example of system use. For readability, the language of discussion is English text and explanatory comments are added in italics. The actual implementation uses a combination of menus and text input to facilitate interaction.

The only information about the design that the novice is sure of is that the fire engine needs to carry six firefighters, they need to be able to use the pumper as a command center, and they would like to have hydraulic ladders on the truck. The truck should be made of aluminum.

Once this data has been entered, a rule-based system is used to translate these initial specifications into specific structural constraints. The following interaction represents the design process (throughout the examples, we italicize embedded comments, discussion, and explanations, and underline feature and case names):

Computer: The preceding requirements have been translated. The following constraints were used to select a solution:

    Cab Capacity: 4
    Motor Location: Rear
    Pump Panel Location: Midship
    Cab Canopy: Yes
    Material: Aluminum
    Accessories: Hydraulic Ladders

The cab capacity, material, and accessories goals are direct requests of the user. The other three requirements are created by the rule-based system that translated the user's request that the pumper be a command center.

Based on this information, the following case was retrieved:
    CASE 8
        Cab design:
    Capacity: 4
    Cab canopy
    Enclosed cab
    Frame: Wishbone
    Material: Aluminum
    Pump Panel Location: Driver's side
    Hose Connections: Front(1), Passenger Side(1), Driver's
Side(1)
    Water Tank
    Capacity: 500 Gallons
    Construction: Steel
    Hoses: 1500 feet of 2.5" hose, 400 feet of 1.5" hose, 3 hard
suction hoses
    Ladder:
    Location: Passenger's Side
    Accessibility: Standard
    Storage Compartments: Hinged
    Lighting: Light Bar
    Accessories:
    Horns, top mounted
    Siren, Front mounted
The following changes were made to the case by reinstantiating
the ladder subassembly with that of another case:
    Ladders:
    Location: Top
    Accessibility: Hydraulic

Originally, the retrieved case had a standard ladder; PANDA found a piece of another design that satisfied the hydraulic ladder requirement, replaced the standard ladder, and in the process critics were used to adopt the location of the ladders from passenger's side to top.

```
The following constraints are still unsatisfied:
    Pump Panel Location: Midship
Cannot find a case to satisfy this constraint.
```

PANDA knows of other cases with pump panels located in the middle, but these cases are too dissimilar from the one being adapted. PANDA will not reinstantiate using components from very different cases, so it cannot adapt the case. It must retrieve a more abstract adaptation and finally it reaches the prototype.

```
The following changes were made to the case by reinstantiating
the ladder subassembly with that of a prototype:
    Pump Panel Location: Generic
```

PANDA gives up and indicates that a pump panel should be designed, but it does not know how. The user can now work with the system to decide how to design the pump panel.

User: What alternatives are there to the pump panel location?

Computer:
```
RETRIEVED CASE #2
    Pump Panel Location: Side
    Advantages:
    Standard location. Cost effective.
    Disadvantages:
    Limited view of the fire scene.
    Possible limited view of hose connections.

RETRIEVED CASE #8
    Pump Panel Location: Midship      Advantages:
    This location allows the engineer a full range of vision while
controlling the pumps. It also allows access from either side of
the pumper.

Disadvantages:
This location generally increases the overall length of the
pumper or decreases the cab capacity. It also requires either a
front or rear mount engine.

RETRIEVED CASE #11
Pump Panel Location: Rear
Advantages:
Better view of the fire scene than standard side mount.
    Disadvantages: Reduces allowable tank capacity.
```

User: I would like information on the air horns.

These queries allow the user to evaluate the design, consider alternatives, and make final decisions. The information presented by PANDA is contained in the cases as explanations and annotations, and in the partonomic hierarchy as descriptors of the generic components.

5. BENTON: A Multi-Agent CBR Tool that Designs Software Specifications

BENTON is a multi-agent, blackboard-based design system that transforms informal user requirements into formal specifications. BENTON assists its user by translating requirements expressed in a simple attribute-value form into a formal specification in Larch/Modula-3 (Jones, 1991), a Larch interface language for Modula-3 (Nelson, 1991). Such assistance includes automatically handling routine problems as well as larger problems requiring innovative solutions. The resulting specification is a collection of Modula-3 interface modules containing LM3 specifications and Larch Shared Language (Guttag, Horning, and Modet, 1990) traits to support new constructs when necessary.

BENTON uses an adapted version of the ASP-II reasoning system to specification fragment and design plan reuse. BENTON differs substantially from ASP-II and PANDA in that it is a multi-agent system in which case the base is distributed among multiple several agents; it reuses not only solution fragments, but also solution methods; and it implements several problem solving methodologies among its agents, implementing a form of task analysis. The ASP-II and PANDA design systems only store previous designs, thus using only transformational analogies. BENTON adds design plans supporting derivational analogies. The result is an application of CBR to the design process, as well as the design itself.

As in ASP-II and PANDA, subcases play an important role in the BENTON reasoning process. BENTON agents retrieve and reuse component fragments and subplans from design plans. Thus, parts of solutions and parts of solution methodologies may be reused. Likewise, during adaptation activities, BENTON agents replace solution and design plan fragments using the ASP-II adaptation by replanning approach. Thus, adaptation of solutions and design plans is achieved by replacing failed components. This combines the specific techniques used in ASP-II, whose case base contains only plans, and PANDA, whose case base contains only structures.

The most significant use of case structure in BENTON occurs when manipulating a design plan. A *design plan* is a partially ordered collection of instructions to be executed by a single agent. Some of these instructions will initiate communication with other agents, requesting them to solve sub-problems, suggesting problem-solving strategies and other metalevel activities. Each action that causes communications with other agents, particularly those initiating subdesign activities, represents a piece of the overall design activity. ASP-II retrieved and reused plan fragments based on pre- and post-conditions. BENTON achieves the same result when reusing a plan action. If all agent actions initiated by a design plan were combined into a single sequence, the result is a fully instantiated design plan executable by a single reasoning system, exactly analogous to the ASP-II methodology. However, the multiagent approach supports the development of problem-solving specialists, compartmentalizing subdesign activities and reduction of complex design activities to a single high-level action. This significantly reduces the complexity of indexing and retrieval algorithm development, feature design and adaptation activities.

5.1. THE BENTON DESIGN PROCESS

The BENTON design process is based on a three-phase design model (Chandrasekaran, 1990; Gero, 1990; Maher, 1990). This design model decomposes the design task into synthesis, analysis, and evaluation subtasks. Synthesis generates a hypothesis from requirements, analysis predicts the behavior of the hypothesis, and evaluation determines if the hypothesis' predicted behavior satisfies initial requirements and determines the next action. Together, these tasks are referred to as a synthesis-analysis-evaluation (SAE) design process.

For any design task, a number of methodologies exists to achieve its goal. Task analysis involves selecting a methodology for a generic task using characteristics of the problem as selection criteria (Chandrasekaran, 1990). Problem characteristics and the problem-solving environment (Barletta and Mark, 1988) provide information for methodology selection. BENTON starts its problem-solving activity with an SAE design task breakdown and instantiates each task with methodologies based on problem characteristics. The three primary means of achieving task analysis in BENTON are implementation of methodologies in knowledge sources, execution of design plans developed using CBR and skeletal planning, and multiagent reasoning.

Multiple knowledge sources may exist for achieving each design task. The blackboard control system determines what knowledge source(s) to apply, using results from applying knowledge source preconditions. Design plans (Brown and Chandrasekaran, 1985; Mostow, 1990) allow a BENTON agent to specify partially ordered actions for achieving tasks, thereby supporting decomposition of design tasks. Implementing actions allowing design plans to send messages to other agents supports generation of subtasks and multiagent reasoning.

5.2. THE BENTON AGENT STRUCTURE

BENTON is a collection of agents constructed around the SAE design model. Each BENTON agent is a blackboard based problem solving system (Erman, Hayes-Roth et al., 1980; Nii, 1986a; Nii, 1986b). An agent implements the design model using blackboard spaces to hold information for each design task and knowledge sources to implement the design task transformations. Knowledge sources transform and move information from one blackboard space into another, implementing the SAE process. The blackboard architecture supports convenient implementation of task analysis using knowledge sources to implement problem-solving methodologies and preconditions to determine when methodologies apply. The blackboard also provides a convenient framework for building agents and simulating agent communication.

A BENTON agent is comprised of three primary blackboard spaces containing requirements, hypothesis, and behavior units. Three types of knowledge sources implement SAE methods by transforming units from one space into another. When a unit is added to the requirements space, synthesis knowledge sources trigger, generate hypotheses, and add units to the hypothesis space. When a unit is added to the hypothesis space, analysis knowledge sources trigger, generate behaviors, and add units to the behavior space. When a unit is added to the behavior space, evaluation knowledge sources trigger, evaluate behaviors, and take appropriate action based on the results. This comprises the SAE loop in the BENTON agent.

The blackboard control module handles execution of BENTON knowledge sources using a prioritized queue scheduling algorithm. Execution is a four step process of triggering, determining priority, scheduling in the execution queue, and actual execution. A knowledge source triggers as a result of events signaled by the blackboard. Adding, changing, deleting, and moving blackboard units all generate events that can trigger knowledge source execution. All BENTON knowledge sources of the same type trigger on the same events.

5.3. SINGLE AGENT EXAMPLE

This example documents a BENTON agent's activity during the specification of a simple data structure. In this example, the data structure specification agent (the `data` agent) designs a specification of a type representing an object that can take on one of four values:

```
(:object "Status"
  :list-of-values
  ("Enrolled" "NotEnrolled" "Probation" "Graduated"))
```

SAE processes are each attempted in sequence, driven by knowledge-source transformations. Note that design of this simple data structure, achieved by a single agent, primarily involves predominantly traditional reasoning techniques.

5.3.1. Solution Synthesis

The problem is added to the `data` agent's requirements, space triggering its synthesis-knowledge sources. In this example, two knowledge sources execute and attempt to produce LM3 specifications for the problem. The first, a CBR knowledge source is discussed here. A second schemata-based reasoning knowledge source also produces a solution; however, its reasoning process is not presented, as it does not involve CBR.

The CBR knowledge source uses the ASP-II CBR approach. Its knowledge-source precondition determines that it can perform the desired task and detects nothing that would indicate CBR will fail. Thus, the precondition returns a high priority value. Conditions that might decrease the priority of CBR knowledge sources include problems involving arbitrary iteration and domains where small changes in case structure result in large changes in case behavior.

The knowledge source considers using a TEXT type because of the alphanumeric nature of the values, as well as BOOLEAN and subrange types. The BOOLEAN type is rejected because it can only represent sets of cardinality 2, and the subrange is rejected because no type is available to restrict appropriately. The CBR knowledge source chooses an LM3 specification using a TEXT data type as an initial solution.

```
TextType =
    <* BASED ON Text
    INITIALLY t = empty *>
        TEXT;
```

The case-based knowledge source adapts the initial solution to fit the problem using rules that replace the name of the type. This results in the following potential solution:

```
StatusType =
    <* BASED ON Text
    INITIALLY t = empty *>
        TEXT;
```

This synthesis activity ceases and the potential solution is added to the hypothesis space.

The schemata-based knowledge source produces a similar specification based on a user defined enumerated type. This alternative solution is involved in the analysis and evaluation processes, thus it is included here:

```
StatusType =
    <* BASED ON StatusType-set *>
        SET OF
            (Enrolled,Probation,Graudated,NotEnrolled);
```

The synthesis activity halts with two proposed solutions, one text-based and the other an enumerated type.

5.3.2. Solution Analysis

When a knowledge source adds a unit to the hypothesis space, analysis knowledge sources trigger and attempt to predict its behavior. Like synthesis knowledge sources, the analysis knowledge sources employ CBR, schemata-based reasoning and procedural knowledge.

The simplest analysis knowledge source embeds the data type specification in an appropriate stub and calls the Modula-3 compiler on the result to test syntactic correctness. The knowledge source executes because it recognizes the hypothesis as a Modula-3 code fragment as well as an LM3 specification. If the hypothesis is not recognized as a Modula-3 code fragment, the precondition returns 0 and the knowledge source is not scheduled for execution. The results of this activity are then added to the behavior space. This result says nothing about the correctness of the specification with respect to initial requirements. However, an evaluation knowledge source can declare the hypothesis a syntactically correct specification, satisfying an implicit domain requirement.

Two additional knowledge sources suggest proofs and/or demonstrations of correctness. The first attempts to prove that the data type includes all values specified by the requirements. The second attempts to prove that the data type includes only values specified by the requirements. These knowledge sources execute because they recognize the LM3 specification that represents the type of data structure for which they can generate analysis information.

First consider the TEXT-based hypothesis. The syntactic-correctness knowledge source easily embeds the type description in a Modula-3 stub and calls the Modula-3 compiler on the result. Compilation succeeds and the knowledge source adds a unit to the behavior space indicating syntactic correctness.

Using a CBR approach, the two remaining knowledge sources attempt to retrieve instructions for automated proofs and/or demonstrations from a problem involving another TEXT type. The first attempts to show that all desired elements can be represented by the hypothetical data type. The data agent has no proof for this characteristic, but does have access to a demonstration program. The agent prefers a proof, but the demonstration suffices when none exists. Figure 11.4 shows the Modula-3 code fragment retrieved from a previous activity, and the code adapted to the current problem. The demonstration succeeds and a unit is added to the behavior space, indicating the type can represent all necessary values.

Using a CBR approach, the final knowledge source attempts to retrieve instructions to prove the TEXT type represents only the desired values. In this case, no such proof exists because the TEXT type is not restricted to the values specified. Thus, the knowledge source adds a unit to the behavior space indicating that the type can represent more than the required set of values.

```
MODULE Main;                      MODULE Main;
  IMPORT Wr, Stdio;                 IMPORT Wr, Stdio;
  TYPE GradeType =                  TYPE StatusType =
    <* BASED ON t: Text              <* BASED ON t: Text
       INITIALLY t = empty *>          INITIALLY t = empty *>
       TEXT;                           TEXT;
  VAR                               VAR
    TestVar : GradeType;             TestStatus : StatusType;
  BEGIN                             BEGIN
    TestVar := "A";                  TestStatus := "Enrolled";
    TestVar := "B";                  TestStatus := "NotEnrolled";
    TestVar := "C";                  TestStatus := "Probation";
    TestVar := "D";                  TestStatus := "Graduated";
    TestVar := "F";                 END Main.
  END Main.
```

          (a)   (b)

Figure 11.4. Listing of (a) the retrieved code fragment for demonstrating the type represents all necessary values; and (b) the code fragment adapted for the current problem.

Now consider the enumerated type generated by the schemata-based knowledge source. As before, the first knowledge source embeds the specification in a Modula-3 stub and calls the compiler. The specification is syntactically correct; therefore, it compiles correctly and the knowledge source adds an appropriate unit to the behavior space.

The next knowledge source attempts to prove the data type can represent all specified values. The knowledge source retrieves a proof used for a different enumerated type. It then adapts the proof to fit the new specification. The initial and adapted proof implemented using the Larch Prover (Garland and Guttag, 1991) are shown in Figure 11.5. The proof succeeds for the SET-based specification and the knowledge source adds a unit, indicating this to the behavior space.

The final knowledge source attempts to prove the hypothetical data type represents only specified values. This time, the case-based reasoner finds a proof for a similar enumerated type and adapts it. The original and the adapted proof are shown in Figure 11.6.[3] Unlike the TEXT type, the proof completes successfully for the enumerated type. The knowledge source then adds a unit to the behavior space indicating proof results.

Analysis completes adding three units to the behavior space representing characteristics of the two candidate solutions.

---

[3]Note that the variable declaration section is omitted for brevity. It is the same as the previously retrieved proof.

```
declare variables              declare variables
  Grade: Elem                    Status: Elem
  GradeType: Set                 StatusType: Set
..                             ..
declare ops                    declare ops
  A, B, C, D, F : -> Elem        Enrolled, Probation,
..                               Graduated, NotEnrolled : -> Elem
assert                         ..
  A \in GradeType              assert
  B \in GradeType                Enrolled \in StatusType
  C \in GradeType                Probation \in StatusType
  D \in GradeType                Graduated \in StatusType
  F \in GradeType                NotEnrolled \in StatusType
..                             ..
prove                          prove
  A \in GradeType                Enrolled \in StatusType
  & B \in GradeType              & Probation \in StatusType
  & C \in GradeType              & Graduated \in StatusType
  & D \in GradeType              & NotEnrolled \in StatusType
  & F \in GradeType            ..
..                             qed
qed
              (a)                              (b)
```

Figure 11.5. Listing of (a) the original value inclusion proof retrieved from the case base; and b) the proof adapted to fit the current problem.

```
prove                          prove
  when Grade \in GradeType yield   when Status \in StatusType yield
  Grade = A | Grade = B            Status = Enrolled
  | Grade = C | Grade = D          | Status = Probation
  | Grade = F                      | Status = Graduated
..                                 | Status = NotEnrolled
  complete                      ..
  qed                             complete
                                  qed
              (a)                              (b)
```

Figure 11.6. Listing of (a) the original exclusive value proof retrieved from the case base; and (b) the proof adapted for the current problem.

5.3.3. Solution Evaluation

The three analysis knowledge sources produce different analysis results indicating three aspects of the specification's ability to satisfy requirements. One unit represents syntactic correctness, another that indicates elements of this type takes values only from the desired values set, and another indicates that the type covers all desired values. In isolation, none of these results indicate whether the specification satisfies initial requirements, thus the evaluation knowledge sources must consider them together. Unfortunately, analysis knowledge sources generate these results in an arbitrary order and evaluation knowledge sources trigger each time a unit is added to the behavior space.

Three knowledge sources evaluate the generated specifications. The first knowledge source's precondition recognizes when the triggering behavior unit indicates syntactic correctness. If the check succeeds, this knowledge source declares that the behavior satisfies the requirements and returns the hypothesis as a solution. The second knowledge source's precondition recognizes when the triggering behavior unit indicates syntactic correctness or the specified type represents all desired values. When either of these units triggers the knowledge source, it checks the existence of the other type in the behavior space. If it does not exist, the controller does not schedule the knowledge source. If it does exist, the controller schedules the knowledge source for execution. If the behavior units indicate syntactic correctness and the specified type represents all desired values, this knowledge source declares that the behavior satisfies the requirements and returns the hypothesis as a solution. Finally, the third knowledge source's precondition recognizes the same units as the second, plus a unit indicating the specified type represents only desired values. When one of these units triggers the knowledge source, it checks the existence of the other two in the behavior space, and the controller schedules the knowledge source for execution appropriately. If the units indicate the specified type represents all necessary values, represents only necessary values, and is syntactically correct, this knowledge source declares the behavior satisfies the requirements and returns the hypothesis as a solution.

These three evaluation knowledge sources represent varying degrees of satisfaction from minimal syntactic correctness to a strong proof of representational correctness. Knowledge source preconditions not only check the presence of necessary units, but also determine when their correctness assessment methodology applies. Problem requirements and knowledge of synthesis methodologies help determine the appropriate type of evaluation. If synthesis techniques generate correct solutions with a high degree of confidence, (correctness preserving transformations, for example), then a weak, syntactic evaluation may be in order. In this situation, the syntax checking knowledge source's precondition returns a high priority value. When using more heuristic synthesis techniques, the syntax-checking knowledge source is scheduled with low priority or ignored completely. By default, BENTON agents prefer the strongest form of correctness. Scheduling of evaluation knowledge sources is a prime example of task analysis in the agent.

Both solutions are generated by heuristic agents; thus, there is no guarantee of correctness. In this situation, evaluation prefers the strongest form of satisfaction, and the knowledge sources checking compilation, or compilation and representation, trigger but are not executed. The knowledge source implementing the strongest correctness check does execute and rejects the TEXT-based hypothesis because the type represents more than desired values. In reaction to this failure, the agent deletes the TEXT-based hypothesis. However, the same knowledge source accepts the SET-based hypothesis because it is syntactically correct and represents only desired values. In reaction to this success, the agent returns the SET-based hypothesis as a solution.

5.4. BENTON DESIGN PLANS

Thus far, a single BENTON agent solves problems using a single knowledge source to directly transform information. In the single agent example, each knowledge source implements an SAE method. Through schemata instantiation, case adaptation, and procedure execution, BENTON effectively reuses solutions from previous problems, implementing a form of transformational analogy. BENTON agents also implement derivational analogy by reusing solution methods from previous problems. These methods take the form of design plans. Through the use of design plans, a BENTON agent can generate a plan for achieving a design subtask, execute that plan, and indirectly obtain a solution.

5.4.1. Design Plan Structure

BENTON design plans are procedural networks (Sacerdoti, 1975) implementing partially ordered collections of actions. A BENTON design plan uses three action types, split, join, and common actions. Common actions implement functions, whereas split and join actions implement parallelism and provide synchronization. Any action executes when the action(s) directly preceding it completes. If an action has no actions preceding it, then the action represents the first action in the plan and executes immediately. If an action has no actions following it, then the action represents the final action in the plan and its execution terminates plan execution. A well-formed plan has only one initial action and only one final action.

A common action has an associated macro that implements the action's effect. A common action has zero or one preceding action and zero or one following action. Thus, a common action executes immediately following the completion of its only preceding action. A split action has zero or one preceding action and one or more following actions. When a split action executes, all paths directly following it execute in parallel. A join action has one or more preceding actions and zero or one following action. A join action executes when either all actions directly preceding it complete or when one action preceding it completes. A parameter in the join indicates what trigger condition it uses. The split action generates parallel threads and the join action synchronizes their completion.

The send action is a special common action that implements communication with other agents using string-based message passing. The send action sends a message to an agent and awaits a response. On receiving the response, the send action terminates and the next action executes. The most common message asks an agent to solve a problem. Such a message is of the form (add <req>) where <req> is a requirements set. The receiving agent processes this message by adding a new unit representing <req> to its requirements space. This initiates problem solving in the receiving agent. When the receiving agent finishes its problem-solving activity, the send action is again used to return the result. The receiving agent indicates the success or failure of its attempt and returns any resultant structures.

5.4.2. Design Plan Applications

In the previous single agent example, three analysis knowledge sources used different techniques to analyze hypotheses. Evaluation knowledge sources look for groups of behaviors indicating that each behavior represents a part of the desired analysis results. However, each analysis result was independently generated and existed in the behavior space without reference to the others. Using a design plan, the analysis agent could coordinate generation of each analysis result and consolidate that information in the behavior space.

Figure 11.7 shows a procedural network representing a BENTON design plan for achieving the same analysis results. The plan develops and executes the same three proofs in parallel and composes the results into a single behavior unit. This design plan shows how a design task is achieved by using an ordered collection of functions.

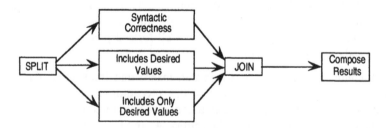

Figure 11.7. Design plan for performing analysis done in the three-agent example by three analysis knowledge sources.

In contrast, a design plan can decompose a task into ordered subgoals achieved by independent problem-solving activities. Consider the design of a RECORD type. Because a RECORD consists of several fields also having types, the BENTON data agent decomposes it into the design and composition of types for several fields. The BENTON data agent uses a knowledge source to design records by generating requirements for each field, adding each field's requirements to its requirements space, designing data types for each, and composing the results into a RECORD type. The design of each field is an independent problem handled by the data agent. In this case, the design task is achieved by generating a collection of subgoals for the agent.

A more general use of design plans for subgoal generation is sending requirements sets to other agents. Using the send action, a plan may indirectly add requirements to the requirements spaces of other agents. When receiving a message of the form (add <req>) where <req> is a requirements set, an agent adds a unit containing <req> to its requirements space.

An example common in BENTON is design of abstract data types. When designing an abstract data type for storing and retrieving information, one must design a data type to represent the information, a container to store the information, and a search function to retrieve information. A BENTON design plan decomposes this problem as shown in Figure 11.8.

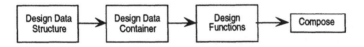

Figure 11.8. A plan for designing a simple data storage and retrieval abstract data type.

Specifications for the data type are sent to the data agent, the container type to the dataorg agent, and the search routine to the search agent. Note that these design activities do not occur in parallel because the data container design requires information from the data structure design, and the search routine design requires information from the data container design. Note also that the data agent's plan used for designing RECORD structures could employ send actions to send requirements to itself or another data agent. Adding each field's requirements directly to the requirements space avoids communications overhead.

Using design plans allows BENTON to structure the design process and reuse process information as well as solution information. ASP-II and PANDA use a single methodology for solving each new problem. BENTON generalizes design methodologies forming the SAE process. The system adds detail to the SAE process only at design time, based on the problem environment. Thus, features of the problem influence the selection and adaptation of design processes. The use of subcases allows process component reuse and replacement in the same fashion as ASP-II supports solution component reuse and replacement. Effectively, BENTON adapts the view of a solution as a composite structure to solution methodologies, extending the ASP-II reasoning approach to derivational analogy.

5.5. MULTI-AGENT EXAMPLE

The following example demonstrates how BENTON uses a design plan involving four agents to generate a complex specification. The problem is to design a specification representing a simple record system. This record system must keep track of students and classes, providing a link between each class and the students enrolled in it. In prose, the initial requirements have the following form:

"Each student has an associated name, 6 digit ID and enrollment status. Possible enrollment status values include Enrolled, NotEnrolled, Probation and Graduated. Each class has an associated 6 character name and a collection of no more than 40 enrolled students. Must support search of the student records by ID and class records by name."

In BENTON's informal specification language, the initial requirements have the following form:

```
(:specification "ClassRecord"
 (:object "Student"
    (:object "Name" :alphanumeric t)
    (:object "ID" :min 0 :max 999999 :numeric t)
    (:object "Status" :legal-values
      ("Enrolled" "Probation" "Graduated" "NotEnrolled")))
 (:object "Class"
    (:object "Name" :alphanumeric t :length 6)
    (:object "Students" "Student" :finite 40))
(search "Student" "ID" :av-time :reasonable)
(search "Class" "Name" :av-time :reasonable))
```

5.5.1. Solution Synthesis

To initiate problem solving, the user sends the requirements to the `manager` agent. A knowledge source implementing the ASP-II reasoner generates an initial solution based on the structure of the requirements. The knowledge source recognizes that two problem-solving activities may occur at once. Using this fact, it retrieves a high level plan for a parallel design activity. This plan is shown in Figure 11.9.

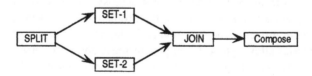

Figure 11.9. Initial plan schemata generated by synthesis knowledge source.

The knowledge source specializes the solution using constraints from the problem, constraint propagation rules, and CBR. Using the skeletal plan shown in Figure 11.10, the knowledge source specializes each parallel subproblem to design data structures, containers, and functions respectively. Thus, the component is replaced with a more specific component generated using the initial plan structure and characteristics of the problem. This is analogous to ASP-II replacing plan components due to problem characteristics. This activity results in the plan shown in the following figure.

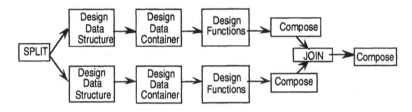

Figure 11.10. First specialization of plan schemata for student record problem.

Finally, the knowledge source specializes the solution for the specific problem by generating requirements sets for each plan action from the original requirements. Using this plan, the synthesis knowledge source generates each data structure and search routine by sending a data-type design problem to the `data` agent, followed by a data structure problem to the `dataorg` agent, and finally a search routine problem to the `search` agent. Each `send` action sends a requirements set to an agent and waits for a result. The top path handles the design of student-related components and the bottom path handles the design of class-related components. On subproblem completion, the `join` action synchronizes execution. Finally, the `compose` action composes the subproblem results to form a single solution. Figure 11.11 shows the final plan executed by the `manager`'s synthesis knowledge source.

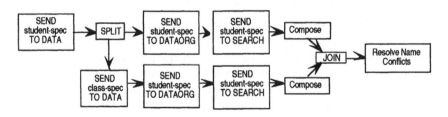

Figure 11.11. Final plan generated by `manager` agent for solving student record design problem.

When specializing the plan, the manager agent recognizes that the student record structure is needed to design the class record structure and therefore schedules the student-structure design task before the split action. This insures that the student data structure will be available before the class structure is designed. The manager agent's plan modification knowledge sources work much like critics (Sacerdoti, 1975) in assessing the generated plan and making necessary modifications. Specifically, the agent's knowledge sources use a constraint-posting approach (Stefik, 1981).

In producing this design plan, each plan action is treated both in isolation and as a plan component. During the design of the high-level plan, the problem and plan are treated as single structures. As detail is added, the reasoner begins to manipulate individual plan actions as subcomponents of the larger plan. Looking at single plan actions enabled the generation of problems for other agents. Looking at the plan as a whole enabled detection and correction of an ordering problem. Thus, the reasoning system views the plan as a composite structure.

During specialization of the design plan, adaptation of each design action involved only the manager agent's knowledge of how to solve the problem, namely, that a problem could be generated for another agent. The agent, given the task of completing each plan activity, views the action as a goal and either retrieves a design plan or a potential solution. But the plan action is analyzed using local knowledge of solving that specific problem. Structuring the reasoning process in this manner dramatically decreases the complexity of constructing case and knowledge bases. It is a much simpler task to design feature types for agents specializing in data structure, algorithm, and abstract data type design than to construct a single, monolithic case base for the overall problem domain.

Note that plan adaptation occurs in exactly the same manner as in the ASP-II system. Problems are generated from the high-level plan actions and CBR employed to generate potential solution actions. These actions may exist in the case base in isolation, or as a part of a larger plan.

Figures 11.12 and 11.13 are a representative portion of the solution generated by executing the instantiated design plan. Figure 11.12 shows the data types and interfaces whereas Figure 11.13 shows the generic package instantiated by the solution. Note that the solution reflects the structure of the plan. The TYPE section results from work done by the data agent. For each object described in the initial requirements, the data agent defines a data structure. When dealing with composite data, RECORD structures are used with types defined for each field. This reflects the data agent's decomposition of RECORD structure design into the design of each field and composition of all results. The plan executed by the manager agent reflects only the general structure of the problem—each plan action sending a subproblem to an external agent. By decomposing the problem in such a manner, specialists perform lower-level design activities, simplifying case base construction and feature design.

The resulting specification fragment is added to the hypothesis space and, like the single agent example, it is analyzed and evaluated. BENTON's capabilities for analyzing large, composite solutions is somewhat limited. Beyond component analysis done by participating agents, the analysis of the resulting specification involves only syntactic correctness. For brevity, the process of generating and executing such a test is not presented here.

```
TYPE
 StudentType
 <* BASED ON StudentType-tuple *>
    = RECORD
       Name : NameType;
       ID : IdType;
       Status : StatusType;
       END;
 IdType
 <* BASED ON IntegerEnumeration
     INVARIANT last = 999999
     AND first = 0 *>
     = [0..999999];
 StatusType
 <* BASED ON StatusType-set *>
     = SET OF {Enrolled,Probation,Graduated, NotEnrolled};
 ClassType
 <* BASED ON ClassType-tuple *>
    = RECORD
       Name : NameType;
       Students: StudentsArray;
       END;
 NameType
 <* BASED ON r:Text
    INITIALLY t = empty
    INVARIANT length(r) <= 6 *>
       = TEXT;
  StudentsArray
  <*BASED ON array(Student) *>
       = ARRAY [0..39] OF Student;

INTERFACE
 StudentBinarySearchTree=
 BinarySearchTree(StudentType,StudentContainer);
 END StudentBinarySearchTree.

INTERFACE
 ClassBinarySearchTree=BinarySearchTree(ClassType, ClassContainer);
 END ClassBinarySearchTree.
```

Figure 11.12. Data types and interfaces developed for the student record design problem.

```
GENERIC INTERFACE
 BinarySearchTree(Element,BTree);
 <* USING
 BinaryTree(Element FOR E, BTree FOR C)
 *>

 EXCEPTION Error(ErrorCode);

 TYPE  BTree
 <* BASED ON T: BinaryTree
      INITIALLY size(T) = 0 *>
     <: REFANY;
 ...
 PROCEDURE New : BTree;
 <* MODIFIES NONE
  ENSURES
   FRESH(RETURN\post)
   AND size(RETURN\post) = 0 *>
 ...

 PROCEDURE Search(READONLY T: BTree; READONLY K: KeyType) : Element
      RAISES (Error);
 <* MODIFIES NONE
  ENSURES
   Key(T) = K => RETURN\post = Contents(T)
   AND Key(T) > K => RETURN\post = Search(T.Right,K)
   AND Key(T) < K => RETURN\post = Search(T.Left,K)
   EXCEPT isLeaf(T) => RAISE\post = Error(NotFound) *>

PROCEDURE Insert(VAR T: BTree; READONLY E: Element);
 <* MODIFIES T
  ENSURES
   isLeaf(T) AND Key(E) > Key(T AND T.Right\post = E
   OR Key(E) < Key(T) AND T.Left\post = E
   OR NOT(isLeaf(T)) AND Key(E) > Key(T) AND Insert(T.Right,E)
   OR Key(E) < Key(T) AND Insert(T.Left,E) *>
```

Figure 11.13. Generic module included in the student record design solution.

5.5.2. Agent Organization

A side effect of design plan execution is the organization of BENTON agents. Initially, no agent organization exists, except that the manager agent assumes the responsibility of accepting initial requirements. When the manager agent executes a design plan and sends problems to the data, dataorg, and search agents, a hierarchical arrangement results.

In this example, the data agent generates appropriate date type specifications for each aggregation of information and declares them to be records. Notice that the ClassRecord type contains an array. The data agent does not deal with containers; thus, to generate this type, it executes a plan sending requirements (:object "Students" "Student" :finite 40) to the dataorg agent. The dataorg agent designs the array and returns the result for inclusion in the record structure.

A side effect of the data agent directly communicating with the dataorg agent is the violation of a strict hierarchy. If BENTON agents adhered to a strict hierarchical organization, the data agent would send requirements to the manager agent. Figure 11.14 shows the organization of agents at various times during plan execution. The dynamic organization of BENTON agents avoids unnecessary communications overhead. Multiagent reasoning research demonstrates the inefficiency of purely hierarchical agent organizations. Furthermore, the use of design plans supports organization of BENTON agents in a manner deemed best for the current problem rather than using an organization selected *a priori.*

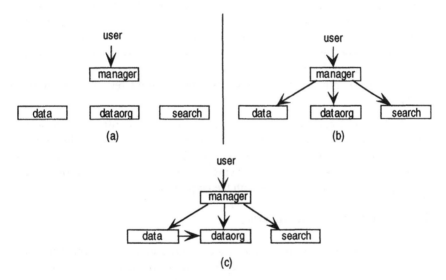

Figure 11.14. Organization of BENTON agents; a) before plan execution; b) after initial execution; and c) during the design of the student record database.

6. Related Work

Our work in CBR-based design is influenced by a lot of other work in CBR, CBD, and intelligent design. Due to space restrictions we cannot compare our work to all CBD systems, but we limit ourselves to systems that have directly influenced us.

Kolodner's (1991) vision of how a Design Assistant should function greatly influenced the capabilities that we implemented in ASP-II and PANDA.

Kolodner's other work has also influenced some of our decisions in storing designs in inheritance and partonomic hierarchies; for example, JULIA (Kolodner, 1987). Similar ideas about the organization of designs are used in other systems, as, for example, in ARCHIE, a case-based architectural design system (Domeshek and Kolodner, 1992; Goel, Kolodner, Pearce, and Billington, 1991). Other recent CBD systems include the work described in Zhao and Maher (1992), Huhns and Acosta (1988), Hinrichs (1992), and so forth.

Our adaptation technique is a combination of parameterized and derivational adaptation. Parameterized adaptation (tweaking) is a very common adaptation method. Our method of derivational adaptation is somewhat similar to the one used by Barletta and Hennessy (1989) in the domain of designing layouts for autoclave loads and to decompose-and-recombine used by JULIA (Kolodner, 1987). This technique is appealing for adaptation in CBR systems because one reason for using cases is that it is assumed that the cases in the case base are well thought out and optimized for the current situation. This often means that certain portions of the design are put together in such a way as to optimize performance. During adaptation, if one of these well thought out portions of the design case are substituted into another design case, they should retain their optimum performance.

Finally, most current CBD assistants will deal with only retrieval or case adaptation, leaving the other to the designer, as for example, the work by Mriryala and Harandi (1991), Domeshek and Kolodner (1992), Hua, Smith and Faltings (1992) and others. Our systems address both issues by retrieving and adapting cases, albeit sometimes with the help of the user.

7. Summary and Conclusions

The implementation of the three systems presented here exemplifies the usefulness of CBR techniques applied to design. Initial specifications on any level of abstraction, and possibly incomplete and inconsistent, are translated into a consistent vocabulary of elementary structural requirements. Old designs are stored in a case base that organizes cases in inheritance hierarchies with skeletal, uninstantiated design prototypes being on the highest level and fully instantiated designs being on the lowest level. Our systems use a weighted average similarity for retrieval. Designs are adapted by simple parametric adaptation (tweaking) and by reinstantiation, where solution components are replaced by components from other cases. The component replacement is guided by critics that establish and propagate constraints. This way we combine pieces of designs into a coherent whole. In ASP-II, the user is presented with the finished design; PANDA can discuss the design with the user and provide information concerning its choices, alternative designs, and alternative components; BENTON treats the user as an agent, querying it and sending tasks when appropriate. Also, BENTON adds a metareasoning ability to the design component and distributes its problem-solving components over a blackboard.

Our work has made some significant contributions: We combine historical, CBD knowledge with prescriptive generic design prototypes in the form of skeletal plans. We can deal with inconsistent and incomplete design specifications by using a rule-based translator that moves all specifications on the same level of elementary structural requirements. We allow the adaptation of retrieved cases by pieces of other cases, based on constraints and a simple heuristic that allows that only two similar cases may exchange components. We also use domain-specific knowledge and critics to tweak the cases and to make sure that adaptations are propagated throughout the design. Whenever the system cannot adapt a case, we allow the inclusion of uninstantiated design prototypes that can be used as prescriptive guidelines by the designer. In PANDA, we allow the designer to discuss with the system the advantages and disadvantages of alternatives, to browse solutions, and to explore the design space. In BENTON, we have shown the usefulness of dividing the CBR problem-solving components into separate knowledge sources, and of using CBR to guide the metareasoning of a distributed problem solver.

Acknowledgments

This work was supported in part by a KTEC grant to the Center of Excellence in Computer-Aided Systems Engineering (CECASE). The authors wish to thank CECASE for its continuing support of system design research.

References

Alexander, P.: 1992, *The Design and Implementation of a Specification Design System,* Doctoral Dissertation, The University of Kansas.

Alexander, P., Magis, P., Holtzman, J., and Tam, D.: 1989, An integrated workstation for cosite EMC analysis, *Poceedings of the 5th Annual Review of Progress in Applied Electromagnetics,* Monterey, CA, pp. 16–22.

Alexander, P. and Tsatsoulis, C.: 1991, ASP-II: An experiment in combining case-based and skeletal planning, *International Journal of Expert Systems: Research and Applications,* 4(2), 221–247.

Barletta, R. and Hennessy, D.: 1989, Case adaptation in autoclave layout design, *Case-Based Reasoning Workshop,* AAAI Press, Menlo Park, CA, pp. 541–546.

Barletta, R. and Mark, W.: 1988, Breaking cases into pieces, *AAAI Case-Based Reasoning Workshop,* AAAI Press, Menlo Park, CA, pp. 12–16.

Brown, D. C. and Chandrasekaran, B.: 1985, Plan selection in design problem solving, *AISB Conference of the Society for the Study of Artificial Intelligence and the Simulation of Behavior,* Warwick, UK, pp. 2–19.

Chandrasekaran, B.: 1990, Design problem solving: A task analysis, *AI Magazine* 11(4): 59–71.

Domeshek, E. and Kolodner, J.: 1992, A case-based design aid for architecture, *in* J. S. Gero (ed.), *Artificial Intelligence in Design '92*, Kluwer Academic, Dordrecht, NL, pp. 497–516.

Garland, S. J. and Guttag, J. V.: 1991, A guide to LP, the Larch Prover, *DEC Systems Research Center Technical Report*, DEC Systems Research Center, Palo Alto, CA.

Gero, J. S.: 1990, Design prototypes: A knowledge representation schema for design, *AI Magazine*, 11(4), 27–36.

Goel, A., Kolodner, J., Pearce, M., and Billington, R.: 1991, Towards a case-based tool for aiding conceptual design problem solving, *Case-Based Reasoning Workshop*, AAAI Press, Menlo Park, CA, pp. 109–120.

Guttag, J. V., Horning, J. J., and Modet, A.: 1990, Report on the Larch Shared Language: Version 2.3, *DEC Systems Research Center Technical Report*, DEC Systems Research Center, Palo Alto, CA.

Hammond, K. J.: 1989, *Case-Based Planning: Viewing Planning as a Memory Task,*. Academic Press, Boston.

Hinrichs, T.: 1992, *Problem Solving in Open Worlds: A case study in design*, Lawrence Elrbaum Associates, Hillsdale, NJ.

Hua, K., Smith, I., and Faltings, B.: 1992, Adaptations of spatial design cases, *in* J. S. Gero (ed.), *Artificial Intelligence in Design '92*, Kluwer Academic, Dordrecht, NL, pp. 559–575.

Huhns, M. N. and Acosta, R. D.: 1988, Argo: A system for design by analogy, *IEEE Expert*, 3(3), 53–68.

Jones, K. D.: 1991, LM3: A Larch Interface Language for Modula-3. A definition and introduction, *DEC Systems Research Center Technical Report*, Prentice Hall, Englewood Cliffs, NJ.

Kolodner, J.: 1987, Extending problem solver capabilities through case-based inference, *Machine Learning Workshop*, Kaufmann, San Mateo, pp. 21–30.

Kolodner, J.: 1991, Improving human decision-making through case-based decision aiding, *AI Magazine*, 12(2), 52–68.

Maher, M. L.: 1990, Process models for design synthesis, *AI Magazine*, 11(4), 49–58.

Mostow, J.: 1990, Design by derivational analogy: Issues in the automated replay of design plans, *in* J. Carbonell (ed.), *Machine Learning: Paradigms and Methods*, MIT Press, Cambridge, MA, pp. 119–184.

Mriryala, K. and Harandi, M. T.: 1991, The role of analogy in specification derivation, *6th Annual Knowledge Based Software Engineering Conference*, AAAI Press, Syracuse, NY, pp. 521–526.

Nelson, G. (ed.): 1991, *Systems Programming with Modula-3*, Prentice Hall, Englewood Cliffs, NJ.

NFPA: 1991, *NFPA 1901 Standard for Pumper Fire Apparatus*. National Fire Protection Agency, Quincy, MA.

Nii, H. P.: 1986, Blackboard systems: Blackboard application systems, blackboard systems from a knowledge engineering perspective, *AI Magazine*, 7(3), 82–106.

Nii, H. P.: 1986, Blackboard systems: The blackboard model of problem solving and the evolution of blackboard architectures, *AI Magazine*, 7(2), 338–353.

Roderman, S.: 1992, *PANDA: A Hybrid System to Aid in Routine Design*, Masters Thesis, The University of Kansas.

Sacerdoti, E. D.: 1975, The nonlinear nature of plans, *4th International Joint Conference on Artificial Intelligence*, Kaufman., Palo Alto, pp. 206–214.

Stefik, M.: 1981, Planning and meta-planning (MOLGEN: Part 2). *Artificial Intelligence*, 16, 141–170.

Zhao, F. and Maher, M. L.: 1992, Using network-based prototypes to support creative design by analogy and mutation, *in* J. S. Gero (ed.), *Artificial Intelligence in Design '92*, Kluwer Academic, Dordrecht, NL, pp. 773–793.

chapter twelve

CASE DESIGN SPECIALISTS IN FABEL

ANGI VOSS
German National Research Center for Information Technology

From a project manager's perspective, major issues, achievements, and decisions in the FABEL project are reviewed. They concern the plan of the project that was changed to support an exploratory approach, the software architecture that was designed in a strictly decentralized way, the representation of designs and cases that provides a common format that is further interpreted by the individual methods, and the set of methods that consists of universalist case-based methods and specialized knowledge-based ones.

1. About FABEL

The aim of the FABEL project is to investigate how CBR can be integrated with heuristic and MBR as applied to architectural design. A prototype software system is being developed, running in distributed hybrid hardware and software environments to support designers of, for example, industrial buildings.

FABEL is a joint research project conducted by a consortium of six partners led by the German National Research Center for Information Technology (GMD), and partly funded from July 1992 to June 1996 by the German Ministry for Education and Research (BMBF). There are over 20 members of the project, 17 of whom are supported by BMBF funding, and there are also about a dozen students who are contributing to the project.

It was not easy planning such a large, distributed research project. The original strategy was to twice loop through a sequence of modeling and implementation. It was soon recognized as too rigid. An incremental strategy was adopted that divided the project into smaller tasks. These tasks were approached in an exploratory fashion, as the meaning of design was not at all clear at the start of the project, and methods of handling complicated designs were practically nonexistent. We started by developing several of our own methods for each task that would operate as independent tools, mostly complementary to, but sometimes competing with, other tools on the same materials or designs. Our software architecture accounts for the tool metaphor: It is open to any other methods operating on our design material.

This chapter reviews major issues, achievements, decisions, and results, not only from my personal perspective as manager of the project, but also as leader of the GMD group. Therefore, descriptions of methods are rather biased toward our own developments with which I am naturally most familiar. In addition, this chapter expresses my own subjective opinions that are not necessarily shared by other members of the consortium.

2. Major Strategic Decisions in FABEL

2.1. HOW TO PLAN THE PROJECT?

The original plan of the project was oriented toward a twofold waterfall model of software development. Six months were to be spent getting acquainted with the matter, the next two years in building a conceptual model of the domain, problem solving, and implementing it. The rest of the time was to give us the opportunity for remodeling and re-implementation.

The best part of this schedule was the first half-year. It allowed us to break down the main task of design into finer tasks: retrieval of useful designs, adaptation of a design to a new problem, assessment of designs, the elaboration of designs without precedents using more abstract knowledge, and planning what to do next. Learning was viewed as a meta-activity for the automatic acquisition of cases and abstract knowledge for incrementally improving the system. We agreed to pursue these tasks more or less sequentially and to produce a sequence of software prototypes with increased functionality. The subsidiary task of knowledge acquisition by machine learning was to accompany all other tasks.

This left us to decide in which order to carry out the tasks. If we had tried to maximize synergy between different qualifications in the project by assigning a task to an individual partner it would have been counterproductive. The CBR paradigm suggested starting with retrieval, but then offered a choice of either doing assessment and then adaptation, or adaptation followed by assessing its result. Smith and Keane (1994) argued that one should retrieve useful cases, and because a case is useful if it is easy to adapt, so one should first study adaptation. We chose to start with retrieval because the architects in our project said they expected most immediate profit from this functionality. We then wanted to switch to assessment because we believed it to be prerequisite to adaptation (Bakhtari and Bartsch-Spörl, 1993).

What we actually did in the project was to start with retrieval and pursue the other tasks somewhat later and more in parallel than we had originally planned. Thus, we got a lot of feedback between the different tasks, and the number of prototypes planned could be reduced from a maximum of six to three; that is, two for retrieval and the third growing incrementally to full functionality.

From today's perspective, I would not impose any *a priori* order on the tasks, but would try to maximize the users' immediate profits so as to raise their motivation. Another criterion is feasibility of the tasks, which might be hard to assess from the start. In any case, our incremental strategy is much more robust and less risky than the original give-it-a-second-chance strategy.

2.2. HOW TO APPROACH THE TASKS?

Model-based approaches to knowledge acquisition (prominent ones are KADS (Schreiber Wielinga, and Breuker, 1992), role limiting methods, generic tasks, and the method-to-task approach (for a comparison, see Karbach, Linster and Voss, 1990) recommend identifying the tasks to be solved, the methods for solving the tasks, and the knowledge needed by the methods. Having identified the tasks, we faced a dilemma: Should we, for each task, first agree blindly on a method and then try to acquire the knowledge it needed, risking not getting that knowledge? Or should we first acquire knowledge broadly and then hope to find a method that would exploit some of it? This dilemma had never occurred to me before because FABEL was the first complex project where we had such a fragmented model of the domain and of the problem-solving approach taken by experts.

Our approach was exploratory. In our institute, researchers started by investing a little effort in knowledge acquisition but quickly changed to a particular method that was, in turn, tuned by experiments. Such exploratory behavior has resulted in a broad choice of implemented methods for each type of task. To our surprise, the tasks were more interrelated than expected. A matching method developed for adaptation has been turned into an independent retrieval method. Most adaptation methods can also be used for assessment and elaboration; an assessment method is growing into an elaboration and adaptation method; and an elaboration method is turning into an adaptation method. The most adventurous journey in task space led one method from retrieval via adaptation to elaboration. The reason behind this seems to be that our initial division into tasks was too coarse.

When exploring unknown territories, there is no recommendable procedure. The tasks should be approached from any direction and, in doing so, they may even mutate.

2.3. WHAT KIND OF SOFTWARE ARCHITECTURE?

We came up with many methods per task and many tasks per method. As the set of methods and the tasks a method has to cope with are still being evolved, the software architecture of our system must be so designed as to allow for easy addition of multipurpose methods.

Our methods are quite independent. Each retrieval method has its own case description and case memory. Each assessment method has its own encoded knowledge and makes its own inferences, as do adaptation and elaboration methods. These independent methods have their advantages and drawbacks. As an advantage, the software architecture is easy to extend and is insensible to changes of individual methods. As a drawback, there is no common knowledge base that would grow with the addition of more methods. Even worse, the interaction hypothesis warns us that not only the knowledge requirements may vary with the methods, but also knowledge representation. To give an example, adaptation by autonomous agents and a constraint-relaxation method would probably have knowledge deposited in different data structures. Independence of methods and flexibility of the system were more important for our evolutionary approach. So we left the issue of knowledge integration for the time being and built an open framework as shown in Figure 12.1. There is a common server for building projects and cases. It serves independent modules that can perform various tasks. The user interface is modular.

Our first prototype was just an experiment in coupling a design editor with one retrieval method. The second prototype system, completed in Spring 1993, offered four retrieval methods. The next (and as it happened, the last) prototype, developed by the end of 1995, was to contain an additional 12 methods, two for retrieval, at least two for assessment, four for adaptation, and four for design elaboration.

To support a complex design process, there are a multitude of complementary and competing methods, and this set of methods will grow with time. This requires an open software architecture with independent modules operating in a common data pool. A challenge facing the end of the project will be suggesting to the user the right method at the right time, to turn soloist methods into a cooperating orchestra.

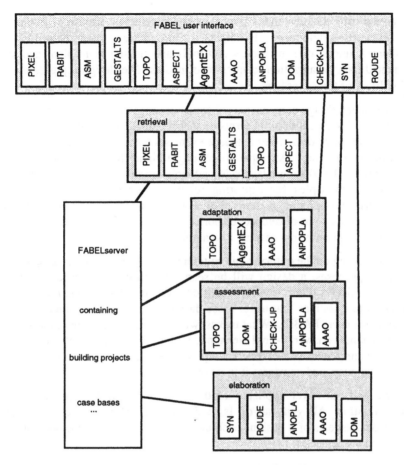

Figure 12.1. A task-oriented survey of the FABEL system.

3. Representation of Designs

3.1. WHAT IS (NOT) IN A DESIGN?

The spectrum of FABEL methods has grown, historically, in our attempt to cope with a new domain. But there are more substantial reasons why I believe a design support system can provide a pool of different methods.

Commercial CAD systems started as drawing tools, and the objects they treated were purely geometric; that is, lines, polygons, rectangles, volumes. These basic CAD systems were extended to application-specific tools; for example, CADE tools for engineers or CAAD tools for architects. Rather than geometric objects, modern CAD tools manipulate domain-specific objects, which I call design components. Examples for an architectural domain are walls, windows, doors, or staircases. CAD tools are moving from plan- and slide-oriented data organization to integrated models. The design representation in FABEL is of this latter kind.

However, design components are only part of the vocabulary in an architect's language. Architects think in terms of spaces, topologies, gestalts, symmetries, patterns, abstract ideas. Their language expresses many requirements, constraints, and design decisions. Attempts at defining a higher language can be found in Alexander's (1979) pattern language, and more recently in Oxman's (1994) issue-concept-form triples for capturing relations between problems, ideas for solutions, and solution patterns. For a new generation of CAD tools, such languages have to be developed, elaborated, and formalized. But will this suffice to express all that is in a design? I do not think so.

Depending on the observer, his cultural background, his personal experience, and his purposes, a design will be seen differently. The entire research on emergent shapes (Gero, 1993) is built on the belief that a design may contain answers to questions that never arose during its creation. Consider one of our first questions in FABEL: What makes two designs similar? Whenever we asked it, we got new answers—until we stopped asking. Each of our retrieval methods gives an alternative answer. Each interprets a design in its own way, represents it in its own way, and compares it in its own way.

So you can never explicate all that is in a design. Designs are open to interpretation. All you can do is to develop specific spectacles to capture individual aspects of a design. Each of our FABEL retrieval methods provides one kind of spectacles.

3.2. THEN, WHAT IS IN A FABEL DESIGN?

A FABEL design contains design components without any interpretations or derived information (Hovestadt, 1993a, 1993b).

A building project, represented in a data structure, is a set of (design) components. It constitutes an integrated building model that is not split into plans with separate layers. Any set of components can be visualized. I use the term design for any set of components, be it an entire building of some 10,000 components, or only a small item of, say, 10.

Each component has a type (from a catalogue of building components) that determines its geometric and semantic attributes. We reason with components as orthogonally oriented cuboids. Position and size are extracted from the geometric attributes (x, dx, y, dy, z, dz). We use only four of the semantic attributes:

- Subsystem: = {space, construction, floor, roof, ceiling, wall, facade, supply air, return air, hot water, cold water, sewage, . . .}.
- Morphology or function: = {use, technical service, connection}.
- Precision or resolution: = {zone, bounding box, element}.
  Zones are sketchy areas whose coordinates are interpreted vaguely. Bounding boxes are precisely located, and elements are concrete components from a catalogue. Our drawing tool visualizes zones in 2-D by ellipses rather than by their surrounding rectangles. This is a clever graphical trick: Overlapping ellipses intersect at a few points only, whereas rectangles share sections of their lines.
- Scale: = {0, 2, 4, 6, 8, 5, 7}.
  0 means the building site, 2 the entire building, 4 a floor, 6 a room, 8 part of a room, 5 transitions between floors and rooms, 7 transitions between rooms and their parts. 5 and 7 refer to the service layer.

Figure 12.2 shows the main hall of the education center of the Swiss railway company in Murten, designed and built by Haller (1988).

Figure 12.2. The main hall of the education center of the Swiss railway company in Murten.

The upper part of Figure 12.3 contains a case with the design of its spaces and climate subsystems (the components are listed following the keyword ":solution-objects"). To the right is the design as visualized by our drawing tool (Hovestadt, 1993a, 1993b).

the problem (with 50 components) problem

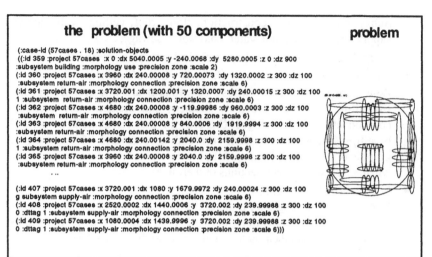

```
(:case-id (57cases . 18) :solution-objects
((:id 359 :project 57cases :x 0 :dx 5040.0005 :y -240.0068 :dy 5280.0005 :z 0 :dz 900
:subsystem building :morphology use :precision zone :scale 2)
(:id 360 :project 57cases :x 3960 :dx 240.00008 :y 720.00073 :dy 1320.0002 :z 300 :dz 100
:subsystem return-air :morphology connection :precision zone :scale 6)
(:id 361 :project 57cases :x 3720.001 :dx 1200.001 :y 1320.0007 :dy 240.00015 :z 300 :dz 100
1 :subsystem return-air :morphology connection :precision zone :scale 6)
(:id 362 :project 57cases :x 4680 :dx 240.00008 :y -119.99986 :dy 960.0003 :z 300 :dz 100
:subsystem return-air :morphology connection :precision zone :scale 6)
(:id 363 :project 57cases :x 4680 :dx 240.00008 :y 840.0006 :dy 1919.9994 :z 300 :dz 100
:subsystem return-air :morphology connection :precision zone :scale 6)
(:id 364 :project 57cases :x 4680 :dx 240.00142 :y 2040.0 :dy 2159.9998 :z 300 :dz 100
1 :subsystem return-air :morphology connection :precision zone :scale 6)
(:id 365 :project 57cases :x 3960 :dx 240.00008 :y 2040.0 :dy 2159.9998 :z 300 :dz 100
:subsystem return-air :morphology connection :precision zone :scale 6)
. ..

(:id 407 :project 57cases :x 3720.001 :dx 1080 :y 1679.9972 :dy 240.00024 :z 300 :dz 100
g subsystem supply-air :morphology connection :precision zone :scale 6)
(:id 408 :project 57cases :x 2520.0002 :dx 1440.0006 :y 3720.002 :dy 239.99988 :z 300 :dz 100
0 :dttag 1 :subsystem supply-air :morphology connection :precision zone :scale 6)
(:id 409 :project 57cases :x 1080.0004 :dx 1439.9996 :y 3720.002 :dy 239.99988 :z 300 :dz 100
0 :dttag 1 :subsystem supply-air :morphology connection :precision zone :scale 6)))
```

aspect	representation of the problem:	representation of the case:	cases

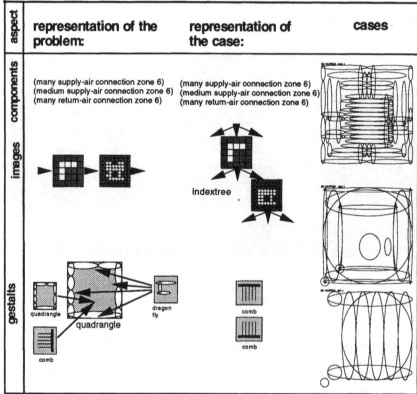

components

(many supply-air connection zone 6)
(medium supply-air connection zone 6)
(many return-air connection zone 6)

(many supply-air connection zone 6)
(medium supply-air connection zone 6)
(many return-air connection zone 6)

images

indextree

gestalts

quadrangle
quadrangle
dragon fly
comb
comb
comb

Figure 12.3. Different aspects of a design.

The four major semantic attributes of our design components allow the decomposition of the design process into some major stages as presented in Figure 12.4. A decomposition as shown in the figure was initially suggested by Janetzko, Börner, Jäschke, and Strube (1994) and by Hovestadt (1993). It further differentiates with respect to morphology and scales. The subsystems cluster around space, construction (including facade, walls, roof, ceiling, and floors), and technical services (water, climate, . . .). During the design process, resolution and scale increase from zones at scales 0–4, to bounding boxes and elements, each at scales 4–8. The arrows indicate major influences, which mainly work middle-out and top-down, from spaces to other subsystems and from coarser to finer phases. As we will see in Figures 12.15 and 12.17, many of our methods can be associated with certain stages in Figure 12.4. So Figure 12.4 grew into a map of our methods, telling us which were overlapping or complementary, and which stages were not covered. Moreover, every field in the table corresponds to certain types of components, so we get a close association between stages, methods, and the components involved.

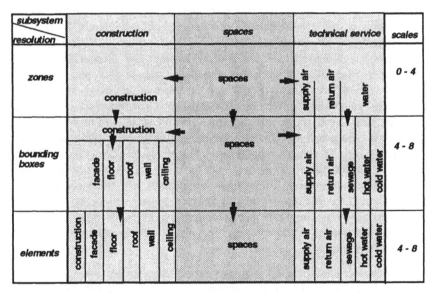

Figure 12.4. Mapping of major stages in building design.

4. Retrieval

The purpose of retrieval is to find designs similar to a given one. The given one is called the *query* or the *problem*, and is defined by selecting some components on the screen of the drawing tool. The designs to be searched for are stored as cases in a case base.

There are two ways of differentiating the retrieval methods in FABEL: by the techniques used, and by the similarity concepts they implement. Let me start with the first.

4.1. WHAT TO RETRIEVE?

Asked "what makes two designs similar?" we heard:

- components: the subsystem they belong to, their function, their level of resolution, their scale;
- visual appearance as images—if you look at them from a distance;
- occurrence of certain layout patterns resembling quadrangles, rows, combs, and more complex gestalts;
- structure or topology.

In Figure 12.3, the upper half shows the design of the spaces and the climate subsystems of the central hall in the Murten building (Figure 12.2) and its visualization by our drawing tool (top right). Under there are different views of the design: as components represented by tuples like "(medium supply-air connection zone 6)," as images represented as pixels of grey value matrices of different grain size, and as gestalts represented by keywords like *comb* or *quadrangle* and visualized by icons. The right-hand side shows the vizualizations of cases that are recognized as being similar with respect to these aspects, and in between are the aspect-specific representations of these cases, which are the basis for comparison. The design recognized as being most similar with respect to the aspect of components is an elaboration of the query. Using the aspect of images, another subsystem with a similar layout was found. And the aspect of gestalts led to a detail for refining the middle part of the query. In general, retrieval by components and topology returns elaborations and alternatives, whereas gestalts and images come up with more surprising, unexpected designs, which may be a source of inspiration.

The aspect-specific views are not explicit in the designs. They must be extracted from or read into the component descriptions. For this purpose, our retrieval methods use different techniques.

4.2. HOW TO RETRIEVE?

Figure 12.5 shows the ingredients of a retrieval method for designs. Both the cases and the new problem (or query) must be transformed or interpreted, yielding an aspect-specific representation. In the case base, the cases are stored both in their original and in their aspect-specific representation. The case base must be accessed, and cases and the query must be compared. A similarity concept is implemented by a combination of case representation and comparison. Such a pair can be combined in turn with case bases of a different structure. Figure 12.6 gives a survey of the different combinations explored in FABEL.

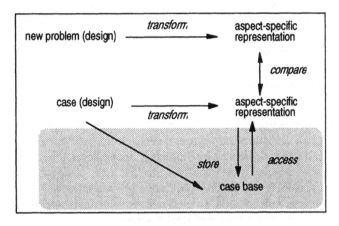

Figure 12.5. Ingredients of a retrieval method.

method	aspect	aspect representation	comparison	case base
ASM	components	keywords	subset	associative memory
RABIT	components	attributes	distance	linear list or tree
ASPECT	components	keywords	subset	multidimensional
GESTALTS + ASM	gestalts	keywords	subset	associative memory
GESTALTS + RABIT	gestalts	attributes	distance	linear list or tree
GESTALTS + ASPECT	gestalts	keywords	subset	multidimensional
PIXEL	images	grey value matrices	fieldwise identity	tree
PIXEL + ASPECT	images	grey value matrices	fieldwise identity	multidimensional
TTOPO + ASPECT	topology	relations	subset	multidimensional

Figure 12.6. Retrieval methods in FABEL.

For instance, we encoded the components view as a set of tuples like "(medium supply-air air connection zone 6)," meaning that there is a medium number of components with subsystem = supply-air, morphology = connection, resolution = zone, and scale = 6. Alternatively, we expressed this information in terms of attributes like subsystems = {supply-air, return air}, and resolution = {zones}, and so forth. We stored the tuples in an associative memory that treats them as atomic units, just like keywords that ordinary text retrieval systems use as indexes (Salton and McGill, 1983). The attributes were stored in a linear list and, alternatively, in a decision tree. There they are compared using distance-based functions that allow arranging the cases by similarity. Both keywords and attribute representations can also be stored in a multidimensional case base using ASPECT (see later).

As another example, we encode images as pixels of grey value matrices of different grain size and store them in a decision tree with the coarsest matrix at the root. The tree is descended by following, at each level, the matrix identical to the matrix of the query. At each leaf there is a set of cases looking like the matrix of that leaf. Alternatively, we store the most finely grained matrix as another dimension in ASPECT's case base. As yet another alternative, which we did not realize, we could have used RABIT's trees.

ASM (Henne, 1990): a shell for associative memories adapted for retrieval by Gräther.

RABIT (Linowski, 1995): a shell for case-based retrieval using attribute-value representations, inspired by PatDex (Richter and Wess, 1991) and by commercial shells, but programmed in a strictly object-oriented way.

ASPECT (Schaaf, 1995; Schaaf and Voss, 1995): a completely new retrieval combination shell.

GESTALTS (Schaaf, 1994): a completely new gestalt recognition method.

PIXEL (Coulon, 1993): specially developed for FABEL, but using techniques known from image recognition (Duda and Hart, 1973; Niemann, 1990).

TOPO (Coulon, 1995): retrieves designs with similar structural relations. Later, we see that TOPO performs graph matching in a second step as a prerequisite for adaptation.

More information can be found in Voss et al. (1994) and Voss and Bartsch-Spörl (1995). The next two sections have a closer look at the innovative approaches, ASPECT and TOPO.

4.3. GESTALTS IN ARCHITECTURAL DESIGNS

There are certain typical layout patterns that often occur in designs. In our domain, they look like combs, fish bones, or quadrangles. Of course, the combs or the fish bones are not explicit in the plans, and because they are only patterns in our mind we have chosen to call them gestalts, a term adopted from gestalt psychology (Helson, 1933).

For retrieval, gestalts have to be detected in the cases (during preprocessing) and in the current problem (during run time). Marr (1982) suggested that humans transform pictures for comparison into an abstract form. We use such an abstract form, called *sketches*. They were inspired by pinman sketches as representations of human limb constellations. Sketches are representations of gestalts that are to make similar gestalts equal. If these sketches are too abstract, dissimilar gestalts will be identified incorrectly. Figure 12.7 shows the eight gestalts we have identified in our domain and the way we sketch them. Each gestalt is defined by one or more of its reference sketches.

fishbone	row	bug leg	comb	regulary filled	H	dragon-fly	quadrangle

Figure 12.7. Examples and sketches of our gestalts.

In order to automatically detect instances of the eight gestalts in a design, we first identify groups of components that constitute a potential gestalt. For that purpose, we filter the design, removing all types of components that do not belong to any reference set. Then we use clustering algorithms to find spatially close groups of components of the same type (the same values for the four major attributes). Treisman (1985) confirmed the cognitive relevance of this approach. Clusters with combinations of component types that do not occur in any reference sketch are discarded. The remaining clusters are sketched.

Figure 12.8 demonstrates how a group of components can be sketched:

1. *Focus on a group of components:* Part 1 shows a design with space zones for rooms and floors.
2. *Attempt to sketch it:* This step shows how a sketch would look if only the centers of components were represented. The problems are that on the one hand, too much information would get lost, whereas on the other

hand, we would get different sketches for constellations of the same gestalt (e.g., if two quadrangles differ in size).

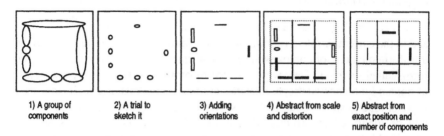

| 1) A group of components | 2) A trial to sketch it | 3) Adding orientations | 4) Abstract from scale and distortion | 5) Abstract from exact position and number of components |

Figure 12.8. How a group of components can be sketched.

3. *Add orientations:* We decided to take the orientation of a component into account (bars). A small circle indicates a missing orientation.

4. *Abstract from scale and distortion:* If the scale and the distortion of a gestalt were considered, it would be impossible to classify gestalts correctly. Humans also neglect these attributes while sketching things and recognizing gestalts. Step 4 shows a sketch that abstracts from scale (by scaling a grid) and from distortion (by distorting the grid in the same way).

5. *Abstract from exact position and number of components:* In the previous sketches, the exact number of components is noticed. To abstract from similarly oriented objects, we defined a way to merge objects into one element. Step 5 shows the result of this merging. Thus, we constructed a sketch that may represent many different examples of the gestalt *quadrangle*.

Having sketched a group of components, we try to classify it as one of the eight gestalts. For that purpose, the sketch is compared with the set of reference sketches. This is first done for the sketch obtained from step 4, and if this fails, we try the more abstract sketch produced in step 5. Fortunately, because the same sketching mechanism is used to represent groups of components in cases and in problems, the recognition of gestalts is insensitive to the quality of the sketches.

The sketches classified successfully yield a set of gestalt names. We use them as keywords, like (2 comb), or as attributes, like gestalts = {quadrangle, comb}, for retrieval by ASM or by RABIT.

4.4. ASPECT: A COMMON ROOF FOR MULTIPLE RETRIEVAL

An initial evaluation of our retrieval methods (Figure 12.3) revealed that they often returned different designs. We wondered which of them was correct or better, but soon saw that they depend on the purpose of retrieval. We came to the conclusion that different case representations have different meanings. Although in the literature, case representation is usually treated as an indexing problem, in design, it is indeed more of an interpretation problem. In contrast to ordinary information system technology, this is not a mistake. Precision and recall cannot be defined in absolute terms but depend on the user, the context, and the purpose (Coulon and Gebhardt, 1994a, 1994b).

Because the methods were more or less complementary (except ASM and RABIT, which both encoded components and gestalts), we wanted to combine them, intersecting or uniting their results. And because they also differed in selectivity and speed, we wanted to combine them sequentially, feeding the output of fast, less selective ones into slower, more selective methods (Voss et al., 1994). It was at that time when my colleague Schaaf argued that there was a better means of arbitrarily combining the methods. Let me use a metaphor: Each retrieval method views a design through colored glasses, say red for component, yellow for images, blue for gestalts, and black for topology. So, what about orange, violet, green, and brown glasses?

To achieve such mixtures, he invented ASPECT, a multidimensional case base, with one dimension for each aspect (or primary color). Given a comparison function, which need neither be a metric nor a distance, for each dimension (aspect or primary color), and given weights specifying the mixture to be obtained, he developed an access method that, at any time, would find the n best cases of the desired blend. This method is called fish&sink.

Figure 12.9 shows how a case is represented in many aspects or dimensions. An aspect corresponds to one side of a polyhedron (here a cube). There are links between the same aspects of any two cases. They are labeled with their (normalized) degree of similarity in this aspect. The entire network constitutes the organization of the multidimensional case base.

The approach trades time for space by precomputing the aspect-wise similarities between all cases: For each direct comparison between the query and a (fished) case, it guesses the dissimilarity of neighboring cases and correspondingly infers their direct comparison (sinks them). The fish&sink algorithm is an anytime algorithm. It is complete and guaranteed to find the best n cases, n increasing with the available time. In contrast, the hill climbing in Goos (1995) or Lenz and Burkhard(1995) looks for better neighbors of good cases and may get stuck at local maxima. Figure 12.10 conveys the metaphor of fish&sink.

From the query and its context, the blend of aspects and their weights are dynamically computed. For instance, we can combine the aspect of components weighted at 0.7, and the aspect of gestalts weighted at 0.3, or combine all aspects with weights of 0.25, or combine the aspect of images (0.6) with gestalts (0.2) and topologies (0.2). Which blends will be useful to capture which intentions of the user—be it green or orange—will be subject to future tests.

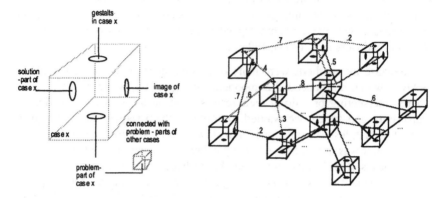

Figure 12.9. The multidimensional case base ASPECT.

Figure 12.10. The metaphor of fish&sink.

To explicate different aspects of a design, semantically (and technically) different interpretations and comparisons are needed. Different purposes of retrieval prioritize different aspects in variable constellations. Such a dynamically combined retrieval is supported by a multidimensional case base that provides a common access and store medium for many interpretation/ comparison pairs.

5. Adaptation

Retrieval of cases may serve various purposes; that is, inspiration, comparison, finding alternatives and, last but not least, elaboration by design adaptation. The purpose of the latter is to transfer parts of one design (a previous solution) to another (the current problem or query). This requires a match between these two designs so as to recognize the differences that are to be exploited by the transfer. Because a design is a set of components, the match must be done between their components. Differences may occur in the geometry (size and position), in the semantics, in the topology (relative positions) of matching components, or there may be unmatched components in the previous solution. In the first case, transfer leads to a modification of existing components in the current problem. In the second case, it elaborates the current problem by inserting new components; that is, those that were unmatched in the previous solution. In any case, the result may violate certain domain-specific constraints whether they be semantic, geometric, or topological. To assess the validity of transfer, it must be checked with respect to the constraints and, if necessary, modified.

Figure 12.11, an extension of Figure 12.5, shows the ingredients of adaptation methods. The comparison may require a precise match in order to establish correspondences between the sets of components in the query and in the previous solution. This is impossible if the aspect-specific representation cannot be transformed back to the original one. Anyway, the transfer from the previous solution to the new problem must be effected on the set of components, which means that the transformation must be an enrichment rather than a colorful interpretation. In FABEL, the transformations essentially compute topological relations from the positions and sizes of the components.

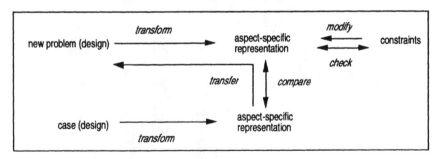

Figure 12.11. Ingredients of adaptation methods.

As for retrieval, we are developing several adaptation methods: TOPO, AAAO, and AgentEX. And again, we can distinguish their semantic scope from the techniques used. The following descriptions vary in the level of detail because the methods are at different stages of development. Also, I am not equally familiar with them all. A more detailed survey is given in Börner (1995).

5.1. WHAT TO ADAPT?

5.1.1. TOPO

Figure 12.12 illustrates the TOPO method in five parts (Coulon, 1995). The designs are examples of furnishing an office room.

1. The query includes placed and unplaced components.
2. Retrieval with TOPO finds part of a former design matching the walls, window, chairs, and tables to the query.
3. Adaptation transfers the objects and relations found in the result of retrieval, including additional shelves. It cannot transfer all topological relations between query and retrieved design because the table and two chairs cannot be placed between the door and the right wall as in the former design. Additionally, the collision of the door with the table and chairs points to a conflict at the lower right corner.
4. A new retrieval for similar components, this time ignoring topology, finds no correct placement within radius RI but a solution is found within radius RII.
5. Design II is found and transferred.

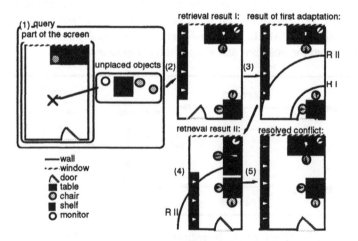

Figure 12.12. TOPO at work.

TOPO accepts arbitrary designs and expresses their topology using the relations touches, overlaps, includes, near-by in all three dimensions. For comparison, it determines the largest common substructure. It inserts into the query those components from the previous solution that do not match with those in the query. Components can be selected by the user or are heuristically chosen. TOPO checks the result by using the same kinds of topological relations as constraints. By scanning our buildings and case bases, it determines statistically usual and unusual topological relations. No manual knowledge elicitation is needed. If it detects any unusual relations in the elaborated query, TOPO retrieves another case with the same kind of components, but with other structures. The elaborated query is then modified by transferring the new topology to the original representation format.

5.1.2. AAAO

As another example, Figure 12.13 shows the AAAO method at work. The architect is designing an office building with the steel frame construction set MIDI (Haller, 1974). The layout shows offices, seminar rooms, and some others.

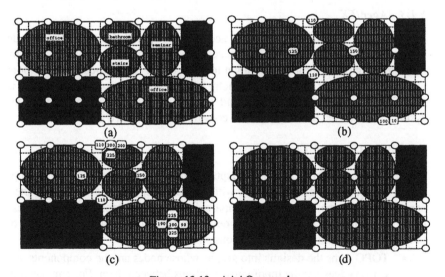

Figure 12.13. AAAO at work.

(a) shows the query with an outline of the building and zones of intended use (indicated as grey ellipses; the dark shadings denote areas outside the building). In addition, there is an initial distribution of columns (small white circles) that do not yet satisfy statical and architectural needs.

(b) shows the situation after all columns outside the building have been removed and the others have evaluated their position. For five columns, a score of over 100 inicates the violation of hard constraints. Those five columns have then evaluated their neighboring positions. They will move to the neighboring position with the least conflict; that is, the lowest score.

(c)   the columns have moved and once again evaluated their position. There are still serious conflicts for four columns.

(d)   the process continues as in (c), but this time, one more column is created. In the final result, at least all hard constraints are satisfied.AAAO (Adami, 1995) accepts a design of spaces and areas of intended use (components with subsystem = space, morphology = use, resolution = zone, scale = 6) as the query and a previous solution that additionally contains columns (components with subsystem = construction, morphology = connection, resolution = zone, scale = 4). It inserts the columns into the query and checks constraints from statics on geometry and topology. These constraints are acquired manually. It repositions the columns using domain-specific heuristics until the constraints are satisfied.

5.1.3. AgentEX

The AgentEX method (Bhat, 1995) accepts any spatial design at floor scale (components with subsystem = space, scale = 4) as a query and elaborates it by inserting supply-air components down to scale 8. For this purpose, it uses more elaborated supply-air cases. The geometry of inserted and existing components is modified until certain geometric and topological constraints for supply-air systems are satisfied in the query. The constraints are acquired manually.

5.2. HOW TO ADAPT?

Figure 12.14 summarizes the three adaptation methods at the semantic level (top) and at the technical level (bottom), which determines how they represent their aspect of a design, how they compare it, how they represent and assess constraints, and how they modify the design in order to satisfy the constraints or to maintain the topology of the previous solution.

- TOPO turns the designs into graphs whose nodes are the components and whose edges are the topological relations between them. For comparison, it determines their largest common subgraph by using a highly tuned algorithm based on Bron and Kerbosch (1973) for finding largest cliques. Constraints are spatial relations between two intervals in three dimensions. For checking and modification, TOPO relies on itself: For checking, it matches the elaborated query with unusual topological relations; for modification, it transfers the topology from the new case.

- AAAO relies on an external comparison. It assumes that the query and the previous problem have similar spaces and just inserts all columns from the latter into the former. Then all components in the elaborated query are represented as autonomous agents that are positioned in a grid where they know their neighbors. The agents have methods for checking the constraints to be satisfied in their neighborhood. For modification, the agents either move into their neighborhood, negotiate with their neighbors, or create new ones.

adaptation method	scope	aspect	transfer by insertion of components	constraints	constraint elicitation	suitable retrieval
TOPO	any zones and bounding boxes	+ topology	unmatched components	topological	automatic	components topology
AAAO	columns	+ topology	all columns	geometric topological	manual	components images topology
AgentEX	supply air	+ topology	all supply-air components	geometric topological	manual	components images topology

adaptation method	aspect representation	constraint representation	assessment technique	modification technique	approach
TOPO	topological graph	relations	match	case-adaptation	centralistic
AAAO	agent for components	objects	procedural	heuristic search + negotiation	distributed
AgentEX	agent for components	methods of agents	procedural	heuristic search + negotiation	distributed

Figure 12.14. Adaptation methods in FABEL.

- AgentEX also relies on external comparison. It assumes that the query and the previous problem have similar spaces, and incrementally inserts various kinds of supply-air components from the latter into the former. Then all components in the elaborated query are represented as autonomous agents and placed in a grid. Agents know topologically related agents. They have methods for encoding the constraints to be satisfied between themselves and their acquaintances. For checking, the agents call their methods; for modification, the agents move and negotiate with their acquaintances, or create new ones.

Adaptation in design transfers components and topology from one design to another. The result has to conform to specific, often domain-specific constraints. Modification techniques vary according to the representation of the constraints.

5.3. HOW MUCH DO THE VIEWS OF RETRIEVAL AND ADAPTATION DIFFER?

Earlier in this chapter, I argued that the way you look at a design depends on its context and purpose, and that each retrieval method in FABEL provides a different view on a design. Colored glasses are used, and the more colored they are, the more fanciful are the designs that can be detected. Now we have seen how our adaptation methods look at a design. Because adapation must be performed on the design components, glasses must be more transparent. All adaptation methods see the design components (transparence) together with their topology (a little color). Unlike retrieval methods, they have a limited field of vision: AAAO only sees part of the construction system, and AgentEX only sees part of the supply-air system, but they see them more clearly than TOPO. Figure 12.15 superimposes the scopes of our adaptation methods on the map from Figure 12.4, and our retrieval methods can operate on any part of this map.

TOPO is an all-rounder in topological adaptation and should be complemented by specialists like AAAO and AgentEX. In fact TOPO, with the help of ASPECT, can retrieve suitable cases for adaptation and insert new components from the case into the current problem. The result will satisfy any topological constraints that are common in building projects. Yet, it may violate more specific semantic and geometric constraints, specific laws and rules that cannot be detected statistically but are acquired manually. In as far as such constraints are local, they can be attached to certain components, and agent-based constraint-satisfaction methods like AAAO or AgentEX can be applied to check and modify the design until they are satisfied.

The techniques behind AAAO and AgentEX are similar, and both methods can be used for the same purposes; that is, for satisfying specific constraints in the neighborhood of certain design components while maintaining a given topology. They follow a distributed approach, whereas TOPO has a more central approach.

The different views between retrieval and adaptation raise an integration problem: How do we find an adaptable case? We have several answers to offer.

First, the designer can manually select a case to be used for adaptation. This attitude is assumed in the CADRE system (Dave Schmitt, Faltings, and Smith, 1994). Second, we can invent special retrieval methods. This was done for TOPO. Afterward, it turned out that its topological matching was not only useful for TOPO's adaptation function, but it has also been turned into an independent retrieval method. Third, we can suitably combine our existing retrieval methods. The most promising candidates are retrieval by components, by images, and by topology (Figure 12.14) and using ASPECT, we can assign to the aspects arbitrary mixes of weights in order to obtain a suitable case. And fourth, we can retrieve a number of cases and the designer selects one of them for adaptation.

Retrieval and adaptation may, but need not, coincide in how they view a design and how they compare them. Adaptation requires a closer and usually more focused look.

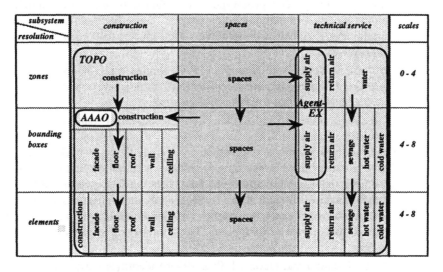

Figure 12.15. Scope of our adaptation methods.

6. More Design Support

6.1. WHAT CAN BE DONE WITHOUT CASES?

In order to support assessment and to cover a broader range of elaboration, we added more knowledge-intensive methods. It turned out that they are closely related to the checking and modification techniques employed for adaptation. The following description is concise. It focuses on the relation between knowledge-based and case-based methods. More details can be found in Börner (1995).

- ANOPLA (Gräther, 1995) assigns pipes (components with 'use = connection', 'resolution = bounding boxes', 'scale = 6') that are temporarily deposited on a grid line on positions that are legal with respect to templates from the installation methodology armilla for technical services (Haller, 1985). There are different templates predefining possible positions for pipes of different diameters.

  The method instantiates agents for the components, places them onto a grid, and lets them move and negotiate with their neighbors.

- SYN (Börner, 1994) connects outlets of any technical service system with trunk pipes by inserting branch and twig pipes. It transforms a design into a tree with the trunk pipe at the root and the outlets at the leaves. Given trees of prototype solutions it determines which one best matches the trunks and outlets of the query and instantiates this tree correspondingly. The prototypes are obtained by extracting suitable supply-air cases from the building projects, clustering them according to similar trees, and then generalizing each cluster to form a common, prototype tree.

- ROUDE (Jäschke and Janetzko, 1994) applies a set of operators for inserting climate components with 'resolution = zone'. The operators encode knowledge that was manually acquired.

- CHECK-UP (Janetzko and Jäschke, 1994) recognizes a couple of complex topological constraints. The constraints were acquired manually, but from our buildings and cases, the method has learned the types of designs that have to satisfy these constraints. It assesses a design by first computing primitive topological relations and then checking the constraints it has to satisfy. Examples of constraints are: All supply-air components are placed within zones of climate components; all supply-air trunk pipes are located within shafts; a zone of supply-air is completely covered by supply-air outlets.

- DOM (Bakhtari and Oertel, 1995a, 1995b) identifies various groups of semantic, geometric, and topological constraints that apply to the heating, ventilation, and air conditioning (HVAC) systems at the resolution of zones and bounding boxes. It assesses a design by first computing primitive topological relations and then checking the constraints it has to satisfy. The constraints are very specific and have to be acquired manually. DOM constraints are interpreted by the inference mechanisms of FAENSY, a FABEL development tool (Oertel, 1994).

Figure 12.16 shows two designs assessed by DOM. The first one specifies the return-air subsystem in a grid for the service spaces. DOM checks spatial and geometric constraints with respect to the grid, collisions with other subsystems that may already have been laid-out, and connectivity. The first design is assessed to be correct. Not so the second one. Here DOM detects a stand-alone outlet that violates the connectivity constraints. The other additional outlet is in conflict with the grid and would lead to a suboptimal solution. Finally, the radius of the horizontal branch-duct is insufficient and has to be corrected.

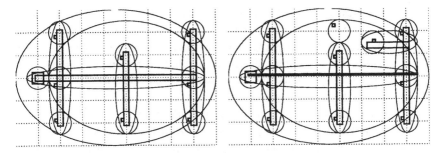

Figure 12.16. Two return-air designs assessed by DOM.

To summarize, Figure 12.17 indicates the scopes of our knowledge-based methods superimposed on the map in Figure 12.4. They focus on technical service subsystems because we had a knowledge source: the armilla methodology (Haller, 1985). However, knowledge-based methods, like adaptation methods, can be extended in scope by acquiring more knowledge.

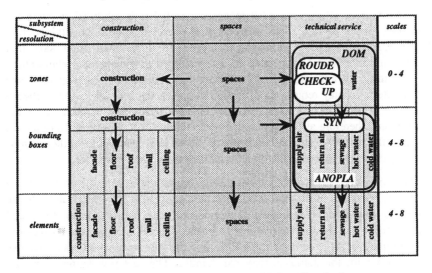

Figure 12.17. Scope of our knowledge-based methods.

6.2. WHICH METHODS FOR WHICH TASKS?

So far, I have described each method as a specialist of one particular task: retrieval, adaptation, assessment, and elaboration. The only exception was TOPO, but there are exceptions.

- AgentEX can be used for assessment because it checks its designs, and for modification because it can repair the constraint violations detected.
- The same holds for AAAO. This method can even start with a standard distribution of columns rather than with a distribution taken from a case. Therefore, it is suitable for case-independent elaboration.
- ANOPLA has much in common with AgentEX and AAAO. Like them, it can be used for assessment, and it could even be used for adaptation because it could initially position the pipes according to a case.
- DOM, originally planned for assessment, can also repair a design by modifying or inserting components, and hence it is good for elaboration. There are even plans to extend it to adaptation using cases and case schemes (Bartsch-Spörl and Bakhtari 1996).
- I dare say that we could link FABEL to the CADRE system (Dave et al., 1994), which assesses topological and geometric constraints and modifies a design by dimensional and structural adjustments, and use CADRE to support not only adaptation, but also elaboration and assessment.

What does all this mean? It means our initial task subdivisions were too coarse. From ASPECT, we learned that retrieval should be divided into transformation and comparison, access and store. We then saw that transformation was also needed for adaptation, assessment, and elaboration. Checking constraints is required for assessment, elaboration, and adaptation, and the latter two may require modifications. In fact, the only difference between adaptation and elaboration is that the former additionally takes a case as a starting point, and therefore also requires a comparison. In short, Figure 12.18 (top row) shows the subtasks I consider elementary. As we have seen, some of them can be approached both in a centralized and in a distributed, agent-based way.

The centralized way may be further differentiated into transfer (from a case or a schema), and into other approaches (heuristic, model-based, weak search). In the second row, I have indicated how retrieval, assessment, adaptation, and elaboration are composed of these subtasks. The third row summarizes the techniques we have covered in FABEL, and the row underneath associates our methods with the subtasks they can handle. The last row summarizes the semantic scope covered by the methods. In Figure 12.18 techniques, methods, and scopes are ordered correspondingly; for example, the first technique is implemented in the first method that covers the first scope. The figure suggests a minimum configuration for the FABEL system. It could consist of ASPECT with its multidimensional case base, transformation and comparison techniques for all aspects, to be taken from ASM, RABIT, PIXEL, and TOPO, and one representative technique for all the others. This could be TOPO for SYN, and, say, AgentEx for AAAO and ANOPLA, and DOM for CHECK-UP. Of course, I assume that the knowledge of the methods can be suitably converted.

access & store	compare	transform	check constraints	modify	insert	
retrieve						tasks
	assess					
		elaborate				
	adapt					
associative linear tree multi-dimensional	sets distances identity maximal cliques	keywords vectors pixels graphs trees	central distributed	central - transfer - other distributed	central - transfer - other distributed	techniques
ASM RABIT PIXEL ASPECT	ASM RABIT PIXEL TOPO	ASM/GESTALTS RABIT/GESTALTS PIXEL TOPO SYN	CHECK-UP DOM TOPO ANOPLA AgentEX AAAO	TOPO DOM ANOPLA AgentEX AAAO	TOPO SYN DOM ROUDE AAAO ANOPLA AgentEX	methods
		components gestalts images topology		statics supply-air HVAC		scope

Figure 12.18. Tasks and methods.

However, Figure 12.18 is as yet speculative. The methods are not yet entirely implemented, and only retrieval methods have been tested and compared. As long as we do not have a complete, comparative evaluation, any ideas about merging methods are speculative. Therefore, the software architecture of the FABEL system is conservative and assumes multiple methods, each of which can support one or more of the original tasks (Figure 12.1). The methods are independent and communicate essentially via globally available data.

Elementary tasks in design seem to be interpretation, comparison, insertion, constraint checks, and modification to comply to constraints. They recombine in different ways to yield supertasks like retrieval, adaptation, elaboration, and assessment.

7. What About Cases?

Naturally, cases are one of the central data structures in FABEL. We had barely touched on the first methods when passionate discussions arose about what should be in a case. The well-known distinction between problems and solutions was maintained by some partners. I objected that design is an evolutionary process that continuously evolves an integrated data model; for example, as in our building project. At any time, the designer focuses on some piece by selecting a view on its screen, and then inspects, refines, or modifies it. A building project does not consist of statically fixed slices that could qualify as cases because there are only dynamically changing views. Moreover, a single view constitutes a solution and, at the same time, a new problem, or actually, the view may constitute many solutions and many problems and there is no explicit record of these relationships (Voss, 1994b). After two years, we have learned that what is in a case depends on what the case is good for. In other words, it depends on the task.

- Cases that represent designs support retrieval for various purposes and elaboration by adaptation. For this reason, it is not necessary that the case is statically split into a problem and a solution. The difference exploited for transfer is computed dynamically by matching the current problem (the query) with a single design in the case. All our retrieval and adaptation methods operate on cases with a single design.

- Cases as sequences of design snapshots are good for learning how to focus on which part of the entire design to elaborate and what to add to it (a kind of specification). Cases with problem-solution pairs are special sequences of length 2. We used them to arrive at our first version of the map in Figure 12.4. This knowledge is used by AgentEX in order to incrementally turn supply-air components into active agents. The sequences were produced by tracing the user's actions with the design editor (Hovestadt, 1993a,1993b).

- Cases with judgements could help assessment. Unfortunately, we do not have any.

- Cases with requirements and constraints could help with specification.

- Cases as sequences of design actions could tell us how a design is to be elaborated. However, the actions in the design editor, which we traced, are too low a level for that purpose. It would be more appropriate to trace the actions in the FABEL system as soon as it reaches a sufficient level of completion.

In order to cope with all eventualities and to put an end to controversial discussions, we decided on a liberal case format. A case contains at least one design, the so-called solution. Optionally, it may contain another design, the problem. It can include the user's comments, and any number of annotations. So far, we only have cases with one design, the solution, and possibly a reference to the building project from which they were taken. Currently, they only contain gestalts as derived information. Other aspect-specific representations, such as topology, are included in method-specific case bases.

The cases are stored in central case bases and case sets. The central case bases are transformed into specific ones for each retrieval method; for example, lists, trees, associative memories, or into the ASPECT memory. Cassettes are used to store results of retrievals, to manipulate them with set-theoretic operations, or to pass them to adaptation methods. For purposes of evaluation, case sets can be named and annotated, and are stored together with a record of how they were obtained.

As provisionally desired by some partners, our data server could be extended to store common knowledge bases and records of design problem solving for learning, and so forth. But up to now, these possibilities have not yet been requested nor implemented.

Our primary data sources are building projects. We store them as a huge set of (thousands of) components. Some partners wanted to enrich them with derived information, like topology, that may be computationally expensive. Originally, this was rejected because projects may be subject to arbitrary changes causing consistency problems. Now we are more tolerant, allowing additional information but delegating its consistency to the responsibility of its creator. So far, our building projects contain no additional information.

As already mentioned, our building projects are not statically sliced into designs. Therefore, we have a serious case acquisition problem (Voss, 1994b). Three answers have been suggested in the project.

- The user can manually identify sets of components to be stored as cases. These cases are statistically unpredictable and will probably contain exceptionally good solutions. They are well suited for inspirational retrieval. They are not really apt for adaptation and elaboration methods with limited scopes (Figures 12.15 and 12.17).

- We can cut the projects into slices according to the stages in Figure 12.4. This can be done automatically in a rather straightforward way. CHECK-UP and SYN use this mechanism for learning the applicability of constraints and for obtaining cases from which prototypes are extracted. Thus, Figure 12.4 also plays the role of a pattern for case cutting.

- As a third alternative, we can totally avoid cutting a project into static slices. The entire building project can be indexed and the size of the slices around the indexes is determined dynamically. TOPO offers this technique, for not only can it represent small cases in terms of topological relations, but also large cases like complete building projects.

Because all communication between the methods is done via global data, the FABEL data server, with its building projects, case bases and case sets, acts as a common medium.

The content of a case depends on the design task it shall support. Typically, cases are uncommented designs. Often, designs are not readily available, but have to be extracted from complex and changing models. A good alternative to cutting static cases might be to index the entire model and access it in dynamically determined bites.

8. Further Topics

During the summer of 1995, we were getting the data for several building projects in the format we finally agreed on. They were imported from MiniCAD. These are a more complete description of Murten; some designs specially produced according to the requirements of our psychologists; two competitive designs for a building project nicknamed "The green meadows," a FABEL meeting house; and some buildings professionally designed by Haller. So far, we only have an incomplete description of the Murten project from which we drew some 128 cases.

All this is ample material to test and evolve our case-cutting routines. The cases so obtained will provide a basis for thoroughly evaluating our methods. Detailed test schemata are currently being set up by our psychologists. A large collection of cases will also push another idea: that of abstracting cases to schemata. I think we can use our retrieval methods for both schemata and cases. The open question is whether our adaptation methods will be as general, or whether new ones will emerge. In the next step, we could connect cases with schemata, and these with more abstract knowledge like the theories in ASA (Giretti, Spalazzi, and Lemma, 1994), or the issue-concept-form triples proposed by Oxman (1994). Issues and concepts could be treated as keywords and stored in our associative memory. But I am pessimistic about getting richer cases; for example, with issues and concepts, or with assessments or external requirements so as to cover a broader spectrum of design tasks in a case-based fashion. Automatic extraction of schemas from cases and of more abstract regularities from schemas will be challenges for our machine learners.

After completion and evaluation of our methods, we will be in a better position to judge their analogies, to see whether all assessment, elaboration, and adaptation methods could start from a common representation of topology, and whether we could find a common scheme for representing constraints and other background knowledge. This would help to answer the question whether there is something like ASPECT for elaboration, adapation, and assessment—an integrating concept that leaves enough room for individual manipulation of aspects.

As soon as we get more familiar with the weaknesses and strengths of the individual methods, we can refine ideas about a scheduler, a user's front-end to the system that would accept fuzzy tasks such as "Retrieve something like that," "Adapt this using this case," or "Help me with this piece," without specifying a method and its parameters. Initial heuristics for such a method have been proposed based on unconsolidated guesses about the suitability of the methods.

Given a fourth chance to develop yet another prototype, we could adapt the software architecture to the finer-grained tasks proposed in Figure 12.18. We could establish a common knowledge representation scheme and a common aspect for representing topology. We would include a scheduler and would link the system with a professional, object-oriented database and a professional CAD system.

Because a fourth prototype is beyond the scope of the FABEL project, such a chance might arise in a more application-oriented transfer project. Such a project might well consider another domain, so that we can test the applicability of our ideas for design in general. One such area might be urban planning, where cases must be linked with background information and justifications, because urban planning is a highly interactive process between different groups of people.

9. FABEL Highlights

Let me conclude by recollecting some advice for building software support in complex design domains:

- *Tasks:* The initial order and decomposition of the tasks may turn out to be suboptimal. Therefore, reserve room in the project plan for a second (or third) chance.
- *Cases:* They may not obviously lie around. Identify cases you might get in a realistic setting. They determine the kind of tasks you can support with them. Make sure that the support outweighs the user's burden of creating cases.
- *Methods:* There may be no standard methods to solve the tasks. Therefore you may have to rely on experiments. Designs need interpretation. Therefore, do not stop with one method per task, but prepare for a multitude of competitive and complementary methods.
- *Software architecture:* It should be flexible and open. Direct dependencies between modules should be avoided in favor of indirect dependencies via

data and possibly a scheduler. In any case, early prototyping to test your ideas should be possible.

Faced with a complex design task, have a look at FABEL for:

- tentative task decomposition for design;
- multidimensional case base for dynamic multi-aspect retrieval (ASPECT);
- retrieval without cases (TOPO);
- collection of retrieval methods supporting graphical queries;
- collection of assessment, adaptation, and elaboration methods;
- autonomous shells for various tasks (RABIT, DOM, ASPECT);
- software architecture for loose coupling of design support modules; and
- there could probably be more developments, as the project runs to June 1996.

Acknowledgments

This research was supported by the German Ministry for Education and Research (BMBF) within the joint project FABEL under contract no. 01IW104. Project partners in FABEL are German National Research Center for Computer Science (GMD), Sankt Augustin, BSR Consulting GmbH, München, Technical University of Dresden, HTWK Leipzig, University of Freiburg, and University of Karlsruhe.

I would like to thank the following members of the FABEL project for their collaboration in the projecct, for helping me with insights related here, and for concrete contributions to and constructive comments the presentation of this chapter.

Raghu Bhat, Shirin Bakhtari, Brigitte Bartsch-Spörl, Katy Börner, Carl-Helmut Coulon, Helge Dürschke, Andrea Enzinger, Friedrich Gebhardt, Wolfgang Gräther, Eckehard Gross, Ludger Hovestadt, Dietmar Janetzko, Janos Jantke, Markus Knauff Wolfgang Oertel, Uwe Peterson, Jörg Walther Schaaf, Barbara Schmidt-Belz, Gerhard Strube, Elisabeth Tammer, Jürgen Walther.

Mrs. Calkin helped to improve the text.

References

Adami, P.: 1995, Adaptation by active autonomous objects (AAAO), in K. Börner (ed.), *Modules Supporting Design, FABEL-Report 35*, GMD, Sankt Augustin, Germany, pp. 46–50.

Alexander, C.: 1979, *The Timeless Way of Building*, Oxford University Press, New York.

Bakhtari, S. and Bartsch-Spörl, B.: 1993, Szenarien für die Beispielanwendung von FABEL, *Fabel-Report 6*, GMD, Sankt Augustin, Germany.

Bartsch-Spörl, B. and Bakhtari, S.: 1996, A support system for building design—experiences and convictions from the FABEL project, in J. Sharpe (ed.), *AI System Support for Conceptual Design*, Springer, Berlin, pp. 279–297.

Bakhtari, S. and Oertel, W.: 1995a, DOM: Domain ontology modeling in architecture and engineering design, *Fabel-Report 33*, GMD, Sankt Augustin, Germany.

Bakhtari, S. and Oertel, W.: 1995b, DOM: An active assistance system for architectural and engineering design, *in* M. Tan and R. Teh (eds), *The Global Design Studio*, Centre for Advanced Studies in Architecture, Singapore, pp. 114–122.

Bhat, R.: 1995a, An agent approach to case adaptation, *Fabel-Report 26*, GMD, Sankt Augustin, Germany.

Börner, K.: 1994, Structural similarity as guidance in case-based design, *in* S. Wess, K. Althoff, and M. Richter (eds), *Topics in Case-Based Reasoning: Selected Papers from the First European Workshop on Case-Based Reasoning (EWCBR-93)*, Springer, Berlin, pp. 197–208.

Börner, K.: 1995, Modules supporting design, *Fabel-Report 35*, GMD, Sankt Augustin.

Bron, C. and Kerbosch, J.: 1973, Finding all cliques in an undirected graph, *Communications of the ACM*, 16, 575–577.

Coulon, C.-H.: 1993, Image retrieval without recognition, *in* M. Richter, S. Wess, K. Althoff, and F. Maurer (eds), *First European Workshop on Case-Based Reasoning (EWCBR'93), Posters and Presentations*, Springer, Berlin, pp. 399–402.

Coulon, C.-H.: 1995, Automatic indexing, retrieval and reuse of topologies, Complex Designs, *Proceedings International Conference on Computing in Civil and Building Engineering (ISCCSE-95)*, pp. 749–754.

Coulon, C.-H. and Gebhardt, F.: 1994a, Evaluation of retrieval methods in case-based design, *Fabel-Report 24*, GMD, Sankt Augustin, Germany.

Coulon, C.-H. and Gebhardt, F.: 1994b, Evaluation of retrieval methods in case-based reasoning, *in:* M. Keane et al. (eds) *EWCBR-94: Second European Workshop on Case-Based Reasoning*, AcknoSoft Press, Paris, pp. 283–291.

Dave, B., Schmitt, G., Faltings, B., and Smith, I.: 1994, Case based design in architecture, *in* J. S. Gero and F. Sudweeks (eds) *AI in Design '94*, Kluwer Academic, Dordrecht, NL, pp. 145–162.

Duda, R. and Hart, P.: 1973, *Pattern Classification and Scene Analysis*, Wiley, New York.

Giretti, A., Spalazzi, L., and Lemma, M.: 1994, A.S.A: An interactive assistant to architectural design, *in* J. S. Gero and F. Sudweeks (eds) *AI in Design '94*, Kluwer Academic, Dordrecht, NL, pp. 93–108.

Goos:, K.: 1995, *Fallbasiertes Klassifizieren. Methoden, Integration und Evaluation*, Doctoral Dissertation, Bayerische Julius-Maximilians-Universität, Würzburg, Germany.

Gräther, W.: 1995, Exact and correct placement of pipes (ANOPLA), *in* K. Börner (ed.), *Modules Supporting Design, FABEL-Report 35*, GMD, Sankt Augustin, Germany, pp. 69–77.

Haller, F.: 1974, *MIDI -ein offenes system für mehrgeschossige bauten mit integriertermedieninstallation*, USM Bausysteme Haller, Münsingen, Germany.

Haller, F.: 1985, *ARMILLA - ein installations model*, IFIB, University of Karlsruhe.

Haller, F.: 1988, *Bauen und forschen*, Ausstellung des Kunstvereins Solothurn, Solothurn, Germany.

Helson, H.: 1933, The fundamental propositions of Gestaltpsychologie, *Psychological Review*, 40, 13–32.

Henne, P.: 1990, Ein experimentelles Assoziativspeicher-Modell, *TASSO-Report 12*, GMD, Sankt Augustin, Germany.

Hovestadt, L.: 1993a, A4-digital building—Extensive computer support for the design, construction, and management of buildings, *in* U. Flemming and S. Van Wyk (eds), *CAAD Futures '93*, North-Holland, Amsterdam, pp. 405–422

Hovestadt, L.: 1993b, *A4-digitales bauen: Ein Modell für die weitgehende Unterstützung von Entwurf, Konstruktion und Betrieb von Gebäuden*, Doctoral Dissertation, Institut für Industrielle Bauproduktion, University of Karlsruhe.

Janetzko, D., Börner, K., Jäschke, O., and Strube, G.: 1994, Task-oriented knowledge acquisition and reasoning for design support systems, *Proceedings of the First European Conference on Cognitive Science in Industry*, Centre de Recherche Public Centre Universitaire, Luxembourg, pp. 153–184.

Janetzko, D. and Jäschke, O.: 1994, Using cases for quality control in design, *in* P. J. Pahl and H. Werner, (eds), *Proceedings of the Sixth International Conference on Computing in Civil and Building Engineering*, Balkema, Rotterdam, NL, pp. 187–192.

Jäschke, O. and Janetzko, D.: 1994, Die Verwendung von Operatoren beim Routine-Design, *Fabel-Report 20*, GMD, Sankt Augustin, Germany.

Karbach, W., Linster, M., and Voss, A.: 1990, Models, methods, roles and tasks: many labels—one idea?, *Knowledge Acquisition*, 2, 279–299.

Lenz, M. and Burkhard, H. D.: 1995, Retrieval ohne Suche, *in* B. Bartsch-Spörl, D. Janetzko and S. Wess (eds), *Fallbasiertes Schließen – Grundlagen und Anwendungen*, Zentrum für Lernende Systeme und Anwendungen, Universität Kaiserslautern, pp. 1–10.

Linowski, B.: 1995, RABIT: Ein objektorientiertes System zum Retrieval attributbasierter Fälle, Diploma Thesis, University of Bonn, Germany.

Marr, D.: 1982, *Vision—A Computational Investigation into the Human Representation and Processing of Visual Information*, Freeman, New York.

Niemann, H.: 1990, *Pattern Analysis and Understanding*, 2nd edn, Springer, Berlin.

Oertel, W.: 1994, FAENSY: Fabel development system, *Fabel-Report 27*, GMD, Sankt Augustin, Germany.

Oxman, R.: 1994, Precedents in design: a computational model for the organization of precedent knowledge, *Design Studies*, 17(2), 117–134.

Richter, M. and Wess, S.: 1991, Similarity, uncertainty and case-based reasoning in Patdex, *in* R. Boyer (ed.), *Automated Reasoning*, Kluwer Academic, Dordrecht, NL, pp. 249–265.

Salton, G. and McGill, M.: 1983, *Introduction to Modern Information Retrieval*, McGraw-Hill, New York.

Schaaf, J. W.: 1994, Gestaltsin CAD-plans, analysis of a similarity concept, *in* J. Gero and F. Sudweeks (eds) *AI in Design '94*, Kluwer Academic, Dordrecht, NL, pp. 437–446,

Schaaf, J. W.: 1995, ASPECT: Über die Suche nach situations gerechten Fällen im Case-Based Reasoning, *Fabel-Report 33*, GMD, Sankt Augustin, Germany.

Schreiber, A., Wielinga, B., and Breuker, J.: 1992, *KADS: A Principled Approach to Knowledge-Based System Development*, Academic Press, London.

Smith, B. and Keane, M.:1994, Retrieving adaptable cases, *in* S. Wess, K-D. Althoff and M. M. Richter (eds), *Topics in Case-Based Reasoning: First European Workshop, EWCBR-93*, Selected Papers, Lecture Notes in Artificial Intelligence, Springer, Berlin, pp. 209–220.

Treisman, A.: 1985, Preattentive processing in vision, in Computer Vision, *Graphics and Image Processing*, 31(2), 156–177.

Voss, A.: 1994a, Similarity concepts and retrieval methods, *Fabel-Report 13*, GMD, Sankt Augustin, Germany.

Voss, A.: 1994b, The need for knowledge acquisition in case-based reasoning—some experiences from an architectural domain, *in* A. Cohn (ed.), *ECAI'94*, Wiley, Chichester, pp. 463–467.

Voss, A. and Bartsch-Spörl, B.: 1995, Retrieval of technical design documents for reuse, *Proceedings International Conference on Computing in Civil and Building Engineering (ISCCSE-95)*, Berlin, pp. 9223–929.

Voss, A., Coulon, C.-H., Gräther, W., Linowski, B., Schaaf, J. W., Bartsch-Spörl, B., Börner, K., Tammer, E-Ch., Dürschke, H., and Knauff, M.: 1994, Retrieval of similar layouts—about a very hybrid approach in FABEL, *in* J. S. Gero and F. Sudweeks (eds), *AI in Design '94*, Kluwer Academic, Dordrecht, NL, pp. 525–640.

author index

subject index